The Spanish Economy in the New Europe

The Spanish Economy in the New Europe

Carmela Martín
Jean Monnet Professor of European Integration
Universidad Complutense de Madrid
and
Director, Departamento de Estudios Europeos
FUNCAS (Fundación de las Cajas de Ahorros)

Translated from the Spanish by Philip Hill and Sarah Nicholson

palgrave

Published by PALGRAVE
Houndmills, Basingstoke, Hampshire RG21 6XS and
175 Fifth Avenue, New York, N. Y. 10010
Companies and representatives throughout the world

PALGRAVE is the new global academic imprint of
St. Martin's Press LLC Scholarly and Reference Division and
Palgrave Publishers Ltd (formerly Macmillan Press Ltd).

Outside North America
ISBN 0–333–77459–0

In North America
ISBN 0–312–23006–0

This book is printed on paper suitable for recycling and made from fully managed and sustained forest sources.

A catalogue record for this book is available from the British Library.

Library of Congress Catalog Card Number: 99–049727

10 9 8 7 6 5 4 3 2
10 09 08 07 06 05 04 03 02

Printed and bound in Great Britain by
Antony Rowe Ltd, Chippenham, Wiltshire

Contents

List of Tables

List of Figures

Preface

In 1986 Spain joined the European Community of the Twelve (today the European Union (EU) of the Fifteen), but to what extent is the Spanish economy truly integrated in this area? In what ways does it resemble its European partners? What are its peculiarities? In what aspects has it tended to converge? And in what others have the differences widened? In short, what is Spain's relative position, and how has it evolved in the process of formation of the new European economy? The answers to these questions are interesting not only to learn what Spain's participation in European integration has brought, but also to discover how it might adapt better to the environment of economic and monetary union (EMU), which has so recently come into being.

If we review the theoretical literature on monetary unions, we find that the crucial aspects that determine their success are in fact the degree of similarity of the countries' economic structures (their productive structures, productivity, competitiveness, for example) and the level of economic interdependence (trade, labour mobility, direct investment flows, for example) between the member countries. An examination of the wealth of literature published in recent years on the economic aspects of the European integration process shows that these questions have not been addressed in a reasonably comprehensive and homogeneous way, as most of them concentrate either on the study of Community institutions and policies or on the analysis of the variables most closely linked to the criteria in the Maastricht Treaty for deciding which countries would qualify for EMU.

The present book seeks to explore these questions, taking into account the theoretical debate and drawing on a new homogeneous and very broad statistical base. It analyses the most relevant economic variables for the 15 countries that now form the European Union – and, to broaden the interpretation of the data, for the United States and Japan as well – in order to arrive at an evaluation of the process of European integration. Here, readers should note that this is a book not only on the Spanish economy but also on the European economy, as practically the same information is given for Spain and for each of its EU partners and, consequently, for those countries which are – since 1 January 1999 – members of EMU.

In keeping with the book's objective, our analysis has taken a twofold approach.

In Part I of the book (Chapters 1–7), we have examined from a comparative perspective to what extent and in what aspects Spain's economy has converged with the economies of its EU partners, and have also identified the main defining features of the Fifteen as a whole with respect to the United States and Japan. To ensure a fairly in-depth analysis, we have had to focus this comparison on several specific questions, and in this respect have opted to give priority to those aspects that affect the real economy, at the expense of monetary and financial phenomena. This decision was dictated not only by professional specialization, but also by the conviction that in recent years the issues relating to the real economy have received, unjustifiably in our opinion, less attention. For the same reason, we decided to highlight the variables that most influence the economy in a medium- and long-run timeframe.

Chapter 1 studies the trends and changes both in the structure of demand and in the composition of output. It thus offers an initial view of the relative weight of Spanish GDP and a description of productive specialization within the European Union. Chapter 2 estimates Spain's productivity (labour and total factor) in relation to that of the European Union as well as its main determinants – the relative factor endowment in the broad sense (physical, technological, human and public capital) – shedding light on the gap that still exists between Spain's per capita GDP and the average of its European partners. Chapter 3 seeks to identify the most salient features and problems of the Spanish labour market, distinguishing between those which are specific to Spain and those which are common to all European economies; in this respect, it reveals Spain's peculiarities in relation to the European Union and the latter's in relation to other industrialized economies – particularly the United States – as regards the size and nature of unemployment and its possible causes.

Chapter 4 then goes on to analyse competitiveness by examining diverse specifications of real effective exchange rates and other complementary indicators that attempt to capture the impact of competitive strategies based on product differentiation. Chapter 5 studies public finances, describing the trends in the size and composition of the budget deficits of Spain and the other EU members over the period in question. It then sets out the terms of the debate on the welfare state in Europe and, in greater detail, in Spain. Chapter 6 describes – through a comparative examination of Spain's balance of payments and the overall balance of payments of the 15 EU countries – the structure of the external transactions of Community economies, giving special attention to the mechanisms employed by Spain to deal with its permanent trade deficits and all too frequent current and capital account imbalances. Chapter 7 closes the first part of the book with what might be considered a balance or corollary of the comparative analysis in the preceding chapters, providing a diagnosis of the progress made by Spain, and by the Fifteen as a whole, towards economic convergence. The concept of convergence is first considered in nominal terms, with reference to the Maastricht criteria for joining EMU. The chapter's most substantive contribution, however, is its evaluation of the achievements in terms of real convergence, on the basis of a composite indicator prepared for this purpose.

The analysis in Part II takes a different approach: it seeks to explore how the economic relations between EU countries have evolved – in other words, to evaluate their actual level of integration – paying close attention to the case of Spain. And, for a broader evaluation of the depth and characteristics of Spain's integration with the other members and of the integration of the EU members as a whole between themselves, it also considers – as a counterpoint – their relations with non-Community countries. Chapter 8, the first of the five which form Part II, analyses trade relations, including a detailed study of the changes in trade specialization, both inter- and intra-industrial, as well as an estimation of the quality differences between the goods imported and exported by Spain. Chapter 9 studies another key channel of economic integration: direct investment. Here again it seeks to document and interpret the changes that have arisen in the economic relations – in this case, those in the form of direct investment – within the European Union and with third countries, singling out those with the former communist countries of Central and Eastern Europe that are set to gain entry into the Community soonest.

Chapter 10 goes on to examine the changes in the intensity and characteristics of migratory flows between EU members and those originating in other countries, and then considers the numerous factors that may lie at the root of the scant labour mobility between EU partners and its implications in the context of EMU. The two final chapters of Part II address two issues of prime importance for our understanding of the new macroeconomic policy regime in the euro area. First, Chapter 11 analyses the changes in the size and structure of the Community budget, and evaluates its stabilizing capacity and, in greater depth, its distributive function or, in other words, its contribution to economic and social cohesion within the European Union. Secondly, Chapter 12 describes the transition to monetary union and the defining features – as envisioned in the Maastricht Treaty and later agreements – of the monetary policy that has been implemented, in a centralized way, since 1 January 1999.

The book also includes an epilogue, covering the main conclusions and their implications for the design of an economic policy that would help Spain make the most of its participation in the Europe of the euro. Finally, two appendices have been included: the first, a chronology of the European integration process, and the second, a methodological discussion of the valuation problems in analyses based on international comparisons and how they have been approached here.

This book was prepared with the assistance, on different tasks, of most of the members of the Department of European Studies of the Fundación de las Cajas de Ahorros Confederadas. I would particularly like to mention the valuable contribution of José María Maté, Patxi Perales, Ismael Sanz and, above all, Francisco J. Velázquez in preparing the broad, homogeneous database that underlies the book's analysis and is one of its main defining attributes. Francisco J. Velázquez also participated in the writing of Chapters 2, 6 and 10, and José María Maté in that of Chapter 9. Finally, Lis Fraile has carried out all the administrative tasks and helped in the management of the bibliographic references, with extraordinary efficiency and dedication.

In addition, Esther Gordo (a researcher at the Bank of Spain's Research Department) and Cecilio Tamarit (Professor of Applied Economics at the Universidad de Valencia) collaborated in Chapters 8 and 12, respectively.

Other people – members of the Fundación and other institutions – also contributed in different ways to the book, and I would like to express my gratitude to them. First of all, Victorio Valle, director of the Fundación, who from the start has shown his enthusiasm for the project and made available the necessary material and human resources. Likewise, Enrique Fuentes Quintana, honorary president of the Fundación, who has given me so much encouragement in my work. My thanks as well to those of my colleagues who have read different chapters of the book and contributed useful suggestions that have helped improve the final version: Julio Segura and Manuel Varela (of the Universidad Complutense de Madrid), Guillermo de la Dehesa (of CEPR), José Marín (of the ECB), Vicente Salas (of the Universidad de Zaragoza) and Soledad Núñez (of the Bank of Spain).

The students who have attended the doctoral course on economic integration in Europe which I have taught for more than ten years at the Universidad Complutense de Madrid – more recently under the auspices of the Jean Monnet programme – have helped me to distil the most substantive ideas of the economic literature on the subject.

I would like to dedicate my final words of gratitude to Luis Ángel Rojo, Professor of Economy and Governor of the Bank of Spain, who since introducing me to the study of economics has been a constant source of encouragement in my professional activity.

In concluding, I would like to point out that the book is primarily intended for students and professionals in the field of economics. But, to make the book more accessible to non-specialists, an effort has been made to present the concepts and premises in the most intuitive way possible. As such, I trust that it will also be of use to readers who, while specializing in other fields, may be interested in learning about the past course, the present situation and the future prospects of the Spanish economy and of its EU partners in the process of building the new Europe, namely an economic and monetary union that is currently in the process of consolidation, and also of enlargement towards Eastern Europe, and, in the final instance, committed to a project of political integration.

Madrid CARMELA MARTÍN

List of Abbreviations

Country abbreviations

A	Austria
BL	Belgium and Luxemburg
D	Germany
DK	Denmark
E	Spain
EUR	European Union, including all 15 members after the last accession
F	France
FIN	Finland
GR	Greece
G-7	'Group of seven' – the world's seven major economies (United States, Japan, Germany, France, United Kingdom, Italy and Canada)
I	Italy
IRL	Ireland
J	Japan
LUX	Luxemburg
NL	Netherlands
P	Portugal
S	Sweden
UK	United Kingdom
USA	United States of America
USSR	Union of Soviet Socialist Republics

ACP	African, Caribbean and Pacific States
ASEAN	Association of South East Asian Nations
CAP	common agricultural policy
CEEC	Central and Eastern European countries
CEFTA	Central European Free Trade Association
CEPR	Centre for Economic Policy Research
CET	common external tariff
CNAE	Clasificación Nacional de Actividades Económicas (Spanish National Classification of Economic Activities)
CPI	consumer price index

EAEC	European Atomic Energy Community
EAGGF-Guarantee	European Agricultural Guidance and Guarantee Fund, Guarantee Section
EAGGF-Guidance	European Agricultural Guidance and Guarantee Fund, Guidance Section
EC	European Community
ECB	European Central Bank
ECOFIN	Economy and Finance Ministers Council
ECSC	European Coal and Steel Community
ecu	European currency unit
EDF	European Development Fund
EDP	excessive deficit procedure
EEA	European Economic Area
EEC	European Economic Community
EFTA	European Free Trade Association
EIB	European Investment Bank
EMCF	European Monetary Cooperation Fund
EMI	European Monetary Institute
EMS	European Monetary System
EMU	economic and monetary union
ERDF	European Regional Development Fund
ERM	exchange-rate mechanism
ESA	European System of Integrated Economic Accounts
ESCB	European System of Central Banks
ESF	European Social Fund
EU	European Union
Euratom	European Atomic Energy Community
Eurostat	Statistical Office of the European Communities
FIFG	Financial Instrument for Fisheries Guidance
GATT	General Agreement on Tariffs and Trade
GDP	gross domestic product
GDP mp	gross domestic product at market prices
GNP	gross national product
HCPI	harmonized consumer price index
ICLS	International Conference of Labour Statisticians
IGC	inter-governmental conference
ILO	International Labour Office
IMD	Institute for Management and Development
IMF	International Monetary Fund
IMP	Integrated Mediterranean Programmes
INE	Instituto Nacional de Estadística (Spanish National Statistical Office)

MERCOSUR	Southern Common Market
MICYT	Ministerio de Industria, Comercio y Turismo (Industry, Trade and Tourism Ministry)
NACE-CLIO (25)	general industrial classification of economic activities within the European Communities, 25 branches
NACE-CLIO (56)	general industrial classification of economic activities within the European Communities, 56 branches
NAFTA	North American Free Trade Agreement
NCI	New Community Instrument
NEER	nominal effective exchange rate
OECD	Organization for Economic Cooperation and Development
OLI	ownership, localization and internalization
PHARE	programme of technical assistance to Central and Eastern European countries
PP	producer prices
PPP	purchasing power parity
R&D	research and development
RCAI	revealed comparative advantage index
REER	real effective exchange rate
SEA	Single European Act
SITC	standard international trade classification
SNA	System of National Accounts
STAN Database	Structural Analysis Database
TACIS	programme of technical assistance to the Commonwealth of Independent States
TARGET	trans-European automated real-time gross settlement express transfer system
TARIC	integrated tariff of the European Community
TEU	Treaty on European Union (Maastricht Treaty)
ULC	unit labour costs
UN	United Nations
UNESCO	United Nations Educational, Scientific and Cultural Organization
UVI	unit value indices
VAT	value-added tax
WEU	Western European Union

Introduction: Changes in the International Economic Setting

As noted in the preface, this book analyses the Spanish economy in the Europe of the Fifteen. Accordingly, it takes as its reference period the years spanning the period from Spain's accession to the Community project at the beginning of 1986 to the present.[1] But this period is not only interesting from the Spanish point of view, for it also encompasses many other events that are important for the Fifteen as a whole and even for the world economy. And, in addition to these developments, no less influential changes have arisen in the field of economic theory. It would seem worthwhile, therefore, to review here some of the main events and ideas that form the backdrop to what has occurred in the Spanish economy and in the other European economies analysed in this book.

We shall begin by recalling the changes the Spanish economy has had to cope with since its entry into the European Community, especially those most directly linked to Europe's integration. Here the first point to be borne in mind is that Spain joined the Community at a time of renewed momentum in the project of European integration, stemming from the signing of the Single European Act in February 1986 that set the goal of unifying the market (including its two new members, Spain and Portugal) by the end of 1992. This integrating impulse was further strengthened in 1989 by the agreement – at the Madrid summit – to begin the first stage in the process of forming an economic and monetary union (EMU) on 1 July 1990, which was to prove a decisive step in the configuration of the new Europe.

The culmination of the single market's creation – albeit more *de jure* than *de facto* – on the agreed date, the enlargement to fifteen partners (with the accession of Sweden, Austria and Finland) in 1995, the process of forming EMU and its launch in January 1999, and the steps to extend the integration process to Eastern Europe together make the book's reference period – beginning with Spain's accession to the European Community – one of the most important in the history of European integration.[2]

The intensity of the changes the Spanish economy has had to face since joining the Community is the result not only of the special vitality of Europe's integration process, but also of the adjustments Spain – like the rest of its partners – has had to make during these years to accommodate other developments with far-reaching consequences in the international setting.

Since 1986 we have witnessed such momentous events as the fall of the Berlin Wall in 1989, the collapse of COMECON and the gradual unravelling of communism in Central and Eastern European countries from then onwards. Besides adding a new dimension to Europe's integration process, which has to date materialized in the rapid unification of Germany and in commitments on the integration of several former communist countries in the not-too-distant future, these decisive events have greatly affected the framework of political and economic relations on a world scale. Note, too, that this has involved the irruption into the international market of a large group of countries previously isolated in a situation of virtual autarky centred on COMECON. This opening up to the Western world is now creating opportunities for trade and investment, while at the same time producing greater competitive pressures and, in one sense, a threat to the output and potential to attract international capital of countries with similar productive structures.

Among the events of worldwide impact in this period, most notable were the advances made in the liberalization of international economic transactions at the last round of GATT, which began in late 1986 and concluded with the agreement signed by 119 countries in April 1994. In addition to a substantial reduction in both tariff and non-tariff barriers on trade in goods and services, including those relating to copyright, the Uruguay Round led to the creation of a new institution, the World Trade Organization (WTO). It replaces the former GATT secretariat and is responsible for safeguarding the compliance with these multilateral agreements.

But, in parallel to the progress achieved in the liberalization of multilateral relations under the auspices of the Uruguay Round, there has also been a proliferation of regional integration initiatives, most notably NAFTA, Mercosur and ASEAN, and a reinforcement of the three hegemonic blocs, the so-called triad formed by the United States, Japan and the European Union.[3] This drive towards regionalism and the consolidation of blocs makes the situation of countries that remain on the sidelines increasingly problematic.

The avalanche of radical technological innovations, which have arisen and spread in this period in many fields, and particularly in information and communications, has also produced major changes in international economic relations. Here it is important to emphasize that, in addition to generating significant cost and time savings in productive activity in general, the enormous advances in communications technologies now allow many services to be marketed where previously the provider's physical presence was required. It has thus become much easier to surmount the institutional barriers in real markets, and in financial markets in particular. In sum, with the introduction of new technologies, firms are having to reorganize their productive strategies and labour relations and, at the same time, require greater skills from their workers.[4]

Together these developments have fuelled the globalization of goods, services and – above all – capital markets, a process led by multinational firms that operate virtually the world over. Since the mid-1980s, the pace of direct investment worldwide and other forms of corporate internationalization has quickened and been spurred by the restructuring of firms, allowing them to take advantage of the increasing opportunities offered by new technologies for communications between productive units which operate at different geographical locations under integrated management.

As a consequence of these many developments, an international scenario has gradually emerged in which events abroad have an increasing impact on the actions of the different agents of national economies. Companies now face intense and mounting competitive pressures, driving them to segment their productive and marketing processes between different countries in order to benefit from the comparative advantages (better infrastructure and lower labour costs, among others) offered by each country. Consumers in turn have easier and faster access to new products, which may emerge in far-off places but are increasingly within their reach. And governments find themselves involved in an ever greater number of international disputes and negotiations at forums where their say – not to mention their vote – is highly problematic unless they have the backing provided by membership of one of the important regional blocs. Furthermore, the growing globalization of markets is increasingly restricting the leeway of governments to apply differentiated economic policies.

Against this international backdrop, it is not surprising that the governments of EU countries have made such determined efforts to meet the requirements in the Maastricht agreements for the constitution of an economic and monetary union, seeking not only to strengthen their own economic development but also to improve Europe's political position vis-à-vis the other members of the triad.

Moreover, it might even be said that the fear of being left behind, economically and politically, in a world characterized by an ever greater globalization of markets and the simultaneous intensification of regionalism, with the United States at the fore, constitutes the great driving force behind the efforts of European countries to integrate; by extension, it is also the main counter-balance to the disintegrating tendencies (or nationalistic resistance) that still prevail in Europe and tend to grow stronger during recessions. But, in other respects, these tendencies have some justification in the many ambiguities in the economic theory on the effects of regional integration agreements. Consequently, even though economic integration clearly appears to generate gains in efficiency and welfare for the area as a whole, very little can be predicted as to their distribution among the individual partners. And, in theory, there is of course room for losers. What is more, the economic literature on the subject is notably unclear as to the effects likely to derive from the ambitious degree of integration achieved so far by 11 EU member countries through the constitution of an economic and monetary union, marking an initiative that has – in the terms in which it was conceived – no true parallel in history.

It is in the light of these many politically and economically momentous developments, which are reshaping the framework of international relations, that we must examine the performance of the Spanish economy in the Europe of the Fifteen and the launch of EMU, despite the lingering uncertainty surrounding the ultimate economic benefits and costs that EMU will bring to each of the member countries.

In the period analysed here, EU economies have also been influenced by the no less important changes in the field of economic theory. Most notable in this respect is probably the change in the concept of the public sector's role in market economies.

Indeed, the widespread view that it is necessary to curb the public sector's sphere of intervention is perhaps the most characteristic feature of an age that has, in a way, seen the consolidation of monetarist orthodoxy.

An eloquent example of the ascendancy of this view is the flood of criticism levelled during these years at the welfare state as it has existed in Europe. From this perspective, the greater size of the welfare state in European countries vis-à-vis that of other industrialized nations, and the United States above all, is considered one of the main reasons for the sluggish growth of output and employment. This line of thought thus implies a rejection of the Keynesian premises on which the interventionist and beneficent concept of the public sector rests and which have, for some time, been questioned.

None the less, in the period covered in this book, diverse lines of thought have emerged in many branches of economics. Specifically, in the area of growth, endogenous growth models constitute a certain counterpoint to monetarism's reductionist ideas about the role of the public sector, and as such lend support to various propositions of Keynesian thought. In fact, by assigning to technology, human capital and infrastructure – especially transport and communications – a key role in growth and by pointing out that public-sector investment in these assets generates very significant positive externalities for private investment, endogenous growth models tend to reinforce the arguments in favour of public intervention in market economies. These are the ideas underlying the defence of active government participation in the development of the above-mentioned factors considered essential to growth. Furthermore, they have drawn attention to the need for special efforts on the part of public authorities to help satisfy the demand for more highly qualified labour, with the new skills required by technological change, which might lie at the root of the structural unemployment that afflicts European economies.

All in all, the basic lines of economic thought in these years could be viewed as a further strand in the traditional debate between Keynesians and monetarists or, what is essentially the same, between those who consider that faced with the dilemma of 'market failure' versus 'government failure', the former or the latter, respectively, is more important. There is a very noticeable tendency towards *laissez-faire,* and none the less, consequently, a loss of confidence in economic policies. In any event, the growing commitment to the market is still vulnerable to confusion and anxiety when faced with the tremendous impact and volatility of the reactions of international financial markets and, of course, the lack of satisfactory solutions for unemployment. Moreover, there are inevitable uncertainties about the implications of the economic policy regime designed for EMU, for it is, in large part, an experiment.

In sum, the events and ideas briefly narrated in the preceding pages are a useful frame of reference for our analysis of the course of the Spanish economy since Spain's accession to the project of European economic and monetary integration in 1986. As we have indicated, while the more immediate purpose of this study is to examine how the relative situation of the Spanish economy has evolved within the Community of the Fifteen, its ultimate aim is to draw conclusions from this experience that will help prepare Spain to make the most of its presence in the final and most ambitious stage of the project, which has just begun: monetary union.

Part I
Comparative Analysis

1 Growth and Structural Changes

1.1 Introduction

We begin the comparative analysis of the development and present situation of the Spanish economy in relation to its European partners by considering GDP per capita. This variable summarizes, in a way, the results of the growth experienced by a country and thus its achievements in terms of economic welfare.

After examining, in Section 1.2, the relative position and path of Spain's GDP per capita during its period of EU membership, the chapter goes on to analyse, in Section 1.3, the changes in the structure of GDP, from the perspective of both demand and supply. It attempts to identify the main characteristics of the Spanish productive system compared with that of the other EU countries, as well as the trends in its specialization. In addition, a view is offered of the functional distribution of income. The chapter closes with a summary of the main conclusions.

1.2 GDP and economic growth

Before comparing the level and path of Spanish and Community GDP per capita, it is worth recalling that Spain is the second largest EU country by area (accounting for 15.6 per cent of the EU total) and the fifth largest in terms of both population and output (10.5 per cent and 8.5 per cent, respectively, in 1997). Note that the latter proportion is the result of comparing Spanish GDP with that of the European Union as a whole in terms of purchasing power parity (PPP). Using the exchange rate instead yields a somewhat lower figure of 6.6 per cent. The disparity between these two figures illustrates the importance in international comparisons of using the most appropriate method to homogenize the values of the variables of the different countries. Accordingly, Appendix II considers the different procedures available, with an analysis and justification of those used here.

From the data for Spanish GDP per capita in terms of PPP (see Figure 1.1, which shows the ranking of Spain and its Community partners), it is apparent that between 1986 and 1997 Spain slipped one place to thirteenth, overtaken by Ireland. Yet, with respect to the European average, Spain's GDP per capita improved significantly, rising from 72.7 per cent in 1986 to 78.6 per cent in 1997.[1]

It should, however, be pointed out that this narrowing of the gap did not take place linearly throughout the period. From 1986 to 1991 there was a very strong recovery in Spain's relative income per capita (albeit without reaching the 1975 level), while in the early 1990s there was a slight distancing from levels of Community welfare, due to the deeper impact of the economic crisis in Spain.[2] Indeed, this is only as might be expected, for there appears to be a general rule in the OECD whereby at times of international economic expansion the countries most behind converge with the average of all the members of the organization, diverging from it during recessions (see Andrés, Boscá and Doménech, 1995). In accordance with this rule, the trend in Spain since 1995 seems to signal renewed convergence with the European average.

Given this situation, it would be interesting to pose the following question: How long will Spain take to reach the average level of European welfare? To answer this question completely is, however, a very complex task.

It is simpler, and also of interest, to determine the number of years Spain would need to reach the EU average, on the assumption that past growth differentials are sustained in the future. Extrapolating from the period spanning from Spain's accession to 1999 (with a growth differential of 0.6 percentage points), 35 years would be required.

Although this projection is in no sense a prediction, it does serve, and therein lies its interest, to illustrate the need for Spain to sustain growth rates well above those of the Community countries if it is to reach the average level of welfare within a reasonable period.

In this respect it should be stressed that the European Union as a whole is committed to converging with the two other major economic powers, the United States and Japan, although in this period no significant progress has been discerned.

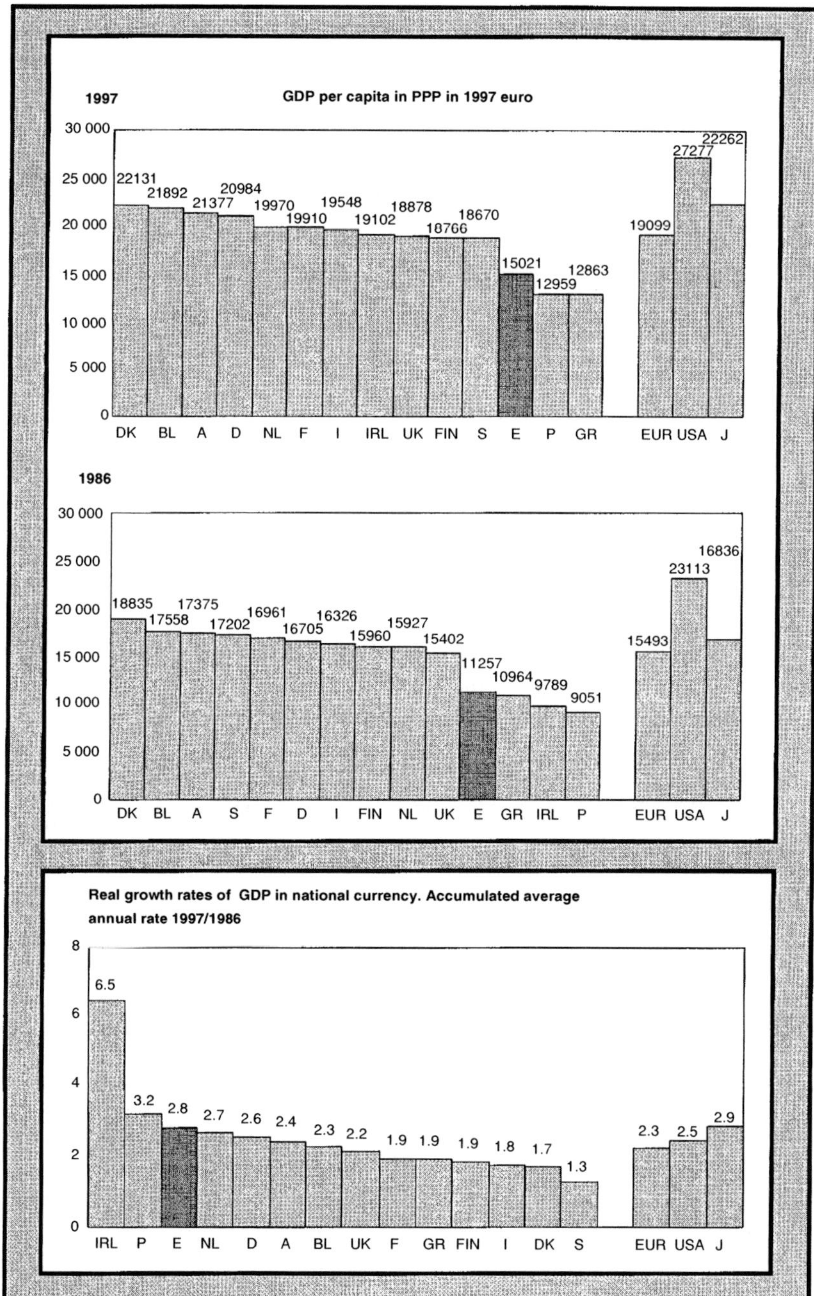

Figure 1.1 GDP per capita

Source: OECD: *National Accounts*, vol. I: *Main Aggregates*; OECD: *Quarterly National Accounts*; Departmento de Estudios Europeos, Fundación de las Cajas de Ahorros.

1.3 Changes in the structure of GDP

The significant growth in the Spanish economy since its entry into the European Union would seem to suggest that the structure of Spain's economic system has changed with respect to that of the other Community members, as these countries, with the exception of Portugal, did not have to cope with such an intense process of opening up.

Consequently, and to obtain an initial idea of the alterations which may have occurred, we shall now look at the changes in the composition of GDP in Spain and in the European Union between 1986 and 1997, on the basis of the data presented in Table 1.1, from three viewpoints: demand, supply and income.

Starting with a comparison of the changes in the composition of demand, most notable in real terms is precisely the magnitude of the increase in the degree of openness to foreign trade. Indeed, as seen in Table 1.1, foreign trade transactions[3] rose in Spain, in relation to GDP, by nearly 25 percentage points, against 19 in the European Union as a whole. Despite this, trade as a proportion of GDP is still almost 6 percentage points below the EU average.

No less relevant is the fact that the economy's opening up has led external demand to make a negative contribution to the growth of the Spanish economy in the period as a whole (–3 per cent), especially given that in the European Union quite the opposite has occurred (a positive contribution of 6.7 per cent).

Another interesting difference between the structures of Spanish and Community demand is the higher relative importance of investment in Spain during this period. On average during the years considered, the weight of gross fixed capital formation in Spain's GDP exceeded by nearly 2 percentage points the EU equivalent. This greater relative demand from investment was the consequence of the Spanish economy's lower capitalization at the beginning of the period, as discussed in the next chapter, and the need to overcome this serious constraint on growth. Here it is important to point out that national saving was not sufficient to finance the extra investment effort made in Spain until 1995, when there was a change in the situation, which continued in 1996 and 1997. On average during the period, the shortfall of saving in relation to gross capital formation amounted to 0.5 per cent of GDP. By contrast, average EU national saving exceeded investment by 0.4 per cent of GDP.

Moreover, there is a difference in the distribution of national saving between institutional sectors which makes Spain's situation more vul-

Table 1.1 Gross domestic product and its components in Spain and the EU (%)

	Spain			European Union		
	1986		1997	1986		1997
	Nominal	Real*	Nominal = Real*	Nominal	Real*	Nominal = Real*
Demand components						
Private national consumption	63.6	64.3	62.4	60.0	60.1	60.2
Government consumption	14.4	14.6	15.8	19.4	20.2	18.6
Gross fixed capital formation	19.3	17.6	20.3	19.5	18.1	18.2
Stockbuilding	0.5	0.5	0.1	0.4	0.3	0.5
Exports of goods and services	19.7	16.3	27.9	26.1	21.5	31.5
Imports of goods and services	17.6	13.2	6.5	25.3	20.3	29.0
Supply components						
Agriculture	5.3	4.4	3.4	3.1	2.3	2.1
Industry	27.3	24.2	23.4	27.3	24.5	22.8
Energy	5.6	5.8	5.6	4.9	4.6	4.2
Manufacturing	21.7	18.4	17.8	22.4	19.9	18.6
Construction	6.1	7.2	7.8	5.2	5.4	4.8
Services	55.4	57.7	59.2	55.3	58.1	59.9
Market	44.0	45.3	45.5	41.4	43.0	46.6
Non-market	11.4	12.4	13.7	13.9	15.1	13.3
Indirect taxes	6.0	6.4	6.3	9.1	9.7	10.5
Income components						
Compensation of employees	45.4		46.3	53.0		50.2
Gross operating surplus	45.5		45.3	36.5		38.1
Taxes related to production and imports	10.7		10.9	13.5		13.9
Operating and import subsidies	1.6		2.4	3.0		2.2

* In 1997 euro.

Source: INE: *Contabilidad Nacional de España*; Eurostat: *National Accounts ESA*; OECD: *National Accounts*, vol. I: *Main Aggregates*, and vol. II: *Detailed Tables*; OECD: *Quarterly National Accounts*; Departmento de Estudios Europeos, Fundación de las Cajas de Ahorros.

nerable: on average over the period, household saving did not even account for 40 per cent of total saving, whereas in the European Union it was more than 55 per cent. None the less, this obstacle seems to have been fading in recent years. According to a survey sponsored by the Fundación de las Cajas de Ahorros Confederadas,[4] this was due, among other reasons, to the increase in household economic insecurity, the uncertainty over the future of the welfare state, the emergence of new saving methods producing higher returns, and the decline in inflation.

Naturally, this difference in the behaviour of household saving during the period is reflected in a share of national private consumption in Spanish GDP above the EU average in most years of the period. The corollary of this, as a result of the late development of the provision of public services and social benefits in Spain, is that the weight of government consumption is less in Spain. In any event, the trend visible over the period is one of convergence of the relative shares of these two components of consumption.

Having looked at the main changes in demand, we shall now go on to analyse the changes which have taken place on the supply side. The importance of its study is shown by the existence of a wealth of empirical evidence, at the national and international level, which suggests that the change in the sectoral composition of output has had a significant effect on growth in the Western economies during the past forty years[5] and that, in addition, the differences in the growth rates of these economies have been caused by the divergences in productive structures (see Dollar and Wolff, 1993).

Most of the transformations in the productive system – in particular, the decline in the importance of agriculture and the growth in the weight of the service sector – are an extension of past trends, and are common to the rest of the Community countries. Somewhat more recent, however, are the reduction in the share of manufacturing industry and the increase in the share of the construction sector.[6]

None the less, it should be noted that some of these trends turn out to be stronger or weaker when real instead of nominal data are considered. This shows the great differences in price behaviour across sectors.

By way of example, the decreases in the shares of agriculture and industry are much greater in nominal terms than in real terms, while in the case of the increase in services the opposite is true. Indeed, some authors point out that the move to a service economy in recent years is more a nominal than a real phenomenon (see Pérez, Goerlich and Más, 1996). It is argued that since the service sector is not exposed to external competition and is strongly regulated in a way which limits the development of domestic competition it has been able to sustain, until recently, much faster price growth than the other productive branches, giving rise to so-called 'dual inflation'. However, greater liberalization seems to be bearing fruit and correcting the disparate growth of the sectoral deflators; at least that is what the available data suggest. In any event, there are certain characteristics inherent to a large number of service branches which stifle their productivity growth and, consequently, tend to make them more inflationary (see Herce, 1995).

As regards agriculture, it is notable that its weight in Spain has continued to move towards the Community average. Between 1986 and 1997, the share of its real added value in GDP fell considerably, and now stands at only 3 per cent of GDP. Within this period, however, two separate phases can be identified. During the first, until 1989, the importance of the agricultural sector held constant or fell slightly as a consequence of the expansionary boost from the economy and the flow of investment (domestic and foreign) into the sector. During the second, from 1989 onwards, there was a general slide in activity, although it has been halted in recent years.[7] This decline was the result of changes in the common agricultural policy (CAP) which tended to limit supply from the sector, a long drought, and the international liberalization of agricultural markets stemming from the Uruguay Round GATT accords.

The share of the Spanish manufacturing sector in GDP fell (in real terms) from 18.4 per cent in 1986 to 17.8 per cent in 1997, considerably lower than the EU average.

Specific studies of the sector (see Martín, 1995b, and the references cited there) have shown that in recent years, in an environment marked by the opening up to trade and growing external competitive pressures, manufacturing firms have had difficulty absorbing significant increases in labour costs and in the prices of inputs obtained from goods and service industries that are sheltered from external competition. This has hampered the development of the sector.

For a more precise characterization of the manufacturing sector's relative situation, it seems worth going into somewhat greater detail in the comparative analysis of its composition. This has been carried out on the basis of the threefold classification of sectors under the NACE-CLIO (25) classification, which involves combining the two criteria normally used by international agencies: the relative buoyancy of demand – frequently seen in the publications of the European

Commission, where the productive branches are grouped on the basis of the growth of apparent consumption of the OECD countries – and technological intensity, a classification created by the OECD, based on various technological indicators of the member countries.

The relative buoyancy of demand is taken to approximate the differences in the income elasticity of the various branches and, therefore, in their capacity for growth. The larger the weight of the branches displaying more buoyant demand, the greater the expected growth of manufacturing as a whole.

In turn, technological intensity is indicative of the potential for productivity growth. Therefore it is also to be expected that the more production is geared towards the manufacturing branches with a higher technological content, the greater the growth of the sector as a whole. It should also be borne in mind that there seem to exist important externalities, or positive spillovers, which boost growth even more (see Sakurai, Papaconstatinou and Ioannidis, 1997).

Combining these two criteria we obtain Table 1.2, from which at least three conclusions can be drawn.

First, we find that those sectors with high demand and technological content have a much lower weight in Spain than in the European Union. And while the share of these activities in Spanish manufacturing as a whole has increased by nearly 3 percentage points to 20 per cent of value added, their weight has increased even more in the European Union, so that Spain's clear under-specialization in these branches has become yet more pronounced in relation to Europe. The situation is especially striking in the branch of office and data-processing machines, whose weight in Spain in 1997 was 40.9 per cent of the EU average. The electrical-goods sector has performed best, since its relative importance has moved towards the Community average. The opposite has occurred in the case of the chemical industry; its weight has increased somewhat, but not to the same extent as in the European Union.

Secondly, the traditional specialization of the Spanish economy in activities with low demand and technological intensity has continued. This is due to the fact that, even though the weight of this group of branches has declined in Spanish manufacturing, the same has occurred in the other EU countries. Particularly well known is Spain's specialization in food, beverages and tobacco, non-metallic minerals and mineral products, and textiles and clothing, leather and footwear. As a whole, this group of sectors has tended to converge, with the exception of food, beverages and tobacco and non-metallic minerals

Table 1.2 Structure of value added in manufacturing in Spain and the EU (%)

	1986			1997		
Structure calculated in 1990 euro	Spain	EU	Spain/EU	Spain	EU	Spain/EU
Sectors with strong demand and intensive technology	**16.8**	**21.0**	**80.0**	**19.7**	**25.8**	**76.4**
Electrical goods	6.4	9.0	71.1	8.5	10.8	78.7
Office and data-processing machines	2.2	3.1	71.0	1.8	4.4	40.9
Chemical products	8.2	8.9	92.1	9.4	10.6	88.7
Sectors with moderate demand and intermediate technology	**23.0**	**29.4**	**78.2**	**25.2**	**28.0**	**90.0**
Rubber and plastic products	4.4	3.8	115.8	4.8	4.3	111.6
Transport equipment	8.8	10.2	86.3	11.5	10.0	115.0
Agricultural and industrial machinery	4.6	10.1	45.5	4.5	8.9	50.6
Other manufactured products	5.2	5.3	98.1	4.4	4.8	91.7
Sectors with weak demand and low technology	**60.2**	**49.7**	**121.1**	**55.2**	**46.3**	**119.2**
Textiles and clothing, leather and footwear	11.1	8.3	133.7	8.2	6.5	126.2
Ferrous and non-ferrous ores and metals	5.5	4.3	127.9	4.5	4.3	104.7
Non-metallic minerals and mineral products	8.2	5.3	154.7	8.5	5.0	170.0
Paper and printing products	6.5	8.2	79.3	6.1	8.3	73.5
Food, beverages and tobacco	21.3	14.8	143.9	20.5	13.8	148.6
Metal products, exc. machinery and transport equipment	7.6	8.8	86.4	7.4	8.4	88.1
Total manufacturing	**100**	**100**		**100**	**100**	

Source: OECD: *National Accounts*, vol. II: *Detailed Tables*; OECD: *Quarterly National Accounts*; Eurostat: *National Accounts ESA, Detailed Tables by Branch*; Eurostat: *Monthly Panorama of European Industry*; INE: *Contabilidad Nacional de España*; Departamento de Estudios Europeos, Fundación de las Cajas de Ahorros.

and mineral products, in which Spanish specialization has increased; in the case of the latter sector, this is possibly due to its close relationship with construction, which, as we shall see below, has grown very substantially in the 1990s.

Finally, there has been convergence in the weight of those sectors with average demand and technological intensity. It should be noted, however, that this basically reflects the growth of the transport-equipment branch (which includes automobiles) and agricultural and industrial machinery.

In the construction sector, the first point to note is its enormous importance in Spain. In 1997 its weight was 3.0 percentage points higher than the EU average. Indeed, some consider that this branch of activity is oversized as a consequence of its expansion during the 1980s, when there was a major investment drive to upgrade Spain's underdeveloped infrastructure (which remains deficient, albeit to a lesser extent).

Currently, the presence of services in Spanish economic activity is similar to that of the European Union. However, within services the disparate performance of market and non-market services is significant, because the relative importance of the latter, unlike the case of the European Union, increased. This asymmetric development may be due, at least in part, to the less developed role played by the public sector in the Spanish economy; in 1986 there was a difference of nearly 3 percentage points in the relative weight of non-market services in Spain and in the European Union.

To study services in greater depth, their productive branches were classified according to whether their productivity has been greater or less than the OECD average for the sector during the 1990s. This ranking allows us to distinguish those activities in which the most radical technological innovations generated in recent years are taking place (and, by extension, where growth potential is greater) from the more traditional ones tied to specific geographic characteristics of the country, in which productivity gains are more limited. The first group of services has been called progressive (because they show notable productivity growth), and the second, stagnant or traditional (because their productivity remains almost unchanged).[8] The result of applying this criterion is displayed in Table 1.3.

The first group of high-productivity activities includes those sectors linked to transport (except domestic transport) and communications, the financial system and other market services (basically business services). As a whole, this group of branches has a much lower weight in

Spain than on average in the European Union. Furthermore, the gap widened in the period 1986–95 (the last year available), when their importance increased by 5 percentage points in the European Union but fell in Spain.

When assessing the seriousness of the Spanish economy's weakness in these high-productivity services it should be borne in mind, as pointed out above, that most of the technological innovations of recent years are concentrated in these activities, and as a result these are the fastest-growing services at the international level. Furthermore, their externalities and backward linkage effects extend not only to the rest of service activities, but to the economy as a whole, and, in particular, to manufacturing. Consider telecommunications services, for example. Their development gives a significant boost to the capital goods industry in a broad sense.

One particularly striking case is that of the credit institutions and insurance sector, which has a relatively higher weight in Spain. In fact, Spain has the second largest financial sector, after Luxembourg, in terms of the value added that it generates relative to the whole economy. This situation is basically a consequence of the great importance the banking sector continues to have in Spain. None the less, largely due to the intense deregulation of recent years and the resulting increase in competitive pressures, the weight of these services in Spain is tending to move towards the Community average.

Turning now to the group of services with productivity levels below the OECD average, the first point to make is that the weight of the lodging and catering sector in Spain is nearly three times the Community average, owing to the importance of tourism in Spain compared with the average in its Community partners, not counting France and Italy.[9]

The distributive trade also has a relatively high weight in Spain, although it has declined in recent years – especially since the early 1990s – leading to a tendency to converge with the European Union. In fact, the introduction of deregulating measures and strong penetration by foreign capital (see Martín and Velázquez, 1996b) have increased competition and reduced its high margins. As a result, a significant portion of the retail sector has been pushed out of the market.

In sum, as in the case of manufacturing, those service branches with the best prospects for demand growth, in which most technological activity at the world level is concentrated and, thus, with higher productivity, are underdeveloped in Spain compared with the European

Table 1.3 Structure of value added in services in Spain and the EU (%)

	1986			1995		
Structure calculated in 1990 euro	Spain	EU	Spain/EU	Spain	EU	Spain/EU
Sectors with higher-than-average productivity	**41.4**	**46.0**	**90.0**	**40.4**	**50.9**	**79.4**
Maritime and air transport services	0.9	0.8	112.5	0.9	1.0	90.0
Auxiliary transport services	1.5	2.0	75.0	1.5	2.0	75.0
Communication services	2.6	3.1	83.9	3.3	3.7	89.2
Services of credit and insurance institutions	10.9	8.6	126.7	8.6	8.4	102.4
Other market services	25.5	31.5	81.0	26.1	35.8	72.9
Sectors with lower-than-average productivity	**58.6**	**54.0**	**108.5**	**59.4**	**49.0**	**121.2**
Recovery and repair services	23.8	20.2	117.8	22.7	19.4	117.0
Lodging and catering services	11.2	4.5	248.9	11.4	4.0	285.0
Inland transport services	3.6	3.6	100.0	3.8	3.6	105.6
Non-market services	20.0	25.7	77.8	21.5	22.0	97.7
Total services	**100**	**100**		**100**	**100**	

Sources: OECD: *National Accounts*, vol. II: *Detailed Tables*; OECD: *Quarterly National Accounts*; Eurostat: *National Accounts ESA, Detailed Tables by Branch*; INE: *Contabilidad Nacional de España*; Departamento de Estudios Europeos, Fundación de las Cajas de Ahorros.

Union. Consequently, the productive specialization of the Spanish economy does not appear to be the best suited to sustaining, in the medium and long run, the high rate of growth required if Spain is to reach a level of development similar to that of its EU partners. In any event, it is important to stress that during this period there has been a slight convergence between Spanish and Community productive structures. The index of similarity between the sectoral distribution of value added in Spain and in the European Union rose by one point for the economy as a whole and remains unchanged when the manufacturing sector is considered on its own.[10]

Finally, to complete this initial picture of the relative progress of the Spanish economy within the European Union, we consider how the primary distribution of income (between factors of production) has developed.

What stands out most here (see Table 1.1) is the growing weight of employee compensation in Spain, versus a decline in the European Union. Another noteworthy feature is that the share of employee compensation is much lower in the Spanish economy, which may be explained by two facts: first, the lower dependent-employment ratio in Spain, and secondly, the higher relative endowment of labour in relation to the European Union, and consequently, the lower remuneration of this factor.

1.4 Conclusions

This chapter began by analysing the path of Spanish GDP per capita in relation to that of the countries which make up the European Union. An examination of the changes in the structure of GDP, from the point of view of both demand and supply, completed this analysis, revealing the changes in the patterns of sectoral specialization of the Spanish economy in relation to the Community. Finally, the way in which all these changes have been reflected in the primary distribution of income was considered.

The main conclusions of this chapter can be summarized as follows.

- Between 1986 and 1997, Spain managed to reduce the negative gap between its GDP per capita and the average of the rest of its European partners by 6 percentage points, increasing its GDP per capita from 72.7 per cent of the average Community income per capita in 1986 to 78.6 per cent in 1997. In spite of this, Spain has fallen one place in the European Union to thirteenth, having been overtaken by Ireland.

- As to changes in the structure of GDP from the viewpoint of demand, it must be stressed that, despite the notable similarity between Spanish and Community demand, Spain is characterized by certain peculiarities. First, the economy is less open. Even though this difference has tended to be corrected over time, opening up has been accompanied by significant trade deficits. Secondly, Spain's government consumption is lower and its investment is very much higher. When it is recalled that the average Spanish and European saving ratios over the period have been similar, it is clear that Spain's saving has been insufficient – in contrast to the evident balance in the European Union – and that this constitutes a limitation on the potential growth of the Spanish economy.
- On the supply side, the lesser importance of manufacturing and the greater weight of construction stand out.
- Descending to the level of disaggregation permitted by the NACE-CLIO (25) classification, it can be seen that the sectors in which Spain is underspecialized are those characterized by more buoyant demand and greater technological intensity, in particular the capital goods and chemical products branches, and business services and services linked to communications. At the same time, the sectors in which Spain is relatively specialized are those characterized by low demand growth and technological content (such as food, beverages and tobacco, for example) or those exploiting some geographic feature (lodging and catering services, due to their relationship with tourism). This pattern of specialization is most obvious in manufacturing. None the less, it should be noted that in the period 1986–97 the Spanish and Community productive structures tended to converge.
- Finally, with regard to the primary distribution of income, the lower weight in Spain of employee compensation should be highlighted. This phenomenon, from any standpoint, is a symptom of the relative scarcity of capital in Spain, which is manifested in its higher relative remuneration.

2
Productivity and its Determinants

2.1 Introduction

Spain's objective of convergence with the Community levels of per capita income can only be achieved if its economic growth is more rapid than that of the rest of its EU partners. To accomplish this goal, one almost indispensable condition is to heighten the efficiency of the use of the factors of production or, more precisely, to increase relative productivity.

It is easily shown that a country's level of GDP per capita hinges on labour productivity and the proportion of the population that is employed. Thus:

$$\frac{\text{GDP}}{\text{Population}} = \frac{\text{GDP}}{\text{Employment}} \times \frac{\text{Employment}}{\text{Population}}$$

Approximately 57 per cent of Spain's per capita GDP growth since its entry into the European Union has in fact been due to the increase in labour productivity. Differential growth in labour productivity must therefore play a central role in moving the level of Spain's GDP per capita closer to the Community average.[1]

But labour productivity is in turn determined by capital, both physical and intangible. For this reason, the present chapter will focus on a comparative analysis of the labour and overall productivity of the 15 member countries, and of Spain in particular, as well as their determinants. Specifically, Section 2.2 presents a comparative evaluation of productivity, or productive efficiency. Section 2.3 then goes on to analyse the relative behaviour of the explanatory factors of productivity growth, which are either derived from the conventional model of economic growth, such as the economy's endowment of physical capital, or emanate from the more recent theories of endogenous growth, including for example technological, human and public capital (in the latter case, with special emphasis on transport infrastructure). As in the other chapters of the book, the chapter closes with a series of conclusions.

2.2 Analysis of productive efficiency

Efficiency gains are one of the prime means of enhancing a country's level of economic welfare. For this reason, as elucidated in the breakdown of per capita GDP described in the Introduction (Section 2.1), labour productivity is the cornerstone of the study of economic growth and the most common indicator of productive efficiency. Labour productivity is, however, an imperfect measure of efficiency, because it only explicitly considers the labour side.

As a consequence, since the mid-1950s other indicators, whose calculation is more complex, have been devised to reflect this phenomenon better. It is now generally acknowledged that total factor productivity constitutes a better measure of efficiency, since it takes into account the labour and physical capital employed in the productive process. None the less, this indicator is not exempt from certain basic criticisms, mainly concerning the very restrictive nature of the assumptions required for its calculation and the omission of other forms of capital, of an intangible nature.

2.2.1 Labour productivity

Labour productivity is defined as the ratio of the output obtained in a productive process to the quantity of labour employed. As such, it indicates the apparent efficiency of the labour factor, and consequently some authors speak of apparent labour productivity.

Here we have taken as the output variable the value added to market prices in real 1997 terms. Given the great disparity in the time actually worked per employee in the Community countries,[2] as a measure of the labour factor we have used the number of hours worked by employees as a whole. Hence what we have calculated is productivity.

As shown in Figure 2.1, Spain stands among the EU countries with the lowest labour productivity during the period studied. In 1986 Spain's hourly productivity was 14.2 euro (in 1997 euro), or around three-fourths (75.1 per cent) of the EU average. Since then it has risen to 17.3 euro per hour.

Note, however, that this increase in Spain's productivity occurred against a general backdrop of intense growth in this variable throughout the 15 EU countries.

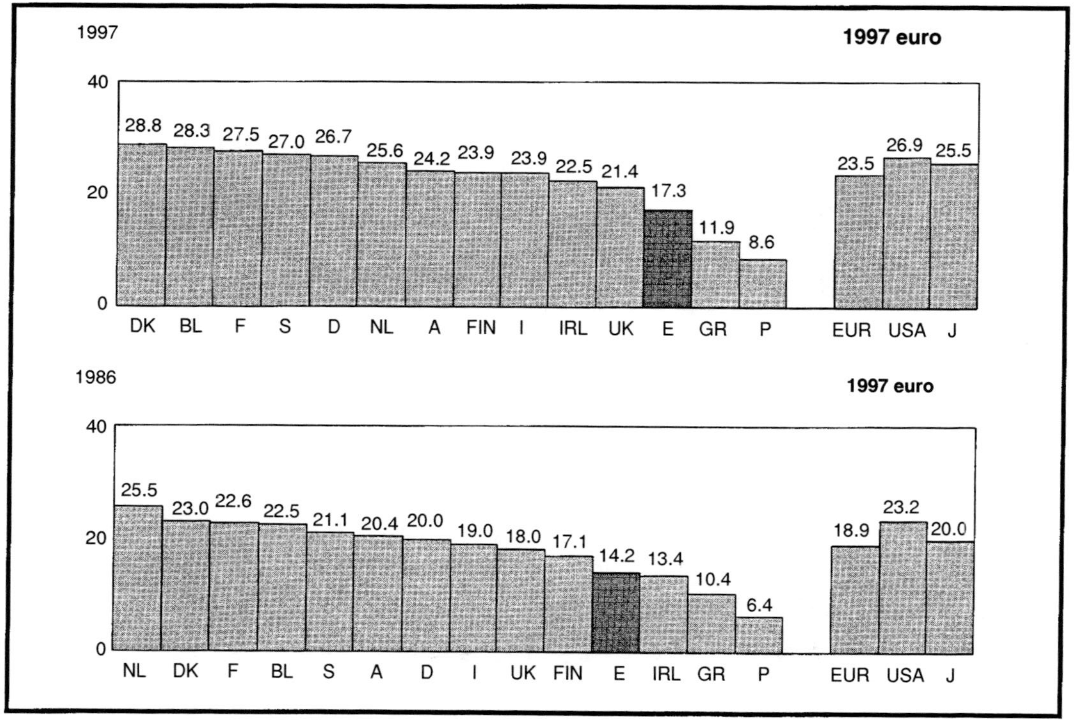

Figure 2.1 Labour productivity (GDP mp per hour worked)

Source: OECD: *National Accounts*, vol. I: *Main Aggregates*; OECD: *Labour Force Statistics*; Eurostat: *Labour Force Survey*; Departamento de Estudios Europeos, Fundación de las Cajas de Ahorros.

Finally, it should be stressed that the productivity differentials within the European Union narrowed during these years, with the variation coefficient falling from 0.28 in 1986 to 0.26 in 1997.

2.2.2 Total factor productivity

As noted above, total factor productivity is considered a better indicator of efficiency than labour productivity. In this respect, its measurement takes us another step forward in our assessment of the level of efficiency at which European economies operate. Yet it is worth recalling that this measure is not immune from criticism, owing to the restrictive assumptions involved.[3]

From the wealth of available indices for measuring total productivity,[4] we have chosen a version of the Törnqvist-Theil index developed by Caves, Christensen and Diewert (1982) – known as the multilateral translogarithmic productivity index – which allows us to compare productivity levels both over time and across countries.[5]

As in the case of labour productivity, value added is used to measure output, but here it is measured at factor cost.[6] Also, labour is calculated in terms of hours worked. The measure of physical capital is more complex. At present, the OECD provides information on the magnitude of the stock of physical capital of some EU countries,[7] although the same methodology is not applied in all cases.[8] To arrive at a homogeneous measure for the Fifteen, we have estimated the capital stock under the perpetual inventory method, in other words by summing fixed capital investment (deflated and adjusted for depreciation). Finally, we have obtained a measure of the capital stock in its hybrid form and at constant replacement cost.[9] Lastly, as an approximation of the remuneration of the two factors, for labour we have taken its share in gross value added at factor cost, according to the definition used in Velázquez (1995a), and for capital the balance of this magnitude.

Figure 2.2 presents the results obtained after calculating, under the method described, the overall productivity for Spain and for the most and least productive EU countries – Germany and Greece, respectively – standardized by the European average. As seen, according to this indicator of total productivity, Spain's position relative to the EU average is considerably better than that reflected in the labour productivity indicator. In fact, in relation to the average of the Fifteen, Spain's efficiency level stands at nearly 87 per cent.

It is worth noting that the disparity between the diagnosis of Spain's situation as reflected in total productivity and that inferred from labour productivity stems from the difference in the degree of capital-

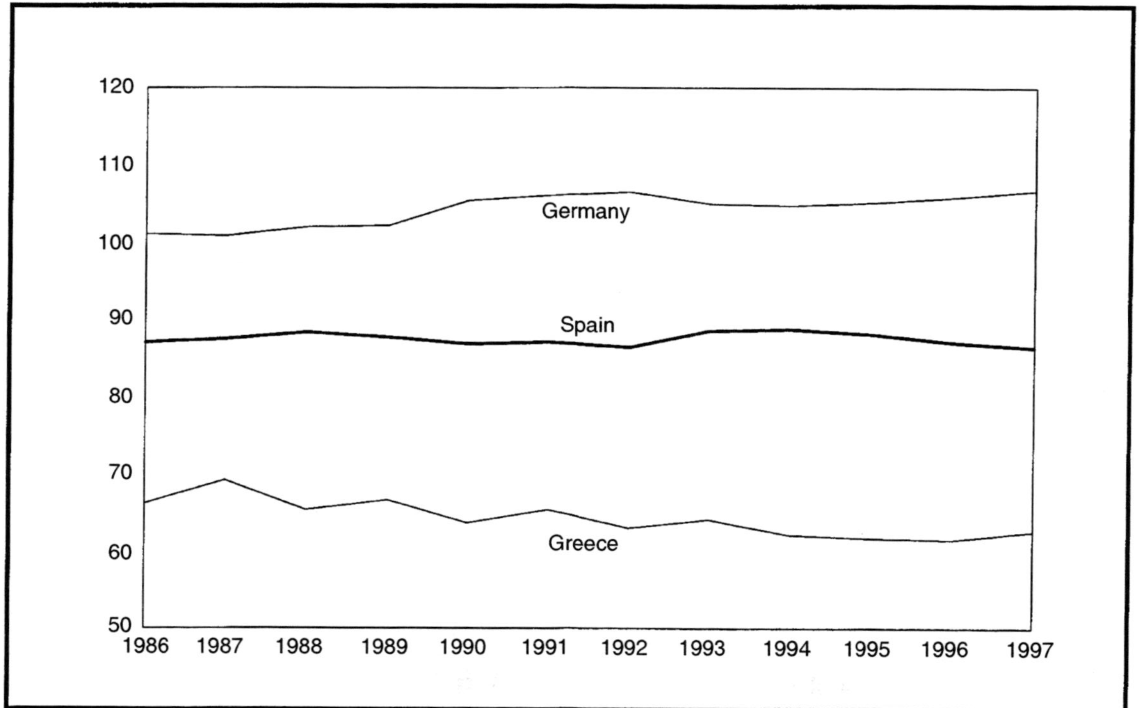

Figure 2.2 Trends in total factor productivity of various EU countries (index of multilateral translogarithmic productivity, EU = 100)

Source: OECD: *National Accounts*, vol. I: *Main Aggregates*; OECD: *Labour Force Statistics*; Eurostat: *Labour Force Survey*; Departamento de Estudios Europeos, Fundación de las Cajas de Ahorros.

ization of the economies compared. More specifically, the results show that Spain is undercapitalized with respect to the EU average (for a more detailed explanation of this subject, see Dowrick and Nguyen, 1989, and Velázquez, 1995b).

2.3 Determining factors of productivity growth

Now that we have an idea of the efficiency level at which the Community economies operate, it would seem interesting to examine the factors that cause the differences between them.

In this respect, the notable progress made since the early 1980s in the economic literature on growth – the so-called endogenous growth models – proves very helpful.[10]

Indeed, when we examine the available theoretical and empirical evidence, we find a marked coincidence in their emphasis on the importance of certain intangible assets, especially human and technological capital, as basic ingredients of productivity and growth. The emphasis placed on these factors does not exclude, however, the relevance of investment in physical capital, and also leaves open the possibility that part of technology is included in capital goods. Another factor that appears to exert significant influence on growth capacity is the composition of government spending. In this respect, the available studies indicate that public equipment in general, and public transport and communications infrastructure in particular, stand out for their special impact on productivity.

Consequently, to explore the reasons for the productivity gap between Spain and the EU average, we will carry out a comparative analysis of their relative endowments in each of the factors mentioned.

2.3.1 Physical capital

While it has long been known that countries' labour productivity – and, in consequence, their growth – is influenced by their endowment of physical capital, until recently the difficulty of quantifying this variable discouraged undertaking studies to measure its exact impact.

The measurement of capital endowment carried out in the present study, however, allows us to calculate the physical capital stock/labour ratios of all the EU countries. The results for 1986 and 1997 are shown in Figure 2.3, expressed in terms of the value of the average Community ratio in 1986. As seen, after a decade-long convergence process, in 1997 Spain had a physical capital/labour ratio of around 74 per cent of the EU average, fruit of its stronger investment efforts

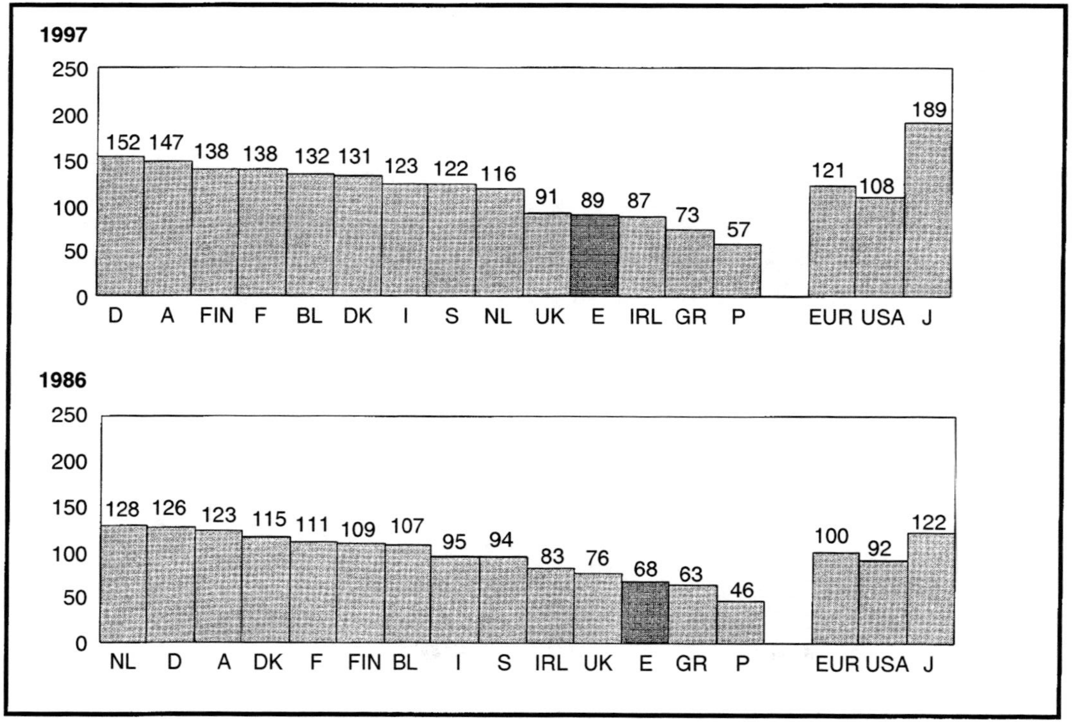

Figure 2.3 Physical capital/labour ratio (ratio of stock of physical capital to employment, EUR in 1986 = 100)

Source: OECD: *National Accounts*, vol. I: *Main Aggregates*; OECD: *Labour Force Statistics*; Eurostat: *Labour Force Survey*; Departamento de Estudios Europeos, Fundación de las Cajas de Ahorros.

since joining the EU. On average during the period, gross fixed capital formation in Spain was 21.6 per cent of GDP, compared with a Community average of 19.4 per cent.

As various studies (see Argimón, González-Páramo and Roldán, 1997; and Velázquez, 1995b) demonstrate, the investment drive in the period – except in the final years – was to a large extent sustained by government investment.

Despite this, Spain still stands in twelfth place in the ranking of the Fifteen in terms of its capital/labour ratios (see Figure 2.3).

2.3.2 Technological capital

As mentioned above, recent growth models increasingly stress the essential role played by technology (see, by way of example, Romer, 1990; and Grossman and Helpman, 1991).

Its measurement, however, still poses many problems. Yet, a consensus exists that the resources assigned to R&D – despite the many possible qualifications – represent a reasonable measure of a country's capacity to generate technical knowledge.[11] For this reason, to measure the stock of technological capital in Spain and the other EU members, we have drawn on the information on the R&D spending of each of these countries and applied the perpetual inventory method.[12]

After estimating the technological capital stock of all the countries in the way indicated above, its relationship to GDP has been calculated. The resulting values of the technological capital ratio, expressed in terms of the average EU value in 1986, are shown in Figure 2.4. From examining these results, we deduce among other things that Spain stands at a far remove from the average of its Community partners. On our estimation, Spain's technological capital stock in 1997 was only 35 per cent of the EU average. Moreover, we find that, even though the technological capital ratio moved towards the EU average between 1986 and 1997 (in 1986 it represented only 20 per cent), Spain's relative position in the ranking of the Fifteen remained unchanged, ahead of Portugal and Greece and behind Ireland, throughout the period.[13]

At the core of this enormous technological insufficiency lie the meagre research efforts on both the public and private fronts. A further worrisome and striking feature is the way the financing of R&D is distributed between the government and the corporate sector: whereas in the European Union the corporate sector accounts for the largest share, financing around 52.5 per cent of R&D expenditure, in Spain this figure is less than 44.5 per cent, clearly indicative of the scant attention paid by Spanish firms to technological activities.

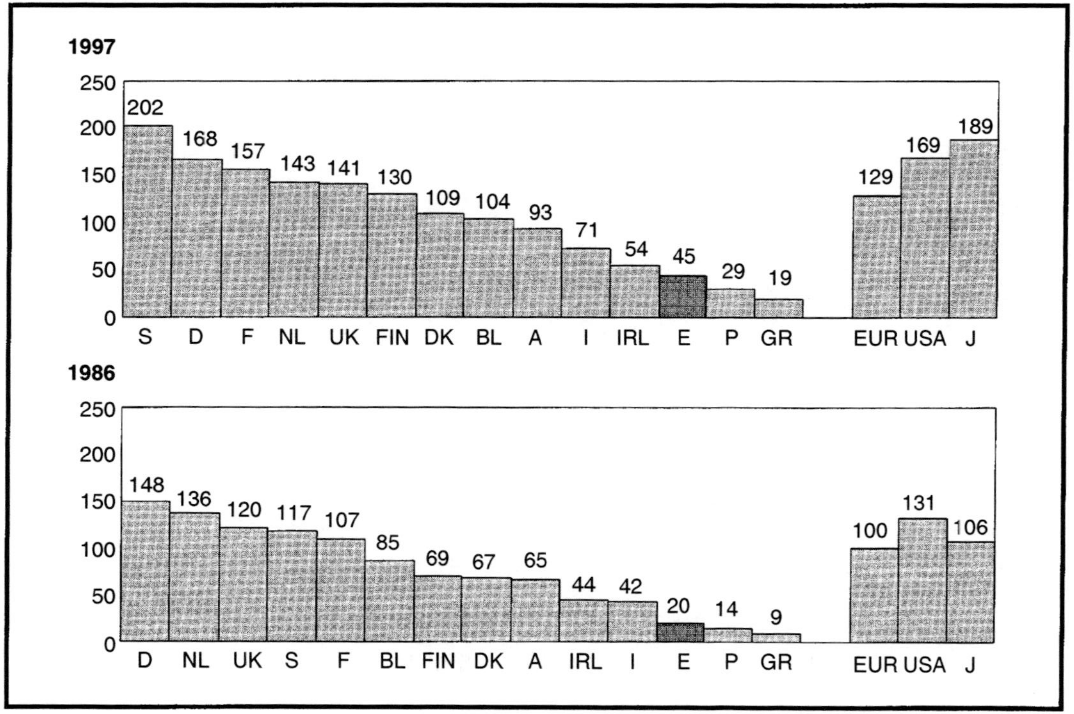

Figure 2.4 Technological capital (ratio of stock technological capital to GDP mp, EUR in 1986 = 100)

Source: OECD: *Main Science and Technology Indicators*; OECD: *Research and Development Expenditure in Industry*; UNESCO: *Statistical Yearbook*; OECD: *National Accounts*, vol. I: *Main Aggregates*; Departamento de Estudios Europeos, Fundación de las Cajas de Ahorros.

2.3.3 Human capital

As in the case of technology, the literature on economic growth places great stress on human capital to explain the differences in growth between countries (see, for example, Lucas, 1988; Romer, 1989; Uzawa, 1965).

Human capital influences growth in two ways. First, the accumulation of knowledge and skills by labour has a direct impact on the productivity of the labour factor. And secondly, human capital affects productivity indirectly by improving the performance of physical and technological capital. Moreover, some studies underscore the importance of human capital in the assimilation of imported technology and in the generation of own innovations (see Benhabib and Spiegel, 1994). Here, however, it should be emphasized that the return on investment in education and training (in other words, investment that increases the stock of human capital) entails – as does R&D spending – a long period of gestation.

Before proceeding to estimate the human capital stock of Spain and its Community partners, it should be pointed out that there is no generally accepted method for undertaking this task.[14] In any case, the procedure most used, albeit not exempt from criticism, is to approach the human capital stock of a country in terms of the level of training of its population (or, better still, the working-age population) according to the years of schooling at all levels of education. In essence, this is the method used here.

Specifically, we have obtained the indicator of human capital through a formulation similar to the perpetual-inventory method;[15] that is, by adding up the number of students enrolled each year since 1930 at all educational levels (primary, secondary, technical and higher education) who are of working age in the year for which the indicator is calculated, previously weighted by the ratio between expenditure per student at each level of education and in each country, and the average total cost of educating a university student in the EU. Moreover, we have considered that the knowledge acquired tends to depreciate[16] if it is not used at work (either through inactivity or through failure to find employment). Finally, the results obtained were divided by the working-age population (15 to 64 years of age) and expressed in terms of the average EU value in 1986. The resulting indicator can therefore be interpreted as the percentage of the working-age population with the equivalent of higher education in relation to the EU average.

The indicator thus calculated, shown in Figure 2.5, gives results that are consistent with the findings for the other productive factors, both

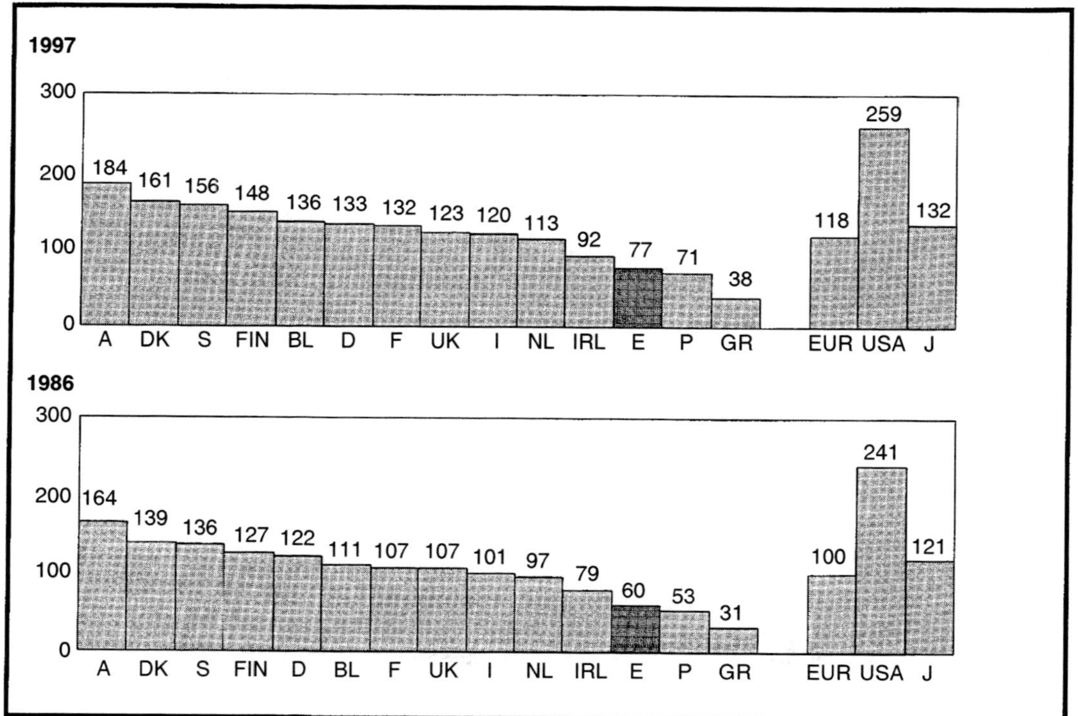

Figure 2.5 Human capital (population with higher education or equivalent, EUR in 1986 = 100)

Source: UNESCO: *Statistical Yearbook*; OECD: *Education at a Glance*; Departamento de Estudios Europeos, Fundación de las Cajas de Ahorros.

in terms of the diagnosis of the present situation and with respect to the trends in recent years. In fact, even though Spain's stock of human capital has increased to a greater extent than that of the EU as a whole, it was not enough to raise its position in the ranking: in 1986 Spain ranked thirteenth, and it remained there in 1997. Admittedly, however, thanks to the improvement made, Spain was able to narrow its gap with the Community, reaching 65 per cent of the EU average.

In examining Figure 2.5, we also find that the human capital endowment improved in all European countries, but by more in those countries with a lower point of departure, thereby shortening the distance between them. Consequently, though possibly venturing too far, it could be said that the European Union – except Greece – appears to have escaped the so-called 'poverty trap' that snares poorer countries when they invest less in education than the richer economies (see Boldrin, 1993).

In any event, returning to the Spanish situation, it should be noted that, if the policy of budget cuts applied to education expenditure in recent years continues, the human capital gap which still exists between Spain and the EU could widen once again. This would have serious repercussions on future productivity levels and GDP per capita, taking into account the externalities and economies of experience implicit in this type of investment.

2.3.4 Public capital and transport infrastructure

Another productive factor, not directly related to the factor endowment of companies, which has recently been incorporated in the explanatory models of growth is the stock of public capital in general, or, more specifically, the endowment of certain types of infrastructure (see Aschauer, 1989; Stern, 1991, and Munnell, 1992).

The public capital stock affects productivity in at least two ways. First, because it provides the equipment (motorways, high-tension networks, among others) that companies require but whose cost cannot be entirely borne by private initiative. Secondly, the availability of this type of capital, particularly transport infrastructure, makes it easier to supply a wider market and, accordingly, to exploit economies of scale.

Thus, from a theoretical standpoint, it seems obvious that the public capital stock has significant positive externalities on the productivity of companies. Here, however, the findings of empirical studies are even more conclusive than what the theory had ventured to predict. Thus, for the Spanish case, Argimón et al. (1994, 1997) and Más et al. (1994) provide cogent proof of the positive impact of public capital on the productivity of the private sector.

Moreover, it appears that companies' decisions on where to locate often hinge on the infrastructure endowment, which illustrates its importance in the productive process.

To measure the public capital endowment, and specifically the transport infrastructure, we have constructed two mutually complementary indicators. The first is the stock of public capital calculated on the basis of the accumulation of gross fixed capital formation of the general government sector, duly updated and adjusted for depreciation. To ensure that the stock calculated is comparable across countries, it has been homogenized by the number of inhabitants and expressed in terms of the EU average in 1986. The second indicator was calculated under the method proposed by Biehl (1986 and 1988).[17] It is the average of two indices, one expressing the kilometres of motorway – or the equivalent in the other road categories[18] – in relation to the total area, and another which relates them to the population, each expressed in terms of the weighted average of the EU countries in 1986.

As to the first of these two indicators – public capital stock, whose EU ranking is shown in Figure 2.6 – Spain's situation is worse than the Community average. It is positioned in a broad group of countries poorly endowed in public capital, including Ireland, the United Kingdom, Portugal and Greece. None the less, in Spain this gap has narrowed during the period of its membership of the European Union. Spain has thus risen from fourteenth to thirteenth place in the ranking of the Fifteen, attesting to its significant investment drive. Specifically, Spain's public capital endowment per head of population has climbed from 37 per cent of the Community average to 64 per cent in 1997. Even so, it still has a substantial deficit.

The indicator of transport infrastructure endowment, shown in Figure 2.7, allows us to analyse that part of public capital with the greatest impact on the productive process (see De Rus, Román and Trujillo, 1995). Although the classification of countries obtained from this indicator is similar to the ranking in terms of public capital stock, there are several differences which refer to countries covering a large territory but with low population density, whose transport system is concentrated in a small area. This is precisely the case of Sweden, which ranks first in public capital per head of population, but stands in ninth place in terms of transport infrastructure.

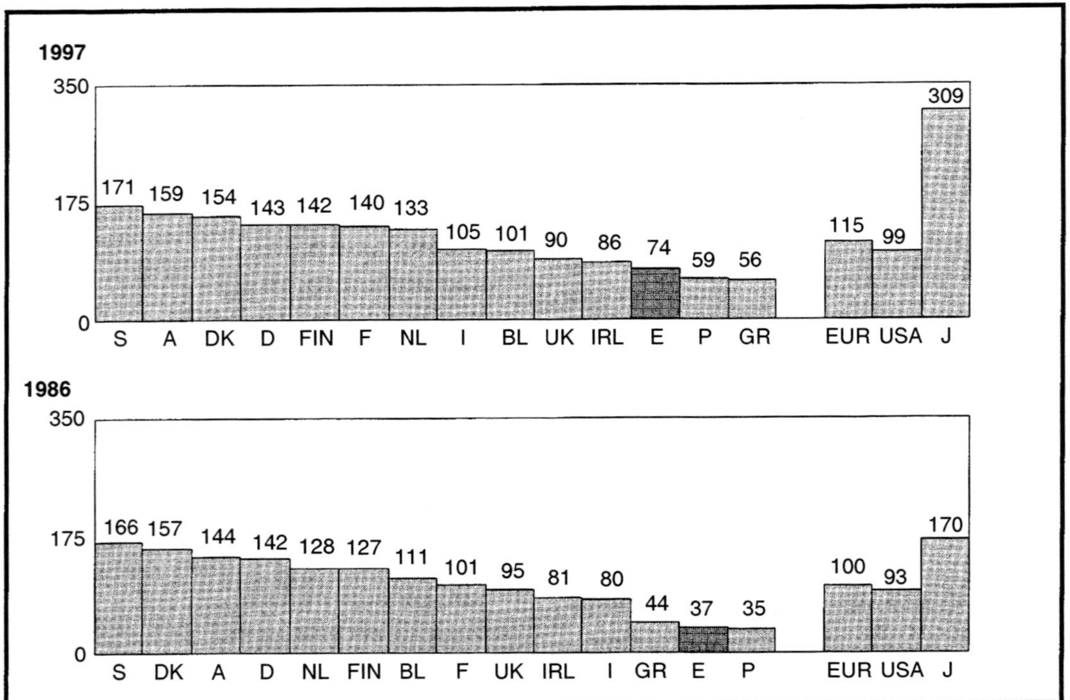

Figure 2.6 Public capital (stock of public capital per capita, EUR in 1986 = 100)

Source: OECD: *National Accounts*, vol. II: *Detailed Tables*; Departamento de Estudios Europeos, Fundación de las Cajas de Ahorros.

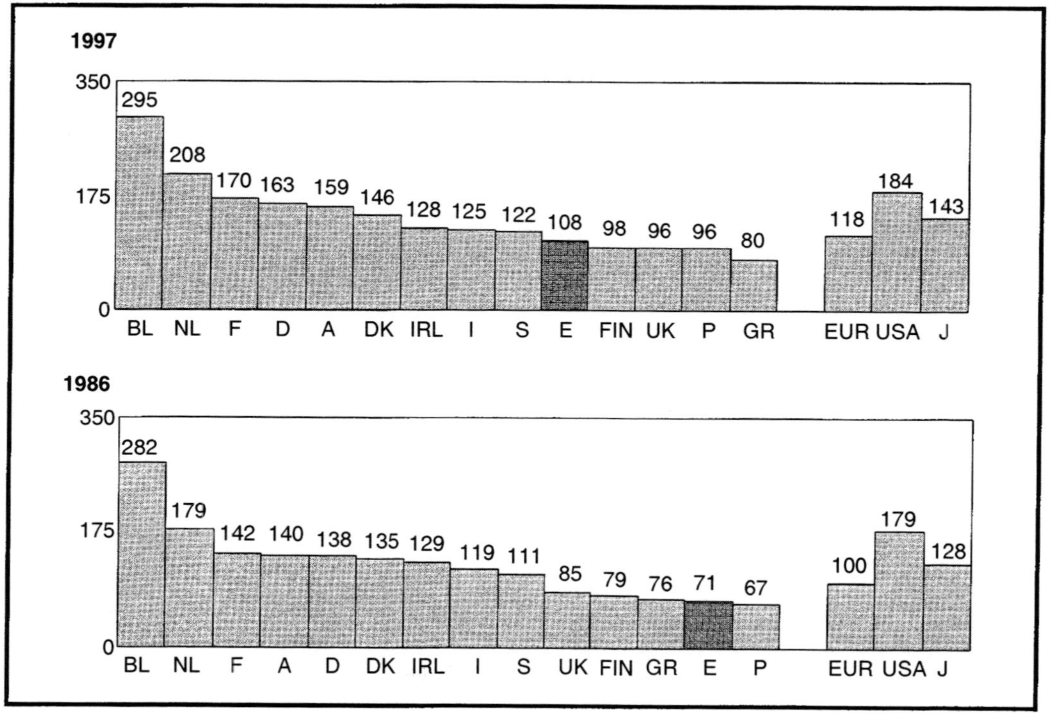

Figure 2.7 Transport infrastructure indicator (EUR in 1986 = 100)

Source: UN: *Annual Bulletin of Transport Statistics for Europe and North America*; Departamento de Estudios Europeos, Fundación de las Cajas de Ahorros.

In the case of Spain, there has been a notable convergence with the average Community values. In 1986, Spain had a significant gap in transport infrastructure as its endowment was only 71 per cent of the average in the European Union. Eleven years later the situation had improved, and this figure had advanced to 92 per cent.

In sum, the relative situation of Spain as regards public equipment is, on the whole, substantially better than that indicated by the other measures of factor endowment analysed in this chapter. Obviously, the improvement during this period is the result of the enormous investment drive carried out by general government agencies, especially in the area of transport infrastructure. Even so, the persistence of a certain lag in Spain vis-à-vis the European Union should be borne in mind.

For this reason, and to conclude, several observations would seem apposite regarding the inappropriateness of the public spending cuts included in recent budgets, within the framework of the fiscal consolidation envisaged in the stability pact agreed by the EMU member countries. In this respect, it is worth recalling that infrastructure endowment is crucial to a country's capacity to attract investment projects from abroad, especially when the country has a peripheral location, as is the case of the Spanish economy within Europe. Moreover, as several authors have stated, cuts in government spending budgets have only a short-term effect on the deficit, at the expense of negative consequences for productivity and economic growth, which are of a permanent nature. It should also be remembered that the endowment of public capital in general and the availability of transport routes in particular have a special impact on the development of tourism activities, so important to the Spanish economy.

2.4 Conclusions

This chapter measures the productivity levels of the fifteen Community countries in order to analyse the productive efficiency of the Spanish economy vis-à-vis its EU partners. As measures of productivity, we calculated apparent labour productivity in terms of output per hour worked, and total factor productivity using a multilateral translogarithmic productivity index. From the results obtained and the subsequent analysis – following the line of the endogenous growth models – of the relative situation of the determining factors at play, we deduce that:

- Spain's level of labour productivity stands at around 75 per cent of the EU average, thus practically the same gap as for GDP per capita.

- The level of total factor productivity (physical capital and labour), however, stands at more than 85 per cent of the Community average. The difference between this measure and the previous one should be interpreted as a deficit in the Spanish economy's capitalization relative to the average in the European Union. Note in this respect that under our calculations Spain's capital/labour ratio is less than 75 per cent of the EU average.
- The determining factors of productivity analysed here signal a significant lag with respect to the European Union. The greatest deficit occurs in technological capital, which reaches only a third of the Community average. None the less, the rest of the factors reflect differentials which, though more moderate, are still worrisome.
- During the period, however, a converging tendency is apparent. The relative situation of all the types of capital analysed has therefore improved during the years of Spain's membership of the European Union.
- Nevertheless, it should be borne in mind that this converging path could founder if budgetary austerity is geared – as now appears to be the case – towards cuts in infrastructure investment or in spending on education and R&D. In this respect, it is worth recalling that the productive factors analysed are cumulative in nature, and therefore any decline in the investment flows that sustain or enlarge them could widen Spain's already existing shortfalls vis-à-vis the EU average.
- It should be pointed out that the greatest investment efforts to generate intangible assets and human and technical capital have been made by the public sector. In fact, Spain's corporate sector does not appear yet to have assumed the more active role played by private initiative in this respect in the more advanced countries of the European Union. In this sense it would be very unfortunate if the human capital generated by the educational system were to be lost due to insufficient training efforts by companies. Indeed, the quickening in the pace of technical change would appear to require increasingly more intense and continuous on-the-job training efforts of this type.
- Briefly, to round off these conclusions, it could be said that, even though Spain has advanced on the difficult path of efficiency growth, it still has a long way to go, and nothing would seem to justify a backward step.

3
Activity, Employment and Unemployment

3.1 Introduction

With high and persistent unemployment rates prevailing in the European Union for so many years – notably higher than in the United States and Japan – studies have sought to explain this phenomenon by examining the idiosyncratic features common to EU economies. They tend to coincide in highlighting, among others, two large groups of factors. The first includes those most directly linked to the peculiarities of the institutional framework, which affect the workings of the labour market itself and the nature of the system of social benefits. The second group encompasses those associated with the productive structure, which determine the capacity of economies to adapt to changes in technology and in international competition.

Naturally, along with the features shared by the EU member countries, unemployment problems are also manifested in ways that are specific to each economy. This is especially true in the case of Spain, where for many years the unemployment rate has been around double the Community average, unquestionably constituting the most disturbing of the imbalances in the Spanish economy.

This chapter will attempt to identify the unique features of Spanish unemployment – aside from its extraordinarily high rate – through a comparison with the situation in the other EU economies. It also examines the main labour market variables with a view to advancing our knowledge of the reasons and possible remedies for unemployment. We begin, in Section 3.2, by analysing the variables relating to activity and to the level and structure of employment. Section 3.3 then goes on to review the variables that best serve to explain the nature and causes of unemployment. Section 3.4 concentrates on a more detailed discussion of one of its causes – the difficulty of adapting to technological change – because this appears to be one of the chief factors in Europe's higher unemployment rates, and in Spain's extraordinarily high rates vis-à-vis its EU partners. Finally, the main conclusions of the analysis are summarized in the hope that useful inferences for a job-promotion policy can be drawn from them.

3.2 Labour force and employment trends

In the period 1986–97, the proportion of the Spanish population aged 15 to 64 – in other words, those potentially active, according to European standards – rose appreciably, and by the end of 1997 surpassed that of the European Union as a whole. In parallel, the labour force as a percentage of the total population, which in the mid-1980s was clearly lower in Spain, gradually increased, moving closer to but not quite reaching the EU average (see Figure 3.1).

Throughout these years, and especially in expansionary periods, Spain's labour force exerted increasing pressure on the labour market, not only because of the natural growth of the working-age population but due in particular to the growing presence of women in the labour force. Figure 3.2 clearly illustrates how Spain's labour force – like that of the United States and Japan – has tended to increase, while that of the EU countries as a whole has tended to stabilize since the early 1990s.

All told, as mentioned, the participation rate of the Spanish economy is still one of the lowest in the European Union, while the EU participation rate is in turn markedly lower than the US and Japanese rates, as seen in Figure 3.3.

In the years ahead, therefore, the Spanish participation rate should continue to move closer to the European average. This forecast is based on the comparatively low rate of female participation that still exists in Spain, the significant improvement in the job skills of women and, in sum, the greater possibilities for part-time employment under the labour reform of 1994. None the less, to a large extent, the impact on the labour force of the growing presence of women in the labour market will be offset over time, in so far as the abrupt decline in the birth rate in recent years is reflected in flat growth rates (see Bover and Arellano, 1995).

Turning now to employment, we should begin by pointing out that Spain's low level of employment is a striking case within the European Union. As shown in Figure 3.4, the number of employed as a

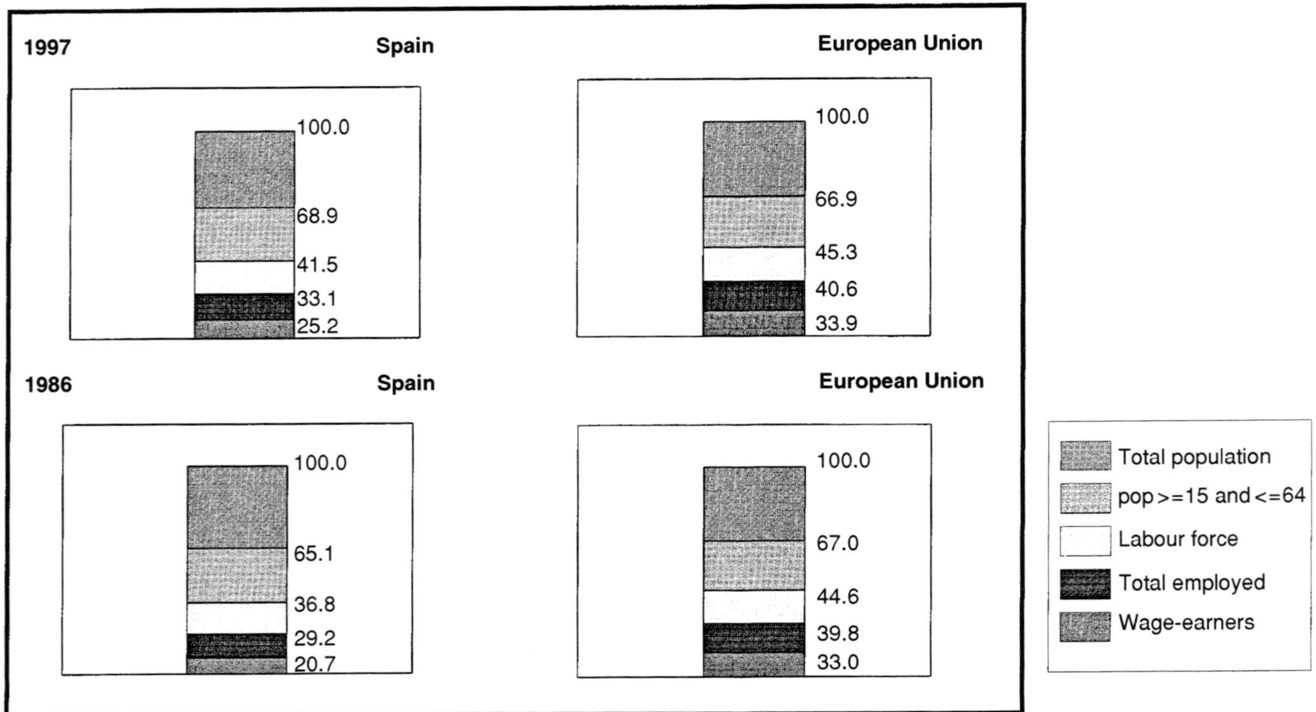

Figure 3.1 Classification of the population in relation to activity in Spain and the EU (percentage of total population)

Source: OECD: *Labour Force Statistics*; Departamento de Estudios Europeos, Fundación de las Cajas de Ahorros.

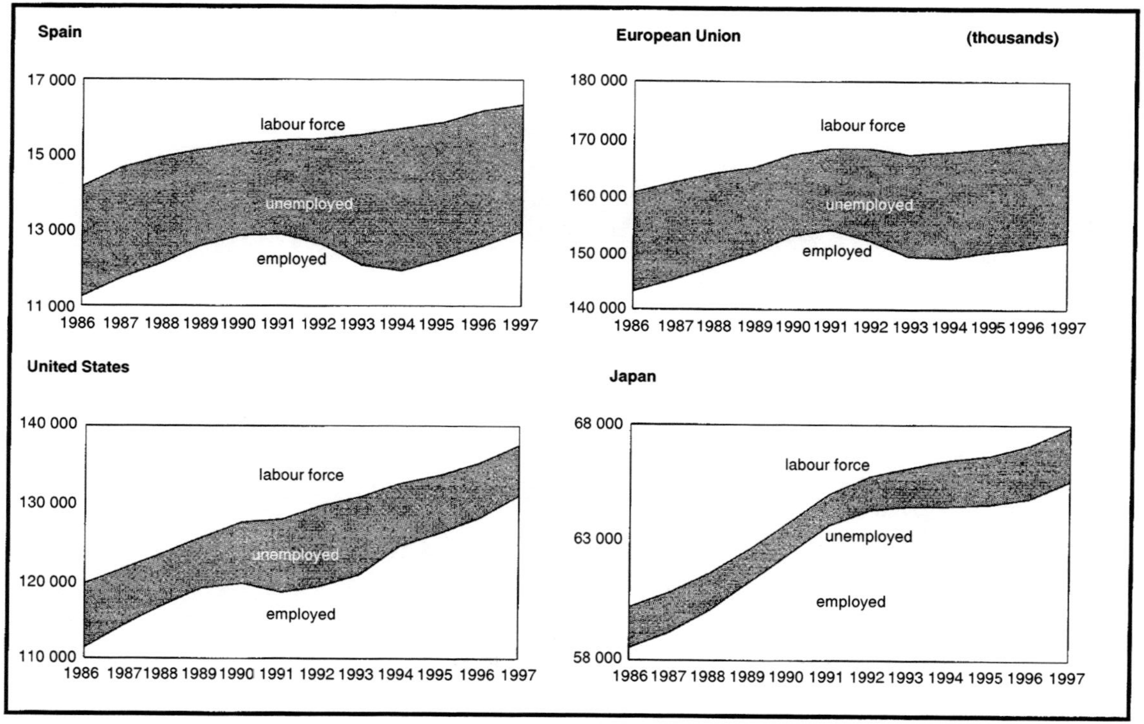

Figure 3.2 Trends in the labour force and total employed in Spain and the EU

Source: OECD: *Labour Force Statistics*; OECD: *Quarterly Labour Force Statistics;* Departamento de Estudios Europeos, Fundación de las Cajas de Ahorros.

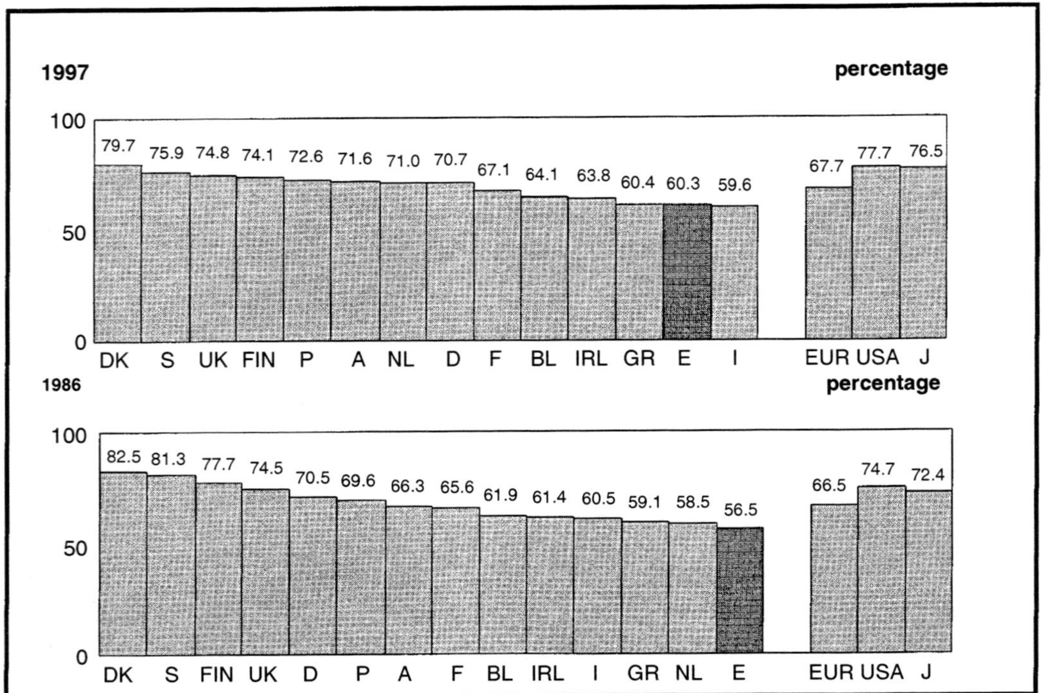

Figure 3.3 Participation rates (labour force as percentage of population aged 15 to 64)

Source: OECD: *Labour Force Statistics*; OECD: *Quarterly Labour Force Statistics;* Departamento de Estudios Europeos, Fundación de las Cajas de Ahorros.

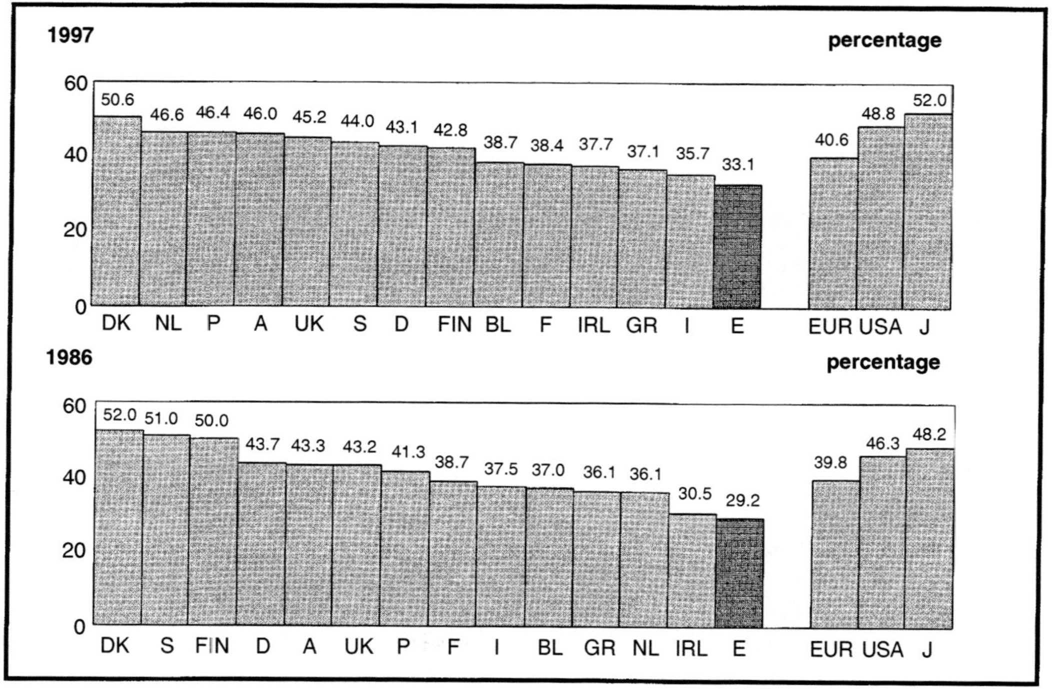

Figure 3.4 Employment rates (employed as percentage of total population)

Source: OECD: *Labour Force Statistics*; OECD: *Quarterly Labour Force Statistics;* Departamento de Estudios Europeos, Fundación de las Cajas de Ahorros.

percentage of the total population was lower in Spain in 1986 than in any other EU country – and this continued to be the case in 1997. Here again, for a correct reading of this figure, it should be borne in mind that the average values of this ratio for the European Union are markedly lower than those of the other OECD countries, especially the United States and Japan.

In fact, as many studies have shown, one of the most distinctive features of the growth process in the European Union as a whole in recent decades vis-à-vis that of the United States and Japan is that increases in production have generated weak rates of job creation.[1] Note that even in a period marked by a certain vitality in employment in Europe – such as the years 1986–97 studied here – there is still a significant gap between the EU growth rate and the US and Japanese rates – 6.1 per cent versus 17.6 per cent and 12 per cent, respectively. None the less, it should be noted that, unlike in earlier periods, between 1986 and 1997 the Spanish economy was notable for its capacity to create jobs, with 15.7 per cent growth in employment, although this was not enough to improve Spain's position as the most laggard EU country in terms of the proportion of the population that is employed.

Continuing with our analysis of employment, another noteworthy point is the change in the sectoral structure of employment since 1986, in line with trends in the past: the relative weight of agriculture and industry fell in favour of services, including market services, but particularly those not distributed through the market. As seen in Table 3.1, this change was obviously the result of very disparate employment trends within the different productive branches, ranging from the creation of jobs in construction, and above all in services, to the destruction of jobs in other branches.

Although in general the sectoral structure of Spain's employed labour force resembles that of its European partners, at least two peculiarities deserve mention. The first is the lower relative weight of manufacturing jobs, which was already below the EU average in 1986 and declined even further during the period studied. This is explained by the drastic loss of jobs during the deep recession of the early 1990s, reflecting the costs of adjusting to the growing external competition induced by the greater integration of European economies. The second is the different nature of the service jobs created in the period, with a larger proportion of public-sector service jobs generated in Spain and, consequently, a lower contribution of jobs in market services.

Here, as when considering production in Chapter 1, it is worth pausing to examine in greater detail what occurred in each branch. In

Table 3.1 Sectoral employment structure and contributions to job growth in Spain and the EU

	Spain		European Union	
Employment structure by sector	**1997**	**1986**	**1997**	**1986**
Agriculture	7.6	14.6	5.3	7.5
Industry	20.7	23.5	22.1	26.0
Energy	0.9	1.4	1.1	1.5
Manufacturing	19.8	22.1	21.0	24.5
Construction	8.9	7.4	7.0	7.3
Services	62.8	54.6	65.6	59.2
Market	41.8	37.4	44.8	41.3
Non-market	21.0	17.2	20.8	17.9
Contribution to job growth	**1997/96**	**1997/86**	**1997/96**	**1997/86**
Agriculture	–2.2	–28.8	1.2	–67.7
Industry	24.0	5.9	–1.0	–102.8
Energy	–2.8	–1.8	–1.6	–10.7
Manufacturing	26.8	7.7	0.6	–92.1
Construction	12.0	16.8	1.8	–3.3
Services	66.1	106.1	98.0	273.8
Market	44.0	64.8	70.4	157.9
Non-market	22.1	41.3	27.6	115.9

Source: OECD: *National Accounts*, vol. II: *Detailed Tables*; OECD: *Quarterly Labour Force Statistics*; Eurostat: *National Accounts ESA*; Departamento de Estudios Europeos, Fundación de las Cajas de Ahorros.

this respect, it would be interesting to learn to what extent the changes in the composition of manufacturing jobs involve, as would be desirable, a shift towards branches combining greater technological vitality and higher expectations for growth in demand.

A close examination of Table 3.2 brings several points to light. It shows the changes arising between 1986 and 1997 in the breakdown of the employed in the 13 manufacturing activities in the NACE-CLIO (25) classification when they are grouped according to the two criteria of technology and demand.

First, we find that, in the job structure of manufacturing industry, the share of branches characterized by weak demand and low technology has lost ground to branches with moderate demand and technology, while the weight of jobs in sectors with better growth expectations – due to stronger demand and greater technological content – has eased somewhat.

Secondly, on closer scrutiny, other interesting points come to light, such as the changes which have arisen in the breakdown of jobs in the

Table 3.2 Structure of manufacturing employment in Spain and the EU

	1986			1997		
	Spain	EU	Spain/EU	Spain	EU	Spain/EU
Sectors with strong demand and intensive technology	**12.8**	**18.6**	**68.8**	**12.7**	**18.4**	**69.0**
Electrical goods	6.2	9.7	63.9	5.8	9.5	61.1
Office and data-processing machines	1.0	2.8	35.7	1.4	2.7	51.9
Chemical products	5.6	6.1	91.8	5.5	6.2	88.7
Sectors with moderate demand and intermediate technology	**27.6**	**31.5**	**87.6**	**31.9**	**32.4**	**98.5**
Rubber and plastic products	3.5	4.1	85.4	3.7	4.6	80.4
Transport equipment	9.8	10.2	96.1	11.3	10.1	111.9
Agricultural and industrial machinery	4.0	10.1	39.6	5.9	10.1	58.4
Other manufactured products	10.3	7.1	145.1	11.0	7.6	144.7
Sectors with weak demand and low technology	**59.6**	**49.9**	**119.4**	**55.4**	**49.2**	**112.6**
Textiles and clothing, leather and footwear	17.4	12.7	137.0	12.4	11.3	109.7
Ferrous and non-ferrous ores and metals	3.9	3.8	102.6	2.5	3.0	83.3
Non-metallic minerals and mineral products	6.5	4.7	138.3	6.0	5.0	120.0
Paper and printing products	5.5	7.8	70.5	6.6	8.3	79.5
Food, beverages and tobacco	15.9	11.3	140.7	15.6	11.5	135.7
Metal products, exc. machinery and transport equipment	10.4	9.6	108.3	12.3	10.1	121.8
Total manufactured products	**100**	**100**		**100**	**100**	

Source: OECD: *National Accounts*, vol. II: *Detailed Tables*; OECD: *Quarterly Labour Force Statistics*; Eurostat: *National Accounts ESA, Detailed Tables by Branch*; Eurostat: *Monthly Panorama of European Industry*; INE: *Contabilidad Nacional de España*; Departamento de Estudios Europeos, Fundación de las Cajas de Ahorros.

production of different kinds of machinery: whereas relative employment in agricultural and industrial machines has risen, it has fallen in electrical goods.

Lastly, it should be noted that the employment structure of manufacturing industry has followed a very similar pattern throughout the European Union.

One area, however, where Spain's singularity particularly stands out is temporary employment. According to the latest available data (1997 figures), nearly 34 per cent of wage-earners are subject to temporary contracts, almost three times the average EU ratio.[2] While this high ratio of temporary to total employment, which places Spain at the head of the European Union (see Figure 3.5), is surely one of the factors behind the intense growth in employment in the second half of the 1980s, it is also a source of serious problems.

Indeed, the studies addressing this issue coincide in pointing out that the high proportion of workers with temporary contracts – linked in turn to the high dismissal costs under permanent contracts – creates strong segmentation, or duality, in the labour market that undermines its efficiency and, worse still, ultimately hinders the creation of jobs.

Several arguments are put forward in this respect. First of all, labour market segmentation gives workers with permanent contracts strong bargaining power, and this power, under the 'job security' conferred by the costs and legal restrictions relating to dismissals, may result in wage demands that conflict with wage moderation.[3] Secondly, the bargaining power of workers with permanent contracts may be expressed in resistance to corporate initiatives involving greater job or geographical mobility within the company that could hamper its adaptation to new technology. Thirdly, another related and possibly counterproductive effect of labour market duality is that it can remove the incentives for occupational training efforts by both employers and workers, and by extension can undermine their capacity to take advantage of the efficiency improvements derived from technological innovations.[4]

In sum, together these arguments help explain why labour market segmentation – either by raising the labour costs of companies and/or by constraining progress in their productivity – is, at least in the medium term, detrimental to job creation.

Another peculiarity of employment in Spain that also seems to be constraining job creation is the negligible use of part-time employment, both in absolute terms and in relation to the other EU countries. As shown in Figure 3.6, while this type of contract gives companies the large margin of flexibility needed to adjust to the dizzying pace of

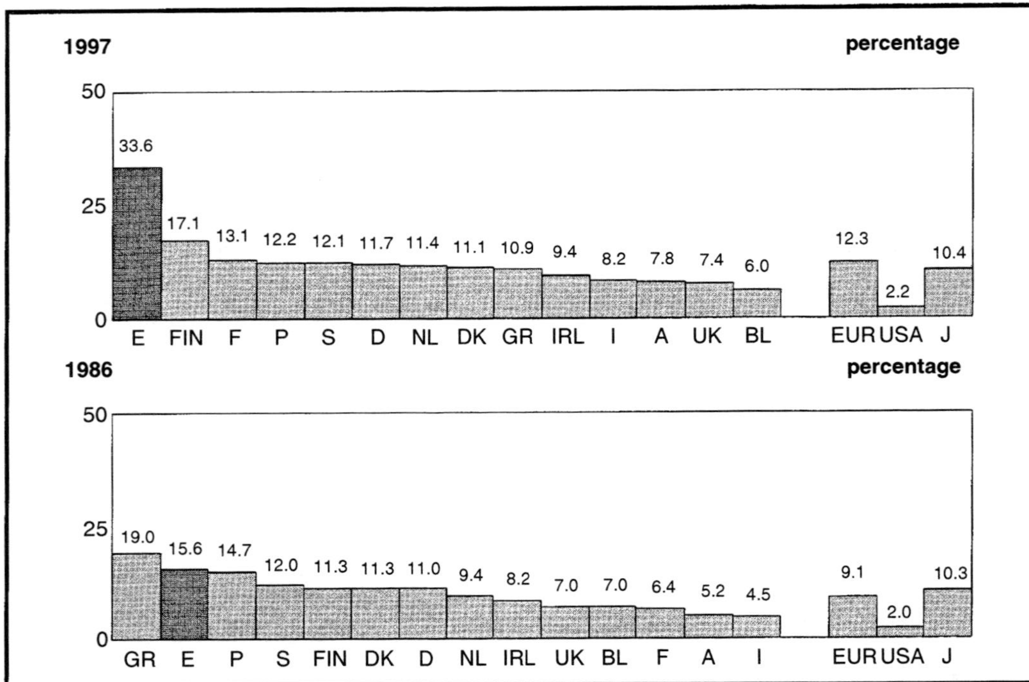

Figure 3.5 Temporary employment (as percentage of wage-earners)

Source: Eurostat: *Labour Force Survey*; Eurostat: *Working Organization and Working Hours;* Departamento de Estudios Europeos, Fundación de las Cajas de Ahorros.

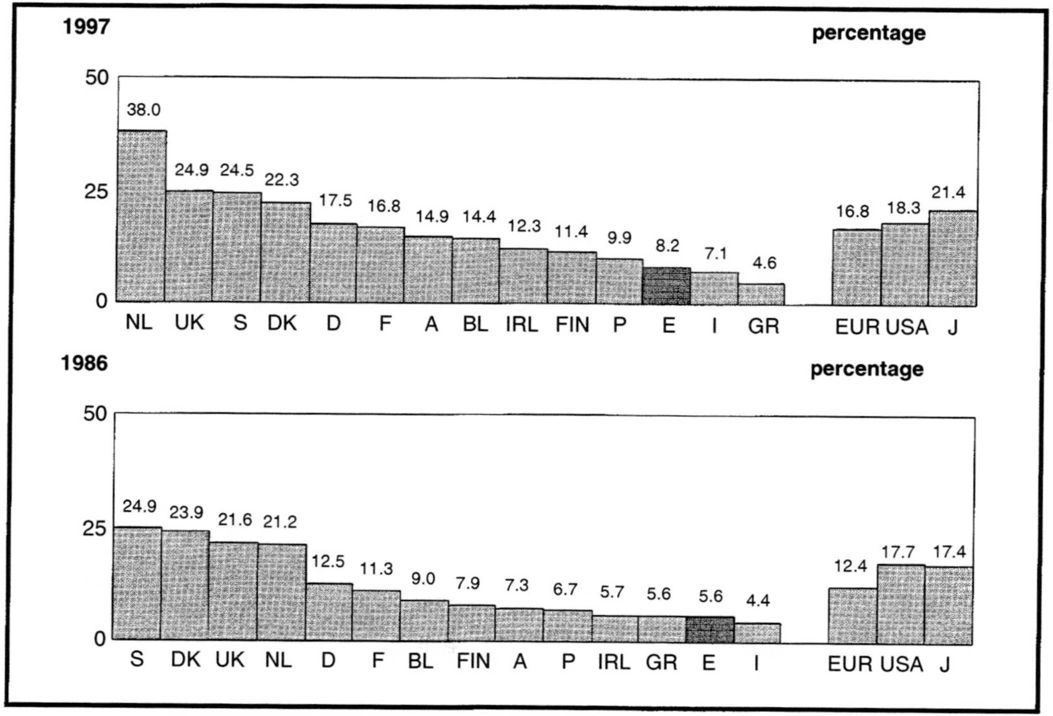

Figure 3.6 Part-time employment (as percentage of total employed)

Source: Eurostat: *Labour Force Survey*; Departamento de Estudios Europeos, Fundación de las Cajas de Ahorros.

change in their competitive environment (induced by technical innovations and the increasing globalization of markets), it is not widely used in Spain, although its use has grown extraordinarily in the past three years.

It is safe to say that the scant use of part-time contracts constrains job creation, especially among female workers, as the available data show that it is women who have a stronger preference for this type of employment. Here it seems fair to assume that this factor is one of the possible reasons for the higher female jobless rate which, as we shall see, characterizes unemployment in Spain.

3.3 The nature and some causes of unemployment

Although in varying degrees, unemployment is a deeply rooted problem in most of the EU countries: it affects more than 18 million people, or 11 per cent of the total labour force. In this context, the situation of the Spanish economy, with more than 3 million unemployed and an unemployment rate of nearly 20 per cent, as shown in Figure 3.7, has no parallel in Europe and even less in the United States or Japan.[5]

Naturally, to comprehend the magnitude of the unemployment problem, it is not enough simply to state that it has reached an extraordinarily high level: to approximate its true dimension requires a complementary examination of its nature. In this respect, it is worth stressing that the first feature, both significant and worrisome, which stands out in Europe's unemployment is its persistence (only partly reflected in Figure 3.7). Thus high unemployment rates emerged before the years included in the graph and, more specifically, date from the mid-1970s; in the case of Spain, however, it could be argued that unemployment existed much earlier but was hidden by the intense migratory flows to other countries in Europe.

Other characteristics of unemployment in Europe and in Spain in particular are shown in Figure 3.8. Notably, unemployment in Europe has a relatively greater impact on women, as they account for a disproportionately high percentage of the unemployed given their presence in the labour force. In this context, the situation of Spain's female unemployed is truly striking and deplorable: even though the female participation rate is much lower than that of males, in 1997 women represented nearly 53 per cent of the total unemployed, clearly much higher than the EU average. Moreover, this higher female unemployment rate has tended to worsen in the European Union as a whole and

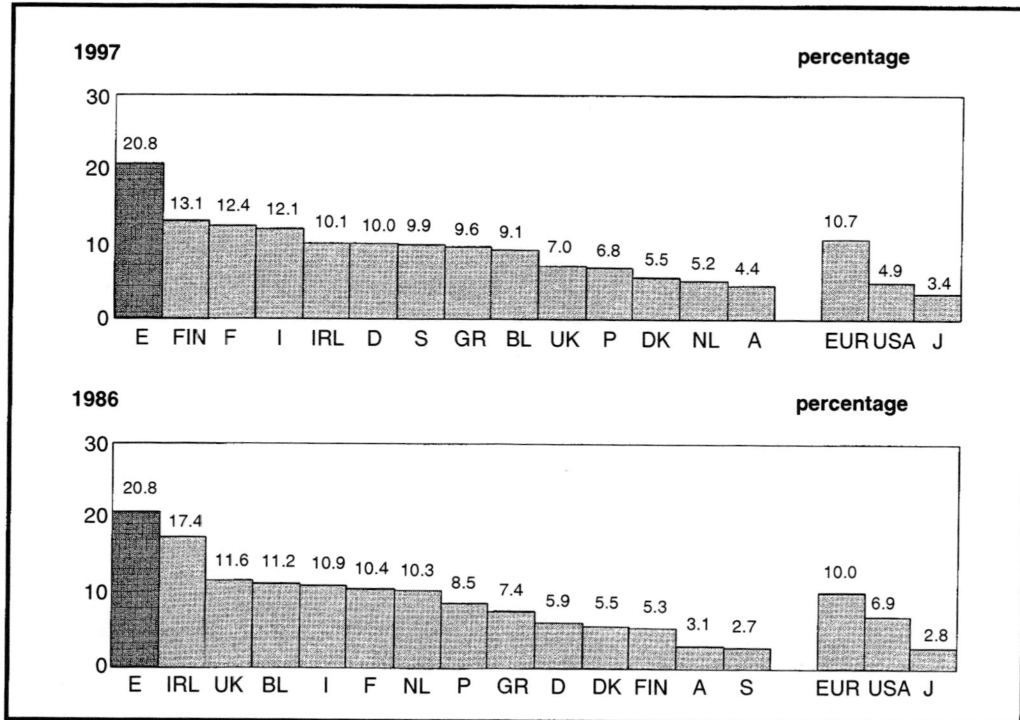

Figure 3.7 Unemployment rates

Source: OECD: *Labour Force Statistics*; OECD: *Quarterly Labour Force Statistics;* Departamento de Estudios Europeos, Fundación de las Cajas de Ahorros.

in Spain in particular. Whereas the female unemployment rates in Spain and the European Union in 1986 were 25.3 per cent and 12.5 per cent, respectively, in 1997 they stood at 28.3 per cent and 12.4 per cent.

Other salient features of EU unemployment, which are also notably worse in the case of Spain, are the predominance of youth unemployment (15- to 24-year-olds) and the significant presence of long-term unemployment. In 1997 youth unemployment still accounted for nearly a third of Spain's total unemployment, against an average of 26 per cent in the European Union. Although, as seen in Figure 3.8, the presence of this group of unemployed has fallen appreciably,[6] it is still very substantial. Among other costs, this means that the section of the labour force with comparatively high levels of training, due to the educational efforts of recent years, is being wasted.

Likewise, Figure 3.8 indicates that the long-term unemployed (more than one year without a job) in Spain represented nearly 52 per cent of the total unemployed in 1997, and around 49 per cent on average in EU countries.

Many studies suggest that long-term unemployment ultimately has hysteresis effects, in that it becomes self-perpetuating. Indeed, the long-term unemployed are more likely to see their professional skills become gradually obsolete and to suffer, as a result, the discrimination of employers, making their integration into the labour market even more difficult. Moreover, the probability of the skills of the long-term unemployed becoming obsolete is of course even greater in periods of radical technological change such as the present, with the spread of major innovations in the fields of information and communications.

The stronger presence of long-term unemployment in Spain would therefore seem to be another of the possible causes of the country's unemployment differential. But there are of course many other reasons. To study them in greater depth, we will first draw up various indicators of labour costs and then explore several factors associated with the institutional and legal framework that determines, to a greater or lesser extent, how the labour market works.

Figure 3.9 shows labour costs per hour worked in 1986 and 1997 (expressed in 1997 euro) in the EU countries, individually and as a whole, and also in the United States and Japan. According to this indicator, the cost of labour in Spain was 71 per cent of the EU average at the beginning of the period; by 1997 it had reached 74 per cent. Although this process of convergence in Spain's labour remuneration towards the higher average EU rates is not surprising in view of the fact

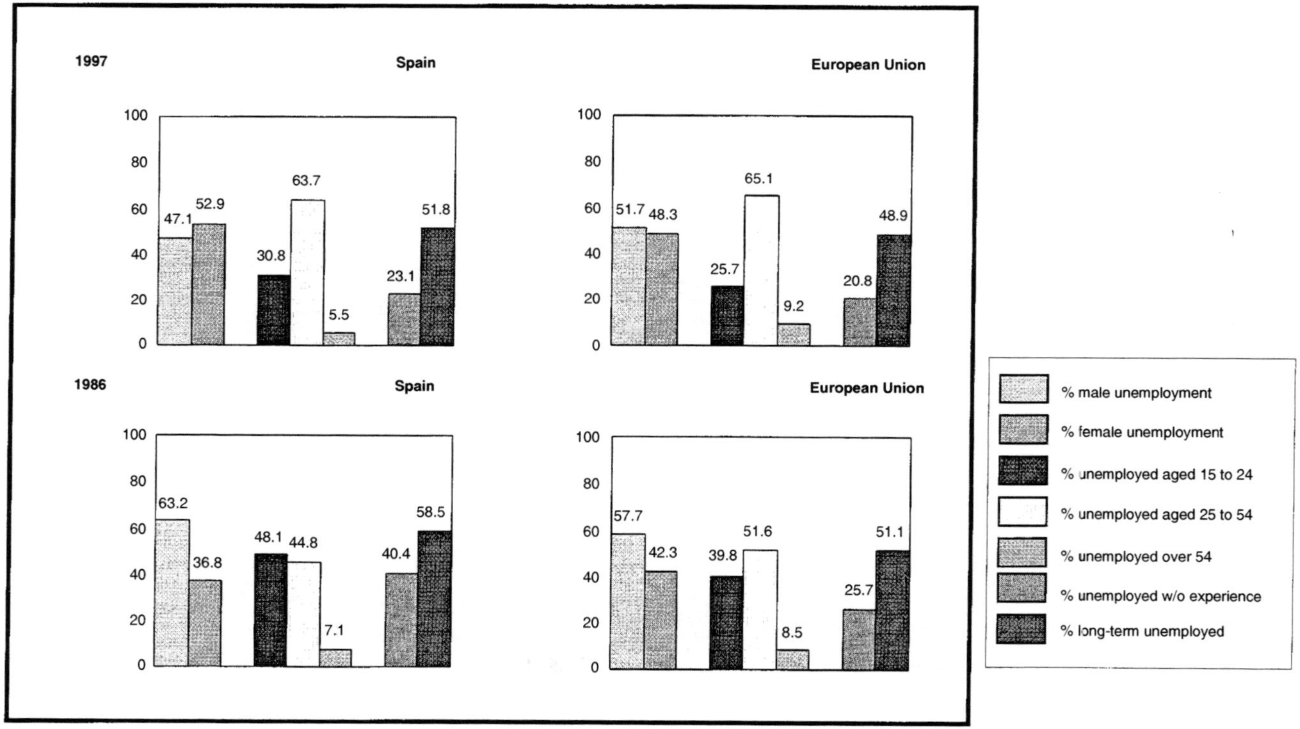

Figure 3.8 Unemployment structure in Spain and the EU (by sex, age and type of unemployment)

Source: OECD: *Labour Force Statistics*; ILO: *Statistical Yearbook of Labour;* Eurostat: *Labour Force Survey;* OECD: *Employment Outlook*; Departamento de Estudios Europeos, Fundación de las Cajas de Ahorros.

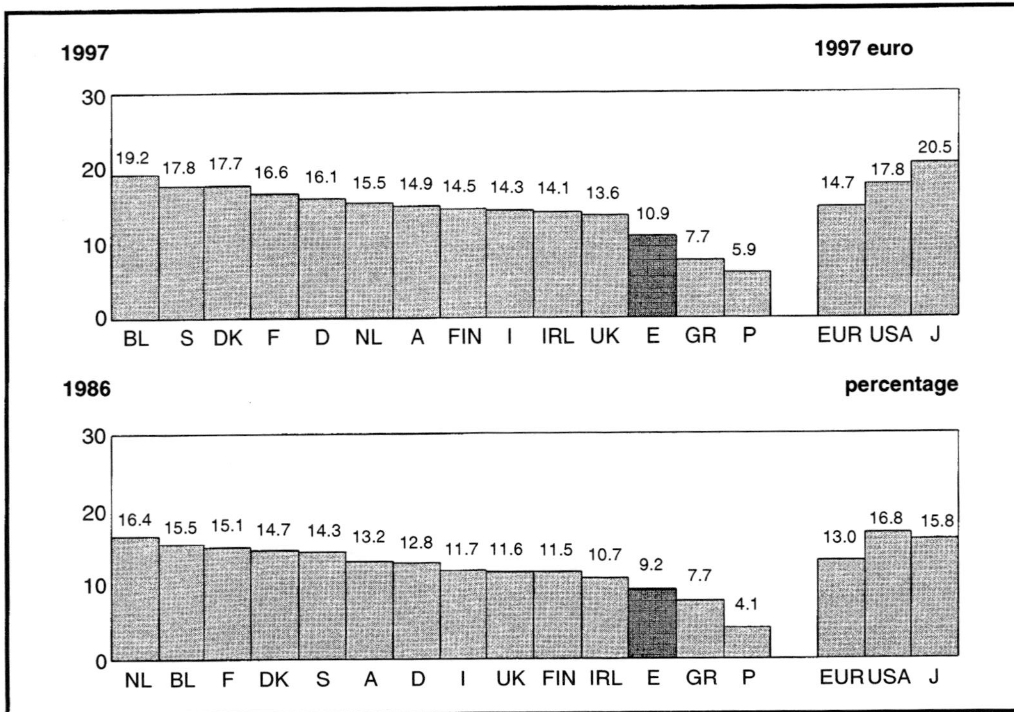

Figure 3.9 Labour cost per hour worked

Source: OECD: *Labour Force Statistics*; Eurostat: *Labour Force Survey;* OECD: *National Accounts*; vol. I: *Main Aggregates*; Departamento de Estudios Europeos, Fundación de las Cajas de Ahorros.

that Spain joined the European Union at the beginning of this period, it is not entirely justifiable when viewed from other perspectives. By way of example, it seems at least debatable whether labour costs should converge to such a degree, given Spain's spectacular and permanent unemployment differential. The combination of these two factors suggests the existence of a certain – worrisome – insensitivity of wages to imbalances in the labour market. In other words, a problem of wage rigidity appears to exist, which might in principle be considered partly responsible for Spain's high unemployment.

None the less, it could be rightly argued that the rise in labour costs need not necessarily be damaging to employment, as long as these cost increases are absorbed by gains in productivity. In examining the trends in unit labour costs in Spain and the European Union during the period (see Figure 3.10), we find that the relative vitality of labour costs in Spain was not accompanied by a similar improvement in labour productivity. As a result, as shown in Figure 3.10, Spanish unit labour costs in most of the years in question grew more swiftly than the average EU rates.

In addition to these findings, the results obtained in econometric analyses provide much more conclusive evidence of the inefficient response of wages to unemployment trends and, by extension, of the negative impact of wages in the fight against unemployment (Andrés, 1995, gives an overview of many of these studies). Note, in any case, that the diagnosis regarding the negative influence of wage pressures on unemployment is not confined to Spain, and is also found in studies encompassing EU countries as a whole.

Wage rigidity is, in fact, one of the factors most emphatically adduced to explain the unemployment gap between Europe and the United States (see OECD, 1995, and the references cited there). One of the clearest symptoms of this rigidity is the widespread application of minimum wages in the European Union. None the less, here it is worth pointing out that the wage flexibility found in the US economy, combined with the relatively meagre system of unemployment benefits (which, as we shall later see, does exist in the United States), appears to be giving rise to a group of workers whose situation is increasingly precarious.

After examining the role of wages, we will go on to explore the possible causes of unemployment in the European Union, and in Spain in particular, from the standpoint of the constraints of an institutional or legal nature, which either directly or indirectly through their impact on another variable – labour costs, for example – produce dysfunctions and inefficiencies in the labour market that worsen unemployment.

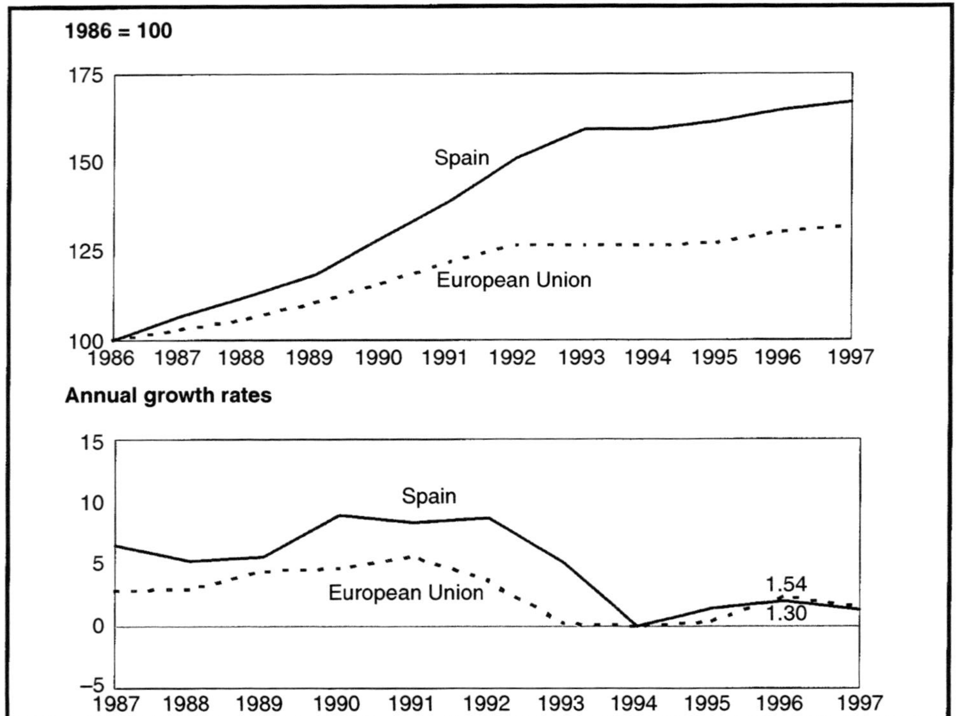

Figure 3.10 Unit labour cost trends in Spain and the EU

Source: OECD: *National Accounts*, vol. I: *Main Aggregates*; OECD: *Labour Force Statistics*; Departamento de Estudios Europeos, Fundación de las Cajas de Ahorros.

Here it is useful to take as our starting point a question that is closely linked to the problem of wage rigidity discussed above, namely the so-called tax wedge, which refers to the labour-cost component formed by social security contributions (paid by both employers and employees). It is therefore a non-wage component of the cost of labour – its purpose is to finance social benefits – and, in a certain sense, acts as a tax on job creation, naturally discouraging growth in employment.

Figure 3.11 shows the relative size and structure of the tax wedge in each of the EU countries, the United States, and Japan in 1986 and 1997. It reflects the enormous disparity between the situation in Europe and that of Japan and, above all, the United States: the weight of social security contributions in the cost of labour is 25.3 per cent in the European Union, compared with a meagre 10.1 per cent in the United States and 13.9 per cent in Japan. This is only one of many manifestations of the concept of the peculiarly European welfare state (analysed in more detail in a later chapter). For the time being, suffice it to say that the relative generosity of the European system of benefits and, more precisely, the importance of social security contributions in their financing may prove counterproductive to the objective of reducing unemployment, since they add a considerable surcharge to the cost of labour.[7]

From the information in Figure 3.11 we also find that the share of social security contributions in labour costs in Spain is somewhat lower than the EU average. Note, however, that Spain figures among the EU member countries in which the weight of social security contributions paid by employers exceeds the European average.

The system of unemployment benefits is another facet of the welfare state in European countries that may significantly affect the level and persistence of unemployment. In fact, this system (which in most European countries comprises two types of benefit, insurance and assistance benefits) has recently met with criticism on the grounds that its relative generosity may undermine the assiduousness with which the unemployed look for jobs.

To test whether this type of benefit is, in fact, especially high in the European Union, we have devised an indicator, calculated as the ratio of unemployment expenditure to GDP, standardized by the differences between each country's unemployment rate and the EU average. The findings, shown in Figure 3.12, eloquently attest to the greater generosity of the EU system vis-à-vis the US and Japanese systems.[8]

But, even though the generosity of the European system is shown, it must still be demonstrated that it is damaging in its effect on

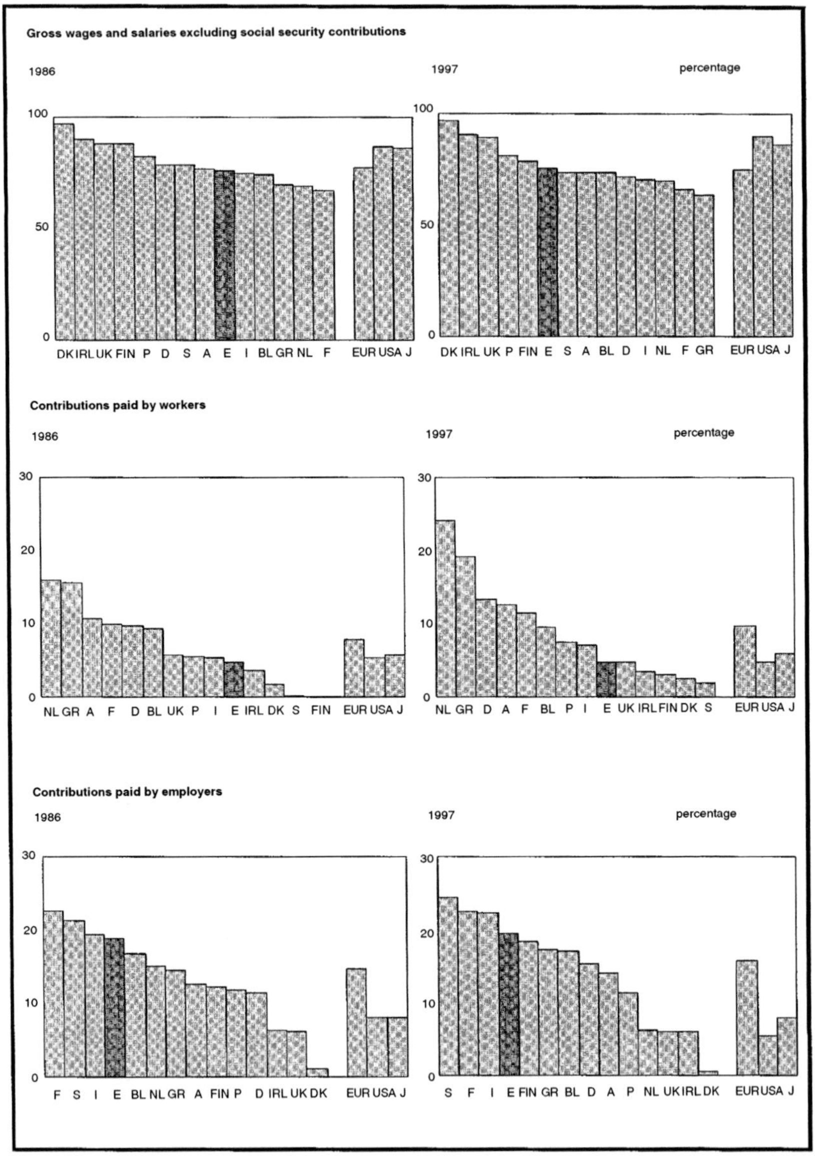

Figure 3.11 Labour cost structure

Source: OECD: *National Accounts*, vol. I: *Main Aggregates*; OECD: *Revenue Statistics of OECD Member Countries*; Departamento de Estudios Europeos, Fundación de las Cajas de Ahorros.

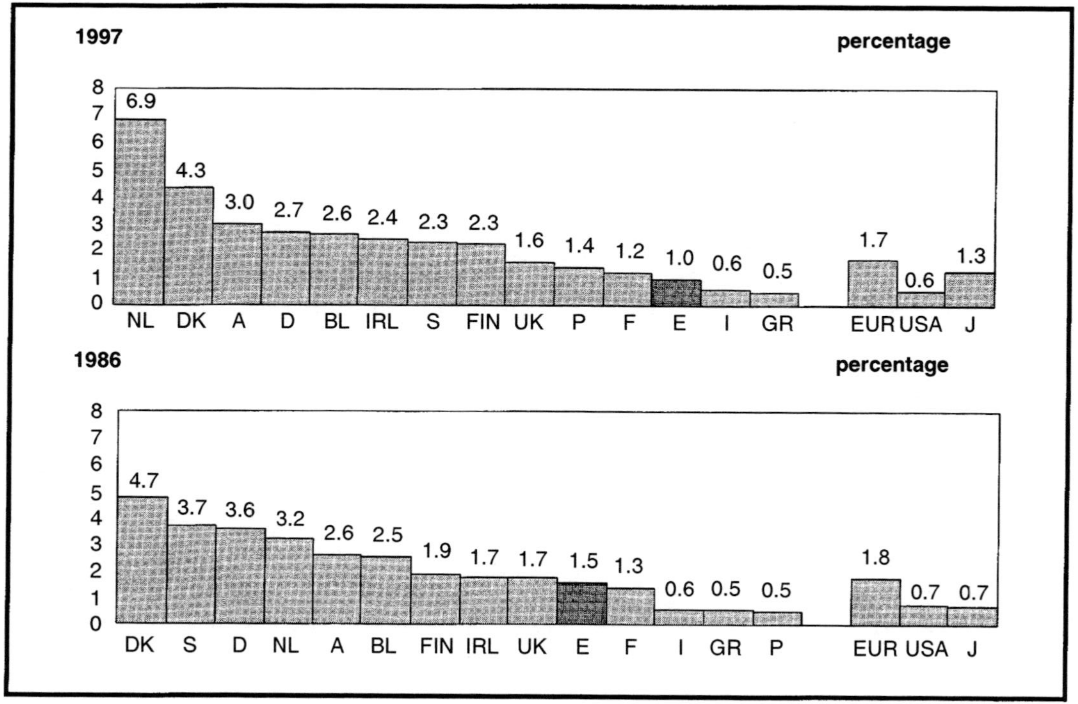

Figure 3.12 Unemployment assistance (expenditure on unemployment benefits as percentage of GDP mp standardized by unemployment rates)

Source: Eurostat: *Social Protection Expenditure and Receipts*; OECD: *National Accounts*, vol. I: *Main Aggregates*; OECD: *Labour Force Statistics*; OECD: *Employment Outlook*; Departamento de Estudios Europeos, Fundación de las Cajas de Ahorros.

unemployment. The economic rationale for believing this to be the case is quite clear: benefits discourage an active search for employment; the empirical testing of this hypothesis is, however, complex. In any event, the available evidence, though scant, suggests that this is the case (see Bover, Arellano and Bentolila, 1995, and the references cited there).

This generosity, however, is not a major explanatory factor in the greater institutional rigidities and labour market inefficiencies, with especially serious consequences for unemployment. In the opinion of most experts on the subject, the two most relevant institutional problems are the nature of the collective bargaining system and, above all, the high cost of dismissals. Let us pause a moment to consider each of these problems separately.

As to dismissal costs, in our discussion of the Spanish economy we noted how – in a legal framework such as Spain's, with many forms of contracts permitted – a restrictive regulation that raises redundancy costs can actually discourage hiring more than firing by creating excessive segmentation in employment (between temporary and permanent employees). The result might be a paradoxical situation whereby a measure designed to protect employment ultimately harms it. And, judging by the numerous mechanisms which, in the specialized economic literature, link dismissal costs to lower employment, this is most probably the situation.

More specifically, the mechanisms through which dismissal costs can lead to lower employment include: the rise in labour costs (both in absolute terms and, naturally, in relation to those of the other productive factors); the strengthening of the bargaining power of workers with permanent contracts to oppose employers' proposals of occupational or geographical mobility which may be necessary for the company's productivity, and the brake on investment stemming from the impact of dismissal costs.

As precise information on the legal framework of dismissals in the EU countries is not available, we have not been able to evaluate the cost differences between one country and another nor, by extension, their impact on employment. We are, however, familiar with the legislation in Spain, and in our view, despite the reforms introduced in 1997, it is still overly restrictive – in other words, the cost of rescinding permanent contracts is still too high.[9] In this sense, we should point out that the costs borne by a company in Spain when shedding personnel derive not only from redundancy payments but also, and at times primarily, from the complex and lengthy legal procedures involved.

Indeed, the mandatory administrative authorization in collective dismissals and the intervention of labour courts in individual dismissals create uncertainties and costly delays. A recent study (see Bentolila, 1996) provides evidence of the high severance payments which are still paid in the case of individual dismissals.

The other institutional feature that can have a more decisive, and possibly more harmful, impact on employment appears to be, as suggested earlier, the nature of collective bargaining. More specifically, one aspect of collective bargaining laws that is generally considered a key determinant of labour market efficiency is the scope of the legislation (covering national, sectoral and company levels). Here it is usually argued that the lower degree of decentralization in collective bargaining in Europe vis-à-vis the United States is one of the factors – together with the many reasons mentioned in this chapter, and others that have yet to be discussed – behind the enormous disparity between the average unemployment rates in the United States and in the European Union.

This diagnosis is largely based on what is considered one of the greatest drawbacks of centralized systems: the fact that they prevent wages from correctly reflecting the differences in productivity between one sector and another and even between companies in the same sector. This, it is argued, has a distortionary effect on the wage structure which, in certain circumstances, can have a very serious and adverse impact on employment.[10]

In addition, there is every sign that centralized bargaining systems discourage the implementation of wage systems with a significant component of variable earnings, which give firms the margin of flexibility they need to accommodate changing technological and competitive conditions.[11]

Before concluding this survey of the main factors linked to the labour market's legal and institutional framework and their apparently adverse effect on the capacity to create jobs in Europe and especially Spain, several observations regarding the latest labour reform of May 1997 are in order, as it includes two legislative decrees[12] that put forward various means of overcoming several shortcomings in the legislation.

The reform's prime concern is to address the problem of the extraordinarily high proportion of temporary jobs in Spain, as discussed earlier, and its impact on the unemployment in various groups (young people, for example). In this respect, it envisages a reorganization of the types of temporary contracts, creates a new permanent contract aimed at promoting jobs in the groups hardest hit by unemployment, and revises the wording of article 52 (c) of the Workers' Statute to clarify the grounds for justified dismissals.[13]

So far we have considered wage rigidity and several factors of a legal or institutional nature that are probably at the core of the particularly serious and enduring unemployment in European economies. Even though the list is not exhaustive, it does contain what are viewed in most studies to be the principal factors. With this in mind, we shall now continue our search for the causes of unemployment in areas other than the labour market in the strict sense. Here our aim is to explore the relationship between technical change and employment or, more specifically, the possibility that high and persistent unemployment levels may in some way be attributable to deficiencies in the productive system's adaptation to the radical technological advances of recent years. This will be the topic of the next section.

3.4 Technical change and unemployment

Through past experience we know that technical change has a twofold impact on employment: technical innovations bring a saving in factors (and, by extension, in labour) but at the same time, by virtue of this gain in efficiency they also produce mechanisms that compensate for the jobs displaced. Admittedly, however, the new jobs generated do not necessarily match either the level or the profile of the skills which have been eliminated.

There are basically three mechanisms induced by technical progress that may compensate for the jobs initially destroyed (or made redundant). First of all, there are mechanisms associated either with capital goods investment (in the case of a technical change that has been incorporated) or with investment in intangible assets (if the technical advance is not incorporated).

A second compensatory mechanism is linked to the growth in demand which will arise in response to the application of the new technology, whether it involves a processing innovation (that is to say, it provides efficiency gains or a cost reduction) or a product innovation (in other words, the launch of a new product on the market). In this respect, note that innovation facilitates the reduction of the price of the product made with the new technology or, if the decrease in the production cost is not passed through to the price, an increase in the innovating company's wages and/or profits. And, in one way or another, this should translate into a stimulus to demand, whose satisfaction would require an increase in production and, consequently, in employment.

It is important to note that the job-creation processes induced by technical change (which has historically facilitated, with greater or lesser adjustment costs, the reabsorption of the labour initially displaced) are not confined to the innovating firms or sectors, but also indirectly affect their suppliers and those who use their products as inputs.

Finally, the third mechanism that may result in the absorption of the labour saved by technical change is the possible decline in wages in response to the drop in labour demand, thereby easing the price of maintaining jobs.

The net impact of technical change on employment would therefore be that resulting from its initial labour-saving effect and the combination of the above-mentioned compensatory effects.

However, even though the history of technical change shows how it has paved the way for the creation of more jobs than it initially destroyed, there is no guarantee that this will continue to be the case in the future. Moreover, it is possible that these compensatory employment effects only take hold over a long period, and in the meantime the labour-saving impact of technical progress predominates, signifying a long period of unemployment.

Thus, in principle, there are not sufficient grounds for ruling out the possibility that technology may, in some way, lie at the root of the severe unemployment problem affecting most economies. In fact, there are increasingly well founded arguments which suggest that one of the reasons behind the intense and widespread increase in involuntary unemployment lies in the difficulties in accommodating the many technical innovations of recent years, especially in the area of information and communications. This diagnosis rests on two types of evidence.

On the one hand, various studies (see Freeman and Soete, 1994, and OECD, 1996c[14]) provide a description of the nature of the new technologies, revealing among other features their radical and versatile nature and their bias towards unskilled labour-saving. Interpreted from the economic standpoint, together these features signify substantial transformations in productive processes (in particular due to the greater need for labour with new skills and higher levels of training), alterations in the composition of what is produced, and important changes in the internal structure of companies towards more flexible and participatory organizational systems and management methods that encourage the creativity of workers.[15] In addition, there are the consequences of what constitutes another of the most defining features of the new information and communication technologies: the enormous savings they generate both in the cost and in the time employed in all stages of production and distribution. This provides greater flexibility for subcontracting and an incentive to relocate certain stages of the productive process (the most labour-intensive ones) to regions and countries with lower labour costs.[16]

On the other hand, there are studies which illustrate the inefficiencies and rigidities in the goods and labour markets in European countries that undermine the full harnessing of the impetus which the new technologies could infuse in production and employment. In this line of argument, we find convincing examples that explain the European unemployment differential vis-à-vis unemployment in the United States. Thus it could be adduced that the greater wage rigidity associated with the more intense regulation of the labour market (in turn framed within a more beneficent concept of the welfare state), which occurs in the EU countries, produces in their labour markets a different response to the new demands arising from technical innovations with a strong labour-saving slant: higher unemployment in Europe as opposed to wage cuts and more precarious job conditions in the United States (see Nickell and Bell, 1995).

Moreover, from this perspective, the lower occupational and geographical mobility of European workers is a further obstacle to the emergence of the potential compensatory effects for jobs destroyed by the technical change discussed above. Of course the same arguments could by extension be applied – and even magnified – when explaining Spain's unemployment differential in the Community context.

In any event, the main determinants of the technological unemployment problem in some countries – those of the European Union for example – appear to lie in the shortfalls in human and technological capital. The reason is that these deficiencies pose a severe obstacle to exploiting the potential expansionary effects induced by technical change in production and employment which could, in turn, counteract the job destruction initially caused by the application of new techniques.

Undoubtedly, the greater the technological and human capital endowment of the country that adopts technical innovations, the greater will be the chance to build a national supply of the equipment, inputs and skilled personnel increasingly needed as these innovations spread. In other words, the countries that apply technical innovations via imports of the equipment incorporating these innovations – and depend on other countries for the technical assistance and the inputs or software which may be required for their proper use – run a greater risk of suffering problems derived from technological unemployment: whereas they will have to continue coping with the displacement of jobs associated with the application of new technologies, they will generally not be able to take advantage of the potential compensatory mechanisms to absorb those made redundant.

In fact, the empirical evidence shows (see Freeman and Soete, 1994, and OECD, 1996c) that the countries at the forefront of technical innovations in the telecommunications field are now enjoying stronger growth in the production of both the manufactured goods and the services associated with them and have comparatively fewer unemployment problems.

Another noteworthy mechanism whereby shortfalls in human capital can translate into a worsening in technology-related unemployment is the intensification of the gap between the level and type of qualifications of the labour made redundant by new technologies and the skills required for their efficient application. Note, for example, that the group of people between 25 and 59 years of age without secondary education qualifications has the highest unemployment rate (in 1996, according to Eurostat, 1997, this rate stood at 12.6 per cent and 21.2 per cent for the European Union and Spain, respectively, compared with 7.6 per cent and 15.8 per cent for those with more advanced secondary studies).

In this respect, it is clear that technical progress requires increasingly frequent updating and improvement in the skills of the labour force. In fact, in some activities subject to a greater rate of technical innovation, there is an acknowledged need for continuous education and training systems.

When all these considerations concerning the relationship between technical change and employment/unemployment are set against the data in the previous chapter on the Spanish economy's endowment of human and technological capital vis-à-vis the European Union, it seems safe to affirm that reasons of a technological nature should occupy – with considerable weight – a place in the diagnosis of the causes of Spain's unemployment differential.

3.5 Conclusions

This chapter has examined the behaviour of the main variables of the Spanish labour market over the past decade within the framework of the European Union and also with respect to the situation in the United States and Japan. With this examination, together with the exploration of other factors only indirectly related to the workings of the labour market, we have sought to arrive at a diagnosis of the nature and causes of unemployment in Spain, which has factors in common with Europe as well as its own peculiarities. This diagnosis can be summarized in the following points:

- Unemployment, which has already reached troubling dimensions in the European Union, is even more severe in the Spanish case: the unemployment rate, at around 20 per cent (versus the EU average of 11 per cent), has no parallel.
- European unemployment affects several groups in particular: women, 15- to 24-year-olds, and the long-term unemployed (more than one year). In all three groups the impact is more pronounced in Spain. In the case of young workers, this is a waste of the section of the labour force endowed with superior levels of training thanks to the more intense investment in education in recent years. In the case of the long-term unemployed, one especially notable cost is the rapid obsolescence of their professional skills, which may eventually block their chances of finding a job.
- In the past decade, Spain's labour force – owing to the growing incorporation of women in the job market – has exerted greater pressure on the labour market than in other European countries, and as such this factor bears a certain responsibility for the gravity of unemployment in Spain. None the less, in this study we have argued that unemployment is basically explained by the factors that have inhibited the demand for labour.
- Trends in unit labour costs in Spain and the European Union during the period analysed – the years spanning Spain's EU membership – show that the growth in Spanish labour costs was not accompanied by a similar improvement in workers' productivity. This would suggest that the productivity factor is one of the possible causes of Spain's significant unemployment differential.
- Spain shares with most of its EU partners an institutional and legal framework marked by strong rigidities in the workings of the labour market. And, despite the reforms carried out in 1994 and 1997, these rigidities are even more pronounced in the Spanish case. Among the many deficiencies in labour market regulations, we concluded that two are particularly relevant: the legislation governing the termination of permanent contracts and, in relation to this, the enormous disparity between the types of contracts, both of which

lead to an excessive segmentation of the labour market. Nevertheless, it should be pointed out that the labour reform of May 1997 was a step towards overcoming these deficiencies.

- Elaborating on the previous point, it should be emphasized that Spain is the EU country with the highest ratio of temporary employment, representing nearly 34 per cent of wage-earners – almost three times the EU average. The present chapter has discussed why this excessive segmentation of the labour market is so damaging to job creation, bearing in mind not only its upward impact on labour costs but in particular its negative impact – via diverse channels – on productivity. In other words, there are clear indications that the high segmentation between permanent and temporary employment in Spain, in turn largely attributable to high redundancy costs, is an important factor in explaining the country's enormous unemployment problem.
- In addition to these factors, the scant use of part-time contracts has most probably constituted a further hindrance to job creation.
- Lastly, but certainly not of least importance, our analysis suggests that a none too negligible proportion of unemployment is due to the failure of the different countries' technological and educational systems to fully harness the potential, in terms of production and employment, of the many technical innovations which have arisen in recent years in diverse fields, above all in the area of information and communications. More specifically, the chapter defends the idea that a technological unemployment problem exists in Europe and to an even greater extent in Spain.

4
Costs, Prices and Competitiveness

4.1 Introduction

After analysing the structure and efficiency of the productive system and the situation and dynamics of the labour market, in the present chapter we shall attempt to evaluate the trends in the Spanish economy's competitiveness since Spain's entry into the European Union as well as its position in the changing corporate environment brought about by EMU. Special attention is given to the loss of the exchange rate as an adjustment mechanism for coping with problems of competitiveness.

Section 4.2 discusses the concept and variables that affect competitiveness. Section 4.3 analyses Spain's competitiveness in terms of its trade performance in the domestic and foreign markets on the basis of three indicators: export market share, the weight of imports in domestic demand, and revealed comparative advantage indices. We then go on to study the factors which affect the competitiveness of the Spanish economy: relative costs and prices and exchange rates, combined in real effective exchange rates (Section 4.4), and a full set of supplementary variables that illustrate the capacity of companies – and countries – to compete on the basis of product attributes other than prices (Section 4.5). Finally, we set out the chapter's main conclusions and attempt to infer from them some economic policy measures which could help to enhance the competitive position of the Spanish economy.

4.2 Concept and measurement of competitiveness

As readers will be aware, in most studies – whether carried out by national or international organizations – diagnoses of changes in the competitiveness of countries are based almost exclusively on analyses of the performance of the real effective exchange rate (REER).

Even though the measurement of competitiveness based on the REER is useful and, because of statistical constraints, is often the only one available for short-term analyses, it has become increasingly clear that this indicator is a partial measure of competitiveness. This is because the REER only contains information on trends in cost differentials (in some cases, adjusted for apparent productivity), prices and nominal exchange rates, thereby leaving on the sidelines the extensive and varied range of attributes and characteristics that make it possible to differentiate products and to affect consumers' decisions. All these characteristics – such as quality, design, brand, guarantees and after-sale technical assistance, for example – can become as decisive as the price factor, at least in the developed countries, where consumer preferences are more sophisticated and, as such, their demands have lower price elasticity.

Indeed, since the work of Kaldor (1978), a wealth of evidence has been uncovered regarding the importance of all these non-price factors in trade performance. Kaldor observed that numerous countries manage to enlarge their market shares in the medium term despite upward trends in their relative costs and prices. This evidence, known as the 'Kaldor paradox', has been confirmed in subsequent studies (by way of example, see the studies of Dosi and Soete, 1988; Fagerberg, 1996, and the references cited there).

In addition to this type of indirect evidence on the relevance of non-price factors in determining a country's competitiveness – and, by extension, the inadequacy of REERs as a measurement – other supplementary evidence has gradually emerged. This reveals that the capacity of companies (and countries) to compete on the basis of all these attributes, which differentiate products and permit gains in market share, are associated with the availability of certain intangible assets: primarily technology, human capital and trade capital.[1]

As a result, increasing efforts have been made to find a concept and a measurement of the competitiveness of nations that are more satisfactory than the REER. This has given rise to a broad debate, reflected in the publications of international organizations and academic journals[2] of recent years, particularly since the publication of the provocative work of Krugman (1994), which refers to the concern surrounding a country's competitiveness as a 'dangerous obsession', in so far as it may – he says – be an excuse for applying protectionist measures.

This debate is still going on, as it has yet to produce a fully acceptable definition of a country's competitiveness, much less an indicator capable of measuring it satisfactorily. A consensus has, however, been reached concerning several important points. Thus it is widely acknowledged that the REER is merely an imperfect indicator of short-term competitiveness, which must be supplemented by others – such as domestic and international market shares – that implicitly reflect non-price factors.

Moreover, in the medium- and long-term competitiveness of a country, the linchpin is considered to be productivity and, by extension, its determinants – in other words, mainly technology and human and physical capital. This does not mean that productivity and competitiveness are synonymous: a country may be more competitive than another with similar productivity, if it is capable of developing a specialization and a sales strategy for its products which allow it to achieve more favourable demand elasticities for its imports and exports.

Finally, within this broader notion of an economy's competitiveness, it is acknowledged that, even though companies are the determining agents of a country's competitiveness, governments also bear a great responsibility because of their power to regulate the workings of goods and factor markets, to influence the macroeconomic environment, and to affect growth in the quantity and, above all, quality of the productive factors as well as the technological capacity of their countries.

In a way, all these ideas are implicit in what appears to be the most widely accepted definition of competitiveness, as formulated by the OECD: '*the degree to which, under free market conditions, a country can produce goods and services that pass the test of international markets and, at the same time, maintain sustained growth in the real income of their citizens*' (OECD, 1992, p. 237). A definition in very similar terms was also used by the European Commission in its 'White Paper on Growth, Competitiveness and Employment' (see European Commission, 1994b).

Unfortunately, however, the advances in the conceptual terrain have not been matched to the same extent by a supply of indicators that would allow this fuller and more precise notion of competitiveness to be put to greater use. In practice, therefore, the REER is still the only measure of competitiveness that is routinely estimated for most countries.

Even though international organizations are now incorporating other supplementary indicators, such as market shares – domestic and international – and various measures that seek to reflect technological capacity, the availability of skilled labour, and other determinants of international competitiveness, measures of this type are still not used in any systematic way. Efforts in this direction are in fact still somewhat sporadic and are often made outside the confines of official national and international organizations.

In this respect, especially notable are the series of reports prepared by the World Economic Forum in Geneva and the Institute for Management and Development in Lausanne. These reports, published annually, give a diagnosis of the progress of competitiveness in a broad group of countries. They draw on a large battery of indicators that seek to approximate the very many macro- and microeconomic factors which underlie the broadest and most widely accepted concepts of international competitiveness, such as those contained in the above-mentioned OECD definition.

The problem, however, is that these reports, while commendable for their focus, are wide open to criticism because of their conspicuous weaknesses both in the method of gathering information on the more than one hundred factors considered relevant for evaluating competitiveness and in the statistical procedure used to combine them in a single measure, which is then used to establish a ranking of the competitiveness of the countries analysed.[3]

In short, to conclude these methodological considerations, it should be noted that substantial progress has been made towards reaching a consensus on the concept of the competitiveness of nations, while there is still considerable disagreement over its measurement.

In view of this situation, in the following sections our diagnosis of the trends in the Spanish economy's competitiveness since Spain's membership of the European Union will draw on a number of indicators: market share, variously specified real effective exchange rates and, finally, several supplementary variables indicative of the ability to compete on the basis of product differentiation strategies.

4.3 Competitiveness according to trade results

This section addresses the path and position of Spain's competitiveness vis-à-vis its European partners by examining trade results. In this respect, it first analyses the change in export shares, and then goes on to evaluate the position in the domestic market by studying the import penetration ratio. Finally and by way of summing up, it calculates the revealed comparative advantage indices.

For the purpose of evaluating Spain's competitiveness in relation to the EU countries as a whole, we calculated the export shares of both Spain and the European Union in different markets.[4]

As shown in Figure 4.1, Spain's export shares in the three markets in question (world, OECD and European Union) have risen continuously since 1986.[5]

It is significant that Spain's export share increased more in the Community market (79 per cent) than in the OECD (38.8 per cent) and the world market (44.6 per cent). This is consistent with the progressive elimination of trade barriers throughout the period in question, owing to the lifting of customs duties consequent upon joining a customs union and also to the additional liberalizing impetus provided by the single market programme. Considering that EU export shares fell by 14 per cent in the OECD, by 9.9 per cent in the world market and by 5.1 per cent in intra-Community trade (trade between EU countries) during the period analysed, the good performance of Spanish exports is even more striking.

Naturally, however, a country's competitiveness is not solely reflected in markets abroad. Trends in international market shares have to be viewed together with the relative capacity to supply the domestic demand for tradables. If we calculate the weight of imports in the domestic demand of the manufacturing sector (which covers most tradables), we find that the presence of foreign products in Spain increases substantially; in other words, in the years since Spain joined the Community, national output has been gradually displaced from the domestic market. In fact, import penetration doubled: from 17.4 per cent in 1986 to 35.9 per cent in 1997.

To evaluate the extent and magnitude of this phenomenon we calculated the same indicator of import penetration for all Community partners. As shown in Table 4.1, Spain is the country where external dependence has increased the most, and this reflects a worsening of its competitive position in the domestic market. None the less, greater dependence on imported products characterizes all the countries in question, and Spain's level of dependence is still lower than the average.

Moreover, the calculation of this indicator by branch of activity shows – as illustrated in Table 4.2 – that the increase in the dependence on imports is widespread in all branches, except in the food, beverages and tobacco sector, but is more pronounced in sectors of moderate and high demand and technology, which would appear to be a symptom of a shortfall in the Spanish supply of their products, especially capital goods. Notable, in any case, is the strong increase in

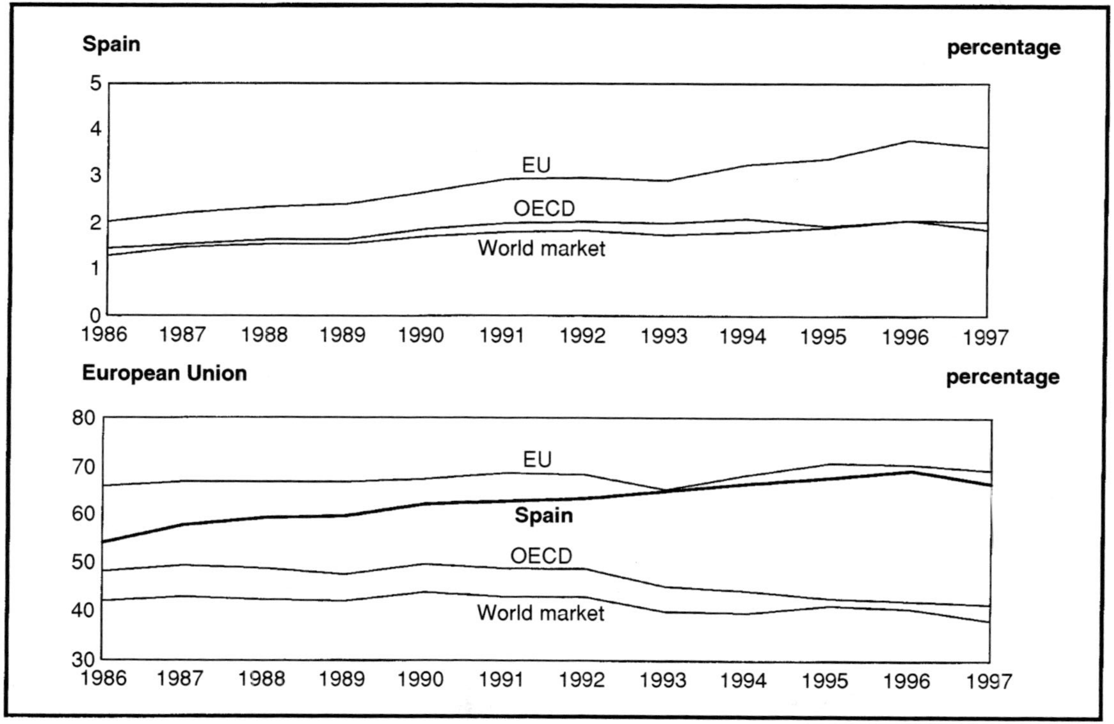

Figure 4.1 Spanish and EU export market shares

Source: Eurostat: *Foreign Trade: Statistical Yearbook*; Eurostat: *External and Intra-European Union Trade*; IMF: *Direction of Trade Statistics Yearbook*; Departamento de Estudios Europeos, Fundación de las Cajas de Ahorros.

Table 4.1 Share of imports in domestic demand for manufactured products (%)

Country	1986	1997	1997/1986
1. Austria	35.9	49.3	37.1
2. Belgium–Lux.	69.3	92.3	33.3
3. Denmark	49.7	59.1	19.0
4. Finland	29.6	41.7	40.8
5. France	26.3	39.5	50.1
6. Germany	22.6	32.1	41.9
7. Greece	36.4	52.9	45.5
8. Holland	61.3	87.1	42.0
9. Ireland	55.2	65.7	19.0
10. Italy	20.1	28.6	42.4
11. Portugal	24.8	49.2	98.0
12. Spain	**17.4**	**35.9**	**106.3**
13. Sweden	36.6	39.7	8.4
14. United Kingdom	29.4	41.7	41.9
European Union	30.1	43.1	43.1
Japan	4.2	8.7	107.8
United States	13.6	19.3	41.6

Source: OECD: *STAN Database for Industrial Analysis*; OECD: *Indicators of Industrial Activity*; Eurostat: *External and Intra-European Union Trade*; Departamento de Estudios Europeos, Fundación de las Cajas de Ahorros.

Table 4.2 Share of imports in domestic demand in manufacturing branches (%)

	1986	1997
Sectors with strong demand and intensive technology	**34.9**	**51.9**
Electrical goods	32.6	48.7
Office and data-processing machines	58.3	77.7
Chemical products	29.6	46.9
Sectors with moderate demand and intermediate technology	**24.6**	**50.8**
Rubber and plastic products	16.9	32.5
Transport equipment	23.4	57.7
Agricultural and industrial machinery	45.2	62.8
Other manufactured products	10.3	26.6
Sectors with weak demand and low technology	**11.0**	**14.9**
Textiles and clothing, leather and footwear	11.3	46.1
Ferrous and non-ferrous ores and metals	20.6	46.2
Non-metallic minerals and mineral products	10.0	12.0
Paper and printing products	13.0	31.3
Food, beverages and tobacco	7.0	6.6
Metal products, except machinery and transport equipment	12.8	20.3

Source: INE: Contabilidad Nacional; Departamento de Aduanas; OECD: *STAN Database for Industrial Analysis*; Eurostat: *Monthly Panorama of European Industry*; Departamento de Estudios Europeos, Fundación de las Cajas de Ahorros.

the weight of foreign products in meeting the demand in some branches with low technological content, where Spain has traditionally enjoyed a position of comparative advantage, as in the case of textiles and clothing and leather and footwear.

To summarize, even though the situation of export shares appears to be good, when we consider trends in the domestic market, it is not at all clear that Spanish manufacturers have preserved their competitiveness. In any event, it should be stressed that this duality in external behaviour (simultaneous growth in export shares and in the penetration of imports) is very widespread in all Community countries and in most manufacturing sectors.[6]

In view of this, in an attempt to arrive at a somewhat more precise diagnosis of trends in the competitiveness of the Spanish economy (or, rather, of manufacturers) from the standpoint of trade results, we have built the revealed comparative advantage index (RCAI), defined as the ratio between the trade balance and the volume of trade.[7] Here the RCAI of sector i in period t reflects the deficit or surplus of said sector as a percentage of the total trade in this type of goods. In the absence of strong distortions produced by the existence of trade barriers, we can expect this index to show positive (negative) values in those sectors where the country enjoys a comparative advantage (disadvantage) in relation to other countries. Note that the value of these indices gives no indication of the impact of the sector's surplus or deficit in question on the overall deficit or surplus.[8]

Table 4.3 gives the RCAI for Spanish manufacturing branches. In 1986 Spain's economy showed a trade disadvantage primarily in the manufacturing sectors of machinery and chemical products, while its advantages centred on the so-called light manufactured products and transport equipment (albeit solely due to automobiles, which are included in this branch). Briefly stated, in 1986 Spain had advantages in sectors intensive in non-skilled labour and natural resources and a position of disadvantage in products with a higher content of physical capital and, above all, human and technological capital.[9]

In the early years of Spain's membership of the European Union (to 1989), its RCAI reflected across-the-board deterioration in all branches of activity. Although these indices improved as of that year, it was not enough to offset the worsening during the previous years, except in the case of the non-metallic minerals and mineral products sector and some of the technology-intensive branches, whose situation improved over the period as a whole although they continued to be the areas where Spain had the greatest disadvantage. Thus, curiously enough, those sectors whose situation was worse at the beginning of the period

Table 4.3 Revealed comparative advantage indices of Spain's manufacturing branches (%)

	1986	1997
Sectors with strong demand and intensive technology	**–37.5**	**–27.8**
Electrical goods	–38.0	–19.3
Office and data-processing machines	–51.7	–48.4
Chemical products	–30.2	–26.3
Sectors with moderate demand and intermediate technology	**4.6**	**2.6**
Rubber and plastic products	12.4	–5.0
Transport equipment	20.2	13.5
Agricultural and industrial machinery	–20.9	–19.3
Other manufactured products	11.3	–7.5
Sectors with weak demand and low technology	**8.5**	**–0.5**
Textiles and clothing, leather and footwear	28.3	–0.4
Ferrous and non-ferrous ores and metals	–2.8	–17.7
Non-metallic minerals and mineral products	18.9	35.4
Paper and printing products	0.2	–9.9
Food, beverages and tobacco	3.4	0.5
Metal products, exc. machinery and transport equipment	4.2	5.2

Source: INE: *Contabilidad Nacional*; Departamento de Aduanas; Departamento de Estudios Europeos, Fundación de las Cajas de Ahorros.

had improved by the end of the period, just the opposite of what occurred in the activities where the Spanish economy had traditionally enjoyed an advantageous position. This somewhat paradoxical behaviour – at least from the standpoint of the conventional models of international trade – appears to be associated with, among other factors, the distortions in the pattern of Spain's relative advantages and disadvantages arising from the tariff structure prevailing before its Community membership.[10]

In any event, these changes in the structure of Spain's relative advantages and disadvantages, within a tendency to move closer to the trends in its more advanced Community partners, could be interpreted positively as a sign of a change in Spain's specialization towards branches of activity with better growth prospects, due to their greater income elasticity in world demand and the lower supply pressures exerted by developing countries.

4.4 Cost and price competitiveness

After analysing Spain's competitiveness in terms of trade results, in this section we examine the indicators, described in Section 4.2, most frequently used to measure price competitiveness: relative costs and prices, exchange rates, and their combination in real effective exchange rates.

For relative costs, we take as our point of departure labour costs per wage-earner and per hour worked.[11] Then, using relative unit labour costs (ULC), we examine to what extent the change in relative labour costs might have been offset by changes in the productivity differential of the labour factor. From there we go on to study the trends in the relative prices of goods, in which the trends in total costs – or, under certain assumptions, those of labour costs[12] – are combined with those observed in profit margins. In this respect, three different price indicators are used: export prices (or if unavailable, the UVI of exports), indicative of competitiveness in goods sold on markets abroad; producer prices, which represent potentially tradable goods as a whole; and the CPI, which encompasses the prices of tradable and non-tradable goods and services.

The comparison of labour costs and export prices reflects – assuming, as seems plausible, that Spanish companies are price takers on international markets[13] – the policy followed by Spanish exporters to accommodate their profit margins to domestic cost conditions and international prices in order to forestall a loss of market share.[14] Likewise, a comparison between external and producer prices – which takes into account the price performance of all domestic products that compete with imports[15] – reveals the existence of price differentiation policies in the different markets in which the companies operate.

In addition, by comparing these price indicators with those obtained by using the CPI, we can deduce the magnitude of the inflationary pressures exerted by non-tradable goods and services, which are responsible for the problems of dual inflation. Dual inflation has negative repercussions on the competitiveness of tradables for two reasons. First, because the persistence of high inflation signifies upward pressures on the labour costs of the economy as a whole, and these pressures are especially harmful in the case of producers of tradable goods, because they have less leeway to pass them through to prices, due to foreign competition. Secondly, because price increases in the non-tradable goods and services used as inputs entail additional pressure on costs, which is also difficult to pass through to prices in the case of companies subject to foreign competition.

Finally, we shall analyse the behaviour of the nominal exchange rate, both separately and in conjunction with all the above-mentioned indicators of relative costs and prices that give rise to the corresponding versions of real effective exchange rates (REER). In this way, we can deduce the role played by exchange-rate policy in competitiveness and also infer the consequences which might be derived from its disappearance upon adoption of the euro.

Beginning, then, with an examination of the labour costs per wage-earner during the years of Spain's EU membership (see Figure 4.2), in the first place we find that these costs grew in Spain by 15.1 per cent, which is significantly higher than the average EU rate of 6.3 per cent (increasing from 72.1 per cent of the average in the European Union in 1986 to 78.1 per cent in 1997). Spain's position in the ranking of EU countries as a whole, however, did not change: it was, and still is, the country with the third-lowest labour cost per wage-earner, after Greece and Portugal.

The second measurement used, the labour cost per hour worked, gives similar results:[16] a deterioration in Spanish costs with respect to those of the European Union (from 68.1 per cent of the EU average in 1986, the percentage rose to 74.1 per cent in 1997).

In sum, in their starting position, labour costs showed a clear comparative advantage, but then gradually worsened over time, although the advantage is still appreciable. Whereas this movement in Spanish costs towards those of the other countries is only logical in view of the process of economic and monetary integration, it is less logical and very worrisome that the converging tendency of costs was not offset by a similar convergence in productivity levels, as we shall now see. As shown in Figure 4.3, the deterioration in relative unit labour costs, which rose in Spain by more than 24 per cent with respect to those of its Community partners, indicates that the greater increase in Spanish labour costs was not absorbed by differential gains in productivity. Moreover, in comparing the growth in the relative unit labour costs of industry with that of its domestic and export prices, we infer that the relative profit margins of industrial firms must have fallen during the period, since the increase in labour costs could not be entirely passed through to relative prices.[17]

Figure 4.3 also shows that, with the exception of a few years, producer prices grew more than the UVI (unit value index) of exports. This seems consistent with the fact that exported goods are more sensitive to international price trends. All told, the most significant behavioural differences are those which arise between producer prices and the CPI,[18] undoubtedly attributable to the higher inflationary pressures from non-tradable goods and services in the Spanish economy in relation to the European Union during these years. In all other respects,

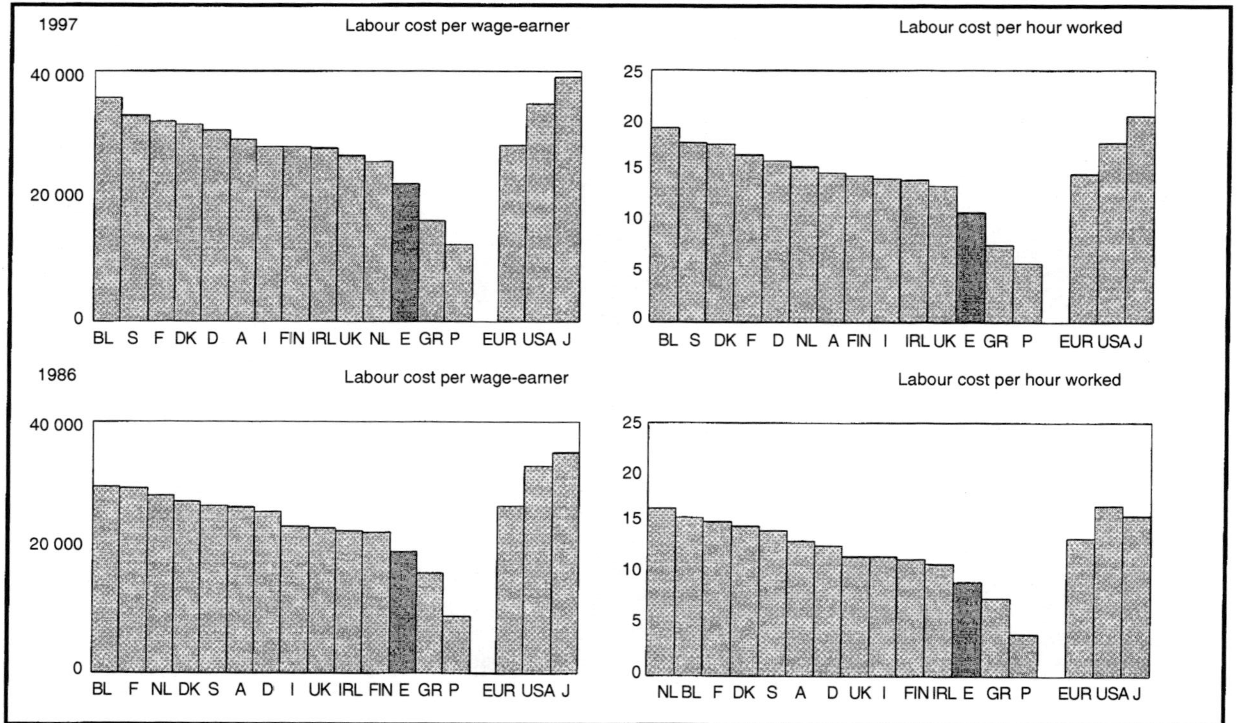

Figure 4.2 Measures of the cost of the labour factor

Source: OECD: *National Accounts*, vol. I: *Main Aggregates*; OECD: *Labour Force Statistics*; Eurostat: *Labour Force Survey*; Departamento de Estudios Europeos, Fundación de las Cajas de Ahorros.

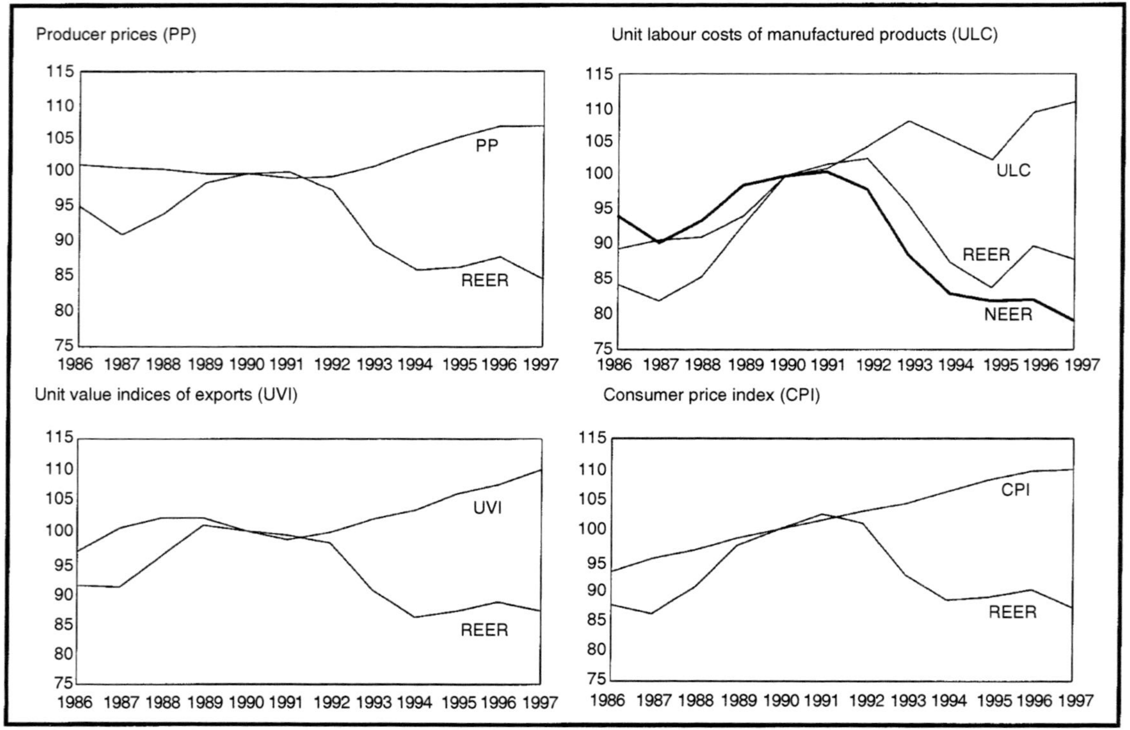

Figure 4.3 Trends in Spain's nominal effective exchange rate (NEER), real effective exchange rate (REER) and relative costs and prices vs the EU (1990 = 100)

Source: Banco de España: *Boletín Económico*; Departamento de Estudios Europeos, Fundación de las Cajas de Ahorros.

these differences evidence the dual nature that was – and still is – characteristic of inflation.

As a result, under whatever measure used, Spanish relative prices have deteriorated considerably over the past decade. The only instrument capable of counteracting this negative price performance is the exchange rate, and, in fact, the nominal effective exchange rate (NEER) fell by nearly 16 per cent between 1986 and 1997. Nevertheless, there were at least three stages in this development. The first spans the second half of the 1980s, when the peseta appreciated substantially, in particular as from 1987. Further opening up of trade and finance produced an abundant inflow of capital, which affected the nominal exchange rate. Thus, between 1987 and 1989, the nominal effective exchange rate appreciated by 9.3 per cent. The second stage began with the peseta's entry into the European Monetary System exchange-rate mechanism (ERM) in 1989, and was characterized by a certain stability in the exchange rate, albeit with a tendency for it to appreciate. In fact, the credibility gained upon entering the ERM strengthened the inflow of capital, leading to an additional appreciation of the peseta. In this situation and with a lax budgetary policy, the response was to apply a restrictive monetary policy that raised interest rates and prompted a further appreciation of the peseta, moving it to the upper limit of the ERM fluctuation band. The third stage began with the devaluations in the early 1990s. Between September 1992 and May 1993, the peseta's central parity in the ERM underwent three realignments, resulting in an effective depreciation of the exchange rate of nearly 16 per cent.[19] Indeed, the peseta trended downwards until March 1995, when it underwent another realignment in the ERM (this time by 7 per cent).

None the less, as noted, these peseta devaluations do not seem to have been entirely passed through to prices, although firms did, to a large extent, take advantage of them to enhance their profit margins.[20]

As a result, the real effective exchange rate[21] shows an improvement in the entire period (1986–97) when calculated with UVIs of exports (–4.3 per cent), producer prices (–11.2 per cent) and the CPI (–0.7 per cent), and a slight worsening when ULCs (4.3 per cent) are used. It could therefore be said that the competitiveness of Spanish tradables improved over the period and that the nominal exchange-rate component was the dominant force in the performance of REERs.

The dominant role of the exchange rate in the price competitiveness of the Spanish economy is a cause for concern from the standpoint of European monetary union, given the loss of the exchange rate as an instrument of adjustment for coping with problems of competitiveness. Hence the need for economic agents to moderate the growth in their remuneration, taking into account the increases in competing countries and the differential increases in productivity.

4.5 Other determinants of competitiveness

In the previous section we saw how the behaviour of the nominal exchange rate offset the deterioration observed in relative costs and prices using different measures, and how, as a result, Spain's export shares trended upwards. But it was also revealed that during the period the share of domestic products in supplying the domestic market declined, while the trade balance relative to the volume of trade also worsened in numerous productive branches. The trends in these indicators would thus suggest a much less favourable diagnosis of the progress of Spanish competitiveness than is deduced from the behaviour of the REER.

This dissociation between the behaviour of the REER and trade results is, as we said, not a new phenomenon, especially since the studies inspired by the pioneering work of Kaldor (1978), which provided evidence that it is a frequent occurrence, illustrative of the relevance of the numerous non-price factors associated with strategies of product differentiation that are also important in competitiveness.

As also noted in the methodological considerations in Section 4.2, the ability to compete successfully on the basis of product differentiation is closely linked to technological capacity, the human capital endowment and the relative availability of trade capital, as reflected in the possession of known brands and consolidated sales networks – in other words, with the exception of the latter, the same kind of intangible assets that are so essential to productivity.

Even though Section 2 cited studies that corroborate the positive and significant impact of all these intangible assets on competitiveness (at all levels: company, sector and country), it is worth adding several others which refer to the specific case of Spain.

In this respect, beginning with the factor most studied – technology – Martín and Moreno (1993) find that technological intensity, measured in terms of R&D spending, exerts a positive and significant influence on competitiveness (after estimating an econometric panel model to explain the performance of Spanish industrial exports, disaggregated into 14 branches, in the Community market). This evidence is corroborated in the studies of, among others, Martín and Velázquez

(1993a), for the group of companies which report to the Bank of Spain's Central Balance Sheet Office, and Merino and Moreno (1996) and Moreno and Rodríguez (1996), for the sample of firms included in the corporate strategy survey conducted by the Ministry of Industry and Energy.

As to the likewise positive influence of human capital on competitiveness, the empirical evidence for Spain is more limited. In any event, the results obtained from the estimates of the factor content of Spain's trade flows (see Rodríguez, 1993, and the works cited there) are consistent with such a hypothesis.

Finally, there are also studies which demonstrate that trade capital, generated by investment in advertising and the creation of own sales networks, is beneficial to exports. Thus Múgica and Yagüe (1993) show the association between the advertising expenditure of companies and their market shares. Alonso and Donoso (1996) hold that trade results depend to a large extent on the ability and expertise of the company management in conducting business abroad. In addition, Merino and Moreno (1996) present evidence that the availability of own distribution channels helps the export activity of firms. In this respect, it is worth mentioning that several studies – for example, Martín and Velázquez (1996a) and Maté (1996b) – find that direct international investment is also an efficient way of consolidating export markets.

When all this evidence pointing towards the relevance of technology and other intangible assets in determining an economy's competitiveness is contrasted with the findings in Chapter 2 on Spain's pronounced gap in all these areas vis-à-vis the European Union (its main customer and supplier), it becomes clearer why the gains in competitiveness reflected in the performance of the REER have not led to significant improvement in the trade balances of the different branches of activity.

4.6 Conclusions

In this chapter we have analysed the trends in Spain's competitiveness since its entry into the European Economic Community (now the European Union). To this end, after several observations on the concept and determinants of an economy's competitiveness, we calculated various indicators of trade results. As a second step, we examined several of the factors that could lie behind these trends. The main conclusions drawn from our analysis are summarized in the following points:

- The analysis of Spanish and Community export shares in different markets reveals the higher relative growth of Spain's export activity between 1986 and 1997, although this does not mean that the export GDP rate has reached the average level of the EU countries as a whole. In a setting in which the export shares of EU countries rose moderately, the growth in the presence of Spanish products in all markets, and the EU market in particular, stands out (79 per cent in the period studied).
- None the less, a notable displacement of national products by imports to meet domestic demand for tradable goods was also found: the relative presence of imports in the apparent consumption of manufactured products doubled to 35.9 per cent in 1997.
- In considering foreign and domestic markets together, it is not evident therefore that Spanish manufacturing industry has preserved its competitiveness since Spain's joining of the European Union. In fact, the simultaneous increase in export shares and the penetration of imports in the domestic market has led to a deterioration in the revealed comparative advantage indices (the trade balance in relation to the volume of trade) in most branches of industry. In any case, it is worth emphasizing that the deterioration during the period as a whole is largely the outcome of what occurred in the early years of the period.
- From this examination of Spain's costs and prices relative to the European Union, our conclusion is that, despite their across-the-board increase, the real effective exchange rate improved significantly, due to the depreciation in the nominal exchange rate in the period as a whole. Consequently, to make the most of membership of monetary union, economic agents (workers and businessmen) must accommodate their remuneration to the levels prevailing in the European Union and to the differential increases in their productivity; if not, the Spanish economy's competitive position will deteriorate, with the resulting cost in employment and welfare.
- Finally, this chapter has provided evidence of the importance of factors other than costs, prices and the exchange rate for an economy's competitiveness. Here we refer to factors linked to product differentiation, on the basis not only of quality but also of other attributes related to consumer familiarity with the product, which in turn depends on the availability of intangible assets (tech-

nology and human and trade capital) accumulated through systematic and prolonged investment efforts. Thus, drawing on the results obtained in other studies and on the information provided in different parts of this book, it has been shown that the weakness of Spain's competitive position is largely due to deficiencies in human and technological capital and also to the meagre investment in generating recognized brands and in creating sales networks abroad (trade capital) conducive to the consolidation and enlargement of markets.

5
Public Finances and Fiscal Policy

5.1 Introduction

Since at least the early 1980s, the size of the budget deficit in nearly all European countries and the need to restrain it have been a source of mounting concern, which governments have addressed through diverse and often dissimilar measures.

Only naturally, the efforts to find, and to follow, the best policies for consolidating budget deficits intensified after the signing of the Maastricht Treaty, because of the requirement that EMU member countries keep their deficits and debt at less than 3 per cent and 60 per cent of GDP, respectively.

More recent debate has therefore focused not so much on the need to reduce the deficit – on which a broad consensus already exists – as on the most efficient way of achieving this goal and, in particular, on the composition of budget adjustments. And, of course, at the centre of the debate on which expenditure items should bear these cuts lies the polemic over possible reform of the European welfare state.

The above observations summarize the setting in which the questions studied in the present chapter should be framed. Here our purpose is, first, to compare the volume and composition of the budget deficits of Spain and the other EU members during Spain's membership of the Community, and then – after considering the evidence on the magnitude of their indebtedness – to comment on some of the problems derived from the growing volume of debt required to finance them (Section 5.2).

Secondly, a brief summary is given of the ideas that best explain the relationship between the budget deficit and growth, and more specifically, the way in which the growth potential of output and employment in EU economies may be affected by the policies of fiscal discipline that EMU countries will have to follow in order to comply with the stability pact (Section 5.3).

The next section will attempt to outline the basic arguments in the debate on the welfare state in Europe, taking into consideration the qualifications, if any, needed to adapt it to the Spanish case.

We shall then go on to evaluate the leeway which remains for the fiscal policies of the member countries after monetary unification, as well as the advisability of reinforcing the stabilizing role of the Community budget.

The final section presents the conclusions drawn, emphasizing – in line with the general focus of the book – the issues that most directly affect Spain.

5.2 Generation of the deficit and the problems derived from its financing

This section will start evaluating the trends in the public finances of Spain and its EU partners by examining revenue and expenditure; it will then consider general government balances and the debt accumulated as a consequence of the generalization of the deficit and the resulting interest payments.

Note that restricting the period studied to the years 1986–97 – for the sake of uniformity with the rest of the book – does not allow proper consideration of several interesting developments, such as the gradual worsening in the deficit in the years prior to that period and the delay in this process in Spain owing to the belated and subsequently rapid introduction of the welfare state. In view of this, we shall attempt to document these points with supplementary data to those presented in the tables and charts referring to the period 1986–97.[1]

5.2.1 Government expenditure and revenue

On average in the European Union public spending as a proportion of GDP stabilized in the years 1986 to 1997 (see Figure 5.1). But, on two counts, this result needs to be qualified. First, from a geographical standpoint, to highlight those countries where the weight of public spending in GDP fell, most notably the case of Ireland where the decline was especially sharp. And secondly, from the standpoint of time, it should be borne in mind the final years of the period were characterized by discipline in expenditure (while not perceptible in Figure 5.1, it is apparent in a graph discussed later).

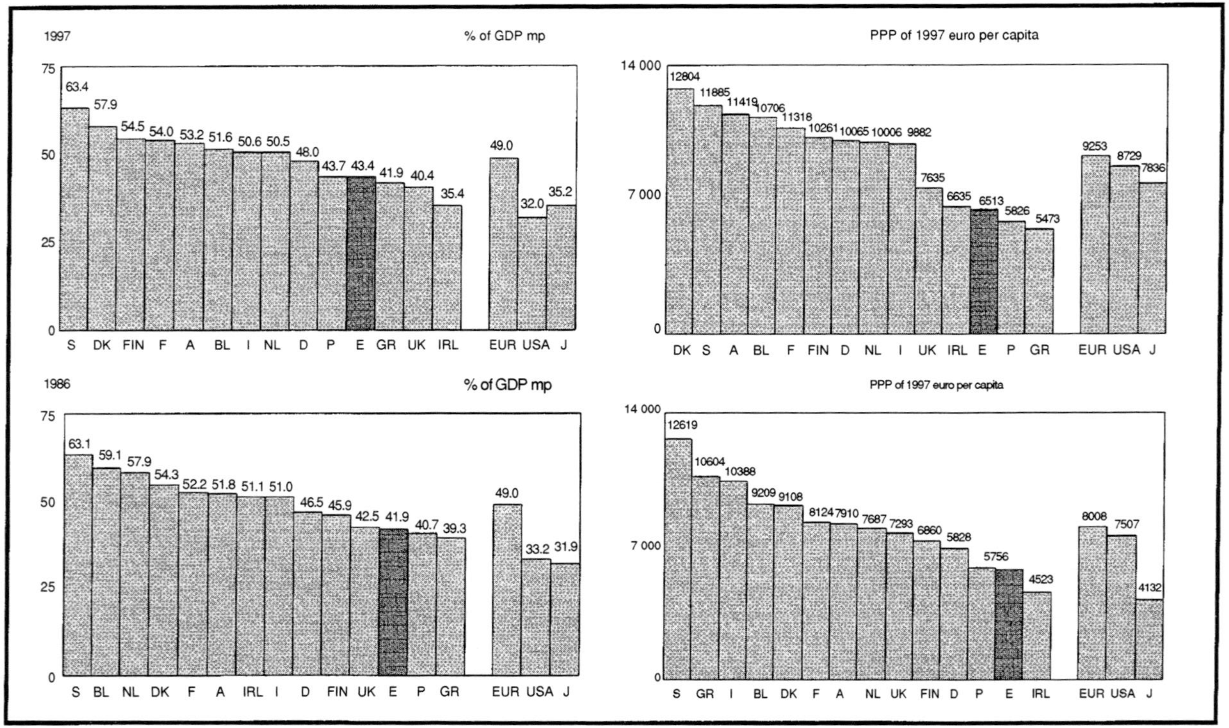

Figure 5.1 Government expenditure

Source: European Commission: *General Government Data*: OECD: *National Accounts*, vol. I: *Main Aggregates*; Departamento de Estudios Europeos, Fundación de las Cajas de Ahorros.

Within this panorama, Spain stands out as one of the countries with the most dynamic public spending. The greater vitality of public expenditure in Spain – already appreciable in the early years of democracy – is associated with the measures taken by various democratic governments to endow the country with public services and benefits similar to those which have long prevailed in other industrialized countries. In other words, the intense expansion in expenditure in those years was essentially an attempt to redress the paltry situation of Spain's public sector in previous years. By way of example, in 1975 Spanish public spending absorbed only 25 per cent of GDP, whereas the Community average was already around 40 per cent.[2]

These belated efforts in Spain to match the conduct of the public sector in the other Community countries were not only beset by problems of precipitation but they were also cut short by the pressures of fiscal discipline associated with the Maastricht agreements.

Figure 5.2 clearly illustrates the growing tendency for restraint in public expenditure in relation to GDP by the year 1994 in the EU countries as a whole and the somewhat greater stringency in Spain. As a result, the weight of Spanish public spending in GDP, at 43.4 per cent, is still well below the Community average of 49 per cent.

Even though this restraint in Spanish public spending is justified for the reasons already discussed, it is still worrisome when judged in the light of Spain's low level of public infrastructure in comparison with the other EU economies, as described in somewhat more detail in Chapter 2.

The closer alignment of Spanish public spending with Community levels not only affected expenditure as a percentage of GDP but affected also, as is only natural, its structure. Thus, from a starting position in the mid-1970s marked by a striking difference in the composition of expenditure, reflecting among other things the paltry development of welfare benefits, the composition of Spain's public spending has since converged towards the average in the European Union.

Figure 5.3 shows the salient features of the convergence in Spain's spending structure in the past 12 years. Here we see that the Spanish system of welfare expenditure, both in relation to pensions and in services provided free of charge (mainly health and education), gradually moved towards the levels that had already prevailed for so many years in most Community countries. Thus, in the expenditure breakdown considered here, we find that Spain's structure is now fairly similar to Europe's, even though a few disparities still exist, such as the greater

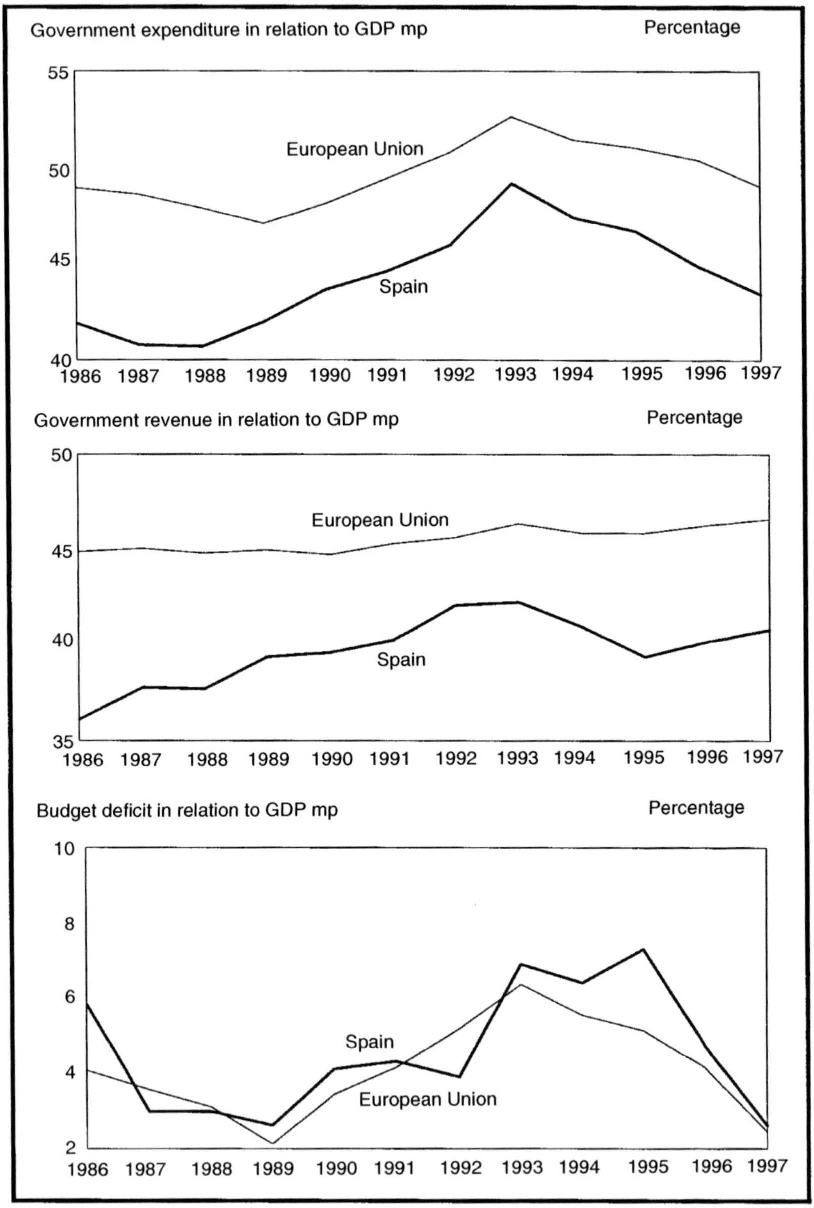

Figure 5.2 Revenue, expenditure and budget deficits in Spain and the EU

Source: European Commission: *European Economy*; OECD: *National Accounts*, vol. I: *Main Aggregates*; Departamento de Estudios Europeos, Fundación de las Cajas de Ahorros.

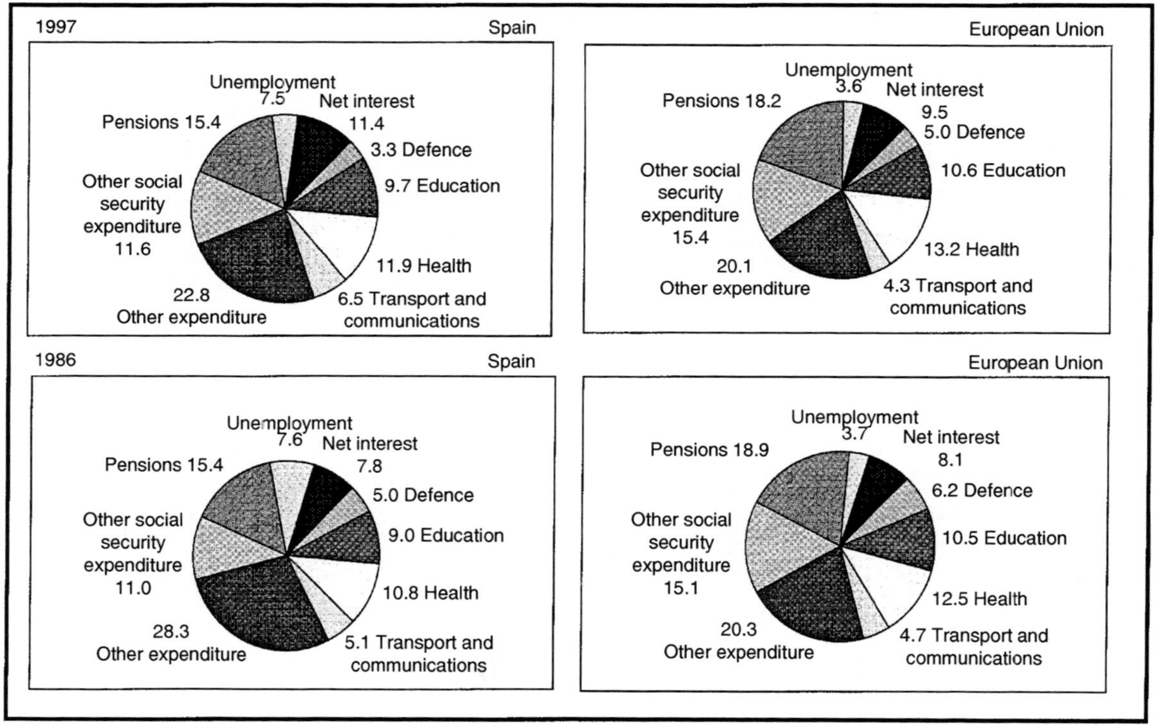

Figure 5.3 Government expenditure structure in Spain and the EU

Source: OECD: *National Accounts*, vol. II: *Detailed Tables*; Eurostat: *Social Protection Expenditure*; Departamento de Estudios Europeos, Fundación de las Cajas de Ahorros.

relative weight of unemployment benefits, associated with the particular gravity of the unemployment problem.

Turning to government revenue, we should begin by pointing out that, owing to similar efforts to remedy a situation completely different from the Community norm, Spanish government revenue has been rising since the mid-1970s at higher rates than the EU average, albeit at a slower pace than that of expenditure. The successive tax reforms in the wake of the Moncloa pacts managed to palliate the serious shortfall in tax revenue – concealed at the time owing to the small scale of spending – under the previous tax system. At the same time, the fairness and flexibility of the Spanish tax system improved, gradually moving towards European models.

Yet there are still several differences between the Spanish and the EU systems with respect to both the level and the structure of revenue.

First, government revenue as a proportion of GDP is lower in Spain – 40.8 per cent compared with 46.5 per cent in the European Union – despite its stronger growth in the period analysed (see Figure 5.4) and also during the previous decade.

Secondly, as regards the composition of revenue, the most striking distinguishing feature is the still lower relative weight of income tax, a vestige – now very slight – of a more regressive tax system (see Figure 5.5).

5.2.2 The deficit and the explosiveness of debt

Combining the data on revenue and expenditure, we find that budget deficits, with the obvious cyclical variation, were a constant phenomenon during the period analysed (1986–97) in nearly all EU countries and, by extension, in the area as a whole. Throughout these years, Spain's deficit in proportion to GDP was generally higher than the average Community levels except in the years 1987–9 and 1992 (see Figures 5.2 and 5.6).

According to the OECD's estimates, in recent years most of the deficit has been structural in nature. Specifically, according to this organization, the structural component accounted for 80.6 per cent and 75 per cent of Spain's deficits in 1995 and 1996, respectively.[3]

Consequently, even though an improvement in the cyclical situation might be expected to have an automatic and favourable effect on the deficit (because government revenue is a positive function of income, and there is a negative correlation between a large part of expenditure – mainly unemployment benefits – and the cycle), no great hopes should be placed on the ability of this mechanism to correct public-

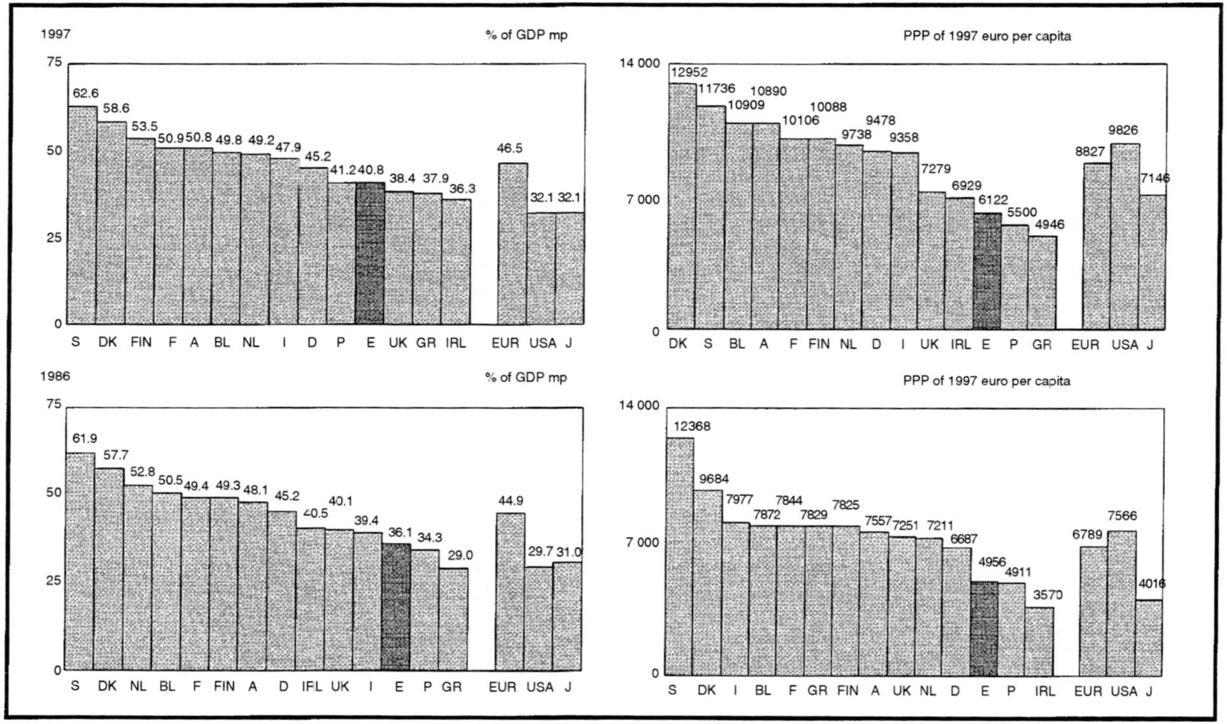

Figure 5.4 Government revenue

Source: OECD: *Economic Outlook*; OECD: *National Accounts*, vol. I: *Main Aggregates*; Departamento de Estudios Europeos, Fundación de las Cajas de Ahorros.

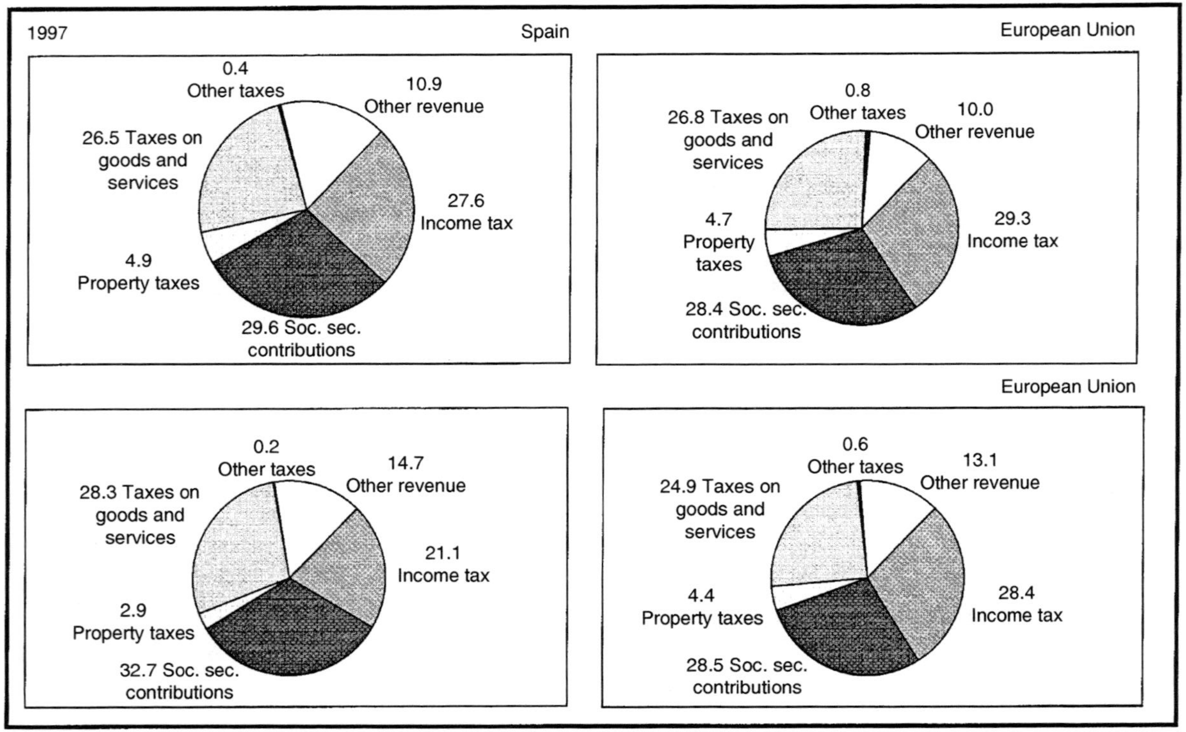

Figure 5.5 Structure of government revenue in Spain and the EU

Source: European Commission: *General Government Receipts, Expenditure and Gross Debt*; OECD: *Revenue Statistics of OECD Member Countries*; Departamento de Estudios Europeos, Fundación de las Cajas de Ahorros.

sector imbalances. And not only because of the fact that the cyclical component does not account for more than a small part of the deficits of recent years, as we have just indicated, but also because it would not seem realistic to predict that high economic growth rates can be achieved in the setting of the anti-inflation policies that will in all probability characterize the period of consolidation of EMU.

Added to this is the fact that the patterns of population growth – and especially the persistence of the trend for the population to age – will continue to be a further element of pressure on public spending, basically in the areas of pensions and health, whose relative weight in expenditure is high.

These trends in the deficit have naturally brought about a swift increase in the indebtedness of European countries, whose debt-to-GDP ratios have reached levels that generally exceed the 60 per cent stipulated in the Maastricht Treaty. Moreover, the accumulated debt in some economies – Belgium, Italy and Greece – has even surpassed the magnitude of their gross domestic product.

Although Spain's debt ratio is, as shown in Figure 5.6, considerably lower than the EU average – 68.8 per cent versus 72.2 per cent – it, too, exceeds the limit imposed by the Treaty on European Union.

The increase in indebtedness has led to spectacular growth in the public-spending item of debt interest payments. Indeed, this item is now one of the main expenditure components; moreover it has become a mechanism whereby the deficit is self-perpetuating. As such, according to the latest available data (see Figure 5.7), debt-servicing accounts on average for 10.2 per cent of the total public spending of EU countries.

The notable weight of the government debt burden is cause for concern, given the uncertainty over its sustainability. The findings of studies that evaluate the sustainability of government debt in EU countries by calculating the so-called primary gap[4] are, in fact, hardly reassuring.

The estimate here suggests that, even though progress was made with respect to the sustainability of debt throughout the period, it is not likely to have a long-lasting effect. Focusing on the case of the Spanish economy, we find that Spain's unsustainable debt situation in 1986 was corrected in subsequent years, as illustrated in Figure 5.8. None the less, as of 1990, the dynamics of public indebtedness once again gave rise to a problem of sustainability, reflected in the positive sign of the primary gap of that year. Fortunately, after the change of course in public expenditure in relation to GDP as of 1994 (see Figure 5.2) and after the

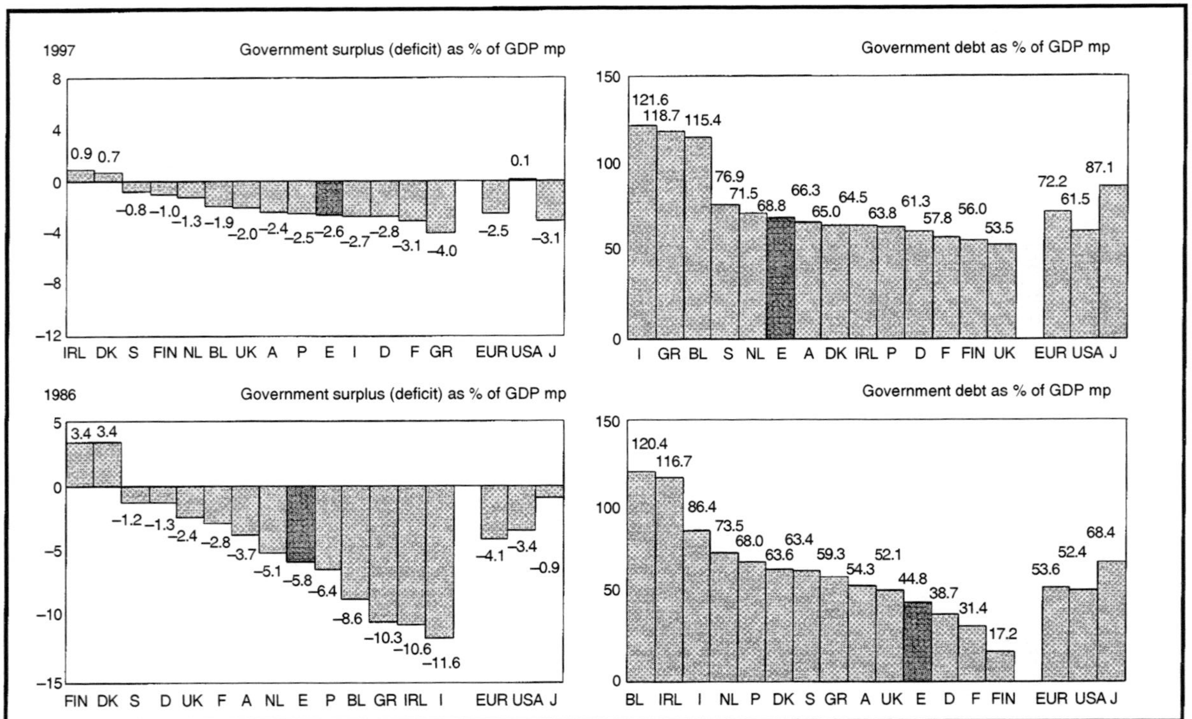

Figure 5.6 The deficit and government debt

Source: European Commission: *European Economy*; OECD: *National Accounts*, vol. I: *Main Aggregates*; Departamento de Estudios Europeos, Fundación de las Cajas de Ahorros.

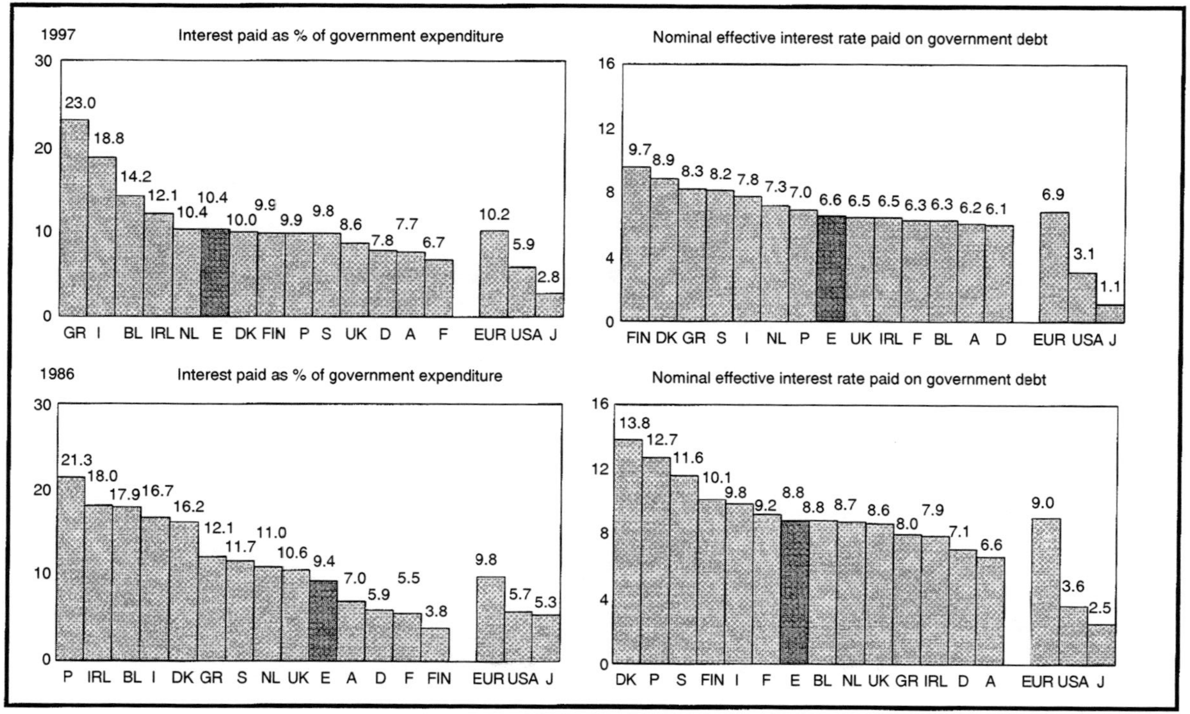

Figure 5.7 Interest paid and the nominal effective interest rate on debt

Source: European Commission: *General Government Receipts, Expenditure and Gross Debt*; Departamento de Estudios Europeos, Fundación de las Cajas de Ahorros.

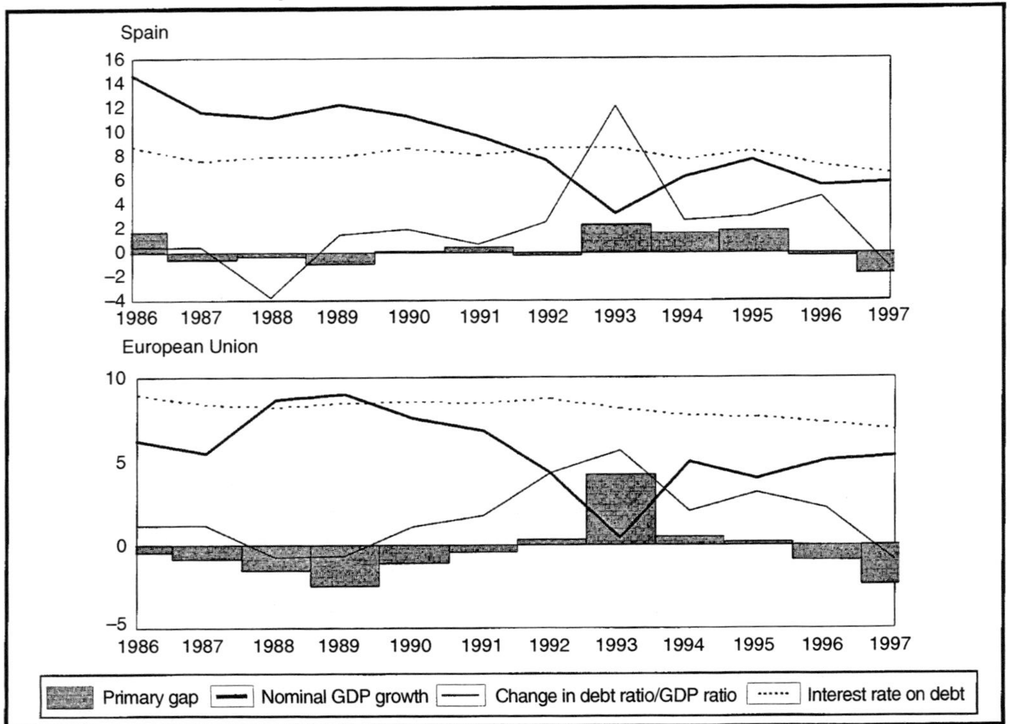

Figure 5.8 Sustainability of government debt in Spain and the EU

Source: European Commission: *European Economy*; Departamento de Estudios Europeos, Fundación de las Cajas de Ahorros.

restrictive adjustment implemented from 1996 onwards, the problem now seems to be resolving itself.

It should be borne in mind, however, that as long as the effective interest rate on government debt is greater than the growth rate of GDP, each considered in real terms, the problems of debt sustainability will persist.[5]

All in all, this signals the need to apply more efficient budget policies, to carry fiscal consolidation further and to keep debt at sustainable levels.

Identification of the categories of revenue (which would have to increase) and/or expenditure (which would have to be reduced) that are capable of achieving a lasting reduction in the deficit without eroding the economy's efficiency and competitiveness is, however, as relevant as it is difficult. Here the difficulty is of a technical and political nature.

From a technical or economic standpoint, the main problem lies in our scant knowledge of the effects of the different fiscal adjustment options on the principal macroeconomic aggregates. Until very recently, in fact, the macroeconomic literature on fiscal policy focused primarily on the study of its impact in terms of whether it was expansionary or contractionary, with very little attention paid to the composition of the budget.

As emphasized in more recent studies[6], however, the composition of budget adjustments appears to be decisive. And, even though the research on the question is still at a very provisional stage, there is evidence that the impact of such adjustments on growth and employment differs substantially depending on the composition of the adjustment; specifically, adjustments based on income tax increases and cuts in public-sector investment expenditure seem to have a negative effect on growth in output and employment, whereas this need not be the case if the adjustment is based on cuts in public spending and social benefits (see Perotti, 1996, for references on this question, which we shall address in greater detail in the next section).

It should be stressed that the political difficulties involved in implementing fiscal discipline become apparent when the numerous sources of inefficiency in budgetary decisions that are observed in modern analyses of public finance based on public choice theory are taken into consideration. There appear to be two main difficulties.

First, there is the possible bias in the electoral process against decisions by those in government that would involve a maximization of the welfare of the country's citizens as a whole, and in favour of the more immediate interests of the groups they represent. And secondly, the time frame used to evaluate the costs and benefits associated with budgetary decisions is distorted, with an overstatement of possible short-term benefits – since these may generate greater political returns, taking into account the election calendar – and consequently, an understatement of the medium- and long-term benefits and costs associated with current decisions.

Furthermore, a recent ambitious study of the experience of budget readjustment in 20 OECD countries since 1960[7] demonstrates that the adjustments which achieve the most lasting and efficient improvements are usually the ones which encounter the greatest social resistance and whose implementation entails the greatest political cost. In consequence, governments – influenced by the election calendar – are reluctant to apply them. In this respect, the studies of the processes that determine budget policy decisions (see Hagen and Harden, 1994 and 1995, by way of example) argue that politicians have incentives to pursue policies involving increased expenditure, especially when these policies affect easily identifiable groups – pensioners, among others – which can help them to preserve or increase their votes, but whose financing is none the less distributed among all the country's citizens.

Similarly, it might be argued that underlying the fiscal consolidation policies of recent years, with their preference for cuts in investment and for indiscriminate privatization of publicly owned companies, is a problem of erroneous perception by government officials of the future costs of this option in terms of growth and employment.

In sum, as a corollary to these observations, two points may be highlighted. The first is the need for structural reforms to combat the considerable problems of structural deficit and accelerating debt which beset European economies. The second is that designing and implementing these reforms is tremendously complex, given the many technical and political difficulties involved.

It is no coincidence, therefore, that the debate on the best way to achieve an effective reduction in government budgets in Europe has gained increasing prominence in academic and political forums.

At the core of this debate lie two issues, which are addressed in greater detail in the sections below: first, the impact of stringent fiscal policies on growth and employment; and, secondly, the viability and advisability of maintaining in present circumstances the generous welfare state that, albeit with certain differences between one country and another, is a defining feature of EU countries with respect to other industrialized nations.

5.3 Fiscal adjustment policies and economic growth

In view of the grave unemployment problem in most European countries, and especially in Spain, unquestionably one of the major challenges faced by EU member countries, and Spain in particular, is how to incorporate in their budgetary policies measures capable of both reducing the budget deficit and strengthening employment.

Unfortunately, however, such measures inevitably involve a certain element of trial and error, because we lack sufficient knowledge and experience of the impact of stringent fiscal policies on growth in output and employment. Here it should be borne in mind that the increasing globalization of markets – especially financial markets – and the formation of EMU are novel developments, which alter the margin for manoeuvre and impact of member countries' fiscal policies in ways that are hard to predict.

Indeed, the most recent studies call into question several of the hypotheses on the impact of fiscal consolidation policies on growth that were generally considered conventional wisdom; at the same time, they are helping to reveal others that have not hitherto been contemplated.

With respect to the revision of conventional explanations, empirical evidence[8] has been found which suggests that a reduction in expenditure and/or increase in taxes may lead to a crowding-in effect, which might more than offset the fall in aggregate demand predicted by a standard Keynesian model. This effect is the result of the great importance that the 'credibility effect' associated with stringent fiscal policies (in other words, the reduction in the risk premium in interest rates on international financial markets, in response to a country's fiscal stringency) appears to have acquired.

What is more, the results of one study referring to OECD countries – Giavazzi and Pagano (1996) – are consistent with the existence of crowding-in effects in consumption in response to the application of fiscal adjustment measures.

Therefore, judging by the evidence in these studies, the idea advanced by Keynes that restrictive fiscal policy leads to a reduction in aggregate demand and, by extension, a reduction in output and employment can be called into question.

However, together with these findings, there is other evidence, obtained by applying the new endogenous growth models, which would tend to support the Keynesian propositions concerning the negative consequences of restrictive fiscal policies on economic activity and employment, especially those involving cuts in public-sector investment.

In recent years numerous studies seeking to identify the determinants of economic growth and its uneven intensity across countries (discussed in Chapter 2) coincide in demonstrating that government investment significantly increases productivity. This is particularly so in the case of investment in areas such as education, research and development (R&D), and transport and communications, which generate more externalities with a positive impact on the productivity of private investment.

In addition, there is equally substantiated evidence that the relative supply of this type of infrastructure seems to be of great importance in the decisions of firms as to where to locate their foreign direct investment projects. Here it is safe to say that the growing integration of the European market and the projected incorporation of Eastern European countries into the process will continue to spur the reorganization and relocation of the productive activities of multinational firms. As a result, transport and communications infrastructure and skilled labour supply will increasingly be decisive in attracting foreign direct investment projects. Here it is worth stressing that Spain's peripheral location with respect to the core countries of the European economic space is an obstacle to its choice as a site for these projects, and therefore this will have to be offset by special efforts in other areas. Note, too, that the likely integration of Eastern European countries may produce a shift in the centre of gravity of European economies, which would make Spain's peripheral location more pronounced. Moreover, the extraordinary labour-cost advantages of these emerging market economies heighten the need to promote private and public investment in transport and communications infrastructure, education and R&D in order to ensure that Spain can offset its wage differentials with higher levels of productivity.

From another standpoint – that of the positive effects of public spending on the productivity of economies – all these arguments and factors tend to reinforce the fears aroused by Keynesian models as to the possible damage to the growth capacity of output and employment produced by the implementation of fiscal consolidation policies, or at least those focusing on cuts in public investment.

Briefly stated, the available evidence on the repercussions of fiscal policy options on economic activity and employment falls far short of providing an adequate basis for determining the most appropriate measures. None the less, several suggestions may be inferred that warrant consideration. Let us examine the main ones.

First, it seems clear that in countries where the tax burden is high, as in the majority of EU member states, the most effective measures in a stringent fiscal policy are spending cuts rather than increases in revenue, as the latter could dampen savings. In this respect, attempts to increase government revenue by raising social security contributions would appear to be the most counterproductive measure, because it would increase the relative cost of labour, with damaging effect on employment. By contrast, many believe that, if it is decided to increase government revenue, the best way is to raise the rates charged for certain public services.

Secondly, with respect to measures aimed at reducing expenditure, the most convincing studies coincide in pointing out that it is much more advisable to cut current spending rather than cut investment. This proposition, supported by many econometric studies (see, for example, Argimón, González-Páramo and Roldán, 1997, and the references cited there), is based on the fact that government investment (but not current expenditure) has significant effects, or positive externalities, on the productivity of companies. In relation to current expenditure, the dominant opinion, especially in the more recent studies, is that the most appropriate method is to reduce expenditure on welfare transfers.

Finally, it is worth noting that opinion is, of course, unanimous that the most satisfactory way to achieve budgetary consolidation is to enhance the efficiency of public administration, both on the tax side (via the eradication of tax evasion and fraud) and in expenditure (via improved cost-efficiency in public-sector activities). But this method of restraining budget deficits is difficult and slow, as it requires substantive structural reforms and equally significant changes in the incentive structure which guides the actions of public managers.

5.4 Sustainability of the welfare state

As noted in the previous section, in many of the studies which seek to ascertain the most appropriate fiscal policy for steering the budget deficits of European countries towards levels compatible with the criteria established for the formation of EMU, the reduction in expenditure on social benefits is found to be one of the most advisable – or, in any case, least objectionable – measures from the standpoint of output and employment.

However, the debate on whether Europe's welfare state should undergo more or less substantial reform rests on other arguments more directly related to the development and workings of the system itself. Here there are basically two types of argument. First, those stressing the problems which have gradually accumulated in the system, due among other circumstances to the profound changes in the demographic and economic conditions which prevailed in Europe during the development and consolidation of the welfare state (the 1950s, 1960s and early 1970s[9]). And secondly, those pointing out the erosion of incentives to work and save, in addition to the administrative costs of the bureaucracy set up to handle the spectacular growth of the system.

As to the problems derived from the growing gap between the current (and future) situation of European economies and the situation which existed during the boom years of the welfare state, we might begin by noting that they all culminate in a single problem: the system's growing financial difficulties.

In fact, the many studies undertaken not only by international organizations[10] but also by the countries themselves[11] coincide, concluding that the welfare state faces a risk of 'financial strangulation'.

The factors contributing to the financial problems that now cast doubts on the system's viability include in particular demographic changes, which have led (and will continue to lead) to a progressive ageing of the population and, consequently, an increase in the number of people receiving social benefits, both in absolute terms and in relation to the number of social security contributors.[12]

But the deterioration in the system's financial capacity is also attributable to changes in the economic scenario, which have caused an erosion of revenue and at the same time an increase in expenditure, basically evidenced in the moderation in the growth rate of European economies since the mid-1970s (not only due to the crises that have occurred but also to the fact that growth rates during cyclical expansions have been more modest than in the two preceding decades) and, in particular, the emergence of a grave and persistent unemployment problem.

And finally, a third factor has been the reforms introduced during the years of the system's consolidation – coinciding with the years of vigorous growth in output and employment – that gradually improved the coverage and level of social benefits, which in some cases even became universal. Notable in this respect for its special contribution to the increase in welfare expenditure (pensions in particular) has been the policy of linking increases in monetary benefits to the consumer price index.

In sum, all the above-mentioned demographic and economic circumstances have steadily fuelled the growth in welfare expenditure, not only by enlarging the number of the system's beneficiaries but also by raising the amount of the payments, while at the same time checking the expansion of revenue from social security contributions. As a result, a situation has arisen of increasing uncertainty over the system's financial viability, which is set to become more severe in future years.

So far the studies which have explored this question are unanimous in their verdict (based on the projected demographic trends that unequivocally signal a continued, strong process of ageing in the populations of European countries): a worsening in the financial prospects of the social protection system as a whole and, in particular, the component that absorbs the largest volume of resources, namely pensions.

The second type of argument put forward in favour of reforming the current system of social benefits in European countries is, as already indicated, based on the well founded suspicion that serious problems exist in achieving efficiency, which even include fraud in the administration of certain benefits. Here it is usually adduced that the intense and accelerated growth in the number of beneficiaries was not accompanied by the institutional reforms needed to ensure the proper administration of the system and the prevention of abuse and fraud by recipients.

Both types of argument – financial unviability and administrative inefficiencies – thus provide grounds for the need for reforms in different areas of the welfare state, and pensions in particular, in European countries. The conviction of the need to reform the system is, in fact, now widespread, at least in professional spheres. However, this has not prevented considerable controversy over the nature of such a reform, or popular resistance to the measures taken in some countries, a recent case being the strongly disputed initiative of extending prescription charges in Spain.

Pensions lie at the core of this polemic, and specifically the extent to which the state pay-as-you-go system of distributing pensions should be trimmed and privately funded schemes promoted.

Most of the proposals, both in Spain and in the other EU countries, advocate reforms which preserve this state pension system, although others call for its complete replacement by private funded schemes. Needless to say, the latter are not only in the minority but also appear to pose enormous technical – not to mention political – problems in the transition from one system to another.

If we confine our discussion to the type of reform that seems most realistic in the short term – reforms which do not call into question the essence of the present system – here, too, we encounter discrepancies over more specific issues, such as how the base salary used to calculate the pension entitlement should be obtained and the system for updating pension payments.

It is beyond the scope of this chapter to give a detailed rundown of the discrepancies between the many proposals now being studied within the European Union. Therefore, after describing the broad lines of the debate in EU countries as a whole, we shall consider only those referring to Spain.

We shall begin with pensions, which, as in most other countries, is the benefit that has drawn most of the attention of experts and politicians. The fruit of the political debate on this question was the so-called 'Toledo pact', which was subscribed to by all political parties and is the reference point for the reforms now being studied by the government.[13] As to the proposals in the studies of the subject, recently summarized in Herce (1997), we should begin by noting that only the study by Piñera and Weinstein (1996) categorically opts for replacement of the pay-as-you-go state pension system; the others contain proposals for reforms aimed at guaranteeing the financial sustainability of the unfunded system, although they also tend to favour supplementary private funded schemes.

Moreover, most of these studies rule out the option of tackling the problem of future financial shortfall via increases in social security contributions or taxes. Instead, they propose more or less ambitious formulas for reducing expenditure, primarily through the following measures: postponement of the retirement age, an increase in the number of years considered in the calculation of the base salary, updating of pensions by less than the growth in the CPI[14], and improved inspection systems to prevent fraud in the collection of pension payments.

As to health benefits, the second largest item in terms of the volume of expenditure, there has also been a long-running debate on the need for reforms to check their spectacular growth, especially in the area of pharmaceuticals, and above all to rectify the problems of administration and quality in the provision of services, in which crowded hospitals and long waiting lists for surgery appear to be merely the tip of the iceberg.

The report of the Commission for the Analysis and Evaluation of the National Health System, generally known as the Abril Commission, issued in 1991, provides a good diagnosis of the pressures and problems afflicting Spain's health system as well as a list of proposals[15] for dealing with the problems. The report is still the starting point for all discussions on the reform of Spain's health system, despite the time that has passed since its publication.

In general, the reforms discussed do not intend to alter the basic core of solidarity, which is the essence of the present health system, but only – albeit no small matter – to promote mechanisms for reducing costs by improving efficiency in the use of human and material resources and also to enhance the satisfaction of service users. Here many proposals take as their basic criterion the separation of the financing (public) from the provision of services (public and private) in order to introduce a certain degree of competition among the providers and to foster the freedom of choice of users.

One of the most debated points in relation to reform of the health system focuses on the best way to secure the rationalization and control of pharmaceutical expenditure, given its magnitude and rapid growth. Here there is a consensus as to the existence of unnecessary consumption and an undesirable bias towards the use of high-priced products. For this reason, many experts advocate measures to reduce the costs of distributing pharmaceuticals, to re-channel consumption towards less expensive products and brands (promoting generic medicines) and – most controversial of all – to increase the user's share of the cost.

As to unemployment benefits, the general thrust of the reforms proposed is to continue with the two lines of action already initiated in 1992 and 1993.[16] In other words, to reduce the level of benefits and, at the same time, to reinforce and improve supervisory mechanisms, not only to penalize abuses by beneficiaries but also to raise the possibility of the unemployed finding work.[17]

Finally, in the area of education, there appears to be little margin for introducing reforms to cut spending. The strategic nature of education as an essential factor in growth means that it would be ill advised to make it the basis for consolidating social expenditure, especially considering that, as shown in Figure 5.9, expenditure per student in Spain is appreciably lower than the EU average at all levels of education, making Spain one of the lowest-ranking EU countries in this respect.[18] On the contrary, the reasons adduced earlier would appear to suggest the need for increased spending on education.

Moreover, the reforms already undertaken at both secondary and university level could fail for lack of funds. The application of these reforms is, in fact, the target of increasing criticism. It is argued that implementing the reforms without the financial backing contemplated in their design has, among other problems, led to a deterioration in quality.

In this context, the proposal that students should bear a larger share of the cost of university education makes increasing sense, especially since higher education is precisely where the private appropriation of the benefits is greatest, or in other words, where the positive externalities for the rest of society are smallest.[19] Part of the resources obtained in this way could be used to release funds to improve the lower levels of education, where between 1986 and 1997 the erosion in relative spending per student in Spain – particularly in the case of secondary schools – vis-à-vis the European Union was greatest.

In a setting like the present one, in which budget consolidation is essential, there appears to be no better policy than to guarantee the quality of state schools at the educational levels that are crucial to job opportunities and whose benefits to society are greatest, namely primary and secondary education. Nor would it seem easy, without recourse to a substantive increase in university fees to achieve, a public system of higher education that meets European standards of quality.

Here, from the standpoint of fairness, it is possible to argue against a system of financing higher education such as the present one, in which households with strong economic capacity pay academic fees which are a mere fraction of the real cost. This argument gains force in a context of insufficient resources to meet educational needs at basic levels, and ongoing fiscal restraint, such as contemplated in EMU under the imperative of the stability pact.

5.5 National fiscal policies in the context of EMU

The preceding sections have shown how the deficit conditions established in the stability pact require the application of fiscal consolidation policies by all EMU countries. Although these conditions are, in principle, beneficial for macroeconomic stability, they entail a risk of inducing the adoption of measures inappropriate to a strategy of sustained growth in output and employment.

Under the stability pact, whose conditions were agreed at the European Council meeting in Dublin and ratified at the Amsterdam Summit, EMU countries must maintain, on a permanent basis, the

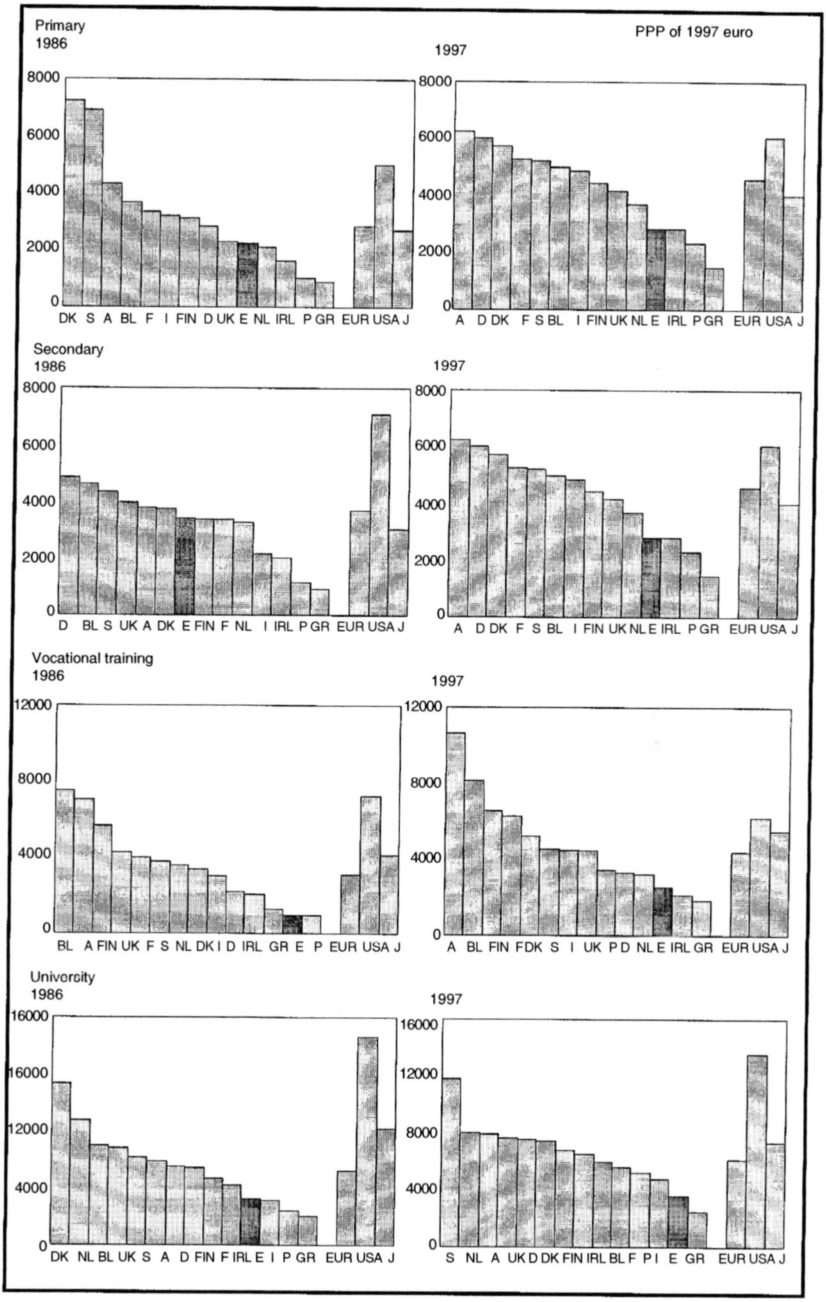

Figure 5.9 Expenditure per student by educational level

Source: UNESCO: *Statistical Yearbook*; OECD: *Education at a Glance*; Departamento de Estudios Europeos, Fundación de las Cajas de Ahorros.

same levels of stability in their public finances as were required for accession to EMU. More specifically, according to the Amsterdam agreement, EMU member countries are required to keep their budget balance close to equilibrium, under penalty of heavy sanctions.[20] These will be automatic, unless the real GDP of the country in question falls by 2 per cent or more. In the event the decline in economic activity lies in a range of 2 per cent to 0.75 per cent, they will be decided by the Council of Ministers, in the absence of the offending country.[21]

As in the case of the Maastricht fiscal-deficit criterion, the stability-pact criterion applies irrespective of the nature of the deficit, the cyclical position or the existing level of public infrastructure in member countries. This makes the requirement quite stringent and, in a sense, penalizes countries whose stock of public capital and welfare systems are less developed, as well as those countries more likely to be affected by shocks as a result of the weaknesses in their productive structures.

In fact, under the stability pact, there is relatively little room for national fiscal policies to address not only infrastructure deficits but also the possible shocks of an asymmetrical type – or even those of a general nature but with specific consequences in a particular economy. Moreover, it is highly improbable that EMU monetary policy, in its conception oriented towards price stability, could be of help to countries beset by specific economic troubles. Finally, the meagreness of the EU budget means that there is little hope that a country weathering economic difficulties could count on this stabilizing instrument.

Given the context of fiscal rigour and the scant leeway for national stabilizing policies within EMU, it would seem worthwhile to ask whether additional stabilizing instruments on a European scale might be necessary.

This question was indeed formulated insistently at the time of the preparatory studies of the diverse initiatives for the implementation of monetary union. In fact, the MacDougall Report (1977), prepared at the request of the EC Commission specifically to answer this question, recommended the institution of a Community fiscal policy to exercise a stabilizing function, in addition to playing a broader redistributive role. But these recommendations went unheeded owing to their rejection by the governments of several member states. Moreover, in contrast to the MacDougall Report's proposal that progress towards monetary union be accompanied by gradual and substantial increases in the budget to the region of 5 per cent to 7 per cent of GDP, a later report – also requested by the Commission[22] – made quite a different proposal: 'that EMU's stabilizing and redistributive requirements be met with a low budget of around 2 per cent'.

But, as the latter report itself acknowledged, this proposal, which was in a certain sense reflected in the principle of subsidiarity in the Maastricht Treaty, stands in contradiction to the propositions of the theory of optimum monetary unions (a good reference for this theory is found in De Grauwe, 1997, and Mélitz, 1995) and to the conclusions of many of its empirical applications to the case of the EMU countries.

The studies applying the tenets of this theory (García Solanes, 1995, and Masson, 1996, offer an overview of these works) do, in fact, cast serious doubts on the adequacy of national fiscal policies to cope with eventual shocks within the monetary union. This conclusion is based on two types of argument; the first type maintaining that among EMU partners several circumstances coincide which suggest that there is a strong probability of shocks with an asymmetrical nature and/or effects (the evidence provided in various chapters of this book being consistent with this verdict), and the second type being based on the weakness of EMU's stabilizing mechanisms. Together with the loss of the buffer provided by exchange-rate fluctuations and the lack of autonomy in monetary policy, as discussed earlier, this argument alludes to the additional restriction on member countries' stabilizing capacity derived from the negligible level of intra-European migration.

Briefly stated, from the standpoint of economic rationality, it would seem advisable to reinforce the Community budget to endow it with a stabilizing capacity[23] in the euro area as a whole in order to prevent asymmetrical shocks from unleashing serious problems of recession and unemployment. But this option is hardly feasible without further progress towards political integration.

5.6 Conclusions

This chapter has offered an analysis of the situation of Spanish public finances in comparison with that of its EU partners since Spain's entry into the Community. After examining the trends and changes in the structure of general government expenditure and revenue and the budget deficit, it evaluated the problem of the high level of debt with which most European economies are now saddled. Finally, an attempt was made to identify – starting with an overview of the most recent theoretical and empirical literature on the subject – the room for manoeuvre for governments to tackle the delicate task awaiting them: the establishment of stringent fiscal policies compatible with the budgetary stability required by EMU but which do not arrest either the growth possibilities of output and employment or the essence of the welfare state in European countries.

The following points review the most conclusive facts and concepts.

- Between 1986 and 1997, the years encompassed in the period analysed, public spending in most EU countries grew at a rate similar to that of economic activity, and as such its weight in GDP remained unchanged. Against this background, Spain is one of the countries with the greatest vitality in expenditure, attributable to the measures of various democratic governments aimed at endowing the country with services and social benefits similar to those which had long prevailed in the other Community countries. This vitality was, however, cut short by the pressures of fiscal discipline which have arisen since the approval of the Maastricht agreements. As a result, in 1997 Spain's ratio of public spending (43.4 per cent of GDP) had still not reached the average of the Fifteen (49 per cent).
- The convergence of Spanish government expenditure with EU standards has affected not only its level as a percentage of GDP but also its composition. As a result, the structure of public spending in Spain closely resembles the average in the European Union.
- On the government revenue side, Spain has also moved closer to Community patterns. But this does not mean there are no differences; the most notable one is that government revenue as a proportion of GDP in Spain (40.8 per cent) is below the EU average (46.5 per cent).
- Growth in government revenue, while substantial, lagged behind that of expenditure, except at the end of the period. As a result, the general trend was one of large deficits of an essentially structural nature. This deficit dynamic has signified a swift increase in the debt of European governments, as evidenced in an average debt ratio of 72.2 per cent in the European Union in 1997 and 68.8 per cent in Spain. In turn, the growth in the volume of debt has resulted in a progressive increase in government expenditure on interest payments to service this debt, which acts as a mechanism to make the deficit self-perpetuating. Fortunately, in recent years, the deficit has been reduced drastically, and the growth in debt has been curbed. This fiscal consolidation, however, has been possible thanks to circumstances that will be difficult to maintain in the future, such as: a very favourable economic climate, an enormous reduction in the interest rates on debt, and one-off measures to restrain expenditure

(the freeze on civil servants' wages and the privatization of companies, for example).

- Thus, to ensure the sustainability of the situation of fiscal discipline already attained, there would seem to be a need for reforms capable of reducing the considerable structural component in European budget deficits. Moreover, to help alleviate the grave unemployment problem in the European Union, efforts should be made to ensure that these reforms do not imperil the potential for sustained growth in output and employment. And while the necessary policy of fiscal discipline will, hopefully, resolve the welfare system's inefficiencies, it should not be implemented in a way that would jeopardize the core of the welfare state.
- To achieve budgetary consolidation, while at the same time meeting the above-mentioned objectives, the most acceptable route would be to enhance the efficiency of government administration, both on the tax side (eradication of tax evasion and fraud) and on the spending side (improvement of the cost-efficiency of public-sector activities).
- One area of government expenditure where inefficiency problems appear to be particularly acute is welfare benefits. Moreover, the many studies of this question, both by international organizations and in the countries themselves, coincide in their verdict that – given the demographic trends and the scenario of moderate growth and modest job creation forecast for the years ahead – the welfare state faces a risk of 'financial strangulation' in the not-too-distant future.
- For the reasons discussed above and in view of the ample evidence provided in this chapter on the negative consequences of restrictive fiscal policies that reduce investment in areas such as education, R&D and transport and communications, which generate most externalities for private investment, reforms capable of curbing the growth in social spending, without altering the essence of the system's solidarity, would seem desirable.
- Judging by the findings of the research on the subject, in Spain's case it could be argued that the social benefits with the most room for cost-cutting reforms are pensions, health, and unemployment benefits.
- As to pensions, the problem of potential insolvency could be tackled through measures such as the stricter application of the principle of proportionality between what is paid and what is received and the improvement of inspection systems to eradicate any fraud in the form of wrongful collection of pensions.

- With respect to health, the most advisable course would probably be to continue widening the possibility of private provision of services and promoting the freedom of choice of users, encouraging competition between providers with the aim of lowering costs and improving the quality of services. In the area of pharmaceutical expenditure, stronger measures should be taken to prevent excessive consumption, while also promoting the use of generic medicines, and to reduce distribution costs.
- In the case of unemployment benefits, it would be advisable to apply less generous standards and to improve inspection mechanisms, not only for the purpose of imposing sanctions on improper conduct but also to encourage the unemployed to find jobs.
- Finally, any attempt to consolidate social spending through cuts in expenditure on education is considered harmful. In fact, with the expenditure currently assigned, there already appears to be a risk that the reforms undertaken in both secondary and higher education may fail for lack of resources. In this respect, the present study advocates raising academic fees in higher education as a way of forestalling further deterioration in the quality of state schools at all levels, and particularly at the most basic levels, where the benefits to society are greatest.
- Lastly, as a corollary to the analysis of the implications of EMU membership for the fiscal policy of member countries, this study supports the proposal that the euro area be endowed with a substantially larger budget than it now has, to enable it to cope with the greater stabilizing and redistribution needs that may arise under economic and monetary union.

6
The External Sector

6.1 Introduction

The balance of payments of a country reflects all the current, capital and financial transactions of its residents with the residents of the rest of the world and, by extension, offers a global view of the way and extent to which an open economy achieves external equilibrium. In a sense, it also shows up both the weaknesses and strengths of a country's productive system, and indeed helps identify some of the consequences of the structural problems afflicting an economy. Thus, balance-of-payments disequilibria, and current-account deficits in particular, are always an important point of reference for macroeconomic policy measures.

With this in mind, the present chapter analyses the main features of the Spanish balance of payments in relation to that of the EU countries as a whole in order to investigate the possible links between the imbalances encountered and the weaknesses of the productive system. Section 6.2 examines in detail the principal entries in the current and capital accounts. Section 6.3 then comments on the characteristics of the financial account, with an emphasis on the most relevant flow from the standpoint of the real economy: direct investment. The chapter ends with a summary of the main conclusions.

6.2 Current and capital accounts

As readers will be aware, the balance of payments on current and capital accounts[1] is the most relevant one for assessing a country's overall trade position with the rest of the world. In this respect, the presence of a negative balance may be interpreted from various perspectives, and two in particular. First, it may be understood as an excess of domestic absorption or expenditure[2] beyond the country's disposable income; this would point to the need for economic policy measures to balance income and expenditure.[3] Secondly, it may be seen as a shortfall in the domestic savings available to finance the country's gross capital formation.

This section will therefore review the main items of the Spanish balance of payments on current and capital accounts since Spain's entry into the European Union, in order to identify the chief features which distinguish it from that of the EU countries as a whole and also the factors behind the Spanish economy's tendency to run prolonged current-account deficits. In the course of this analysis, we shall comment on several possible problems of a domestic origin that could underlie these external imbalances.

Beginning with the merchandise balance, which reflects all the goods traded with the rest of the world, it is symptomatic that in the period 1986–97 Spain recorded an average deficit of around 4.2 per cent of GDP at market prices (see Table 6.1), the maximum being more than 7 per cent in 1989, while its Community partners on average ran a slight surplus. This different performance is attributable to the spectacular growth of Spanish imports, which was much higher than that of exports, even though the latter performed better than in the European Union on average.

From the analyses in earlier chapters, we presume that such a remarkable expansion in imports following Spain's accession might be the result of the lower competitiveness of Spanish industry, stemming from its weakness in the manufacture of quality goods or goods of high technological content and also from productive rigidities, which gradually became apparent as the Spanish economy became more integrated into international markets (in the same vein, see Gordo, 1996). This explains why the deficit widened as domestic activity expanded.

Illustrative of this situation is the fact that a recent econometric study, conducted by the European Commission for the purpose of adjusting the functions explaining the trends in intra-Community trade balances,[4] found that Spain is the country with the greatest income elasticity in the entire European Union.[5] This explains why the trade deficit rose so notably in a period of such substantial economic growth as the second half of the 1980s. From this standpoint, we would not be the first to speak of the existence of an external constraint on growth.

At least three factors might lie at the root of the problem. First, the technological shortfall existing in Spain's productive system with respect to that of the Community, making the system more dependent

Table 6.1 Balance of payments of Spain and the EU (average in the period 1986–97)

As % of GDP mp	Spain			European Union		
	Receipts	**Payments**	**Balance**	**Receipts**	**Payments**	**Balance**
Current account	**24.0**	**25.2**	**–1.2**	**35.8**	**35.8**	**0.0**
Goods	13.6	17.8	–4.2	22.2	21.6	0.6
Services	6.8	3.5	3.3	6.4	6.0	0.4
Income	1.7	2.7	–1.0	5.9	6.2	–0.3
Current transfers	1.9	1.2	0.7	1.3	2.0	–0.7
Capital account	**0.6**	**0.1**	**0.5**	**0.1**	**0.1**	**0.0**
Current account + capital	**24.6**	**25.3**	**–0.7**	**35.9**	**35.9**	**0.0**
	Change liab.	**Change assets**	CL–CA	**Change liab.**	**Change assets**	CL–CA
Financial account	**6.3**	**5.1**	**1.2**	**8.7**	**8.8**	**–0.1**
Spanish foreign investment		1.3	–1.3		4.0	–4.0
Direct		0.7	–0.7		1.7	–1.7
Foreign investment in Spain	4.0		4.0	4.0		4.0
Direct	1.8		1.8	1.1		1.1
Other investment	2.3	2.6	–0.3	4.7	4.6	0.1
Reserves		1.2	–1.2		0.2	–0.2
Errors and omissions	**–0.5**		**–0.5**	**0.1**		**0.1**
Financial account + errors and omissions	**5.8**	**5.1**	**0.7**	**8.8**	**8.8**	**0.0**

Source: Eurostat: *Balance of Payments*; Banco de España: *The Spanish Balance of Payments*; IMF: *Balance of Payments Statistics Yearbook*; OECD: *National Accounts*, vol. I: *Main Aggregates*; Departamento de Estudios Europeos, Fundación de las Cajas de Ahorros.

on imports which incorporate innovations, both of capital goods and of intermediate goods used in the productive process. In addition, exports in those sectors where demand is more dynamic might also be expected to perform poorly. In relation to this question, numerous studies provide evidence of the positive (negative) influence of a country's technological intensity on the behaviour of exports (imports).[6] Here it should be noted that the sectors of machinery and other capital and intermediate manufactured goods are largely responsible for the worsening of the trade deficit in the years in question.

Secondly, it seems highly probable that one explanatory factor in the growth of the trade deficit is the behaviour of foreign investors, who have long held a large and, moreover, increasing proportion of the share capital of Spanish firms. As shown in Martín and Velázquez (1993b), firms with foreign capital appear to have a much higher than average propensity to import than national firms. Thus, even though the average export propensity of firms with foreign capital is also somewhat greater than that of national firms, their trade balance is worse than that of companies with no foreign shareholders. This suggests therefore that the multinational companies located in Spain are primarily geared towards supplying the domestic market, and consequently appear to be of no great help in correcting the trade deficit. A counterpoint to the Spanish case is Ireland. The multinationals located there have specialized in supplying foreign markets, thereby contributing to the substantial improvement in Ireland's trade deficit in recent years.[7]

In this respect, the increase in the presence of foreign capital in the distributive trade in Spain, which rose from nearly 12 per cent in 1985 to more than 40 per cent in 1993, according to the estimates of Martín and Velázquez (1996b), could account for the extraordinary growth in consumer goods imports, mainly in the branches of food, beverages and tobacco, and other manufactured goods. Similarly, the increase in the presence of foreign capital in other sectors manufacturing capital and intermediate goods – mainly non-metallic minerals and mineral products, office and data-processing machines, and transport equipment – could be one of the causes of the larger volume of imports of manufactured goods of this type.

The evidence discussed above on the trade carried out by firms with foreign capital – so far considered as a possible factor to explain the increase in Spanish industry's propensity to import – could be interpreted in a different way: it might indicate that for investor countries direct investment is an appropriate channel to enlarge and consolidate foreign markets. From this point of view, Spain's scant foreign direct investment in relation to GDP may constitute a constraint on Spanish exports and, by extension, a further cause of Spain's large trade deficit.[8]

Lastly, another important factor in explaining the trade deficit is Spain's well known dependence on external primary energy, reflected to a certain extent in the value of the income elasticity of energy demand, which is well above 1.0.[9]

In sum, there are various indications that the persistence of the Spanish economy's trade deficit is to a large extent due to the inadequacies of the productive system and the unavailability of energy resources. Consequently, the correction of this chronic deficit and its alignment with Community levels in the medium or long term will require an active policy to improve productive efficiency and energy saving, as well as to increase agility in capturing markets, by either promoting trade or providing incentives to foreign direct investment.

The services balance, which on average has generally tended towards equilibrium in the European Union, has traditionally been a key compensatory element in Spain's trade deficit. None the less, throughout the period studied, worrisome changes have been observed in its performance. As a general rule, prior to Spain's entry into the European Union, the surplus run by the services balance was notably higher than the trade deficit, and it was capable of securing a balanced current account; after the country's accession and until very recently, however, the compensatory capacity of the services balance steadily waned.

This might be partly explained by the pro-cyclicality of the most important item in the services balance: tourism receipts. Here it is worth recalling the crisis in the tourism sector in the late 1980s and early 1990s brought about by the recession in the world economy, the increase in Spanish prices and, in the final analysis, the growth in tourism to alternative sites, primarily North Africa,[10] which resulted in a 15.6 per cent fall in Spain's tourism receipts in real terms between 1989 and 1991. After that, however, the situation improved considerably, thanks to more moderate price rises in the sector, political instability in rival countries, and the launch by government officials of programmes to upgrade the quality of tourism and moderate its seasonality through the promotion of alternatives to the 'sun and beach' formula, emphasizing other natural resources and culture.[11]

Aside from cyclical swings, however, Spain clearly commands a predominant position within the European Union as regards its capacity to generate receipts through the export of tourism services. None the less, the growth in the level of Spain's per capita income has contributed to an increase in payments for imports of tourism services, which grew by 90.1 per cent in real terms between 1986 and 1997. In any event, the balance of tourism services is very high, representing 4.2 per cent of GDP in 1997.

As to the other services items, especially notable is the increase in the payments under those associated with the penetration of foreign capital and with foreign technological dependence, which have contributed to the decline in the surplus on the services balance. This is the case of items such as merchanting and miscellaneous business, professional and technical services and, in particular, royalties and licence fees, where receipts did grow, but at a slower rate.

In the case of the investment-income balance, what stands out in particular is the overwhelming predominance of items linked to capital, which in EU countries as a whole represent more than 97 per cent of the total income entered under this heading. At present, Spain is no exception to this tendency, as the growth of these items in the period was spectacular: whereas the volume of income (credits plus debits) in 1986 was 2.2 per cent of GDP (9.0 per cent in the European Union), by 1997 this figure had risen to 6.1 per cent (12.8 per cent in the European Union).

In addition, the structure of income derived from capital (investment income) has changed, in line with the changes in the financial account, and also, in response to the liberalization of cross-border capital flows. None the less, the growing volatility of international financial markets translates into lower stability in the receipts and payments included under this heading, due to the greater ease with which agents can respond to changes in expected yields.

In Spain, payments under public-sector financing transactions and the distribution of dividends linked to foreign investment stand out in particular. On the receipts side, those relating to the build-up of reserves predominated until 1992, and from then onwards those derived from the redeployment of deposits following the liberalization of financial flows. This heading ran a deficit throughout the period.

The last caption in the current account records current transfers. The receipts side reflects part of the EU economic and social cohesion policy, basically consisting of transfers from the European Social Fund and the European Agricultural Guidance and Guarantee Fund (Guarantee Section). Among other items on the payments side are the contributions of each member country to the EU budget. In the Spanish case, while receipts have increased, payments have also risen since Spain's accession, albeit to a lesser extent.

By contrast, in most countries of the European Union, payments on current transfers as a whole[12] are much higher than receipts. In addition to Spain (with a surplus of 0.7 per cent of GDP), the exceptions to this tendency are the EU members with lower levels of per capita income, that is Greece and Portugal.

The other EU cohesion policies, implemented via the European Regional Development Fund, the European Agricultural Guidance and Guarantee Fund (Guidance Section), the Financial Instrument for Fisheries Guidance, and the Cohesion Fund, are reflected in the capital-account balance.

Analysing Community policies as a whole – broadly reflected in the aggregate balance of current and capital transfers – Spain is found to have received the largest volume of transfers in 1997 in absolute terms. But, if these contributions are viewed in relation to the GDP of each of the receiving countries, Spain – as discussed in greater detail in Chapter 11 – is found to rank fourth, after Ireland, Greece and Portugal.

The combined effect of all the above-mentioned transactions on Spain was a deficit on current and capital accounts during most of the years after its accession to the European Union (see Figure 6.1), which is still a source of concern despite the clear improvement since 1995. Thus, of the 12 years considered, only four saw a current-account surplus: 1986, 1995, 1996 and 1997. In the deficits of the other years, those between 1989 and 1992 were particularly severe, exceeding 3 per cent of GDP. This situation led to a series of devaluations of the peseta between 1992 and 1995 which resulted in an improvement in the Spanish economy's external performance.

It should be borne in mind, however, that Spain is not the only EU member to suffer a recurrent external imbalance. Deficits on current and capital accounts also reached significant proportions in Italy (between 1987 and 1992), Germany (1991–6), the United Kingdom (1987–94), Finland (1986–93), Sweden (1986–93) and Greece (1986–97).

6.3 Financial account

Obviously, because of the accounting structure of the balance of payments, the results of the financial accounts must cancel out the deficits which may exist on the current and capital accounts, through net capital imports and/or the sale of foreign reserves.

The different forms of deficit cancelling have, however, different effects. As a simple indicator of the sustainability of the current-

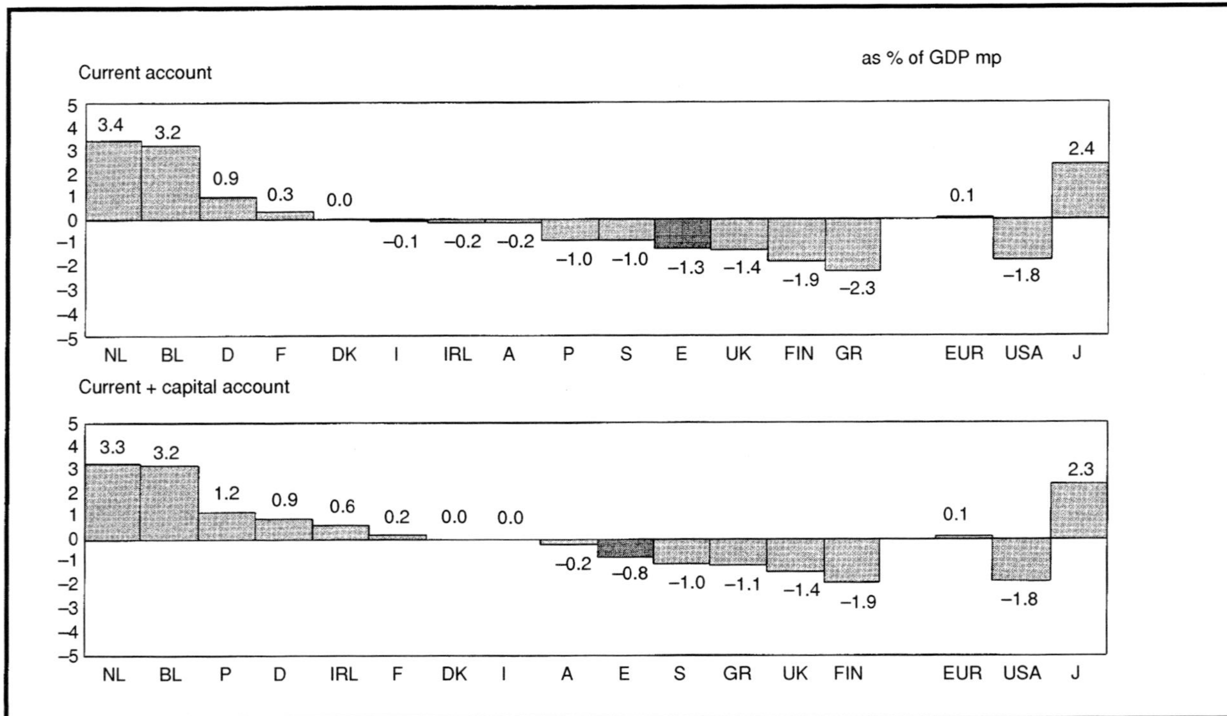

Figure 6.1 Balance of payments on current and capital accounts (average in the period 1986–97)

Source: Eurostat: *Balance of Payments*; Banco de España: *The Spanish Balance of Payments*; IMF: *Balance of Payments Statistics Yearbook*; OECD: *National Accounts*, vol. I: *Main Aggregates*; Departamento de Estudios Europeos, Fundación de las Cajas de Ahorros.

account deficit, the so-called basic balance is generally used. This is defined as the sum of the current-account balance (excluding net interest payments on debt), the capital-account balance, and net investments which do not entail explicit interest payments. Thus, when the basic balance is in equilibrium, the country is considered to have no explicit obligatory payment commitments in the future, and its current-account deficit is therefore considered sustainable. Spain only recorded basic balances close to zero in the years 1991 and 1992. Nevertheless, the improvement since then – due, to a large extent, to the peseta's successive devaluations – in the current-account balance, as well as the increase in the transfers of Community funds recorded in the capital account, has in recent years resulted in positive balances for this indicator of external sustainability.

Dolado and Viñals (1992) and Anchuelo (1995) argue that, if the Spanish economy has not suffered a problem of external sustainability in recent years, this has been due to the exchange-rate adjustments made to correct the excessive growth in Spain's external indebtedness. In this respect, Mauleón and Sastre (1996) postulate – on the basis of the estimation of a simulation model which allows alternative scenarios to be considered – that Spain's external sustainability might become problematic in a situation characterized by a fixed exchange rate and high international mobility of capital. From these studies it can therefore be inferred that, in a context in which the exchange rate is no longer an instrument of adjustment when problems of price competitiveness occur (as in the context of EMU), problems of relative impoverishment may arise. Pursuing this idea further, Dornbusch (1996) holds that the exchange rate has been a basic instrument of economic policy whose use has contributed to external equilibrium, when used immediately and prudently and not anticipated by agents.

Other studies, however, minimize the role of the exchange rate as a tool capable of facilitating macroeconomic adjustments, given that this variable does not respond to real asymmetrical shocks but, rather, to shocks of a monetary and financial nature (see, for example, the work of Viñals, Vallés and Canzoneri, 1996). What's more, other studies show that certain devaluations may have undesired real effects that entail a slowing in the growth of domestic demand, an increase in inflation, and a loss of credibility both at home and abroad.[13]

For the European Union as a whole, external sustainability is unquestionable, because there have been no long periods of current- and capital-account deficits, and when they have arisen, they have been small in size. Recall, however, that we refer here to the aggregate balance of the European Union, which thus consolidates deficit situations of some member countries.

After these general observations regarding the financial account transactions, we shall now examine the characteristics of Spain's external financing in relation to that of the other EU countries.

The globalization of financial markets, brought about by the liberalization of capital movements, especially within the European Union, has spurred the expansion of financial flows, diversification of the instruments used – some were previously restricted – and greater substitutability not only between instruments but also between the economic agents responsible for transactions.

Basically three financial flows predominate both in the European Union and in Spain: flows linked to the credit system, to government debt, and to direct investment. Let us briefly look at what has occurred in each one.

The intense growth in the credit sector's cross-border operations during the years in question is the result of the lifting of the legal barriers that had prevented these flows, both between member countries of the European Union and between it and the rest of the world. It must be stressed, however, that these flows are very sensitive to exchange-rate pressures and to expectations about the growth and macroeconomic stability of the economies. For this reason, it is hard to extract, beyond what has already been said, patterns of conduct for such a broad set of countries and for such a long period as the one studied here.

Most notable, in the case of flows associated with government debt, is their vitality, which is linked to the growth in the financing operations of the general government sector and its need to resort to international markets to finance its debt.

Finally, on the direct investment side, we should begin by saying that its relevance does not lie solely in its role as an instrument for financing the capital- and current-account deficit, but above all in its importance for the real economy. From the perspective of the receiving country, direct investment provides support for national savings, and at the same time gives access to new methods of production and organization that usually entail an increase in efficiency. In turn, from the standpoint of the country that carries out the investment, it is a channel for optimizing the processes of production and distribution of its firms – in that they are able to benefit from the advantages offered by the countries where the investment is located – and also for facilitating the enlargement and consolidation of export markets.

In analysing direct investment flows received and produced by EU countries – whose data are presented in Figure 6.2 – we find that Spain stands out among its European partners for two reasons. First, because of the significant weight of foreign direct investment in its economic activity; thus, for the period 1986–97, this investment represented an average of 1.8 per cent of GDP, compared with only 1.2 per cent in the European Union. Secondly, because of the lower relative presence of Spain's investment abroad, at 0.6 per cent of GDP, whereas the EU average is 1.7 per cent.

The fact that Spain receives a considerable flow of capital in the form of direct investment is consistent with what might be expected in the light of the main theories of foreign investment. Spain does actually enjoy numerous advantages of location, such as its condition as a large and expanding market and the availability of relatively low-cost labour in the context of the European Union.[14]

However, the low weight of Spain's direct investment abroad is not consistent with the level of the Spanish economy's development, as this investment is far lower than the average of its European partners. None the less, it should be borne in mind that the low level of Spanish direct investment abroad on average in the period may, to some extent, be explained by the restrictions on capital outflows which existed in Spain in the early years of the period analysed and also by the existence of high interest rates, which discouraged the outward flow of capital (see Maté, 1996b).

Moreover, two stages should be distinguished: the first, to 1990, marked by a constant widening in the gap between the volume of investment received and effected, and the second, from that year onwards, when this difference tended to diminish sharply owing to the decline in inflows and the intense growth in outward flows.

The slide in the inward flow of direct investment in the early 1990s was a widespread phenomenon in OECD countries as a whole. It is therefore likely to be yet another effect of the recession in industrialized countries during that period. But there are also indications that the deceleration in direct investment is, in addition, linked to a possible reorientation of investment towards countries in Eastern Europe (for the arguments behind this thesis, which will be discussed further in Chapter 9, see Martín, 1995c).

As to the increase in investment abroad, where Spain has a particularly noticeable deficit, this may be due – as noted – to the elimination of the existing obstacles to the outflow of national capital and also to the reaction of firms and the government to the evidence that not only

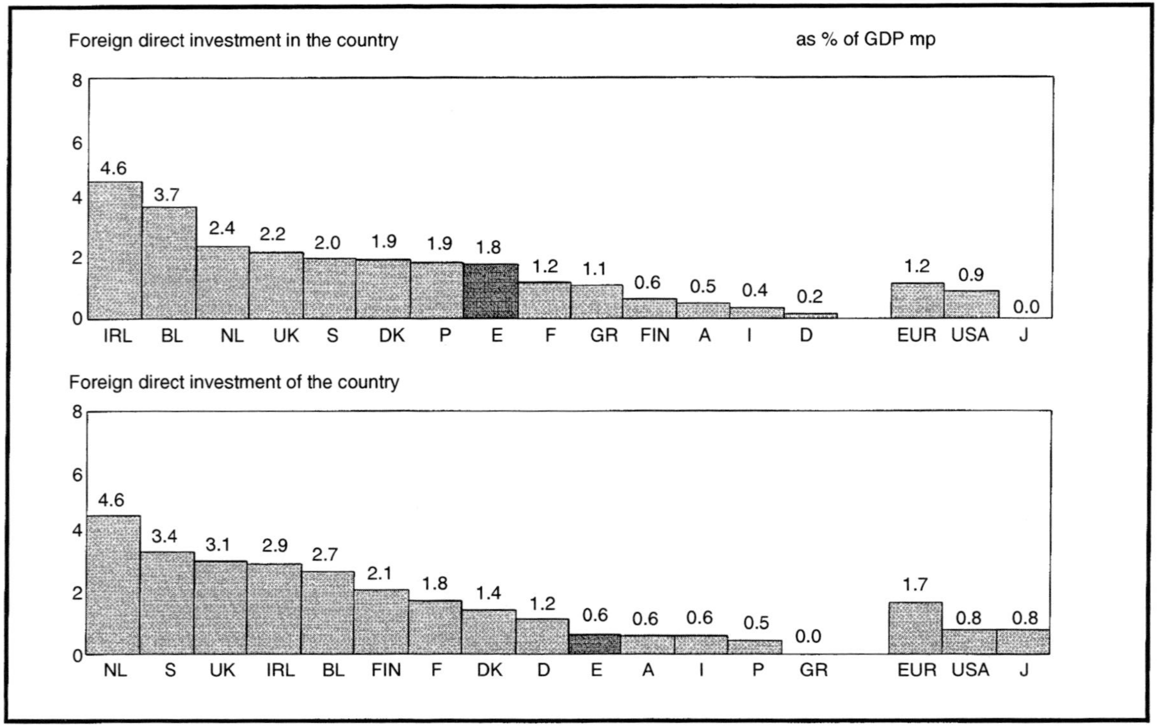

Figure 6.2 Direct investment flows (average in the period 1986–97)

Source: Eurostat: *Balance of Payments*; Banco de España: *The Spanish Balance of Payments*; IMF: *Balance of Payments Statistics Yearbook*; OECD: *National Accounts*, vol. I: *Main Aggregates*; Departamento de Estudios Europeos, Fundación de las Cajas de Ahorros.

the improvement, but even the maintenance, of competitiveness requires a greater presence of Spanish firms abroad. Yet, despite the excellent performance of recent years, Spanish foreign direct investment has still not acquired the weight warranted by Spain's economic position in the European Union.

6.4 Conclusions

In analysing the main features of the Spanish balance of payments vis-à-vis that of its EU partners, the present chapter has attempted to find the links between the external imbalances and the weaknesses, or strengths, of the productive system. The main conclusions are set forth below:

- Since joining the European Union, Spain's trade deficit has stood at around 4.2 per cent of GDP, in contrast with the slight surplus in the European Union as a whole. Although this imbalance has moved in line with the trends in the main variables determining trade flows (demand and the real effective exchange rate), in none of these years – except in the past two – was it possible to reduce this figure to less that 3 per cent of GDP. Also, the figures for the past indicate that the trade deficit is of a structural nature.
- Among the possible factors at the root of Spain's persistent trade deficit, the chapter emphasized three: (a) the technological inadequacy of the productive system; (b) the need for energy supplies, and (c) the strong presence of foreign firms, primarily in the manufacturing and distributive trade sectors. These factors, among others, may explain why Spain has a much higher income elasticity in demand for imports than that of its Community partners, and therefore, why Spain's growth capacity is more constrained by the behaviour of the external sector.
- The balance of services is, thanks to tourism receipts, still the key compensatory element in Spanish trade deficits. The rise in net payments for miscellaneous business, professional and technical services, and royalties and licence fees, explains the deterioration in the services balance.
- The investment-income balance, where capital income predominates, is marked by great variability, in consonance with the growing volatility of financial movements.
- The Community's social and economic cohesion policy, of which Spain is a net beneficiary, is reflected in the current transfers and

capital accounts. Accordingly, the positive balances of these two items have increased, especially since the reform of Community funds in 1992 agreed at the Edinburgh Council. In 1997 the balances of both accounts exceeded 1.6 per cent of GDP. But, even though Spain is the largest beneficiary of Community funds in absolute terms, when these funds are expressed in terms of GDP, it ranks fourth after Ireland, Greece and Portugal.

- Since joining the Community and with the exception of the past three years, the Spanish economy has run a deficit on its current and capital accounts, in contrast to a small surplus in EU countries as a whole. The studies evaluating the sustainability of the Spanish economy's external imbalance conclude that in the past the exchange rate was a basic tool for redressing excessive current-account deficits.
- Finally, in the case of direct investment – the financial operations which are most stable and which have the greatest impact on the productive system – the inward and outward flows are not symmetrical. Here Spain stands out as one of the EU countries which has attracted the most foreign investment and, at the same time, as one of the most laggard in the ranking of investment abroad, although direct investment flows from Spain have surged in the past three years. The still meagre presence of Spanish firms in other countries via investment projects is a strong handicap when it comes to competing in an international environment increasingly dominated by multinational firms.

7
Nominal and Real Convergence

7.1 Introduction

To round off the comparative study of Spain's main economic variables vis-à-vis those of the other EU countries, in this final chapter of Part I we shall examine whether economic convergence in the European Union has actually advanced since Spain joined the Community.

Specifically, Section 7.2 discusses the meaning of the concept 'economic convergence' and the most common methods of measuring it. Section 7.3 then explores the process of nominal convergence in Spain in relation to that of its European partners, taking several of the criteria established in the Treaty on European Union, or Maastricht Treaty, as its starting point: price stability and the position of public finances (balance and debt).

Section 7.4 briefly reviews the main ideas of the economic literature on the factors that determine the capacity of countries to raise their per capita income to levels closer to those of the more advanced economies (in other words, to converge in real terms) and considers the implications of economic and monetary unions for the member countries' real convergence. It then examines real convergence in terms of a number of indicators – GDP per capita, the unemployment rate, human and technological capital, and expenditure on social benefits – both separately and combined in a composite indicator of real convergence. A final section summarizes the main conclusions.

7.2 What does economic convergence mean?

Economic convergence in an area formed by different countries (regions) is generally understood to mean the increasing alignment of the economic variables considered, within a general tendency for improvement or, in other words, owing to the greater advance of the laggard countries (regions), and not to the deterioration of the more developed ones.

Two meanings of economic convergence are usually considered: nominal and real. Nominal convergence refers to the tendency towards greater uniformity of nominal variables (those indicative of macroeconomic stability). Real convergence expresses the approximation of the levels of economic welfare.

It is widely agreed that real convergence – or 'economic and social cohesion', as it is known in the Community – should be the ultimate concern of the economic authorities of the less developed EU countries. Whatever the case, nominal convergence is a desirable goal, given the benefits derived from price stability and budgetary discipline in themselves and because it is conducive to real convergence.

The above definition of economic convergence is not, however, very useful in the sense that it cannot be used to arrive at a clear-cut diagnosis of a specific situation. For this reason, the specialized literature has devised more precise concepts based on statistical indices. The ones most often used are the so-called β and σ convergence. Thus, β convergence is present if the growth rate of the variable analysed is inversely related to its initial level or, what is the same, if the poorly positioned countries (regions) advance at a stronger rate than those which are better positioned, and σ convergence is achieved when there is a narrowing in the spread of the variables among the countries (regions) as a whole.[1]

But when – as in the present case – we wish to evaluate the convergence of a single country with respect to a given reference area, an even simpler indicator is generally used: the difference with respect to the average.

In this chapter, we shall use the σ convergence measurement to assess the overall trends in economic cohesion within the European Union,[2] and the difference in relation to the average to evaluate the case of Spain.

7.3 Nominal convergence

This section analyses Spain's nominal convergence in relation to that of the other EU members on the basis of several of the criteria established in the Maastricht Treaty that were used to decide which countries qualified for EMU. Specifically, of the five Maastricht criteria, we have taken the three considered to be the most important (see Table 7.1): prices, government debt, and budget deficits.

Table 7.1 Convergence criteria of the Treaty on European Union

The founding Treaty on European Union, in article 109j (1) and Protocol 6, establishes the following criteria for accession to the third stage of monetary union:

Price stability:
The Member States shall have sustainable price performance and an average annual inflation rate that does not exceed by more than 1.5 percentage points that of the three best-performing Member States in terms of price stability. Inflation shall be measured by the harmonized indices of consumer prices (Council Ruling 2494/95).

Public finances:
The general government financial position must be sustainable, a condition that is fulfilled on reaching a budgetary position with no 'excessive government deficit'. An excessive deficit is considered to exist (article 104c(6)) if:
(a) the government deficit is 3 per cent of GDP (Regulation 3605/93 on the application of the excessive deficit procedure), unless the ratio has diminished substantially and continually, and its level comes close to that of the reference or if this reference value is exceeded only exceptionally and temporarily and the ratio remains close to said figure;
(b) the government debt exceeds 60 per cent of GDP, unless the ratio is sufficiently diminishing and approaching the reference value at a satisfactory pace.

Long-term interest rates:
The average annual interest rate of the Member States must not exceed by more than 2 percentage points that of the three best-performing Member States in terms of price stability. Interest rates shall be measured on the basis of long-term government bonds.

Exchange-rate stability:
This will be understood as the observance – for at least two years, without devaluing against the currency of any other Member State – of the normal fluctuation margins of the exchange-rate mechanism of the European Monetary System.

Other factors:
Other factors will also be taken into account, such as: the results of the integration of markets, the situation and development of the balances of payments on current account, unit labour costs, and other price indices.

As a general rule, the economic literature considers price stability as conducive to attaining sustained economic growth. For the OECD countries, Andrés and Hernando (1996) provide evidence of the negative effect of inflation on per capita income in the long run. Similarly, Raymond (1993), in addition to finding a partial negative correlation between the growth rate and the inflation rate for the EU Twelve, presents evidence of the relationship between the level of inflation and its variability, and points out the distortionary effects of both on the allocation and distribution of resources. Likewise, several studies – mentioned in Chapter 5 – show the pernicious impact of budget deficits and excessive debt on the economy.

As seen in Figure 7.1, prices in the European Union have undergone a very significant process of moderation and convergence.[3] The σ convergence statistic indicates a 74 per cent reduction in the inflation differential between the fifteen member countries in the period 1986–97. Most notable in this respect was the sharp decline in Spain's inflation rate from 1992, especially after the Bank of Spain became autonomous on 1 June 1994, ushering in a change in monetary policy. The intervention arrangements were redirected from two levels (fixing intermediate targets for monetary aggregates) to a single level, with direct targeting of the final variable (the rate of inflation), the prime objective being price stability.

Despite the application of restrictive monetary policies for many years and the progress in curbing inflation in Spain, the excellent performance of prices in various member countries meant that until 1996, when the budget deficit came under stricter control, Spain was unable to narrow its spread with the European Union.

Significantly, the countries that have made the most headway in correcting inflation – Greece, Portugal and Spain – are those that started out with the highest rates.

As regards the budget deficit, the strongest consolidation efforts have taken place in more recent years, following the recession of the early 1990s. Since 1993 the Community countries as a whole have managed to advance towards the Maastricht objective of a maximum deficit of 3 per cent of GDP (see Figure 7.2). In Spain's case, the efforts to restrain the deficit have intensified notably since 1996.

Meanwhile, government debt as a percentage of GDP grew non-stop in both the European Union and Spain (see Figure 7.3). None the less, until 1993 Spain was still one of the EU countries with the lowest percentages of debt in relation to GDP. In fact, it was not until that year that Spain failed for the first time to fulfil the debt requirement – less than 60 per cent of GDP – for joining EMU.

7.4 Real convergence

Real convergence, or alignment with the levels of economic welfare enjoyed by the most advanced EU countries, should be the ultimate goal, to compensate for the notable efforts made – particularly by the less developed EU countries – to enter and remain in EMU.

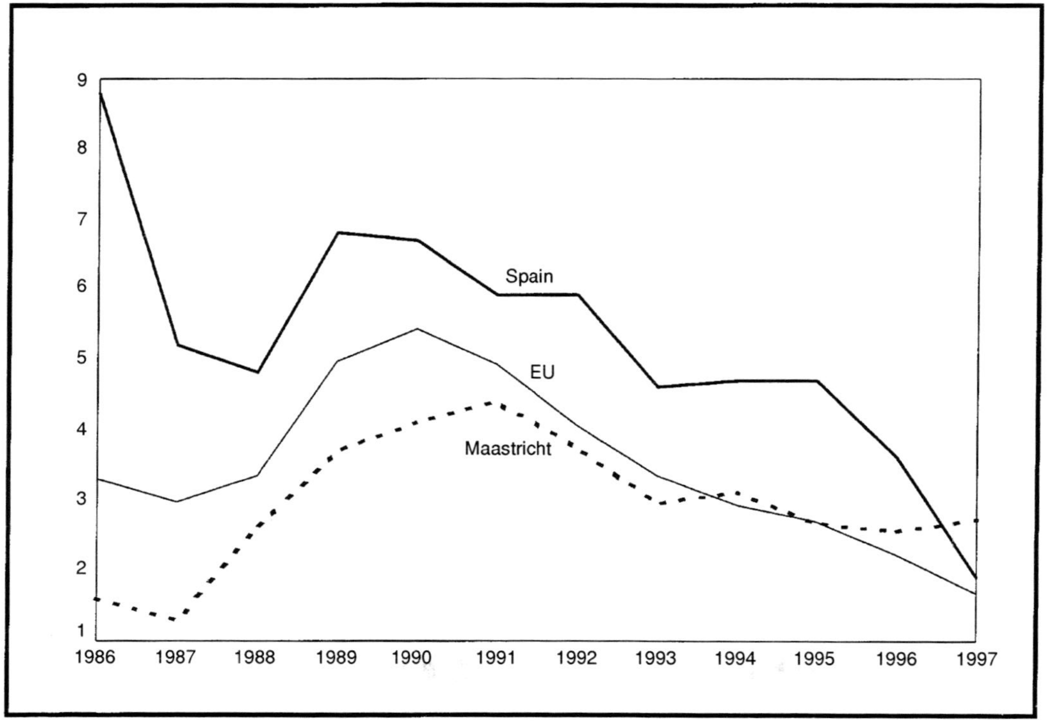

Figure 7.1 Price convergence

Source: Eurostat: *Money and Finance*; OECD: *Main Economic Indicators*; Banco de España: *Boletín Estadístico*; Departamento de Estudios Europeos, Fundación de las Cajas de Ahorros.

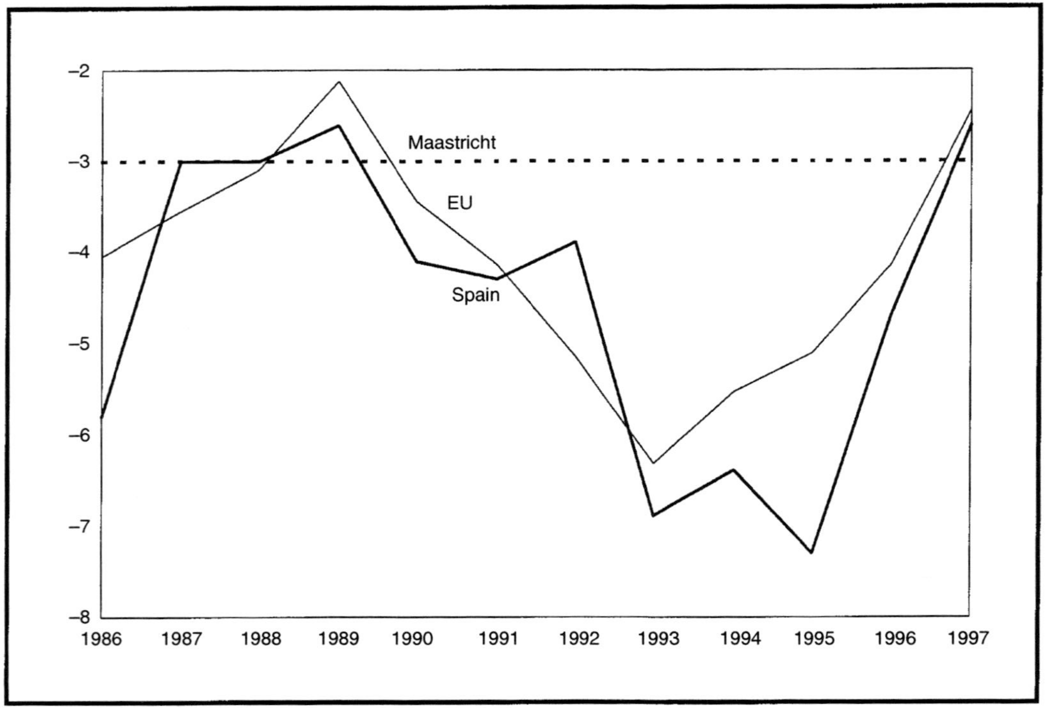

Figure 7.2 Budget deficit convergence

Source: European Commission: *European Economy*; Eurostat: *Money and Finance*; Departamento de Estudios Europeos, Fundación de las Cajas de Ahorros.

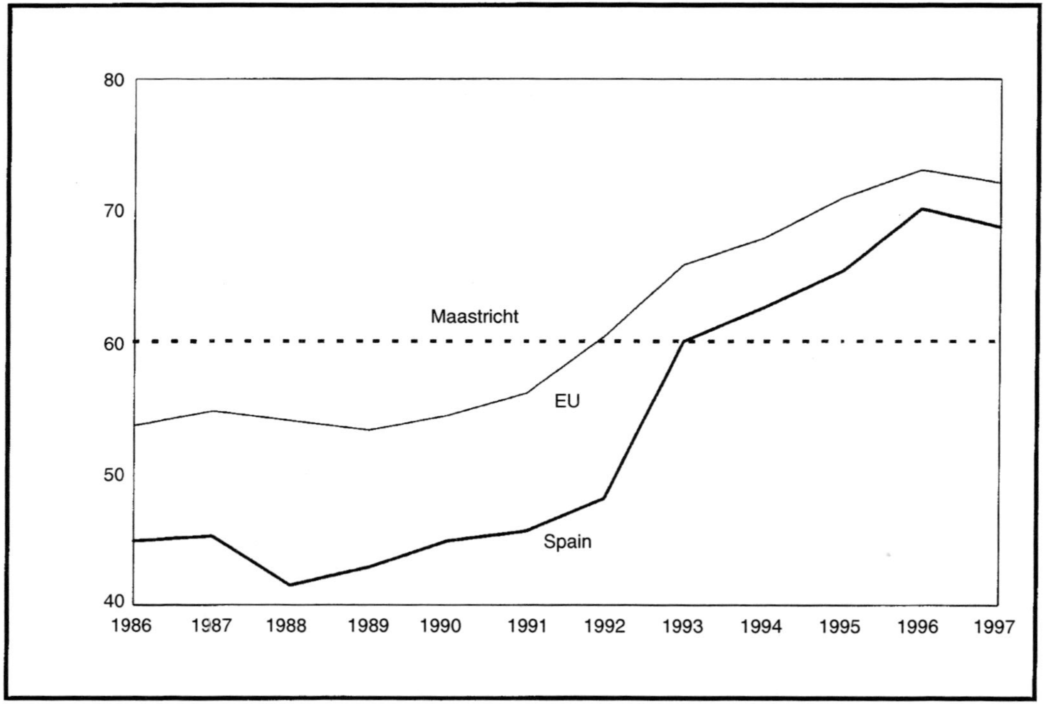

Figure 7.3 Government debt convergence

Source: European Commission: *European Economy*; Eurostat: *Money and Finance*; Departamento de Estudios Europeos, Fundación de las Cajas de Ahorros.

To achieve this objective, macroeconomic stability is necessary, as the studies mentioned in the previous section have shown, but it is not enough. Furthermore, the objective of fiscal discipline required under the stability pact may, in some circumstances, actually curb economic growth. Note in this respect that the most recent research on economic growth – endogenous growth models – emphasizes the decisive role of human and technological capital, a type of intangible asset that has several features in common with public goods and therefore requires government investment.

In any case, for a more precise picture of the possibilities of the most laggard EU economies converging towards the most advanced ones, it is worth reviewing the main ideas in the theoretical literature on the implications of integration processes for the growth of the member countries. Note here that under the neo-classical model, and its assumption of perfect competition in goods and factor markets,[4] the elimination of barriers to international economic transactions stemming from any agreement to form a single market enhances not only the efficiency of the integrated countries but also the equity between them.

As the recent theoretical models postulate, however, the impact on real convergence of forming a single market becomes uncertain when consideration of the existence of economies of scale, external economies, differentiation of goods and productive factors, technological inequality between countries, and restrictions on the free dissemination of technology is allowed. The more advanced countries, owing to their greater technological capacity and/or the different types of economies of scale or external economies (in particular those of agglomeration), may preserve or even increase their advantages vis-à-vis the less developed countries. (See Martín, 1996, and De la Fuente, 1997, for an overview of this type of model.)

When economic and monetary union is the agreed goal of integration, additional mechanisms that are capable of producing both divergent and convergent tendencies in economic and social cohesion are identified. Most notable among the convergent tendencies are the beneficial effects on economic growth stemming from greater price stability and budgetary discipline (the latter via the application of the stability pact), in so far as they prompt a reduction in the risk premiums on interest rates, so providing the necessary incentive for investment in the less developed countries.

As regards EMU's potentially negative effects on real convergence, the disappearance of the exchange rate as an instrument of economic stabilization stands out in particular, due to the greater risk of situations of recession and unemployment, because without this instrument it is harder to deal with asymmetrical shocks. This is especially true if we consider the notable differences in the productive structures of EMU countries and the insignificance of the potentially stabilizing mechanisms, including labour mobility and the distributive capacity of EU fiscal policy in particular. As regards the first of these mechanisms, the empirical evidence (see Chapter 10) reveals the insensitivity of migratory flows to the different economic situations in EU countries; as to the second, the insignificance of the EU budget and the small distributive dimension of Community policies as a whole (see Chapter 11) means that little can be expected of the stabilizing and distributive capacity of fiscal policy.

In sum, the main message to be drawn from these observations is that the possibilities of the laggard countries, such as Spain, aligning their per capita income levels with those of the more advanced members will depend more on the measures taken by each country – particularly their capacity to invest more, and more efficiently, than the central EU countries[5] – than on the effects of belonging to EMU.

Bearing in mind the above considerations, let us look at how Spain's real convergence has evolved vis-à-vis that of the other member countries, individually and as a whole. Note that there is no consensus on which variables should be used in this comparison, although the most frequent one is GDP per capita, with the unemployment rate occasionally used as a complementary variable. While both are relevant in an assessment of real convergence, the inclusion of other complementary variables is also useful, especially if the variable incorporated reflects more clearly the differences in the countries' levels of welfare. In theory, the most appropriate one would be an indicator of personal income distribution. But, in practice, it has proved impossible to find a homogeneous measure for all EU countries during the period analysed. In the absence of a measure of this type, we have used another indicator that expresses – albeit to a lesser extent – economic welfare: expenditure on social benefits in relation to gross domestic product.

Moreover, when estimating the capacity of a country (Spain, for example) to converge towards the higher levels of economic welfare enjoyed by others (the EU average, for example), it would seem appropriate to take into account the factors which, according to the most credible studies, constitute the main determinants of growth in the medium and long run: technology and human capital.

Our examination of real convergence in the European Union is therefore based on the following indicators: per capita GDP, the unemployment rate, and three others constructed for the purpose of estimating the above-mentioned factors.

As shown in Figure 7.4, in the period analysed Spain's per capita GDP has moved towards the average of the EU countries, reducing the gap by 6 percentage points with respect to its European partners as a whole, from 72.7 per cent of average per capita income in 1986 to 78.7 per cent in 1997. This increased alignment is above all the result of the stronger growth of Spanish per capita GDP in the early part of the period, coinciding with Spain's accession to the Community. As suggested in the analyses covering a longer time span – see Fuentes Quintana, 1995 – than that taken in the present chapter (for the sake of uniformity with the rest of the book), this greater alignment may be simply another episode of the general pattern of behaviour exhibited by the Spanish economy during the past few decades: the association of periods of economic expansion (recession) with periods of convergence (divergence) of Spain's per capita GDP with respect to the EU countries.

As regards the other EU members, Ireland is a striking case. In 12 years it has managed to narrow its per capita GDP gap by some 37 percentage points, reaching the average EU level in 1997. At the other extreme, Greece stands out, for having occupied the lowest position in terms of per capita GDP throughout the period.

On the other hand, the σ convergence statistic, which measures the dispersion of the EU countries' per capita income, reveals no significant reduction. This is consistent with the result obtained in Andrés and Doménech (1996): in comparing the trends in the real convergence of the Community and of the OECD between 1960 and 1993, they conclude that integration does not appear to have exerted any appreciable influence on the alignment of the member countries' per capita GDP.

Spain's relative position in terms of the rate of unemployment is much less favourable, as it stands at more than twice that of the Community (see Figure 7.4). One feature that makes the Spanish situation even more worrisome is that it has no parallel in the group of countries with the lowest income levels. Several factors (see the analysis of activity, employment and unemployment in Chapter 3) are to blame for this deplorable situation, including in particular: rising labour costs with no similar improvement in labour productivity, rigidities in the labour market conducive to its segmentation, and the

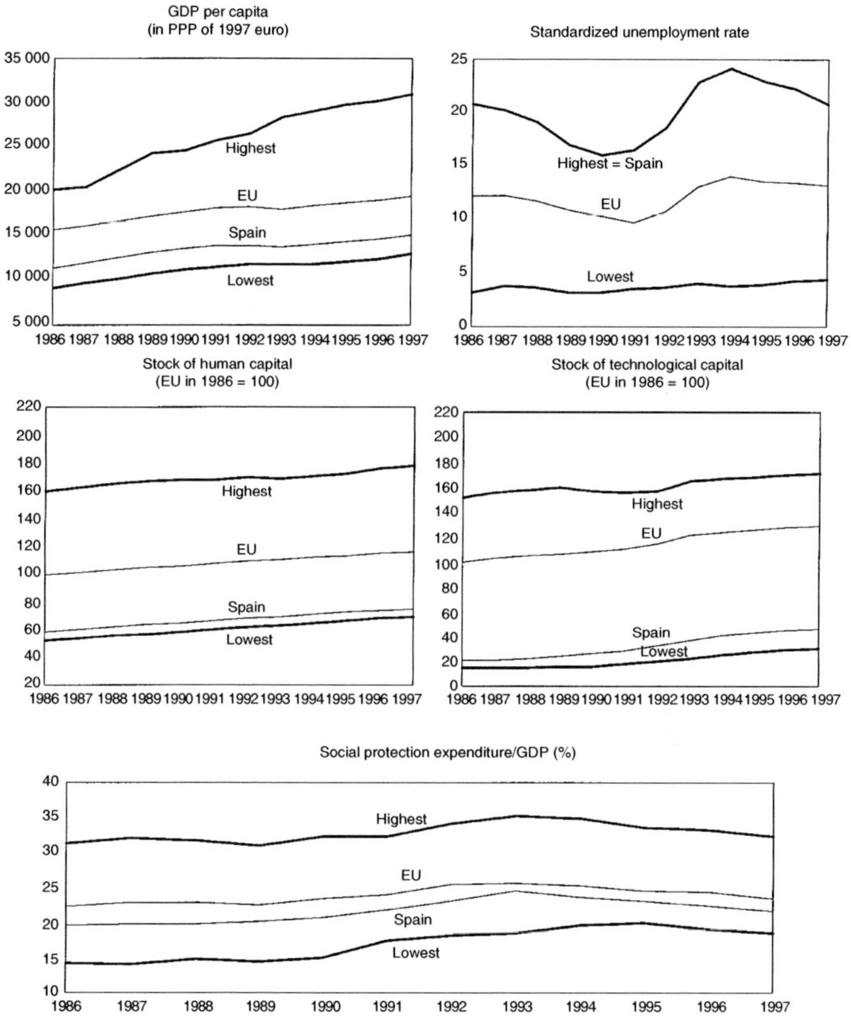

Figure 7.4 Trends in Spain's real convergence with the EU

Source: OECD: *Main Science and Technological Indicators*; OECD: *Research and Development Expenditure in Industry*; OECD: *National Accounts*, vol. I: *Main Aggregates*; OECD: *Education at a Glance*; OECD: *European Surveys: Japan*; US Government Printing Office: *Economic Indicators*; Eurostat: *Unemployment*; Eurostat: *Social Protection Expenditure and Receipts*; UNESCO: *Statistical Yearbook*; Departamento de Estudios Europeos, Fundación de las Cajas de Ahorros.

deficiencies of productive and technological systems that make it impossible to exploit the potential, in terms of employment and production, of technical innovations.

The dispersion of unemployment rates within the European Union has narrowed by 7 per cent. However, the reason lies in the growth in unemployment in most of the member states.[6]

As regards human capital, the third indicator used to evaluate real convergence, Spain has narrowed its gap with respect to the EU average by 6 percentage points, from 60 per cent of average human capital in 1986 to 66 per cent in 1997. This indicator was estimated for each of the EU countries as the proportion of the potentially employed population (aged 15 to 64) that attended school during a period equal to the duration of higher studies, taking into account the quality of education.[7]

For the member states as a whole, the value of the σ statistic shows that the dispersion of human capital endowments has narrowed by 7 per cent in the EU area, thanks to the progress made by the countries with a worse starting position.

The fourth indicator, the stock of technological capital,[8] was included – as in the case of human capital – because it too is one of the main determinants of economic growth. It shows (see Figure 7.4) a notable converging of the situation in Spain with that of the EU average (15 percentage points). None the less, the lag, which – in spite of this convergence – still persists, is truly spectacular. The ratio of Spain's technological capital stock to GDP was still only 35 per cent of the EU average in 1997. In addition to Spain's enormous technological lag, the years 1996 and 1997 have seen a notable slowing in the rate at which it has moved towards the Community average, a truly deplorable development that must be redressed as soon as possible in view of its potentially very negative impact on the growth possibilities of the Spanish economy.

In this case, there has also been a narrowing – by 22 per cent, according to the σ statistic – in the differences between the EU countries. This is explained by the stronger rate of accumulation of technological capital in the most backward countries during most of the period and by the slowdown in R&D investment in some countries, such as Germany, which have a larger stock of technological capital.

Finally, the fifth and last indicator used in this examination of Spain's real convergence within the European Union – expenditure on social benefits as a percentage of GDP[9] (see Figure 7.4) – gives results similar to the findings for per capita income: a narrowing of more than 5 percentage points in the gap with respect to the EU average, with

Spain's ratio of expenditure on social benefits to GDP rising from 74 per cent of the EU average in 1986 to more than 79 per cent in 1997. Moreover, the reduction in the dispersion within the European Union has been practically zero. One significant development has been the turnaround since 1994, partly owing to the fiscal consolidation processes, which began that year. These have led to more restrained government expenditure with reductions in spending on social benefits.

To summarize, the analysis of the five indicators clearly shows that, since Spain's accession to the European integration project, the Spanish economy has advanced in terms of real convergence vis-à-vis the EU countries as a whole. None the less, it still has a long way to go before reaching the average level of economic welfare in the European Union. This is particularly true from the standpoint of its tenuous progress in the area of unemployment, and also considering that Spain still lags far behind with respect to the variables on which sustained economic growth depends – human and technological capital – not only in relation to the Community levels but, even more worrisome, with respect to the relative size of the Spanish economy (relative GDP per capita). Moreover, there has been a slowing in technological capital, and this will have a negative impact on Spain's real convergence capacity in the years ahead.

The analysis based on these five indicators has shed light on both the differential and the path of economic welfare in Spain vis-à-vis the other EU countries since its accession to the Community. However, the construction of a composite indicator, combining the data presented above, provides a more intuitive diagnosis, as it allows the EU countries to be ranked, and thus gives a more clear-cut view of the relative position of the Spanish economy.

We have constructed a composite indicator of real convergence by taking a weighted average of the values of the five variables already analysed – expressed in terms of the EU average, which is assigned five points – based on the following weights: 50 per cent for per capita GDP and 12.5 per cent for each of the other four variables. The decision to assign a larger weight to per capita GDP is justified by the fact that all the determinants of real convergence ultimately come together in this variable. In fact, in most of the studies, this is the only variable used as a reference when evaluating the economic welfare of a country in a given area.

Table 7.2 shows the composite indicator of real convergence for each of the fifteen member states in 1986 and 1997. It confirms that during

Table 7.2 Composite indicator of real convergence

Country	1986	(ranking)	1997	(ranking)
1. Austria	5.6	(4)	5.7	(3)
2. Belgium	5.5	(6)	5.4	(7)
3. Denmark	5.7	(3)	5.8	(2)
4. Finland	5.2	(9)	5.3	(9)
5. France	5.5	(7)	5.5	(6)
6. Germany	5.9	(1)	5.7	(4)
7. Greece	3.1	(14)	3.0	(15)
8. Holland	5.5	(5)	5.4	(8)
9. Ireland	3.6	(12)	4.4	(12)
10. Italy	4.8	(11)	4.8	(11)
11. Luxemburg	5.1	(8)	5.9	(1)
12. Portugal	2.9	(15)	3.4	(14)
13. Spain	3.4	(13)	3.7	(13)
14. Sweden	5.8	(2)	5.6	(5)
15. United Kingdom	5.2	(10)	5.1	(10)
EU average	**5.0**		**5.0**	

Source: OECD: *Main Science and Technological Indicators*; OECD: *Research and Development Expenditure in Industry*; OECD: *National Accounts*, vol. I: *Main Aggregates*; OECD: *Education at a Glance*; OECD: *Economic Surveys: Japan*; US Government Printing Office: *Economic Indicators*; Eurostat: *Unemployment*; Eurostat: *Social Protection Expenditure and Receipts*; UNESCO: *Statistical Yearbook*; Departamento de Estudios Europeos, Fundación de las Cajas de Ahorros.

the period in question Spain has managed to advance in terms of real convergence (from 3.3 to 3.7) with respect to the EU average (5), although this advance has not significantly reduced the lag observed: in 1986 Spain ranked 13th, where it still remained in 1997, ahead of only Greece and Portugal.

7.5 Conclusions

This chapter has analysed Spain's situation and performance in terms of economic convergence with respect to the other EU countries and the European Union as a whole. After reviewing in the first section the two main meanings of the concept of economic convergence – nominal and real – and the method of measuring it, we have examined the position and course of each. The following points encapsulate the main ideas and conclusions drawn from this analysis.

- In the area of nominal convergence, a process of increasing price control was observed. Spain has thus been able to reduce its inflation rate to less than the 2 per cent EU average. Very substantial progress has also been made in curbing debt and, above all, the budget deficit. In this respect, it can also be said that the European Union and EMU have become areas of macroeconomic stability.

- The conclusion regarding real convergence or 'economic and social cohesion' – the ultimate goal towards which economic authorities should focus their attention, as it signifies an improvement in the welfare of individuals – is that it is not at all guaranteed by the advances made towards integration. On the contrary, it is argued that, in certain circumstances, the income inequalities between the member countries could widen. Thus, if the laggard members are to share equally the benefits of EMU, special efforts must be made by the economic and social agents in these countries.
- In this respect, the findings signal, on the one hand, Spain's progress towards real convergence since joining the Community, especially in terms of GDP per capita and expenditure on social benefits, where it has advanced by 6 and 5 percentage points, respectively, vis-à-vis the European Union; on the other hand, they reflect the dismal situation of the unemployment rate and of the economy's relative position with regard to the human and technological capital ratios, which stand at only 66 per cent and 35 per cent of the Community average, despite the investment efforts made. The analysis has also shown that the differences between the EU countries have narrowed, albeit insignificantly.
- But the problem of the Spanish economy's real convergence is most evident when we consider its position in the EU ranking based on a composite indicator, constructed with the above-mentioned variables (per capita GDP, the unemployment rate, human and technological capital, and expenditure on social benefits in relation to GDP). Indeed, in 1986 Spain ranked 13th, and it still occupies this position.

Part II

Evaluation of the Integration Process

8
Trade Relations

8.1 Introduction

A process of economic integration as profound and extensive as the one now under way in Europe has far-reaching implications for the economies involved. Because Spain joined this project late – at the stage of customs union and with the single market in the process of formation – from 1986 onwards the Spanish economy had to confront a radical transformation in the regulatory framework of its foreign trade relations. Since 1986 Spain has had to dismantle the physical and economic borders with its new partners, adapt its systems of protection vis-à-vis third countries to those prevailing in the European common market, and assume the existing commitments in exchange-rate and monetary matters, as well as in areas relating to the freedom of movement of productive factors, areas in which the member countries had gradually advanced until the foundations for the construction of economic and monetary union were in place.

The lifting of barriers to trade and to the free movement of factors opens the way for greater efficiency in the allocation of resources between the member states, which is further enhanced in the case of monetary union by the reduction in transaction costs and the elimination of foreign-exchange uncertainty, and consequently, of the latter's inhibiting effects on the volume of trade. Foreign trade and movements of workers and capital are therefore the channels through which mechanisms that can ultimately heighten the general welfare of the member countries operate. For this reason, analysis of their trade flows is essential not only to evaluate the degree of integration actually achieved by the countries in question, but also because it allows us to draw inferences as to the impact of integration on their income and employment.

To this end, the present chapter analyses the more general features of the adjustment in the trade relations of the Fifteen and then, in greater detail, with reference to the Spanish economy in the period 1986–97, while later chapters deal with trends in labour and capital movements. The chapter is structured as follows: after this introduction, Section 8.2 briefly reviews the basic theoretical principles governing the implications of economic integration schemes for the member countries' trade patterns and structures, and then outlines the possible consequences of these schemes for the efficiency of, and distribution of, income between the countries. Section 8.3 analyses the transformations in the trade relations of EU members, and of Spain in particular, both within and outside the Community, in order to evaluate the progress towards trade integration in the European Union, and its implications, focusing once more on the case of Spain. Finally, the most important conclusions are summarized.

8.2 Economic integration and foreign trade

The elimination of barriers to free trade and, above all, of restrictions on factor mobility between the signatory countries of an agreement on regional integration makes it possible for productive factors to be reallocated to more efficient activities, reflected in the structure of the member countries' productive specialization and, by extension, in the volume and pattern of their trade.

Theories of international trade and economic integration[1] allow us to distinguish two basic approaches, each yielding different propositions as to the nature of the trade adjustment derived from integration agreements. In addition to their diverging predictions of the trade impact, the two approaches also differ in their prognoses of the adjustment costs and, what is possibly more important, in their conclusions regarding the likelihood of convergence in the levels of the per capita income of the participating countries.

This section briefly reviews both approaches. The first is that of the traditional theory of regional economic integration developed during the 1950s and 1960s, inspired by the pioneering work of Viner (1950). Its basic assumptions are the same as those of the neo-classical model of international trade (Heckscher-Ohlin model): the existence of perfectly competitive markets, constant returns to scale, homogeneity of goods and productive factors, and equality of consumer preferences and technology.

Under these assumptions, international trade is explained on the basis of comparative advantages, or, in other words, the differences in the relative costs and prices between the countries, which in turn stem from the differences in their factor endowment. In this context, by reducing or removing the restrictions on free trade and factor mobility, regional integration agreements permit each country to specialize in the production and export of goods requiring the intensive use of the factor of production which the country possesses in relative abundance, so that its relative costs are lower than those of its trade partners. This shift in production – the argument goes – would provoke an increase in the demand for these abundant factors and, in consequence, in their remuneration; the cost differentials existing between one economy and another before integration would therefore tend to disappear. At the same time, the differences in the signatory countries' productive structures would tend to become more pronounced, and their trade and factor movements would intensify until the cost differentials between the countries were eliminated.

Briefly, the neo-classical model predicts the levelling-out of the member countries' prices, costs and income levels, with international trade and international factor mobility acting as the levelling-out mechanisms. None the less, this process of convergence in the countries' income, prices and remuneration of productive factors has different effects on different branches of activity, and is associated with adjustment costs arising from factor re-allocation, which may be significant but are not of a permanent nature.

The process described would in any case lead to an increase in trade of an inter-industrial type, which would reach greater intensity the greater the disparities between the countries. From this perspective, the neo-classical model is appropriate for analysing and explaining the trade flows between countries with very different productive characteristics and levels of development. Its suppositions and some of its predictions, however, are not easily reconciled with reality.

In fact, in practice many industries show increasing returns to scale and external economies. Likewise, a large proportion of international trade now takes place between industrialized countries with great similarities in their factor endowments. Moreover, a large part of this trade is of an intra-industrial nature – in other words, it involves the simultaneous trade of products that are so similar that they are classified in customs statistics within the same branch, even when these statistics are in their most disaggregated form.

The corroboration of all these circumstances has paved the way for a new theoretical approach, now known as the 'new theory of international trade'. While acknowledging the existence of imperfections in goods and factor markets, it offers a complementary explanation of international trade and, specifically, helps to explain the existence of intra-industrial trade.[2] In particular, from the standpoint of supply, the theory emphasizes the presence of monopolistic competition or oligopolistic structures, which make corporate strategies of product differentiation especially important, given the market power they can yield and the existence of economies of scale in production. From the standpoint of demand, consumer preference for product variety stands out.

In this setting, additional efficiency gains can be obtained through economic integration. Specifically, the enlargement of markets allows greater exploitation of economies of scale and enhances the welfare of consumers by widening the possibilities of satisfying their preference for variety. Furthermore, the lifting of trade barriers may intensify competition between firms, thereby narrowing their price–cost margins.[3] However, in these circumstances, predicting the distributive effects of integration agreements becomes more complex and uncertain. The economic literature has tended to highlight the fact that, when integration processes entail an intra-industrial trade adjustment, the adjustment costs stemming from specialization are lower, because each country will tend to produce a given number of varieties of the same product, without the need to transfer resources and productive factors between different sectors. This hypothesis is, however, based on models of monopolistic competition with horizontal product differentiation.

But if the existence of vertical differentiation or differences in the level of product quality (whose origin is found to be closely linked to the countries' different technological capacity) is allowed, then the conclusions are not as optimistic. In particular, it may be that the process of integration between countries with different levels of technological development entails sizeable adjustment costs. Specifically, those countries with a lower degree of development are likely to see a shift in demand towards the higher-quality goods produced by their new trade partners, due to the fall in relative prices induced by the removal of trade barriers. As a result, local products of lower quality might be crowded out by imported products, whereas it is unlikely that consumers in countries with higher income levels will increase their demand for low-quality products. Therefore, countries with lower income might suffer significant adjustment costs, at least in the short run, and even a relative impoverishment vis-à-vis partners with a more favourable starting point.[4] Here it should be ascertained whether the intra-industrial adjustment is based on horizontal or vertical product differentiation, because the implications for the distributive effects and adjustment costs arising from these two patterns of specialization may be very different (see Motta, 1992, for the details of this line of argument).

Briefly, economic integration theory does not permit general conclusions to be drawn for all the integration projects in which diverse countries are involved, or even for all the productive sectors of one country. Thus, in theory, there is a wide range of predictions of the way a regional integration accord might affect the volume and structure of the signatory countries' trade. There are also many possible conjectures as to the size and duration of the adjustment costs and the impact on the countries' income derived from integration – and this is key – which depend on the characteristics of the trade adjustment. For this reason, to draw inferences on all these aspects, it is essential to analyse the nature of the trade adjustment in the Spanish economy during the period 1986–97.

8.3 Trade adjustment in the Europe of the Fifteen

This section analyses the main features of the trade adjustment which took place in the Spanish economy in the years after Spain joined the European Union – when, as readers will be aware, the unification of the European market took place – setting them against the most substantive changes which arose in EU trade patterns in the same years. It begins by describing the performance of exports and imports of goods in aggregate terms, distinguishing between the Community market and the rest of the world. It then goes on to examine trade trends by productive branch, with special emphasis on the transformations in both inter- and intra-industrial trade.[5]

In the period after Spain's accession to what is now the European Union, Spanish foreign trade changed radically. During these years Spain's trade flows – imports and exports alike – grew at very strong rates, leading to a substantial increase in the participation of both variables in the economy's gross domestic product. Meanwhile, this steady intensification of trade flows was accompanied by a significant deterioration in the trade balance.

The disaggregation of foreign trade figures by geographical area reveals that the expansion in trade was characterized in Spain and most Community countries by increasingly stronger trade relations with partners at the expense of third countries (see Figure 8.1 and Table 8.1).

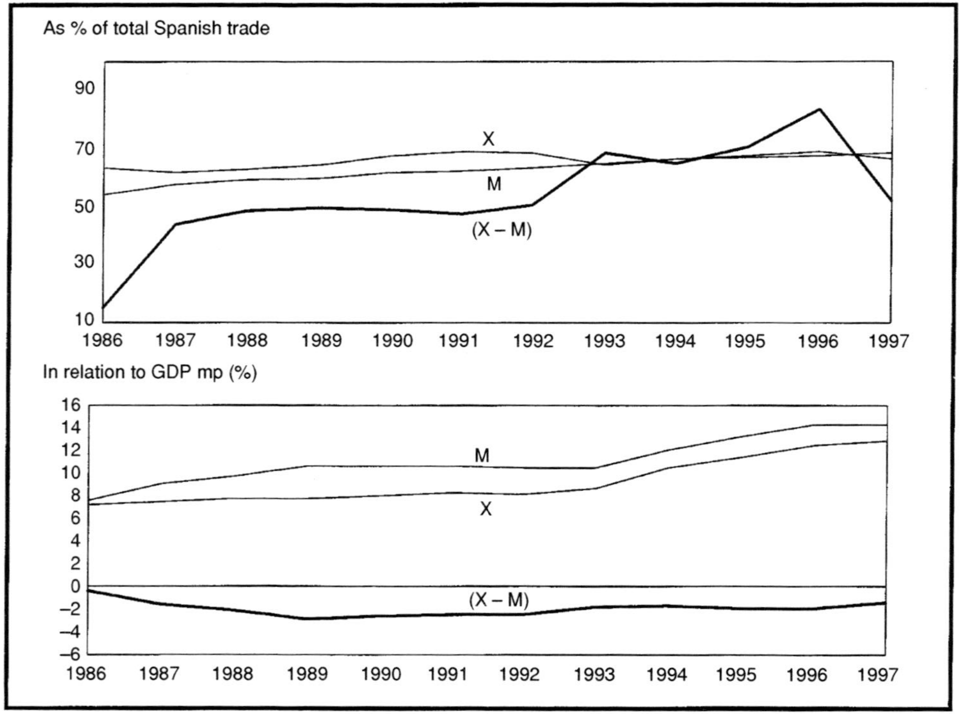

Figure 8.1 Weight of the EU in Spanish trade flows

Source: Eurostat: *External Trade Statistical Yearbook*; Eurostat: *External and Intra-European Union Trade*; Departamento de Estudios Europeos, Fundación de las Cajas de Ahorros.

Table 8.1 Weight of intra-community trade in total trade flows

Imports Country	1986	(ranking)	1997	(ranking)	**Exports** Country	1986	(ranking)	1997	(ranking)
Austria	69.5	(4)	73.1	(2)	Austria	64.1	(6)	61.8	(8)
Belgium–Lux.	73.4	(2)	71.7	(3)	Belgium–Lux.	78.1	(2)	75.0	(3)
Denmark	49.8	(13)	70.7	(4)	Denmark	62.2	(8)	66.8	(6)
Finland	47.4	(14)	64.4	(9)	Finland	50.5	(14)	53.6	(13)
France	67.6	(5)	65.8	(7)	France	57.1	(11)	62.0	(7)
Germany	58.1	(10)	58.3	(12)	Germany	60.2	(9)	55.5	(9)
Greece	62.2	(8)	64.0	(10)	Greece	68.6	(5)	45.4	(14)
Holland	64.7	(6)	58.1	(13)	Holland	81.3	(1)	78.8	(2)
Ireland	75.9	(1)	64.8	(8)	Ireland	73.9	(4)	67.9	(5)
Italy	59.9	(9)	60.4	(11)	Italy	55.2	(12)	54.4	(12)
Portugal	62.8	(7)	75.0	(1)	Portugal	75.5	(3)	80.0	(1)
Spain	54.4	(12)	66.6	(6)	Spain	63.7	(7)	68.7	(4)
Sweden	72.3	(3)	67.5	(5)	Sweden	57.4	(10)	55.2	(10)
United Kingdom	55.3	(11)	53.5	(14)	United Kingdom	52.2	(13)	55.1	(11)
European Union	**61.8**		**62.0**		**European Union**	**62.2**		**61.6**	

Source: Eurostat: *External Trade, Statistical Yearbook*; Eurostat: *External and Intra-European Union Trade*; Departamento de Estudios Europeos, Fundación de las Cajas de Ahorros.

As inferred from Table 8.1, the process of trade concentration on an intra-regional scale is particularly pronounced in those countries, such as Spain and Finland, which started from a more geographically diversified trade structure.[6] The relative shares of intra-Community trade in most countries have thus tended to level out.

A more detailed analysis of the Spanish case, as seen in Table 8.2, shows that the increase in trade with EU countries was greater in imports than in exports, although the latter already showed a stronger orientation towards this market in 1986. The easing of customs barriers after Spain's accession helps explain the spectacular growth in imports from the European Union, given that the degree of customs protection prevailing in Spain in the pre-accession years was especially high in the case of products from the Community, because they were mostly consumer and capital goods subject to very high tariffs.[7] Meanwhile, the restrictions applied to Spanish products by European countries were comparatively milder, because the preferential agreement with European countries dating from 1970 had already brought about a substantial easing of trade barriers that was conducive to the concentration of exports in these markets before Spain's accession.

Table 8.2 also reflects the changes in the relative weight of each of the EU member countries in Spain's imports and exports. Here, one of the most striking aspects is the enormous increase in the relative presence of Portugal in Spanish cross-border trade flows. In addition, the same table clearly shows that Spain's trade balance with Community countries – with the exception of Portugal and Greece – has deteriorated across the board. This is a reflection of the sharp growth in imports from the European Union over the past decade, and it evidences the difficulties that Spanish firms have had to face due to the mounting competitive pressures associated with the liberalization of trade.

As expected, since Spain's accession, the weight of the Spanish economy – as both customer and supplier – in the trade of its partners has also risen. In any event, Spain's relative importance in the imports and exports of EU member countries – shown in Table 8.3 – differs sharply from one country to another. Thus in 1997 the share of Spanish exports was particularly significant in the imports of Portugal and France, at 31 per cent and 9.8 per cent, respectively. Likewise, Spain's role as a client is stronger in these countries, given that the Spanish economy is the destination of 16.6 per cent and 12 per cent of Portuguese and French exports, respectively.

Having described the performance of aggregate trade, we shall now look at what occurred in Spain's foreign trade, broken down by produc-

Table 8.2 Weight of each EU country in Spanish trade flows

Spanish imports from* (%)			**Spanish exports to* (%)**			**Bilateral trade balance (millions of euro)**		
	Share			Share				
Country	1986	1997	Country	1986	1997	Country	1986	1997
1. Austria	1.3	1.5	1. Austria	1.1	1.2	1. Austria	–32	–296
2. Belgium–Lux.	4.9	5.7	2. Belgium–Lux.	4.7	4.0	2. Belgium–Lux.	–48	–1379
3. Denmark	1.2	1.1	3. Denmark	1.2	1.0	3. Denmark	–5	–185
4. Finland	1.4	1.1	4. Finland	0.8	0.6	4. Finland	–97	–371
5. France	22.3	26.5	5. France	29.2	26.5	5. France	1162	–1887
6. Germany	28.2	22.7	6. Germany	18.1	19.1	6. Germany	–1902	–3778
7. Greece	0.4	0.3	7. Greece	0.8	1.4	7. Greece	60	656
8. Holland	5.2	7.4	8. Holland	7.6	5.3	8. Holland	408	–1839
9. Ireland	1.1	1.7	9. Ireland	1.2	0.6	9. Ireland	27	–792
10. Italy	13.6	13.5	10. Italy	13.3	14.2	10. Italy	–83	–582
11. Portugal	2.4	4.0	11. Portugal	5.8	12.9	11. Portugal	612	5041
12. Sweden	3.6	2.0	12. Sweden	1.9	1.4	12. Sweden	–317	–507
13. United Kingdom	14.4	12.3	13. United Kingdom	14.3	11.8	13. United Kingdom	–77	–1174
European Union	**100**	**100**	**European Union**	**100**	**100**	**European Union**	**–292**	**–7093**
Share of EU imports**	54.4	66.6	Share of EU exports**	63.7	68.7			

* As percentage of Spanish intra-Community trade.
** As percentage of total Spanish trade.
Source: Eurostat: *External Trade, Statistical Yearbook*; Eurostat: *External and Intra-European Union Trade*; Departamento de Estudios Europeos, Fundación de las Cajas de Ahorros.

Table 8.3 Weight of Spain in intra-Community trade flows

Imports Country	1986	1997	**Exports** Country	1986	1997
1. Austria	1.2	1.6	1. Austria	3.1	3.5
2. Belgium–Lux.	2.0	2.4	2. Belgium–Lux.	3.5	4.1
3. Denmark	2.2	1.9	3. Denmark	2.7	2.9
4. Finland	2.0	1.9	4. Finland	2.2	3.9
5. France	7.5	9.8	5. France	10.4	12.0
6. Germany	4.1	5.7	6. Germany	6.4	6.0
7. Greece	3.4	5.4	7. Greece	2.4	3.8
8. Holland	2.5	3.8	8. Holland	3.2	3.6
9. Ireland	0.9	1.6	9. Ireland	3.0	3.4
10. Italy	5.2	7.9	10. Italy	8.1	9.2
11. Portugal	21.7	31.0	11. Portugal	18.4	16.6
12. Sweden	1.9	1.9	12. Sweden	2.6	3.8
13. United Kingdom	4.1	5.1	13. United Kingdom	6.9	7.1
European Union	**4.2**	**5.6**	**European Union**	**6.0**	**6.7**

Source: Eurostat: *External Trade, Statistical Yearbook*; Eurostat: *External and Intra-European Union Trade*; Departamento de Estudios Europeos, Fundación de las Cajas de Ahorros.

tive branches in the same period (1986–97).[8] As seen in Table 8.4, at the time of Spain's accession, the structure of Spanish exports showed a certain specialization in sectors with intermediate or low demand vitality and technological intensity, whereas the relative share of sectors with more intensive technology and more vigorous demand was very small. Most notable in the composition of imports was the high share of sectors with greater technological content and more dynamic demand. Together, these features describe a trade structure in Spain that was quite different from that of the more developed EU countries (for more details, see Gordo and Martín, 1995). In short, to a certain extent they reveal the weaknesses that existed in the Spanish productive system in the manufacture of goods requiring the use of more complex technologies, a situation – described in greater detail in Chapter 1 – that tended to generate a high dependence on imports to meet the demand for goods of this type.

None the less, in examining the changes in Spain's trade pattern in the years following accession, we find a certain narrowing of the gap in the Spanish trade structure vis-à-vis that of its more developed partners. Indeed, on the export side, the Spanish trade pattern tended to move towards sectors of intermediate technological intensity and demand, owing to the notable growth in the transport equipment

Table 8.4 Changes in Spain's trade structure

	Exports			
	European Union		Rest of the world	
	1986	1997	1986	1997
Sectors with strong demand and intensive technology	**18.3**	**18.8**	**18.6**	**22.9**
Electrical goods	5.8	7.7	4.5	9.0
Office and data-processing machines	4.4	2.5	1.5	2.8
Chemical products	8.1	8.6	12.6	11.1
Sectors with moderate demand and intermediate technology	**42.8**	**46.9**	**24.5**	**34.9**
Rubber and plastic products	4.2	4.1	4.9	3.5
Transport equipment	27.1	34.3	7.8	17.0
Agricultural and industrial machinery	8.3	6.0	8.4	10.9
Other manufactured products	3.2	2.5	3.4	3.5
Sectors with weak demand and low technology	**38.9**	**34.3**	**56.9**	**42.2**
Textiles and clothing, leather and footwear	9.2	7.4	12.0	9.0
Ferrous and non-ferrous ores and metals	8.4	6.1	15.5	6.6
Non-metallic minerals and mineral products	3.5	3.4	6.2	6.8
Paper and printing products	3.6	2.8	4.4	3.7
Food, beverages and tobacco	9.8	10.8	12.8	11.0
Metal products, exc. machinery and transport equipment	4.4	3.8	6.0	5.1
Total manufactured products	**100**	**100**	**100**	**100**

Table 8.4 continued

	Imports			
	European Union		Rest of the world	
	1986	1997	1986	1997
Sectors with strong demand and intensive technology	**33.2**	**30.8**	**42.3**	**32.3**
Electrical goods	8.9	10.5	13.9	10.8
Office data-processing machines	7.5	5.2	12.8	10.1
Chemical products	16.8	15.1	15.6	11.4
Sectors with moderate demand and intermediate technology	**34.1**	**39.6**	**16.8**	**26.5**
Rubber and plastic products	3.5	4.1	2.3	3.1
Transport equipment	15.0	22.8	4.6	11.1
Agricultural and industrial machinery	13.8	10.6	6.5	7.5
Other manufactured products	1.8	2.1	3.4	4.8
Sectors with weak demand and low technology	**32.7**	**29.6**	**40.9**	**41.2**
Textiles and clothing, leather and footwear	4.[illegible]	5.3	7.1	11.4
Ferrous and non-ferrous ores and metals	10.6	7.4	10.6	9.2
Non-metallic minerals and mineral products	2.5	1.7	3.3	2.2
Paper and printing products	4.1	3.8	2.3	2.1
Food, beverages and tobacco	6.3	7.6	15.1	14.0
Metal products, exc. machinery and transport equipment	4.9	3.8	2.5	2.3
Total manufactured products	**100**	**100**	**100**	**100**

Source: Departamento de Aduanas, Instituto Nacional de Estadística; Banco de España.

sector.[9] By contrast, the relative share of sectors with a lower technological content and less dynamic demand tended to decline. There was an especially sharp slide in the relative share of various branches such as steel, and textiles and clothing, leather and footwear, traditionally very important in Spain's export structure. Among imports, there was an increase in the relative share of sectors with intermediate technology and moderate demand, at the expense of sectors where these two variables are higher. But, despite these changes, the structure of Spain's trade specialization still differs appreciably from that of its main European partners. Broadly, the latter specialize in exports of technologically more advanced goods and depend less on imports of goods of this type in comparison with the Spanish economy.

After this examination of the trends and basic changes in the geographical structure and composition of Spanish trade flows during the period in question, we shall now analyse the volume and trends in inter- and intra-industrial trade. As discussed in the preceding section, the determinants of these two types of trade may differ greatly, and the implications for the distribution of the costs and benefits associated with integration may also be very different, depending on which type of specialization predominates.

Recall that inter-industrial trade is explained by the cost and price differentials between countries, which – under the assumptions of conventional trade theory – are in turn determined by the existence of disparities in their factor endowment. However, given that the differences in relative costs are hard to quantify and observe, empirical studies generally use an approximation based on revealed comparative advantage indices (RCAI)[10] when attempting to evaluate the pattern of this type of trade.

As seen in Table 8.5, the structure of the Spanish economy's comparative advantages has undergone a profound change over the past 12 years. In 1986 Spain's trade with EU countries showed a comparative disadvantage in technologically intensive sectors with strong demand and in various sectors with an intermediate level of technology, such as agricultural and industrial machinery. Its comparative advantages were centred on the sectors with a more intensive use of unskilled labour – such as textiles – as well as several sectors with intensive use of physical capital, such as transport equipment. Compared with the rest of the world, Spain had a position of disadvantage in the more technologically intensive sectors.

The factor content of Spanish trade in the years prior to accession is analysed in greater depth in the works of Fariñas and Martín (1990)

Table 8.5 Spain's revealed comparative advantage indices (RCAI) vis-à-vis the EU and the rest of the world

	European Union		Rest of the world	
	1986	1997	1986	1997
Sectors with strong demand and intensive technology	**–38.2**	**–31.8**	**–36.4**	**–18.9**
Electrical goods	–30.4	–23.0	–49.1	–11.0
Office and data-processing machines	–35.3	–42.1	–77.9	–57.8
Chemical products	–44.1	–35.0	–7.5	–3.0
Sectors with moderate demand and intermediate technology	**0.8**	**0.3**	**21.8**	**11.8**
Rubber and plastic products	–1.7	–8.2	38.0	4.5
Transport equipment	18.8	12.4	28.9	19.0
Agricultural and industrial machinery	–34.4	–35.3	16.2	16.7
Other manufactured products	17.3	–0.2	3.7	–17.2
Sectors with weak demand and low technology	**–1.6**	**–0.8**	**19.3**	**–0.7**
Textiles and clothing, leather and footwear	27.9	8.4	28.7	–13.6
Ferrous and non-ferrous ores and metals	–21.4	–17.4	21.8	–18.1
Non-metallic minerals and mineral products	6.6	24.5	32.7	50.3
Paper and printing products	–16.6	–22.2	34.7	25.3
Food, beverages and tobacco	11.4	8.7	–5.1	–14.4
Metal products, exc. machinery and transport equipment	–15.9	–7.3	43.0	37.1
Total manufactured products	**–10.4**	**–8.2**	**3.1**	**–1.9**

Source: Departamento de Aduanas; Instituto Nacional de Estadística; Banco de España.

and Rodríguez (1992).[11] The conclusions of these studies indicate that Spain stood at an advantage in its trade relations with the OECD in sectors intensive in unskilled labour and natural resources and at a disadvantage in those intensive in physical capital and, above all, human capital. By contrast, in trade with the less developed countries, Spain had an advantageous position in sectors with a relative abundance of human capital and a disadvantage in sectors intensive in natural resources.

Under conventional trade theory, integration into the European Union would be expected to bring about an intensification in the comparative advantages described above. But, between 1986 and 1997, Spain's structure of comparative advantages underwent a transformation that to a large extent contradicts this forecast. Trade in some sectors where Spain had a long-standing specialization deteriorated sharply, reaching a situation of comparative disadvantage in 1997. Particularly striking was the decline in the branches of textiles and food.

In short, the Spanish pattern of comparative advantages has undergone a very profound change reflected, among other aspects, in a loss of the advantages conferred by a factor endowment relatively intensive in unskilled labour. This would suggest that the intersectoral adjustment pattern predicted by the more conventional model of economic integration has failed to materialize.

To round off this analysis of Spain's trade adjustment and to shed further light on its nature, we have analysed the trends in transactions of an intra-industrial type. Intra-industrial trade[12] is measured by taking the index proposed by Grubel and Lloyd (B_i), defined as:

$$B_i = \left[1 - \frac{|X_i - M_i|}{X_i + M_i}\right] \cdot 100$$

The closer the value of this index is to 100, the greater the proportion of intra-industrial trade to the overall trade of a given sector. To avoid the biases arising when this index is measured on the basis of an excessively aggregated classification of trade flows, it was first calculated at the five-digit level of disaggregation of the SITC and was then aggregated in the 13 manufacturing sectors in the NACE-CLIO (25) classification – used in other chapters – by calculating the arithmetic mean weighted by the importance of each in the sector's overall trade.

As seen in Table 8.6, with respect to trade relations with the European Union and third countries alike, intra-industrial trade advanced notably in the years after Spain's accession. Note, too, that much of the increase in intra-industrial trade occurred in sectors where Spain had a comparative advantage in 1986, such as transport equipment, textiles and clothing, leather and footwear, and food. This suggests that, far from a more pronounced specialization in the production and export of such goods, there has actually been a considerable increase in the imports of these goods. From this it can be inferred that the adjustment in the Spanish trade pattern to the changes brought about by accession and the unification of the European market has so far largely been of an intra-industrial nature.

As mentioned in the previous section, the implications in terms of equity and welfare, when this type of adjustment predominates, are much more uncertain. In any case, it may be said that the adjustment costs will be higher when trade in vertically integrated products lies behind the increase in intra-industrial trade.

It is therefore worth ascertaining whether the forces that determine the patterns of behaviour of intra-industrial trade are associated with horizontal (non-qualitative) product differentiation or whether, to the contrary, specialization based on vertical differentiation or levels of product quality has prevailed. In the latter case, the basic question to be resolved is whether the increase in trade within the same industry – in other words, intra-industrial trade – reflects a specialization by Spain in the export of lower-quality products in comparison with its European partners, whose overall level of development is higher.

But how should the quality of Spanish exports and imports be evaluated? Ascertaining the nature of intra-industrial trade and product quality is a complicated task. Assuming that quality levels tend to be reflected in the products' prices, the export and import prices of a single product can be analysed to learn whether a wide difference exists between the two, which might indicate quality differences. But import and export prices are not available. Because of this, unit value indices must be used to approximate prices, even though these indices reflect not only variations in prices but also changes in the composition of trade.[13] In any event, the use of unit value indices is generally accepted for want of a better alternative.

In this chapter we have used the export and import unit value indices calculated at the five-digit level of the SITC, the same level of disaggregation as was used to quantify intra-industrial trade. Intra-industrial trade is considered to be vertical in nature if the unit value index of exports exceeds that of imports by more than 15 per cent (see Greenaway, Hine and Millner, 1994). Hence, if the unit value of the

Table 8.6 Spain's intra-industrial trade with the EU and the rest of the world

	European Union		Rest of the world	
	1986	1997	1986	1997
Sectors with strong demand and intensive technology				
Electrical goods	54.0	57.9	30.7	56.9
Office and data-processing machines	63.7	40.4	23.0	27.4
Chemical products	42.6	51.9	37.5	44.8
Sectors with moderate demand and intermediate technology				
Rubber and plastic products	54.2	71.2	28.4	53.2
Transport equipment	57.3	66.5	38.9	57.2
Agricultural and industrial machinery	53.4	52.5	54.2	47.1
Other manufactured products	39.3	55.8	27.6	31.5
Sectors with weak demand and low technology				
Textiles and clothing, leather and footwear	34.6	58.2	26.4	37.6
Ferrous and non-ferrous ores and metals	67.5	73.2	37.0	46.5
Non-metallic minerals and mineral products	44.6	50.8	11.9	26.0
Paper and printing products	60.2	52.5	23.4	32.6
Food, beverages and tobacco	23.9	38.4	20.9	25.7
Metal products, exc. machinery and transport equipment	34.8	49.2	14.4	17.7
Total manufactured products	**48.7**	**57.8**	**28.2**	**40.5**

Source: Departamento de Aduanas; Instituto Nacional de Estadística; Banco de España.

exports of a product exceeds (falls short of) the unit value of imports by more than 15 per cent, Spanish production is considered to be specialized in goods of high (low) quality vis-à-vis its trade partners. If instead the spreads between unit values are less than 15 per cent, a horizontal differentiation is understood to exist.

Table 8.7 shows intra-industrial trade broken down by these three categories. As seen, the main characteristics of Spain's intra-industrial trade in the period of its EU membership are as follows:

- First, intra-industrial trade of a vertical nature predominates in most industries in trade both with the European Union and with third countries.
- Second, within trade of a vertical nature with EU partners, the quality level of Spanish exports is lower than that of imports.
- Third, the increase in intra-industrial trade after Spain's accession to the European Union largely derives from the growth of trade of a horizontal nature.[14]

In sum, the findings on the nature of intra-industrial trade appear to indicate that during these years the quality of Spanish production moved closer to the highest levels in EU countries. However, the ongoing predominance of trade of a vertical nature, characterized by exports of relatively lower quality, illustrates that Spain continued to lag significantly behind these countries.

In the preceding paragraphs we have analysed the changes in Spain's trade pattern during the period since it joined the European Union, with a special emphasis on the development of its trade relations with the European Union itself.

However, it should be noted that in recent years the international economic order has undergone profound changes, prompted by the opening up of numerous economies which have been increasing their share of international trade flows. Notable, from the perspective of the European Union, is the process of opening up and transformation into market economies that Central and Eastern European countries have recently been confronting. This has spurred their growth and development to the extent that they aspire to form part of the European common market in the near future. In the early 1990s the European Union signed preferential trading agreements with several of these countries, resulting in a gradual easing in the trade restrictions between these two areas.[15] Moreover, some of these economies have already begun formal negotiations to join the European Union.

Table 8.7 Nature of intra-industrial trade: horizontal and vertical breakdown

	European Union				Rest of the world			
	Vertical		Horizontal	Total	Vertical		Horizontal	Total
	High quality	Low quality			High quality	Low quality		
Electrical goods								
1986	26.4	20.9	6.7	54.0	12.7	13.8	4.2	30.7
1997	21.3	21.7	14.9	57.9	15.6	27.5	13.8	56.9
Office and data-processing machines								
1986	41.2	5.5	17.0	63.7	5.9	7.8	9.3	23.0
1997	12.1	13.6	14.7	40.4	14.9	10.4	2.1	27.4
Chemical products								
1986	15.3	20.8	6.5	42.6	15.9	17.3	4.3	37.5
1997	9.0	29.3	13.6	51.9	12.0	25.6	7.2	44.8
Rubber and plastic products								
1986	7.2	42.3	4.7	54.2	2.3	19.4	6.7	28.4
1997	29.3	16.6	25.3	71.2	18.6	20.4	14.2	53.2
Transport equipment								
1986	5.3	46.7	5.3	57.3	20.6	6.3	12.0	38.9
1997	6.1	11.5	48.9	66.5	11.5	18.4	27.3	57.2
Agricultural and industrial machinery								
1986	6.4	38.9	8.1	53.4	11.4	38.8	4.0	54.2
1997	15.6	20.6	16.3	52.5	4.5	26.6	16.0	47.1
Other manufactured products								
1986	7.7	25.1	6.5	39.3	8.5	17.9	1.3	27.6
1997	18.7	24.3	12.8	55.8	16.1	6.0	9.4	3.5

Table 8.7 continued

	European Union				Rest of the world			
	Vertical		Horizontal	Total	Vertical		Horizontal	Total
	High quality	Low quality			High quality	Low quality		
Textiles and clothing, leather and footwear								
1986	10.1	19.8	4.7	34.6	14.9	6.3	5.2	26.4
1997	22.3	16.2	19.7	58.2	29.3	4.1	4.2	37.6
Ferrous and non-ferrous ores and metals								
1986	14.9	38.3	14.3	67.5	15.7	16.1	5.2	37.0
1997	20.5	35.1	17.6	73.2	31.6	9.4	5.5	46.5
Non-metallic minerals and mineral products								
1986	6.2	27.5	10.9	44.6	2.7	8.4	0.8	11.9
1997	15.7	22.3	12.8	50.8	8.2	14.0	3.8	26.0
Paper and printing products								
1986	10.6	26.8	22.8	60 2	2.9	7.9	12.6	23.4
1997	5.9	26.3	20.3	52.5	4.8	21.1	6.7	32.6
Food, beverages and tobacco								
1986	7.8	10.8	5.3	23.9	11.7	5.4	3.8	20.9
1997	11.0	16.4	11.0	38.4	12.7	9.0	4.0	25.7
Metal products, exc. machinery and transport equipment								
1986	3.3	13.7	17.8	34.8	3.3	5.5	5.6	14.4
1997	7.3	18.8	23.1	49.2	6.5	4.0	7.2	17.7
Total								
1986	11.5	28.2	9.0	48.7	10.7	12.0	5.5	28.2
1997	12.7	18.6	26.5	57.8	14.1	15.6	10.8	40.5

Source: Departamento de Aduanas; Instituto Nacional de Estadística; Banco de España.

Against this background, there has been growing interest in studies of trade relations with these countries, because the opening up of their economies offers an exceptional opportunity for the expansion of EU sales, given the breadth and geographical proximity of these new markets. But, at the same time, Eastern European countries have also begun competing in various market segments, especially in products intensive in unskilled labour, due to their lower relative labour costs. In addition, these countries are highly attractive for foreign direct investment flows.[16] As a result, the opening up and development of these countries could significantly affect the productive specialization of Western European economies, above all in Southern Europe where the aforementioned sectors are still relatively large and where development has to a large extent been driven by the inflow of foreign capital.

To evaluate the structure of trade relations with these countries, Table 8.8 shows the composition of bilateral trade between Spain and the Central and Eastern European countries which have embarked most resolutely on a process of restructuring and trade liberalization, namely Poland, the Czech Republic and Hungary.

In the period between 1986 and 1997, the relative importance of Spain's trade with these countries as a percentage of its total foreign trade is seen to have increased, although such trade remains small in comparison with that with other Western European countries. On the export side, we find that sales abroad in 1986 were heavily concentrated in a small number of industries. The protectionist policies of these countries, where the principle of self-sufficiency guided economic policy, precluded imports of goods other than those needed in productive processes and for which there was no domestically produced equivalent. The bulk of their trade was formed by products of the ferrous and non-ferrous ores and metals, agricultural and industrial machinery, chemical products, and food sectors.

The changes in the structure of Spanish exports in recent years reveal a loss of importance of less technologically intensive sectors, in particular the food and chemical products sectors, while exports of transport equipment and electrical goods increased. The updating of productive equipment in these countries partly explains this result. On the import side, what most stands out is the sharp rise in Spanish purchases of transport equipment. The re-channelling of Germany's direct investment towards these countries, targeted above all at the transport equipment sector, would appear to explain this development (see Hoekman and Djankov, 1996). From this it can be inferred that the impact on Spain's trade position in the European market deriving from the

Table 8.8 Pattern of Spain's trade with Central and Eastern European countries

	Exports		Imports		RCAI	
	1986	1997	1986	1997	1986	1997
Sectors with strong demand and intensive technology	**19.7**	**21.8**	**30.5**	**39.9**	**–26.0**	**–9.4**
Electrical goods	1.6	12.8	8.5	23.2	–71.2	–8.8
Office and data-processing machines	0.2	1.8	1.6	2.0	–75.8	15.2
Chemical products	17.9	7.2	20.4	14.7	–11.2	–15.0
Sectors with moderate demand and intermediate technology	17.3	51.1	24.3	32.2	–21.4	40.9
Rubber and plastic products	3.5	3.0	2.3	3.3	15.5	14.5
Transport equipment	0.2	36.0	3.0	20.3	–90.1	45.4
Agricultural and industrial machinery	10.1	9.7	13.7	5.4	–19.2	45.8
Other manufactured products	3.5	2.4	5.3	3.2	–25.9	7.4
Sectors with weak demand and low technology	**63.0**	**27.1**	**45.2**	**27.9**	**11.9**	**18.7**
Textiles and clothing, leather and footwear	8.2	6.9	10.5	6.0	–17.0	26.6
Ferrous and non-ferrous ores and metals	18.5	1.1	1.8	4.4	81.1	–46.0
Non-metallic minerals and mineral products	2.1	7.9	4.7	3.9	–41.4	50.4
Paper and printing products	0.9	1.6	3.6	3.4	–62.6	–18.5
Food, beverages and tobacco	27.9	5.3	22.7	5.8	5.6	16.7
Metal products, exc. machinery and transport equipment	5.4	4.3	1.9	4.4	44.9	19.1
Total manufactured products	**100**	**100**	**100**	**100**		
Percentage of total Spanish manufacturing trade	0.4	0.5	0.6	0.7		

Source: Departamento de Aduanas; Instituto Nacional de Estadística; Banco de España.

integration of Eastern European countries will depend not only on the Spanish economy's initial advantage in the production of more complex goods with higher technological requirements, but also on its capacity to incorporate technological progress and to continue its drive to increase human capital. This would allow Spain to offset – via improvements in productivity – the enormous labour-cost advantages of these countries as well as the advantages they may acquire in future thanks to the growing presence of multinational companies in their economies.

8.4 Conclusions

This chapter has attempted to evaluate the current degree of integration of the fifteen EU countries in terms of their trade relations, with an emphasis on the nature and implications of trade integration in the case of the Spanish economy. Among the main findings, the following stand out:

- At present a large proportion of the trade of EU countries takes place with other member countries, a development that underscores the significant degree of integration achieved by these economies.
- The trade relations of the Spanish economy have also reflected this tendency towards intra-regional specialization. Integration has therefore greatly affected the geographical distribution of Spain's trade flows, leading to a notable increase in the weight of transactions with the other member countries, at the expense of the rest of the world. This re-orientation has been especially strong in the case of imports, owing to the dismantling of the trade barriers between the Spanish economy and its new trading partners. In the case of exports, however, the changes were fewer, owing to the European Union's preferential treatment of Spanish products as from the early 1970s, which meant that the concentration of Spanish sales in this market was already substantial at the time Spain became a member.
- The progressive intensification of trade relations was accompanied by a sharp deterioration in Spain's trade balance with all of these countries, except with Greece and Portugal. This development highlights the difficulties encountered by Spanish industry in adapting to a more competitive setting.
- In addition to the changes in the volume and geographical distribution of foreign trade, the sectoral composition of Spanish trade has also changed substantially. These changes have taken the form of a

progressive shift in the structure of sales abroad towards sectors with higher technological requirements and more dynamic demand, at the expense of less technology-intensive sectors and those with weak demand, which drove the industrialization process in the 1970s. As a result, over the past 12 years, Spain's trade pattern has moved closer to the average pattern prevailing in the more advanced EU countries.

- At the same time, intra-industrial trade with the other member countries has increased considerably. Yet the findings in this chapter indicate the persistence of the considerable predominance of intra-industrial trade where Spanish exports are characterized by lower quality than those of the other EU countries. All told, this underscores the need for a further drive to incorporate technical progress and to develop human capital in order to move the quality levels of Spanish products closer to those of the products imported from the more advanced EU countries.
- Finally, this chapter has analysed Spanish trade flows with the Central and Eastern European countries that plan to join the European Union in the near future. Although these countries still represent a fairly insignificant proportion of Spanish trade, the opening up and restructuring processes under way may have important consequences for European countries, because, first, they constitute very large markets with high potential demand and secondly, these countries may heighten the competitive pressures in certain sectors due to their low labour costs and the assistance they appear to be receiving from the foreign direct investment flows from the more advanced EU countries.

9
Direct Investment Flows

9.1 Introduction

International (foreign) direct investment can be broadly defined as the long-term (inward) capital flows used for exercising control of a business activity in a country other than that from which the investment activity originates.[1]

These international flows of capital are obviously very closely linked to the emergence and development of multinational firms. And, in a way, they are the product of the supranational geographical diversification of firms, either through the creation of new subsidiaries or through holdings in other already existing companies in the host country.

Their strong expansion since the mid-1980s has been a key element in the increasing globalization of international trade relations, spurred by the advances in information and communications technology, in which multinationals have played – and continue to play – a decisive role.

Likewise, the behaviour of these transnational firms – and, by extension, of international direct investment – has been affected by the proliferation of regional integration agreements in the world economy. In this respect, the process of Spain's accession to the European Union and the stronger integration of its partners since the entry into force of the Single European Act have inevitably had an impact on both the volume and the geographical and sectoral distribution of the capital flows to and from Spain. But, *a priori*, it is not easy to ascertain the exact nature of these effects.

Here several questions arise: (a) Have Spain's membership of the Community and the advances towards the integration of this area propitiated growth in the international direct investment received and made by Spain? (b) If so, has it intensified the investment flows with

Spain's EU partners or with non-Community countries? (c) What is the role played by those countries – especially Eastern European nations – with greater possibilities of joining the European Union, not only in Spain's ability to capture direct investment but also in Spanish investment abroad? In an attempt to answer these questions, the present chapter will analyse the behaviour and structure of the outward and inward direct investment flows of Community countries, and of Spain in particular, in the EU market and in third countries.

The chapter is organized in the following way. First, Section 9.2 briefly reviews the main theoretical contributions concerning the way in which an economic integration process influences the conduct of the partners' international direct investment. From there, Section 9.3 goes on to study the direct investment flows received by and issuing from Spain, as well as the changes which may have occurred during the period of its EU membership with respect to the relative importance of the flows whose origin or destination were the European Union. Likewise, an attempt is made to evaluate the possible diversion of these inward and outward capital flows produced by the increasing opening up of the European Union to Eastern European countries. Section 9.4 studies the geographical and sectoral pattern of Spanish investment flows with the European Union to learn whether Spain's integration with its Community partners is uniform or whether, on the contrary, investment is concentrated in just a few member countries. A final section summarizes the main conclusions.

9.2 Economic integration and international direct investment

When examining how regional integration agreements influence international direct investment flows, it must be borne in mind that these agreements produce an alteration in trade barriers and also – in the case of the creation of a single market – in the control of factor movements, which involves treating partners as favoured nations with respect to the rest of the world.

In any event, to ascertain the way in which integration agreements affect the volume, direction and composition of direct investment flows, we must first identify their determinants. Here, however, we run up against the problem that, despite a wealth of literature on international direct investment and the behaviour of multinational firms, the advances in this respect are far from satisfactory.

As readers will be aware, the first theoretical studies aimed at explaining the phenomenon of international direct investment were based on the assumption of perfectly competitive markets, and, by extension, assumed that markets would generate the necessary mechanisms to correct any imbalances in the countries' relative capital endowments. In this context, processes of international economic integration would be expected to encourage capital flows from areas with relatively abundant capital (in this case, the core EU countries) towards those where it is relatively scarce (here, the less developed EU partners)[2] until the marginal productivities of the factors and their remuneration eventually levelled out, which would also contribute to real convergence between the partners.

None the less, this concept of how an economy works is at several removes from reality, given the many widely known market imperfections, such as increasing returns to capital, the externalities associated with the spatial concentration of productive activity (the so-called economies of agglomeration), the differences in products and productive factors, the gaps in countries' technological capacities, and the restrictions on the international dissemination of technology. This set of circumstances is precisely what explains the large volume of international investment (contrary to the predictions of the more idyllic view, in which the countries' factor endowments become ever more similar) that flows to the more developed, OECD countries.[3]

In a framework that – appropriately – allows all the above-mentioned circumstances, the task of explaining international direct investment flows and estimating the effect of integration agreements on these flows becomes much more complicated. Thus, as to the possible motives for international direct investment, there is a wide range of hypotheses, all of which are encompassed in what Dunning (1974, 1980, 1993a) has called the 'eclectic theory' or the 'OLI paradigm', an acronym for the three explanatory factors: ownership, location and internalization. This paradigm postulates that firms become transnational owing to the confluence of ownership advantages, acquired through the generation of some type of intangible asset which local firms do not possess, and the exploitation of the host countries' location advantages – in sum, the advantages derived from internalization when imperfections exist in international markets, as is commonly the case.

Specifically, ownership advantages refer to the possession of intangible assets of diverse types – management capacity, market reputation linked to brands and/or, in particular, technological know-how –

which in general can be combined with other complementary advantages such as the exploitation of economies of scale.[4]

In turn, the reasons leading a firm to internalize the relations between production and sales centres located in different countries, and therefore to internationalize, are associated with situations of uncertainty and market failure, in which it is more advantageous to exploit ownership advantages directly than to make use of exports, technical-assistance contracts or other indirect channels. In this respect, the importance of intangible assets in the internationalization process, and the asymmetrical information problems involved in their transfer, make technology contracts a poor substitute for foreign investment.[5]

Finally, once the firm has decided to invest, the determinants of the choice of where to invest are those known in the OLI paradigm as location advantages. These can be summarized in the following points: labour cost advantages, availability of natural resources, geographical location, the existence of a large or expanding market, the presence of economies of agglomeration,[6] the incentives offered by the host country, and lastly, albeit without exhausting the list, the existence of historical or cultural – primarily language – ties.

Location advantages are precisely the ones which have been most affected by the unification of the market of the Fifteen. The elimination of intra-Community tariff barriers and other obstacles which had segmented the market – boosting its potential growth[7] – and the lifting of controls on capital movement have possibly had more impact on the decisions of multinational firms already located, or with plans to locate, in Europe than any other changes.

None the less, as Dunning (1993a) points out, the way to exploit the advantages of ownership and internalization has also changed. The reduction and, even more important, the elimination of the abovementioned market restrictions allow better harnessing of 'multi-establishment' economies of scale through the reorganization of economic activity, at both the territorial and the productive levels, to achieve greater efficiency. In any event, it is obvious that the way the factors described above are affected by an integration process will depend on the degree of integration attained and the specific characteristics of the countries involved.[8]

Moreover, when studying the changes in the international direct investment flows which may be induced by an integration process, it must be borne in mind that the strategic behaviour of multinational companies may differ greatly and may change in unpredictable ways when faced with the new market situation. In any case, there is reason to believe that economic integration is likely to encourage direct investment flows.

With respect to the reaction of non-Community investors, it is safe to argue that the European market's integration process, by eliminating intra-Community barriers and maintaining external ones, is an inducement for direct investment projects from the rest of the world to supply the market in a way that avoids the Community's external tariff.

As regards intra-Community direct investment flows, even though the unification of the European market may tend to discourage projects conceived as a defensive strategy in protected markets (because the elimination of trade barriers may favour the substitution of exports for capital movements), in general it will encourage more active investment by European companies by allowing fuller exploitation of the differences between the countries' factor endowments and the restructuring of the international investments of multi-establishment companies in order to take full advantage of economies of scale.[9]

To summarize, in theory we can expect integration to have a positive effect on both intra- and extra-Community investment flows, though it is unclear which of the two flows will be more affected.

9.3 Changes in the size and pattern of direct investment flows

In studying the changes in the pattern of Spain's inward and outward flows of international direct investment, it is important to consider the differences in their administrative treatment: whereas foreign investment had long been encouraged (since the end of the period of economic autarky), the Spanish government did not promote investment abroad until recent years. Upon joining the Community, Spain had to adjust its legislation to EU regulations to meet the terms of the Treaty of Accession and the provisions of the Single European Act.[10] Thus, it is only in recent years that the definition and treatment of both investment flows have become homogeneous.

The analysis of the aggregate direct investment flows received by and issuing from Spain draws on the information contained in the balance of payments compiled by the Bank of Spain,[11] because, even though the data present certain problems for comparisons over time,[12] they give a reasonably faithful idea of the trends.

As shown in Figure 9.1, Spain's inward and outward direct investment flows have traditionally been highly asymmetrical in their

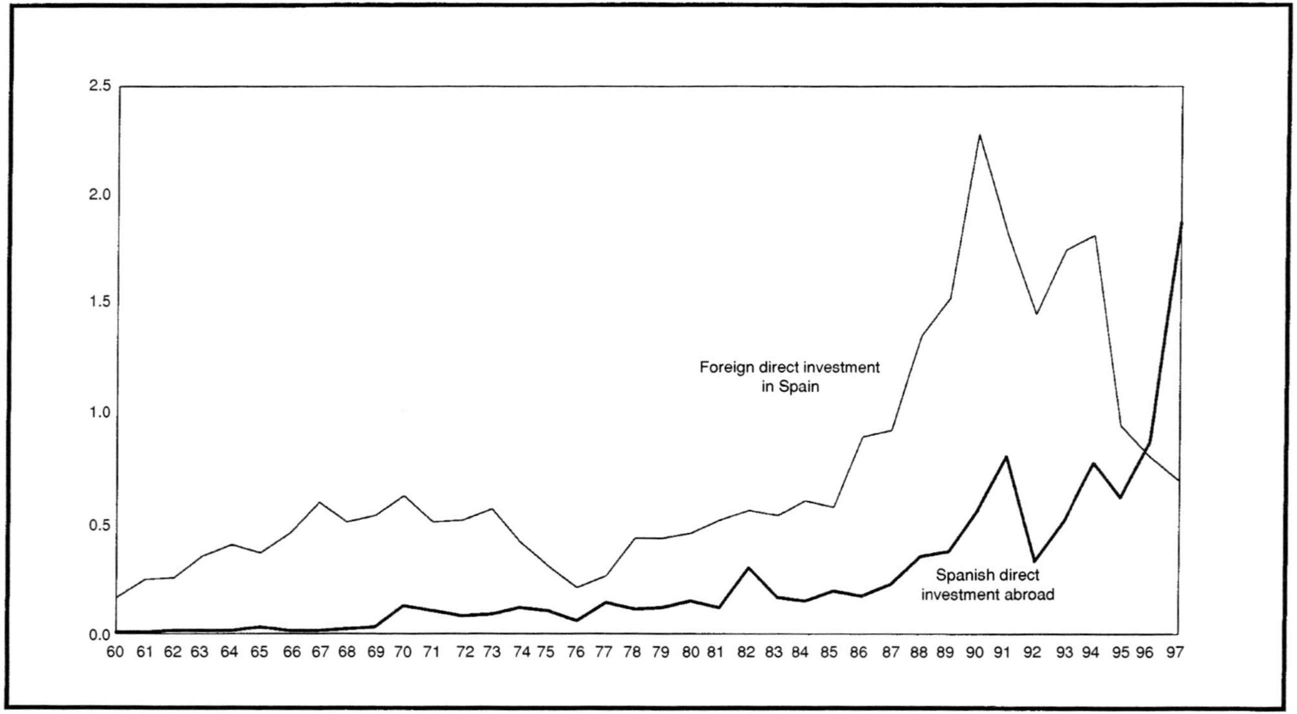

Figure 9.1 Spanish direct investment abroad and foreign direct investment in Spain (as % of GDP)

Source: Banco de España: *Registro de Caja*; Banco de España: *The Spanish Balance of Payments*; Departamento de Estudios Europeos, Fundación de las Cajas de Ahorros.

magnitude. This situation became even more pronounced in the years immediately after EU accession and later eased as a result of the decline in inflows and the rise in outflows. In fact, until the early 1990s, the profiles of the two flows over time are found to rise; afterwards, however, their behaviour is more erratic, and from 1995 onwards they have moved in opposite directions: direct investment received has plunged and investment made has grown spectacularly.

None the less, until the early 1990s the growth of Spanish investment flows – and inward flows in particular – was higher than that of world investment. This signified a notable increase in Spain's share as a recipient of direct investment between 1986 and 1990. In this respect, the econometric studies – Bajo and Torres (1992), Bajo and Sosvilla (1994), and Díaz de Sarralde and Martínez (1996) – conclude that Spain's EU accession is one of the determinants of the strong increase in the inward flow of foreign capital. These findings are in line with those obtained in other studies that evaluate the influence of the accession of Ireland and the United Kingdom to the European Union.

As to the role played by Spain as an issuer of direct investment, note that accession coincided with a sharp increase in capital outflows, spurred not only by more permissive legislation but also by the awareness of the government and economic agents of the need to strengthen international direct investment as a way of competing in an increasingly globalized international setting.

To compare the trends in Spain's international direct investment flows with those of the European Union and the world, we have constructed Table 9.1, in which several Eastern European countries (namely the Visegrad group formed by Slovakia, Hungary, Poland and the Czech Republic) are included as host areas, since they are Spain's possible competitors in capturing international capital, although at the same time they are potential markets for Spain's own foreign investment projects. A breakdown is also given of the least and most developed EU countries, with the former comprising Greece, Spain, Ireland and Portugal (C4) and the latter all others (C11).

The choice of the reference period, 1982–96, was dictated by the availability of data. In the breakdown into stages, the date of Spain's EU accession and the year 1991 were used as the criteria because, as seen above, the latter signals a significant break in the trend in Spain's direct investment flows, while it also marks the point when the transformation of Eastern European countries into market economies became more apparent.

Table 9.1 Geographical structure of international direct investment flows

		Countries issuing direct investment								
		Spain			European Union				World	
		1982–5	1986–90	1991–6	1982–5	1986–90	1991–5	1982–5	1986–90	1991–6
Countries receiving direct investment	EU	23.3	53.8	29.8	29.3	48.4	60.0	29.8	38.3	36.2
	C11*	16.7	42.4	18.8	22.4	39.3	50.4	24.4	32.0	31.1
	C4*	6.6	11.4	11.0	6.9	9.1	9.6	5.4	6.3	5.1
	Spain				**3.3**	**5.4**	**5.2**	**3.7**	**4.9**	**3.5**
	Visegrad**	0.0	0.0	0.3	0.0	0.2	3.0	0.0	0.2	2.2
	Rest of the world	76.7	46.2	69.9	70.7	51.4	37.0	70.2	61.5	61.6
	World	**100**	**100**	**100**	**100**	**100**	**100**	**100**	**100**	**100**

* C4 denotes Portugal, Greece, Spain and Ireland, and C11 the other EU countries.
** The Visegrad group is formed by Slovakia, Hungary, Poland and the Czech Republic.
Source: OECD: *International Direct Investment Statistics Yearbook*; Eurostat: *European Union Direct Investment Yearbook*; UN: *World Investment Report*; Departamento de Estudios Europeos, Fundación de las Cajas de Ahorros.

What first strikes us in Table 9.1 is that the patterns in Spain and the other EU countries coincide with the re-orientation of investment flows towards the Community market itself, and in particular towards the more developed countries, from 1986 onwards. None the less, in recent years the European Union's relative importance as the destination of Spanish investment has diminished substantially in favour of the growing share acquired by Latin America.[13] Moreover, the investments of the rest of the world also share increased interest in the EU market. Whereas in the years 1982–5 the EU attracted 23.3 per cent of Spanish investment, 29.3 per cent of that of the Fifteen and 29.8 per cent of that of the rest of the world, in the period 1991–6 these proportions rose to 29.8 per cent, 60 per cent and 36.2 per cent, respectively.

Restructuring and relocating the economic activities of already installed firms appears to be the main reason behind the growth of intra-Community capital flows (see Cantwell, 1992; United Nations, 1992; and Fernández and Myro, 1995). An alternative data source, which allows the validity of this idea to be tested, is the information on the mergers and acquisitions in which EU firms participated, which is published in the European Union's annual reports on competition. The Commission's data show that the reasons behind the decisions of EU firms to undertake this type of operation are, in order of importance, the search for new markets, expansion, and the streamlining of production.[14]

As to non-Community investors, Aristotelous and Fountas (1996) provide evidence that unification of the European market has been one of the determinants of the growth of non-Community investment in the European Union, particularly in the case of investment from the United States.[15]

As noted earlier – and also reflected in Table 9.1 – a common feature of the investment received by the European Union from countries both inside and outside the Community is its tendency to concentrate in the more developed member nations. This suggests the importance of economies of agglomeration – taking advantage of the externalities produced by the spatial concentration of production – which Krugman (1991) identifies as one of the essential factors in determining the most advantageous geographical location when firms internationalize their activities.

In this respect, some studies – De la Dehesa (1995), for example – have indicated the danger posed to the less developed EU economies by the fact that firms choose to invest in the richer regions with better capital endowments. This would contribute to the increase in the relative decapitalization of the peripheral areas and would therefore be a further obstacle to the difficult objective of achieving real convergence between the Fifteen.

A clear manifestation of the spatial concentration of capital in Europe, and economic wealth in general, is the strip 1500 kilometres long and 200 kilometres wide stretching from northern London to southern Milan, known as the 'hot banana' on account of its shape. This zone is distinguished from the other regions of the European Union not only by its higher degree of industrial concentration but also by its substantially higher per capita income. Furthermore, judging by the greater industrial concentration – as shown in Krugman (1991) – in the United States, the polarization of direct investment within the European Union could increase in the future.

The data on investment flows to Eastern European countries reflect their growth and point towards their possible substitutive role as a substitute for investment flows to Southern Europe. Spain's investment projects in these markets, while growing, are still insignificant.

Naturally it was not until the collapse of the communist system that this group of countries became relevant as a geographical destination for international direct investment projects. Thus, even though the short period of time elapsed since then precludes a well-founded forecast of the likely extent of the diversion of investment towards these emerging markets, the fact that during a period of slowing world direct investment flows such as 1991–6 these nations managed to increase notably the volume of funds received is a sign that the risk of this diversion effect may be significant.

Moreover, the probable incorporation of these countries into the European Union in the not-too-distant future only reinforces the idea of the threat they pose for the investment flows to Spain and other countries on the periphery of Europe. In this respect, Martín (1995c), after analysing the location advantages enjoyed by these countries vis-à-vis Spain, concludes that they have much lower labour costs[16] and a very attractive geographical position[17] for supplying the most prosperous area of the European Union; but it is also concluded that the Visegrad countries' advantages are at least partly offset by the large size of the Spanish market, its political stability, better infrastructure and – albeit with certain reserves arising from the comparison with countries, such as the Visegrad group, whose educational systems are very different – human capital. Meanwhile, Hunya (1996) argues that the Eastern European economies' wage and location advantages are particularly relevant, because the objective of many of the direct investment projects in these countries is to establish a platform for exports to the European market.[18]

Furthermore, the European Union has developed programmes to assist direct investment in the former communist countries of Central and Eastern Europe. This circumstance allows a certain parallel to be drawn between the European Union's measures with respect to these countries and the reconstruction policy implemented by the United States in Japan and Western Europe after the Second World War.

9.4 Changes in the geographical and sectoral pattern of direct investment flows

After seeing in the previous section that Spain's EU accession coincided with an intensification of inward and outward direct investment flows, and intra-Community ones in particular, this section analyses intra-Community flows in greater depth with a view to drawing conclusions about the different degree of integration that Spain has achieved with each of its EU partners via this channel.

As regards capital inflows to Spain from the European Union (see Table 9.2), it is clear that accession has not substantially altered the geographical pattern, because the countries representing the bulk of investment are still France, Germany, Holland and the United Kingdom.

The geographical distribution of Spanish direct investment in the European Union also has a similar structure before and after Spain's accession. Portugal, the United Kingdom, France, Belgium–Luxembourg and Holland absorbed most of Spain's investment abroad during the period.

None the less, these results should be viewed with some caution, because it is hard to ascertain either the origin or the final destination of Spanish investment when there are countries, as in the case of Belgium–Luxembourg, Holland and even the United Kingdom, whose more favourable tax conditions make them a more profitable platform for channelling investment to third countries, both within and outside the European Union. In addition to the relations with these countries, the case of Portugal is particularly striking, as it is the destination of more than 26 per cent of Spanish investment in the European Union. This situation is explained not only by Portugal's proximity but also by the technological lag of Portuguese firms, which allows Spanish investors to exploit certain ownership advantages, and finally by the policy of various major multinational companies of establishing subsidiaries in Spain for their subsequent installation in Portugal.

Table 9.2 Share of each EU country in Spanish direct investment flows

Foreign investment in Spain	Share			**Spanish investment abroad**	Share		
Country	1982–5	1986–90	1991–7	Country	1982–5	1986–90	1991–7
1. Austria	0.1	0.2	0.3	1. Austria	0.0	0.0	0.2
2. Belgium–Lux.	6.3	5.0	8.7	2. Belgium–Lux.	13.4	14.0	8.1
3. Denmark	1.4	0.8	0.9	3. Denmark	0.7	.2	–0.1
4. Finland	0.4	0.5	1.1	4. Finland	0.0	0.0	0.1
5. France	22.6	24.9	19.6	5. France	16.2	11.7	15.2
6. Germany	26.3	13.3	25.8	6. Germany	7.6	7.6	7.7
7. Greece	0.0	0.0	0.1	7. Greece	0.0	0.2	0.1
8. Holland	18.0	30.2	15.9	8. Holland	5.1	15.9	17.5
9. Ireland	0.8	0.1	1.2	9. Ireland	1.0	0.2	1.0
10. Italy	4.7	6.7	8.9	10. Italy	6.7	6.1	5.4
11. Portugal	0.1	0.4	3.3	11. Portugal	27.4	20.8	26.4
12. Sweden	2.6	2.1	1.1	12. Sweden	0.0	0.0	0.2
13. United Kingdom	16.7	15.8	13.1	13. United Kingdom	21.9	23.3	18.2
European Union	**100**	**100**	**100**	**European Union**	**100**	**100**	**100**
Share of direct investment from the EU	40.8	59.7	62.2	Share of direct investment in the EU	23.3	53.8	29.8

Source: OECD: *International Direct Investment Statistics Yearbook*; Dirección General de Política Comercial e Invesiones Extranjeras; Banco de España: *The Spanish Balance of Payments*; Departamento de Estudios Europeos, Fundación de las Cajas de Ahorros.

Table 9.3 provides a closer look at the role played by Spain in the capture and issue of direct investment flows from the standpoint of each EU country. As to Spain's position as a host country, Portuguese investment has acquired an extraordinary significance since the entry of the two countries into the European Union, with its share reaching 52.7 per cent in the period 1991–5. Also striking are the cases of Denmark and France, for whom Spain represents one of the main host countries of their direct investment.

As to Spain's investments in each member country, Portugal is the only one representing a fairly significant volume, while the percentages for the other EU countries are very small.

The last aspect we shall study in this chapter is the change in the pattern of the sectoral specialization of direct investment, which is in a way attributable to the process of European integration. To begin with, we should point out that it is not possible to establish *a priori* precise theoretical hypotheses on the influence exerted by regional integration agreements on the sectoral breakdown of direct investment flows.[19] Here again, we must study the data.

Moreover, the impossibility of using disaggregated data by sector according to the NACE-CLIO (25) classification for a period longer than the one presented in Table 9.4[20] – since 1988 – means that the periods before and after accession must necessarily be compared by referring exclusively to the major sectors. In this respect, other studies – Martín and Velázquez (1996b), Duce (1995), and Bajo and Torres (1992) – show that industry was the main destination of the direct investment received by Spain from the 1960s. These studies also indicate a decline in its relative importance, especially as from 1986. Thus, in the post-accession years, services became the most attractive branch for international investors.

This alteration in the sectoral patterns of investment might be interpreted as a consequence of European integration, because this process entails, among many other changes, the introduction of a significant measure of freedom for the services activities once protected by regulations, which in some cases even prevented the presence of foreign firms. Moreover, given the difficulty of trade in many services,[21] it is only logical to believe that liberalization processes have significantly affected their investment flows.

None the less, in recent years industry has regained a certain importance in the capture of foreign investment. Whereas in the period 1988–90 services absorbed 62.7 per cent of the direct investment

Table 9.3 Spain's share of the direct investment flows of each EU country

Proportion of direct investment issued				**Proportion of direct investment received**			
	Spanish share				Spanish share		
Country	1982–5	1986–90	1991–5	Country	1982–5	1986–90	1991–5
1. Austria	–3.3	0.0	3.3	1. Austria	0.0	0.0	0.2
2. Belgium–Lux.	–1.8	1.7	–1.1	2. Belgium–Lux.	0.0	1.4	–0.8
3. Denmark	5.4	4.2	12.1	3. Denmark	–4.6	–1.0	0.1
4. Finland	2.1	2.7	7.9	4. Finland	0.0	0.0	0.0
5. France	6.6	11.3	7.9	5. France	0.2	0.7	0.5
6. Germany	7.3	8.4	3.9	6. Germany	–0.5	2.5	–0.6
7. Greece	0.0	0.0	0.0	7. Greece	0.0	1.1	0.0
8. Holland	0.0	0.0	6.2	8. Holland	0.0	0.0	0.7
9. Ireland	0.0	0.0	0.0	9. Ireland	0.0	0.1	0.0
10. Italy	3.2	7.4	7.8	10. Italy	0.3	0.4	0.9
11. Portugal	2.3	39.0	52.7	11. Portugal	5.0	13.4	13.5
12. Sweden	1.4	2.7	–0.1	12. Sweden	0.0	0.0	0.0
13. United Kingdom	2.2	3.9	3.3	13. United Kingdom	0.4	0.3	0.1
European Union	**3.3**	**5.4**	**5.2**	**European Union**	**0.2**	**0.7**	**0.3**

Source: OECD: *International Direct Investment Statistics Yearbook*; Eurostat: *European Union Direct Investment Yearbook*; Departamento de Estudios Europeos, Fundación de las Cajas de Ahorros.

received by Spain from the European Union, between 1991 and 1997 they represented 49.8 per cent on average.

In manufacturing, the branches which have received the largest inflows of foreign capital from EU countries are, as shown in Table 9.4, the following: machinery, chemical products, food, and non-metallic mineral products. In other words, all those in which the inflow of foreign capital has traditionally been concentrated.

In the sectoral breakdown of Spain's direct investment in the European Union, we find that the proportion of investment in manufacturing sectors is still very small, and that services still predominate. Within the latter, telecommunications, banking, holding companies and trade services have been the most dynamic.[22]

9.5 Conclusions

This chapter has studied the impact that the process of Spain's integration in the European Union has had not only on the intensity of its investment flows but also on the geographical and sectoral pattern of these flows, arriving at the following conclusions:

- In the years since Spain joined the European Union, the inward and above all outward flows of capital in the form of direct investment have been particularly dynamic. But, more recently, there has been a fall in the investment received that contrasts sharply with the spectacular growth in Spain's investment abroad. Thus, in the period as a whole, the traditional asymmetry in Spain's role as a host (very significant) and an issuer (fairly modest) of direct investment flows has become less pronounced.
- The inward flows of foreign capital to Spain during the period largely originated in EU countries.
- There has been a concentration of investment within the European Union itself, not only in Spain but also in the other countries, especially in the markets of the more developed members. The latter situation highlights the importance of economies of agglomeration and, by extension, the risk that Europe's peripheral economies may find themselves no longer in the running as locations for international direct investment projects.
- In addition, the data suggest that Eastern European nations may become serious competitors of the Southern EU countries in the capture of foreign capital. The location advantages (geographical situation, low labour costs and cultural ties with the central EU

Table 9.4 Sectoral structure of Spain's direct investment flows with the EU

Investment received Sector NACE-CLIO (25)	1988–90	1991–7	**Investment issued** Sector NACE-CLIO (25)	1988–90	1991–7
Agriculture, forestry and fishery products	0.8	0.3	Agriculture, forestry and fishery products	0.8	0.2
Fuel and energy products	2.7	2.6	Fuel and energy products	3.5	2.0
Ferrous and non-ferrous ores and metals	0.4	0.5	Ferrous and non-ferrous ores and metals	0.0	0.7
Non-metallic minerals and mineral products	4.7	7.7	Non-metallic minerals and mineral products	3.1	0.8
Chemical products	5.6	8.6	Chemical products	1.2	1.3
Metal products, exc. machinery and transport equipment	1.5	1.1	Metal products, exc. machinery and transport equipment	0.3	0.2
Agricultural and industrial machinery	0.7	0.9	Agricultural and industrial machinery	0.2	0.3
Office and data-processing machines, precision and optical inst.	1.3	0.3	Office and data-processing machines, precision and optical inst.	0.5	0.2
Electrical goods	1.5	4.0	Electrical goods	0.9	2.1
Transport equipment	5.9	9.4	Transport equipment	1.1	0.4
Food, beverages and tobacco	3.5	7.6	Food, beverages and tobacco	6.5	4.3
Textiles and clothing, leather and footwear	0.7	0.8	Textiles and clothing, leather and footwear	0.2	0.4

Table 9.4 continued

Investment received Sector NACE-CLIO (25)	1988–90	1991–7	**Investment issued** Sector NACE-CLIO (25)	1988–90	1991–7
Paper and printing products	4.4	3.3	Paper and printing products	3.4	2.3
Rubber and plastic products	1.8	1.8	Rubber and plastic products	0.2	0.5
Other manufactured products	0.1	0.3	Other manufactured products	0.2	0.8
Building and construction	1.6	0.9	Building and construction	1.0	0.7
Recovery and repair services, wholesale and retail trade services	8.3	12.4	Recovery and repair services, wholesale and retail trade services	7.1	5.3
Lodging and catering services	2.0	1.8	Lodging and catering services	0.8	0.1
Inland transport services	0.4	0.4	Inland transport services	0.1	0.1
Maritime and air transport services	0.2	0.1	Maritime and air transport services	0.0	0.5
Auxiliary transport services	0.7	0.2	Auxiliary transport services	0.4	0.4
Communication services	0.0	0.5	Communication services	0.8	1.9
Services of credit and insurance institutions and other market services	51.1	33.6	Services of credit and insurance institutions and other market services	67.8	73.7
Non-market services	0.0	0.8	Non-market services	0.0	0.8
Total	**100**	**100**	**Total**	**100**	**100**

Source: Dirección General de Política Comercial e Inversiones Extranjeras; Departamento de Estudios Europeos, Fundación de las Cajas de Ahorros.

countries) which they already enjoyed appear to have been strengthened by the likelihood of their accession to the European Union in the years ahead. However, there are no signs of any notable efforts on the part of Spanish firms to take advantage of the opportunities opened up by the emergence of these former communist countries on the market.

- Even though Spain's direct investments abroad shifted in the direction of its European partners in the first few years of its EU membership, in more recent years several large-scale one-off operations in Latin America have reduced the European Union's weight in overall Spanish direct investment abroad.
- The geographical and sectoral pattern of investment relations with EU partners does not seem to have changed substantially, and not only have the main origins (destinations) of investment inflows (outflows) remained unchanged but also, broadly speaking, their sectoral distribution, albeit with the exceptions discussed.
- As a corollary to these conclusions, it would seem appropriate to consider the need for Spain to develop the location factors that would allow it to continue attracting foreign capital and hence to overcome the increasingly credible threat posed by other geographical destinations, in particular Central and Eastern European countries. Here it would seem essential for Spain to continue upgrading its transport infrastructure – to counteract the disadvantage of its peripheral location in Europe – and its human capital – to offset the clear labour-cost advantages of those countries. In any case, Spain should also attempt – with the same sense of anticipation as its EU partners – to take advantage of the opportunities offered by these emerging markets. With respect to these observations, we should add that the presence of firms abroad is an impetus for growth, because it is highly useful, indeed essential, for consolidating and enlarging external markets, as well as for reducing productive costs through the segmentation of different stages of the productive process and their location in more advantageous places.

10
Migratory Flows

10.1 Introduction

From the outset, the process of European integration has sought to eliminate all barriers to the free movement of workers. The Treaty of Rome, in article 48 and subsequent articles, establishes the freedom of movement for workers in what was then the European Economic Community, and it abolishes discrimination within the Community, based on their nationality, as regards access to employment, remuneration and work conditions. In practice, however, limitations still exist on the full exercise of this principle. Indeed, this is possibly one aspect of the European integration process in which least progress has been made.

Even though the signing of the Single European Act in 1986, the Schengen Agreements in 1985 and 1990 and the Maastricht Treaty in 1992 are landmarks in the creation of a genuinely common labour market in the countries that form the European Union – by incorporating the right to freedom of movement and establishment – the reticence of several member states with respect to uniformity of labour laws, social rights and migration policy continues to be an obstacle to the free movement of workers.[1]

Curiously, in contrast with the massive migration which took place in Europe in the 1950s and 1960s,[2] intra-Community migratory flows slowed practically to a halt in the mid-1970s, despite the progress in the liberalization of the movement of workers and the persistence of considerable differences in the levels of per capita income and welfare between EU countries. Coinciding with the decline in intra-Community migration, the European Union has experienced strong migratory pressures, primarily from countries in North Africa but, after the collapse of the Berlin Wall, from Eastern Europe as well.

These changes in the geographical structure of migratory flows have given rise to an abundance of studies, basically revolving around two questions: the reasons for the low mobility of workers within the European Union, and the possible implications of the coexistence of low intra-Community labour mobility and intense migratory pressures from third countries for the welfare of EMU member countries.

Among others, these questions will be addressed in the present chapter. Section 10.2 will briefly discuss the theoretical contributions as regards the determinants of international migratory flows, as well as the way in which these flows may be affected by economic integration agreements. Section 10.3 will then analyse some of the more relevant data on the scale of migratory flows within the Community and from third countries. Section 10.4 discusses the reasons behind the Community's low labour mobility and also its possible impact on the functioning of EMU, especially in the case of those partners, such as Spain, with lower income levels and higher unemployment rates. Finally, the closing section presents the main conclusions.

10.2 Economic integration and migratory flows

As noted in the previous chapter, the neo-classical model indicates that the lifting of barriers to trade and the free movement of factors, inherent in the processes of international economic integration which reach the stage of a single market, will lead to a relocation of workers from economies where labour is relatively abundant to those where labour is relatively scarce and, by extension, more highly remunerated. As described in Mundell (1957), movements of migrants (and capital) are seen as a substitute channel for trade for levelling out the relative prices of goods and factor remuneration between countries. In this respect – see Krauss (1974) – the studies note that the existence of non-tradable goods and services and/or trade barriers gives rise to factor mobility.

The conclusions reached in the neo-classical framework are nevertheless substantially altered when the existence of increasing returns to capital, economies of agglomeration, labour heterogeneity, technological differences between countries and, in consequence, imperfect competition are taken into consideration, as in the studies of Markusen (1983, 1988) and Ethier (1984, 1985). Indeed, once the existence of all these circumstances – which are, besides, quite consistent with reality – is allowed, it is possible to explain why international flows of labour (and capital) do not occur in accordance with countries' relative factor endowments.

More specifically, when there are substantive differences in workers' skills, the more qualified workers – as explained in Johnson (1980), Borjas (1987) and Razin and Sadka (1995), among others – will probably tend to be located in the same areas as capital – physical and especially technological capital – given the complementary relationship which appears to exist between technological and human capital. The outcome of this process is the phenomenon known as the 'brain drain' that occurs in the less developed countries.

On this basis, it can therefore be explained why skilled labour would tend to concentrate in the core EU countries, which have a greater technological capacity and attract a larger proportion of international investment. By contrast, unskilled labour would tend to relocate in the opposite direction or to remain immobile (see Faini, 1995).

Only naturally, the prognoses based on these two lines of theoretical thought on the meaning and implications of full labour mobility within the European Union differ greatly.

Those who postulate that, were the *de facto* obstacles to migration within the European Union eliminated, labour would relocate according to the member countries' relative factor endowments (and thus from the less to the more developed economies) argue that migration would act as a vehicle for improving the real convergence between EU countries. However, the prognoses derived from the models which incorporate many elements in addition to relative factor endowment to explain migratory flows would be much less categorical.

So far we have summarized the main theoretical contributions that forecast the existence of labour flows in response to the removal of legal impediments to the free movement of workers. But note that there are still numerous obstacles of diverse character which limit these movements, and these will be analysed in Section 10.4. We shall first take a closer look at the changes in intra- and extra-Community migratory flows in recent years.

10.3 Intensity of migratory flows

Even though the best approach would be to analyse the movements of workers, because of statistical deficiencies we have no choice but to study migratory flows as a whole. Since the constitution of the single market, most of the administrative procedures required for undertaking certain labour activities in a Community country other than the country of origin have disappeared, and data can no longer be obtained from the registries which previously contained information on the migratory flows of each country. Information on foreign members of the labour force now comes from the labour force surveys carried out by all European countries, but their breakdown by nationality is very limited. And so, as is often the case, instead of confining our analysis to the movements of workers, we shall have to refer to movements in the population – in other words, migration as a whole – and the related information that can be extracted from population statistics.

By examining this information – shown in a systematic form in Table 10.1 – we find that in the last year for which data are available – 1995 – the number of foreign residents, of both Community and non-Community origin, in the European Union represented 4.7 per cent of the population. For Spain, however, the proportion was much lower, at around 1.2 per cent, in line with Spain's lower degree of economic development in relation to that of its EU partners.[3]

The countries in which the foreign population accounts for a large percentage are, by order of importance, Luxembourg (32.6 per cent), Belgium (9.1 per cent), Austria (9 per cent), Germany (8.6 per cent) and France (6.3 per cent). At the other extreme, in addition to Spain, are Finland (1.2 per cent), Italy (1.2 per cent), Greece (1.5 per cent), Portugal (1.6 per cent) and Ireland (2.7 per cent), precisely those countries where migratory flows were strongest in the 1960s.

Nevertheless, these figures are drastically lower if only Community immigrants are considered. Not including the case of Luxembourg (where 29.5 per cent of the population is from another EU country, Portugal in particular), immigrants from EU countries represent a fairly small percentage of the population in even the main host countries: Belgium (5.5 per cent), France (2.3 per cent), Germany (2.2 per cent) and Sweden (2.0 per cent).

If we compare these percentages with those of 1986, we find that the percentage of Community citizens residing in another EU country has generally remained stable or has even diminished, as in the case of France, one of the major host countries, possibly because of government policies promoting the return of immigrants to their countries of origin.

What is more, the countries with the largest migratory flows in the 1960s – Portugal (with a negative migratory balance of 1.2 million people), Italy (1 million) and Spain (0.8 million) – witnessed a significant repatriation of emigrants during the 1980s. This is eloquently exemplified by the fact that workers returning to their countries of origin accounted for nearly 50 per cent of the migratory flows in the 1980s (see Eurostat, 1995).

Table 10.1 Population of EU countries by nationality

	National citizens		From other EU countries		From the rest of Europe		From Africa		From the rest of the world	
Country	1986	1995	1986	1995	1986	1995	1986	1995	1986	1995
1. Austria	94.3	91.0	1.3	1.4	2.1	4.9	0.6	0.2	1.7	2.5
2. Belgium	90.9	90.9	5.9	5.5	0.2	0.2	1.6	1.9	1.4	1.5
3. Denmark	97.9	96.2	0.5	0.9	0.7	0.7	0.1	0.3	0.8	1.9
4. Finland	99.3	98.8	0.2	0.3	0.2	0.6	0.1	0.1	0.2	0.2
5. France	93.2	93.7	2.8	2.3	0.3	0.3	2.8	2.9	0.9	0.8
6. Germany	94.2	91.4	1.8	2.2	1.3	2.5	0.2	0.4	2.5	3.5
7. Greece	99.1	98.5	0.3	0.4	0.1	0.4	0.1	0.1	0.4	0.5
8. Holland	96.2	95.1	1.2	1.3	0.2	0.2	0.9	1.3	1.5	2.1
9. Ireland	97.6	97.2	1.9	2.0	0.1	0.2	0.1	0.1	0.3	0.4
10. Italy	99.6	98.8	0.2	0.2	0.1	0.2	0.1	0.4	0.0	0.4
11. Luxembourg	74.0	67.4	24.0	29.5	1.0	1.7	0.2	0.2	0.8	1.2
12. Portugal	99.2	98.4	0.2	0.4	0.0	0.0	0.4	0.7	0.2	0.5
13. Spain	99.1	98.8	0.5	0.6	0.1	0.0	0.0	0.2	0.3	0.4
14. Sweden	95.8	93.9	1.9	2.0	0.7	1.9	0.2	0.3	1.4	1.9
15. United Kingdom	97.0	96.4	1.3	1.6	0.2	0.2	0.2	0.4	1.3	1.4
European Union	**96.3**	**95.3**	**1.5**	**1.5**	**0.5**	**0.9**	**0.6**	**0.8**	**1.1**	**1.5**

Source: Eurostat: *Statistiques Démographiques*; Eurostat: *Migration Statistics*; Departamento de Estudios Europeos, Fundación de las Cajas de Ahorros.

In short, recent intra-Community population movements have been very small and have been determined by movements which took place in earlier periods. It is worth noting therefore that the facts have so far confounded the expectations existing prior to the constitution of the single market, of probable massive emigration from the less developed member countries to the core EU economies.

Hence the focus of attention in migratory matters has shifted towards the study of immigrants from third countries, who accounted for 3.2 per cent of the EU population in 1995. The countries with the largest non-EU immigrant population are, by order of importance, Austria (7.6 per cent), Germany (6.4 per cent), Sweden (4.1 per cent), France (4.0 per cent), Holland (3.6 per cent) and Belgium (3.6 per cent). In the less developed EU countries, this proportion is much smaller, at around 1 per cent, similar to the percentage of immigrants of EU origin. In the specific case of Spain, the proportion of non-EU immigrants stands at around 0.6 per cent, according to the latest available data.

Notably, with respect to the origin of non-EU immigration, Eastern European countries have accounted for an increasingly large share in recent years. Germany and Austria have been the main host countries, and this has led to a tightening in their immigration policies. In view of this, expected EU enlargement to include these emerging market economies will potentially entail massive emigration from Eastern to Western Europe.[4]

In fact, even though the information here refers to 1995, and the inflow of labour from the former communist countries of Europe only gathered force after the collapse of the Berlin Wall in 1989, the increase in migratory flows has been so intense that the population of this origin now numbers the same as that of more traditional origins. While there are still other fairly sizeable groups of non-Community immigrants (in particular North Africans and Turks), their growth has been more moderate in recent years. Understandably, immigration policies, albeit restrictive, have been less so with respect to immigrants from Eastern Europe, considering their greater cultural affinity and the expectations about the incorporation of their countries into the European Union in the not-too-distant future.

To summarize, recent European migratory flows have reflected a notable duality: low mobility between Community countries (with returning emigrants predominating), and strong population pressures from third countries, basically Eastern Europe and also, though to a lesser extent, North Africa, despite the special stringency of EU immigration policy towards them.

10.4 Causes and consequences of low labour mobility

In what we have seen so far, it is striking that the period characterized by greater 'legal' freedom of movement for workers between EU countries and by a notable reduction in the cultural differences between them coincided with a drastic decline in labour mobility in comparison with what occurred three decades ago in the same scenario. Moreover, a comparison between the situations in Europe and the United States, where there are also notable differences in per capita GDP between one state and another, only reinforces the diagnosis of the low mobility of Europe's population. This explains the many studies which have addressed this phenomenon, exploring its causes and also analysing its possible consequences for the future of economic and monetary union.

As underscored in the economic literature on migration, the main reason that appears to motivate workers to move to another country is the possibility of bettering their economic situation. And, as we have said, this is why it is so surprising that, in a group of countries such as the European Union, marked by such substantial economic differences, there has been no population shift towards areas with higher per capita income levels.

Recall, in this respect, that in 1997 the average per capita GDP of the three least developed EU countries (Greece, Portugal and Spain) was around 73 per cent of the Community's. Several recent studies – Faini and Venturini (1994) – argue that European migratory flows have slackened over time because the peripheral European countries, which were the focal point of emigration to the more advanced economies in the 1960s and 1970s, have by now acquired a sufficient level of development that provides a reasonable standard of living for most of the population. In other words, they maintain that there is a 'threshold effect' or, what is the same, a minimum income level beyond which emigration rates decline drastically. Specifically, the aforementioned study estimates this threshold at an average income level of around 5000 euro (in 1997 euro), a level not attained by the countries of Eastern Europe and North Africa but amply surpassed by the less developed EU countries.[5]

In this vein, Razin and Sadka (1995) point out that the spread of the welfare state, and in particular the mechanisms of unemployment assistance applied in Southern Europe, has led to an increase in the wage reserve, which has acted as a disincentive to emigration.

Zimmermann (1995) suggests, however, that the main reason behind the standstill of European migration is the high unemployment registered in recent years in the countries that were once the preferred destination of emigrants, and, in consequence, the radical change in their immigration policies. In this respect, it is pointed out that, whereas in the 1960s the more advanced European countries – mainly France and Germany, which then enjoyed a situation of full employment – developed, in collaboration with local authorities, a system of recruiting labour in the Mediterranean region, once the unemployment problem became apparent not only did these countries halt their policies of promoting immigration, but they also introduced programmes to encourage immigrants to return to their countries of origin.

In the same study by Zimmermann (1995), another cause adduced for the decline in intra-Community migratory flows is their replacement by non-Community migration from countries less developed than Southern European economies and, in consequence, characterized by a supply of cheaper labour willing to accept poorer working conditions.

Several studies, such as Straubhaar and Wolter (1996) and Razin and Sadka (1995), also note that the rigidities in EU labour markets may explain the phenomenon of immobility, given that the differences in unemployment rates are not passed through to greater wage differentials conducive to migration.

Another possible inhibiting factor in European labour mobility is, as Gros (1996) points out, the housing market's lack of flexibility, which in varying degrees affects all of Europe. Briefly stated, the problem lies both in the negligible degree of adjustment in housing prices to market conditions and in the preference in some countries for ownership over rentals. This entails an added cost that workers must assume in the event of a move and therefore has a negative influence on decisions to emigrate.

Together with these explanations linked to economic determinants, there are others which refer to psychological and cultural factors. Language differences and the idiosyncrasies of each country naturally represent an obstacle to the mobility of workers. The importance of these differences is evidenced, as shown in Daveri and Faini (1996), in the fact that the massive European migrations of the 1960s led to the burgeoning of areas largely inhabited by immigrants from a single country. Examples are the concentration of Italian immigrants in neighbourhoods of several European cities, forming 'little Italies', and the large Portuguese colony in Luxembourg. The reason for this behaviour lies in the fact that – as Carrington, Detragiache and Vishwanath

(1996) sustain – the concentration of immigrants of a given nationality in a country reduces the cost not only of gathering information on the place of destination but also of adapting to the new environment.

In any case, these arguments of a sociological character, while useful for understanding certain patterns in migratory flows, do not help explain why recent decades have seen a halt in the intra-European migration of earlier decades.

After reviewing the principal reasons advanced to explain the current low labour mobility in Europe, both in relation to that of the 1960s and in comparison with the mobility in other integrated markets such as the United States, it is worth asking what consequences this situation is likely to have in the short and long run.

First of all, we might note that low labour mobility prevents the mechanism that has historically levelled out the per capita income of different countries from coming into play. Without migration, the convergence in per capita GDP must basically be achieved through stronger economic growth in the less developed countries, because the only population-related mechanism capable of acting as a channel for narrowing per capita income gaps is a reduction in birth rates and, by extension, population growth in countries with a lower degree of development. Moreover, even though this has in fact occurred in recent years, the impact on real convergence is negligible.

Another very important implication of low labour mobility is that, since factor movements in general, and migratory flows in particular, are a substitute for exchange-rate movements, as Schmidt and Straubhaar (1995) argue, their absence might make it more difficult and costlier to cope with the asymmetrical shocks which could arise in the context of EMU because of the disappearance of the exchange rate as an adjustment mechanism. De Grauwe and Van Haverbecke (1993), in a study addressing this question in EU countries, find that, whereas on a regional scale the movement of labour has been the main adjustment mechanism for shocks, on a national plane the adjustment to specific problems has been achieved through the exchange rate, given people's reluctance to move.

Other studies, such as that of Blanchard and Katz (1992), pursue this idea further, having found that the geographical rigidity of European labour is much greater than that of the United States, where adverse regional shocks have been offset by migration between states. In this respect, Decressin and Fatás (1995) show that changes in the geographical structure of the demand for labour in Europe have been accompanied not by compensatory labour flows, but rather by an adjustment in the participation rates of older workers in the labour market, which has contributed to the slowing in the convergence process.

None the less, this line of argument is disputed in several recent studies, such as those of Gros (1996) and Straubhaar and Wolter (1996), which conclude that Europe's low labour mobility has positive aspects from the perspective of EMU. Their position is that if labour mobility in Europe were to increase, it would very probably take a form contrary to that indicated by the relative endowment gaps between one country and another. According to these studies, the most plausible outcome is that more skilled labour would move from the less developed to the more advanced European economies, because in the latter – by virtue of the economies of agglomeration created around their stronger activity and better endowment of physical and technological capital – productivity and by extension the remuneration of skilled workers would be higher than in the peripheral countries. For this reason, Gros (1996) and Straubhaar and Wolter (1996) suggest that an increase in European migratory flows would be of little help in overcoming asymmetrical shocks that may occur in EMU. In any event, these studies have a highly speculative element, and the dominant line of thought is still the one described earlier, namely that the absence of intra-Community migration signifies the lack of an instrument for cushioning the problems derived from specific shocks which may occur within the context of EMU.

In this situation, policies that help narrow the differentials in per capita GDP in the European Union (see Straubhaar, 1988), such as those implemented through the Structural and Cohesion Funds, gain greater significance.

In essence, these measures seek to support initiatives that promote stronger growth in EU countries with lower income levels by contributing to their development and their capacity to attract new investment. The objective is to achieve convergence in income without the presence of large migratory flows that could mean very high adaptation costs. But, for such measures to fulfil this role and at the same time buffer the effects of possible asymmetrical shocks in EMU, they would have to be increased substantially in the years ahead. Similarly, Straubhaar and Zimmermann (1993) propose a policy similar to the one described for the less developed Community partners in order to halt the population pressure exerted by third countries, although here they also propose the implementation of measures restricting these migratory flows.

10.5 Conclusions

- Since its creation, the present European Union has pursued complete freedom of movement for goods and factors. None the less, there are still several impediments to their full mobility, especially in the case of the labour factor.
- In any event, as this chapter has observed, intra-Community migration has declined radically despite the greater legal freedom for workers to move within the European Union. What is more, the less developed countries with relatively abundant labour have not issued migratory flows, but instead have seen a return of the workers who emigrated to the more developed European countries in the past.
- In addition to the labour immobility between EU countries, the European Union faces pressure exerted by immigrants from Eastern Europe and North Africa, which has led to a tightening of the immigration policies of member states.
- Many studies have tried to ascertain the causes of this situation and, more important, its impact as regards achieving real convergence in the context of EMU. The findings of these studies suggest that the main reasons behind low intra-Community labour mobility are: the attainment – even by the poorer European partners – of an income threshold that discourages emigration, the existence of high unemployment levels in the potential host countries, the application in these countries of active policies to discourage immigration, the presence of third-country migratory flows that tend to act as a 'buffer' in intra-Community migration, the spread of the welfare state in countries which would otherwise be issuers of emigrants, and the rigidity of labour and housing markets.
- In addition to these factors there are others of a psychological and cultural nature that also stifle mobility, including in particular the existence of important language and cultural barriers, unlike the situation in North America, where impediments of this kind are notably milder.
- As to the consequences, it seems clear – in the light of historical experience – that the convergence process in terms of per capita income in the new Europe will be delayed by the lack of an adjustment mechanism in the form of labour mobility. Moreover, the theory of optimum currency areas highlights the importance of factor movements as an adjustment mechanism for possible asymmetrical shocks. The studies differ, however, when it comes to

evaluating the nature of migration and the direction it would take if migratory flows in Europe were to increase. Even though the majority suggest that these flows would be similar to those of the past and would therefore help combat specific shocks to partners with weaker economies, several recent studies postulate just the opposite.

- Consequently, some studies argue that EU policy should focus on promoting the growth of countries with lower per capita income levels via the Community budget. In this way, the advantages offered by the less developed EU countries as regards the localization of productive activity and their attractiveness to foreign capital could be enhanced, thereby easing the substantial income differences which, as seen in other sections of this book, still persist within the European Union. This is also the policy proposed for those non-Community countries which not only exert greater immigration pressure on the European Union but are also more important from the standpoint of Europe's strategic policy.

11
The Community Budget and its Functions

11.1 Introduction

One of the main characteristics of the European integration process has been the scant concordance between the objectives proposed and the actual development of the Community budget to fulfil them.[1]

In the period analysed and also before, the Community authorities have intervened in the member countries' economic activity more through regulatory actions than through the budget. This can be seen in the Single European Act of 1986, with its blueprint for the single market, and in the Treaty on European Union of 1992, which establishes the economic and monetary unification process.

Yet the budget is a kind of barometer of the degree of EU governments' 'European commitment', because it tends to express the extent to which the member countries are willing to cede sovereignty, and it therefore constitutes an essential ingredient for the success of Europe's integration project.

This chapter begins with an analysis of the budget's size in relation to the member states' national budgets and other defining features, in order to assess its capacity to fulfil the functions – stabilizing, allocative and redistributive – that theory has traditionally recognized all budgets as having. It also examines the terms of the debate on the appropriateness of reducing the degree of decentralization of fiscal policy, an issue not without political undercurrents.

Specifically, the sections below examine the trends in the size and composition of the Community budget between 1986 and 1997, as regards both expenditure (Section 11.3) and revenue (Section 11.4). On the basis of the information on the resources received from, and the funds contributed to, the Community budget for each of the member countries, Section 11.5 then seeks to evaluate budgetary policy from the perspective of economic and social cohesion. Section 11.6 presents the Community budget's financial perspective for the period 2000–2006 as formulated by the European Commission in Agenda 2000, which was approved at the summit held in Berlin in March 1999. The chapter closes with the usual conclusions.

11.2 Main characteristics and functions of the Community budget

Since the signing of the Treaty of Rome in 1957, the Community budget has undergone successive reforms.[2] In its present form, the budget reflects all EU revenue and expenditure, with the exception of the operations of the European Coal and Steel Community (ECSC), the European Development Fund (EDF), the New Community Instrument (NCI) for the promotion of investment, the projects of the European Investment Bank (EIB), and other minor ones.

The main features of the EU budget are its complex compiling procedure, its small size, and the requirement that it be balanced. To a great extent these features are explained by the involvement of the member countries' governments in shaping it, which raises a problem of jurisdiction that is played out against the backdrop of a debate on whether the overriding concept is subsidiarity, signifying a more citizen-friendly administration, or unity, which gives greater preponderance to the European Union.

The first of the above-mentioned features – the complexity of the compiling process – is evidenced in the stages involved in producing the budget. The process begins with the Commission, which draws up a preliminary draft that is sent to the European Council. In the second stage, the Council prepares a draft that it sends to the European Parliament for amendments. In the third stage, the Council deliberates on the draft budget and then returns it to the Parliament for definitive approval.

In addition, the EU budget is subject to controls via two channels: the internal control of expenditure by each institution, with its own auditor, and external control, exercised jointly by the European Parliament, which has political control, and the Court of Auditors, which oversees the legality and proper management of the budget.

The second feature – the budget's small size – is clearly evident when we compare the magnitude of the Community budget with the member states' government expenditure and GDP,[3] as shown in Table 11.1. Thus in 1997 the ratio of Community expenditure to GDP was only 1.14 per cent. Furthermore, in the period 1986–97 its growth was insignificant. This stands in contrast not only to the progress made in European integration in the same period (the market's unification and the substantial advance towards EMU) but also to the emergence of the Community objective of economic and social cohesion with its own legislation (in both the Single European Act and the Maastricht Treaty).

Finally, the third defining feature of the budget is that it must be balanced, which means that the European Union is not authorized to resort to debt to cover expenditure.[4]

In sum, taking these features of the EU budget as a whole, it might be argued that they greatly limit its capacity to carry out the functions that theory traditionally assigns to public finances.

Thus, first of all, it is clear that the budget is practically incapable of acting as an instrument of economic stabilization. Indeed, for the Community budget to fulfil this function efficiently, its size would have to be increased, and above all, some way of adjusting its balance according to the needs of stabilization policy would have to be allowed. Specifically, this would involve making expenditure

Table 11.1 Community budget expenditure

Year	Total expenditure (millions of 1997 euro)	As % of national expenditure	As % of Community GDP	Expenditure per capita (1997 euro)
1986	54 420	2.1	1.00	169
1987	52 882	2.0	0.96	164
1988	59 405	2.2	1.04	184
1989	56 295	2.0	0.95	173
1990	57 664	2.0	0.95	176
1991	65 933	2.2	1.05	191
1992	69 644	2.2	1.11	201
1993	73 659	2.3	1.21	212
1994	66 140	2.1	1.06	190
1995	71 521	2.1	1.06	192
1996	80 339	2.3	1.16	215
1997	83 956	2.3	1.14	224
1998*	85 119	2.4	1.15	227
1999**	86 321	2.4	1.13	229

* 1998 budget.
** 1999 preliminary draft budget.

Source: European Commission: *The Community Budget: The Facts in Figures.*

anticyclical and revenue procyclical to enable the budget to act as an automatic stabilizer.[5]

Secondly, as to the budget's allocative function, we need only recall that allocation is affected more by regulations than by the rendering of public goods charged to the Community budget.[6]

Thirdly, the redistributive function, though also constrained by the budget's small size, is the most centralized of the three, albeit only in its geographical facet.

Note that there is no generally accepted criterion for determining the appropriate scope of each of these functions in the Community budget. On the contrary, it is a controversial topic within the general debate over the centralization versus decentralization of fiscal policy. Though long-standing, this debate has recently intensified as the institutional and operating arrangement of EMU monetary policy has taken shape. The contrast now existing between a unified monetary policy and a highly decentralized fiscal policy is certainly controversial.

Advocates of greater centralization of EMU fiscal policy advance the following as arguments: the stabilizing effects to counter asymmetrical shocks, the internalization of the externalities produced by the member states, the greater discipline in terms of debt and the budget deficit as a percentage of GDP, and the improvement in allocative and redistributive efficiency.[7] By contrast, those who favour the maintenance of decentralization argue that the stabilizing function of fiscal policy is more efficiently carried out at the national level. None the less, they generally acknowledge that the stability pact, by its nature, leaves countries with very little room to exercise this function.

After briefly examining the terms of the debate on the appropriate degree of autonomy for Community fiscal policy within EMU, we shall now study the actual extent of this autonomy in recent years. We shall focus our analysis on the distributive facet because, as we have already mentioned, from a territorial standpoint this is where Community policy has had the greatest impact. From this vantage we shall first address how the size and the composition of Community expenditure and revenue have evolved since 1986, the year of Spain's accession to the Community.

11.3 Distribution of expenditure

Since 1986 the composition of expenditure in the Community budget has undergone very substantial changes. The chief one, as seen in Table 11.2, has been the steady decline in the relative weight of its

Table 11.2 Changes in the composition of Community expenditure (% of total expenditure)

	1986	1987	1988	1989	1990	1991	1992	1993	1994	1995	1996	1997	1998*	1999**
General budget														
1. EAGGF-Guarantee	61.7	63.3	62.0	57.7	56.2	56.5	51.4	52.4	53.6	50.4	50.0	49.6	47.7	46.3
2. Structural Measures	15.8	16.2	15.1	18.8	21.0	25.4	30.2	30.7	25.8	28.1	31.1	32.2	33.4	35.2
• Structural funds	15.8	16.2	15.1	18.8	21.0	22.6	25.9	26.8	21.3	22.5	25.5	26.0	26.1	27.4
(a) EAGGF-Guidance	2.2	2.2	2.7	3.2	4.0	3.8	4.7	4.4	4.0	3.7	4.3	4.4	4.1	4.4
(b) ERDF	6.8	7.1	7.0	9.3	10.0	11.5	14.1	14.3	10.3	12.2	13.5	14.1	14.1	14.6
(c) ESF	6.8	6.9	5.4	6.3	7.0	7.3	7.1	8.1	7.0	6.6	7.7	7.5	7.9	8.4
• Cohesion Fund								1.2	1.4	2.5	2.4	2.8	3.1	3.3
• FIFG									0.6	0.4	0.5	0.6	0.5	0.6
• Others						2.8	4.3	2.7	2.5	2.7	2.9	2.8	3.7	3.9
3. R&D	2.2	2.7	2.7	3.6	3.9	3.1	3.1	3.3	4.0	3.6	3.7	3.7	3.5	3.5
4. External Actions	3.0	2.2	1.8	2.5	3.1	4.0	3.5	4.3	5.0	5.0	4.9	4.8	5.3	5.2
5. Administrative Expenditure	4.3	4.7	4.5	4.9	5.1	4.8	4.7	5.0	5.8	5.7	5.1	5.1	5.1	5.0
6. Repayments and others	9.8	7.7	10.4	8.9	7.3	3.5	3.2	1.4	2.2	4.5	3.0	2.6	2.5	2.4
Total	**96.8**	**96.8**	**96.5**	**96.4**	**96.6**	**97.3**	**96.1**	**97.1**	**96.4**	**97.3**	**98.0**	**98.0**	**97.5**	**97.6**
Non-budgetary operations														
EDF	2.4	2.3	2.8	3.1	2.8	2.1	3.2	2.0	2.9	2.3	1.7	1.4	2.3	2.2
ECSC	0.8	0.9	0.7	0.5	0.6	0.6	0.7	0.9	0.7	0.4	0.3	0.6	0.2	0.2
Total Community expenditure	**100**	**100**	**100**	**100**	**100**	**100**	**100**	**100**	**100**	**100**	**100**	**100**	**100**	**100**

* 1998 budget.
** 1999 preliminary draft budget.

Source: European Commission: *The Community Budget: The Facts in Figures*.

most sizeable item: the expenditure of the European Agricultural Guidance and Guarantee Fund (EAGGF), Guarantee Section, in other words, expenditure to finance the main line of action of the common agricultural policy (CAP): prices and markets.

Behind the reduction in the budgetary weight of the EAGGF-Guarantee's expenditure lie various reforms in the CAP whose purpose was to check the severe financial problems arising from the many inefficiencies – primarily, loss of international competitiveness and the build-up of surpluses – associated with its markedly interventionist and protective nature.

The effects of the CAP reforms, and specifically the greater emphasis on structural measures as a way of improving the efficiency of farms, are also evidenced in the increased weight of the expenditure of EAGGF-Guidance (included in the structural funds).[8] All in all, the financing of the CAP and of the EAGGF-Guarantee's measures in particular is still the priority destination of the Community budget's expenditure.

Second in importance in the volume of expenditure comes under the heading of Structural Measures, consisting of the structural funds – the European Regional Development Fund (ERDF) and the European Social Fund (ESF), in addition to the above-mentioned EAGGF-Guidance – and of the Cohesion Fund and Financial Instrument for Fisheries Guidance (FIFG).

Structural measures as a whole have the common objective of financing policies that promote real convergence, or, in the Community jargon, economic and social cohesion within the European Union. Note, too, that the projects covered by 'Structural Measures' are jointly financed by the beneficiary member states. In short, the aim is for these funds to comply with the principle of additionality to prevent them from becoming a mere substitute for national structural assistance.[9]

On examining – in Table 11.2 – the trends in the proportion of expenditure absorbed by all Structural measures, which increased nearly twofold in the period, from a share of 15.8 per cent of total expenditure in 1986 to 32.2 per cent in 1997, we see, first, that the importance of this heading as a whole increased, and secondly, that new instruments emerged. The first of these observations reflects the reforms of the structural funds in 1988 and 1993,[10] while the second is linked to the approval of the Cohesion Fund[11] and the creation of the Financial Instrument for Fisheries Guidance (FIFG).

These developments signal an increasing sensitivity to distributive questions in the course of the integration process and in the four enlargements of the Community. It was, in fact, in the framework of the Single European Act that the structural funds were reformed and substantially increased, and in the context of the Treaty on European Union that the creation of the Cohesion Fund and the FIFG was promoted. In addition, the accession of Spain and Portugal prompted the application of the Integrated Mediterranean Programmes (IMP), as compensation to Greece, France and Italy for the agricultural competition of the newly incorporated members. The sixth objective, referring to the development of regions with low population density, was adopted when Sweden, Finland and Austria joined the Community, although only the former two benefited from the measure.

The third expenditure item of the Community budget includes the European Union's research and technological development programmes, the so-called 'Framework Programmes', aimed at revitalizing R&D activities in order to narrow the gap that separates Europe from Japan and the United States in this field. As seen in Table 11.2, the 'Framework Programmes' share of the Community budget rose steadily until 1994, when Framework Programme IV came into force, effective to 1999.

In 1998 the first action plan for innovation in Europe – whose objective is to increase innovative projects and involve companies in its application – was launched, and Framework Programme V, effective until the year 2002, was approved.

But, as the figures for technological efforts (R&D expenditure as a percentage of GDP) demonstrate, little progress has been made in easing the European Union's notable gap with respect to the United States and Japan.[12]

The far-reaching political changes in Europe in this decade explain the behaviour of 'External Actions', the budget heading that – together with the EDF – reflects the European Union's allocation to development cooperation policy. 'External Actions' distinguishes between (a) horizontal actions, consisting of food and humanitarian assistance and international fishing agreements, and (b) other actions with a specific geographical destination, mainly areas close – and of greater strategic interest – to the European Union: Central and Eastern European countries (CEEC) with the PHARE programme for financial assistance, the former countries of the Soviet Union with the TACIS programme, and the countries of the Mediterranean basin. As seen in Table 11.2, between 1986 and 1997, the share of External Actions in Community expenditure increased, and this trend is likely to continue, to reach 5.2 per cent in 1999.

'Administrative Expenditure' constitutes the fifth heading, representing around 5 per cent of total expenditure.[13]

The last expenditure item of the EU budget is 'Repayments and others'. It encompasses expenses of a very diverse nature, including the funds for environmental policies and the construction of trans-European networks.

As noted earlier, the operations of the ECSC and the projects of the EDF do not figure in the general budget, but instead constitute a separate non-budgetary entry. The EDF is an instrument of development-cooperation policy, while the ECSC is responsible for coal and steel policy.[14]

By now readers will have noticed that there is no heading in the budget specifically reserved for employment policy, although there are several items that implicitly envisage this objective. In numerous reports and documents, the European Union has stressed that job creation is a priority goal in its policies. In 1993 the Commission took the first initiative by presenting an ambitious project, the 'White Paper on Growth, Competitiveness and Employment', intended to create 15 million jobs. A year later the European Council at Essen drew up a strategy based on macroeconomic and structural reform policies aimed at reducing unemployment, and finally, in 1996 the current European Commission President, Jacques Santer, unveiled a programme called 'Action for Employment in Europe: A Confidence Pact', also intended to promote employment. But these initiatives have been only marginally translated into budgetary terms, as seen in the fact that the weight of allocations to items with the greatest potential impact on job creation – trans-European networks, the ESF, and assistance to research and technological development – has risen only modestly, from 9 per cent of Community expenditure in 1986 to 11.6 per cent in 1997. None the less, the summit meeting on employment held in Luxembourg in 1997 has revived expectations that the Community will pay greater attention to unemployment.

In conclusion, from this examination of the trends in the Community budget's expenditure structure, we infer that EU policy has gradually shifted away from protective actions in agricultural markets in favour of other projects, in particular structural measures on which the cohesion policy is based. Despite this, the CAP through its facet of price and market intervention – in other words, its most protectionist and inefficient facet, implemented through the EAGGF-Guarantee – continues to absorb nearly half the funds of the Community budget.

11.4 Forms of financing

As in the case of the distribution of Community expenditure, the composition of revenue has also changed significantly.

Presently the Community budget has five sources of revenue (see Table 11.3). The two traditional ones are agricultural levies and customs duties, which member states administer and, after deducting 10 per cent for administrative expenses, hand over to the European Union.

Agricultural levies include levies and contributions on the production and storage of sugar and isoglucose. Customs duties are obtained by applying the common external tariff (CET) to the value of the imported merchandise.

The size of these two financing channels has been declining, basically because of the international GATT negotiations, in particular from 1986 to 1994 – the Uruguay Round – when the tariffs that had been hampering world trade were progressively reduced. Other types of accords have also had an impact, including the Lomé Convention, the agreement on the creation of the European Economic Area (EEA), and the bilateral accords – the so-called European Agreements – with Central and Eastern European countries. The general growth of imports has not fully offset the slide in tariffs, and thus the ultimate effect has been a decline in the weight of these resources in EU revenue.

The European Union's basic revenue sources – in quantitative terms – are value added tax (VAT) and the fourth – or GNP – resource. While the former is a tax on consumption and hence penalizes the less affluent member states, the latter is fixed at a uniform rate that is applied to the GNP of each country.

In the period analysed, there has been a reversal in the roles played by these two financing channels. The weight of VAT in EU financing has waned, while the fourth resource has steadily gained in importance, until in 1998 it exceeded VAT.

Revenue from VAT consists of two tranches: the first, constituting the system's regressive side, is calculated by applying a rate to a base determined, in the same way for all countries, by the sum of all final goods and services subject to taxation in the European Union; this base is subject to a ceiling of 55 per cent[15] of the GNP of each country, which means that any amount beyond this limit is not taken into account for the purposes of contributions to the European Union. The second tranche comprises the so-called 'British cheque', this being the

Table 11.3 Changes in the composition of Community revenue (% of total revenue)

Type of revenue	1986	1987	1988	1989	1990	1991	1992	1993	1994	1995	1996	1997	1998*	1999**
Agricultural levies	6.8	8.7	6.2	5.2	4.0	4.4	3.3	2.9	3.1	2.6	2.2	2.4	2.0	2.2
Customs duties	24.3	25.0	22.3	22.5	22.1	20.4	18.9	16.8	16.9	16.7	14.5	15.2	13.3	13.8
VAT	66.0	65.6	57.2	57.3	59.1	55.8	58.0	52.5	50.4	52.2	41.8	42.5	40.9	35.2
Fourth resource			10.6	9.8	0.2	13.3	13.9	25.2	26.8	18.9	29.0	33.4	43.0	48.1
Miscellaneous	2.9	0.7	3.7	5.2	14.6	6.1	5.9	2.6	2.8	9.6	12.5	6.5	0.8	0.7
Total	**100**	**100**	**100**	**100**	**100**	**100**	**100**	**100**	**100**	**100**	**100**	**100**	**100**	**100**

* 1998 budget.
** 1999 preliminary draft budget.

Source: European Commission: *The Community Budget: The Facts in Figures.*

amount that the United Kingdom does not pay,[16] which is covered by the other member states.

The European Union's most recent financing mechanism is the so-called fourth resource. Initially envisaged in the Delors I package, it was finally introduced at the European Council of Brussels in 1988,[17] and it acts as an instrument to balance the budget, since it is defined as the difference between the Community's total expenditure and the rest of its revenue. As shown in Table 11.3, it has grown at a notably dynamic pace.

Finally, there is a fifth item of Community revenue, which reflects miscellaneous sources of revenue, including the tax withholdings on the wages of the employees of EU institutions, the contributions to the financing mechanism of the countries of the European Economic Area that do not belong to the European Union, and the surplus, if any exists, from previous years.

Briefly stated, the revenue structure has changed radically since 1988, thanks to the creation of a new resource linked to each member country's GNP. Underlying this transformation in the composition of revenue is the desire to gradually eliminate the regressive element of the financing system inherent in the VAT resource and to replace it with the fourth resource, which, while not progressive, at least does not penalize the less affluent member states.

Before concluding this section, it is worth noting that a proposal is currently being considered that would involve the introduction of a type of Community-wide personal income tax applicable to EU residents.

After analysing the most substantive changes in the European Union's budgetary structure, the next section goes on to evaluate their implications for the economic and social cohesion – or real convergence – of the member countries.

11.5 The Community budget and economic and social cohesion

As the process of European integration has advanced, there has been a growing awareness of the need to broaden the measures to promote economic and social cohesion in the member countries. The goal is to compensate the less affluent regions for their special difficulties in adapting to a competitive setting that is increasingly dominated by market mechanisms and the resulting distributive problems. Nevertheless, it was not until the late 1980s that the Community authorities actually included economic and social cohesion policies among their priority goals.[18]

Naturally, an analysis of EU budget policy from the standpoint of redistribution or real convergence is especially relevant for those countries, such as Spain, which figure among the less economically developed member states.

As a first step towards evaluating the Community's economic and social cohesion policy, we shall examine the trends in the contributions of each country to the EU budget and the resources received by each, as well as the resulting balance. To this end, we have shown these data, expressed as a percentage of the countries' GDP, in Table 11.4.

The information has been divided into periods representing the three stages delimited by the two major reforms of the structural funds in recent years: the 1988 reform, associated with the market unification project, and the 1993 one, implemented after the guidelines for the creation of EMU had been established.

Table 11.4 shows how each stage has marked an advance in the budget's distributive dimension, as on the whole the net revenue of the member states with lower per capita income has steadily increased, while the more developed partners have been net contributors to the EU budget. But, within this general setting, at least two anomalies stand out. First, the EU countries with the highest per capita income, Luxembourg and Denmark, obtained positive budget balances. And secondly, Ireland benefited the most in the period as a whole, even though it is not the country with the lowest per capita income.

Naturally, the fairness of the impact of the budget on member countries has differed in each of its two facets: funds received from the European Union and contributions to the Community budget.

As expected, the changes in the expenditure structure have helped to further economic and social cohesion. In this respect, a comparison of the two Lorenz curves[19] based on the 1986 and 1997 data indicates that the distribution of funds was more equitable in the latter year (see Figure 11.1). Moreover, the growing convexity of the curve in the first decile, which encompasses the cohesion group, suggests that the policy which drives convergence is increasingly concentrated in the countries with lower per capita income.

By contrast, no significant improvements are found with respect to the partners' contribution to the financing of the EU budget. In fact, an examination of the Lorenz curves based on the information for 1986 and 1997 suffices to confirm this diagnosis[20] (see Figure 11.2).

Table 11.4 Community budget: contributions, revenue and net balance of the EU countries

Average annual contributions to Community budget (% of GDP)				Average annual revenue from the Community budget (% of GDP)				Average annual budget balance (% of GDP)			
Country	1986–8	1989–93	1994–7	Country	1986–8	1989–93	1994–7	Country	1986–8	1989–93	1994–7
1. Austria	—	—	1.1	1. Austria	—	—	0.7	1. Austria	—	—	–0.4
2. Belgium	1.3	1.3	1.4	2. Belgium	0.8	1.1	1.1	2. Belgium	–0.5	–0.2	–0.3
3. Denmark	1.0	0.9	1.0	3. Denmark	1.4	1.2	1.2	3. Denmark	0.4	0.3	0.2
4. Finland	—	—	1.0	4. Finland	—	—	0.9	4. Finland	—	—	–0.1
5. France	1.0	1.0	1.1	5. France	0.9	0.8	0.9	5. France	–0.1	–0.2	–0.2
6. Germany	0.9	1.0	1.2	6. Germany	0.5	0.4	0.5	6. Germany	–0.5	–0.6	–0.7
7. Greece	0.9	1.0	1.2	7. Greece	3.7	5.2	5.3	7. Greece	2.8	4.2	4.1
8. Holland	1.3	1.4	1.5	8. Holland	1.6	1.3	0.8	8. Holland	0.3	–0.1	–0.7
9. Ireland	1.2	1.2	1.3	9. Ireland	5.4	6.5	5.2	9. Ireland	4.2	5.3	3.9
10. Italy	0.8	0.9	0.9	10. Italy	0.8	0.8	0.7	10. Italy	0.0	–0.1	–0.2
11. Luxembourg	1.2	1.2	1.3	11. Luxembourg	0.2	1.9	1.4	11. Luxembourg	–1.0	0.7	0.1
12. Portugal	0.9	1.1	1.3	12. Portugal	1.9	3.4	4.3	12. Portugal	1.0	2.3	3.0
13. Spain	**0.9**	**1.1**	**1.0**	**13. Spain**	**1.1**	**1.6**	**2.3**	**13. Spain**	**0.2**	**0.5**	**1.3**
14. Sweden	—	—	1.0	14. Sweden	—	—	0.5	14. Sweden	—	—	–0.5
15. United Kingdom	0.8	0.8	0.9	15. United Kingdom	0.5	0.5	0.6	15. United Kingdom	–0.3	–0.3	–0.3

Source: European Court of Auditors: *Annual Report*; European Commission: *The Community Budget: The Facts in Figures*; Departamento de Estudios Europeos, Fundación de las Cajas de Ahorros.

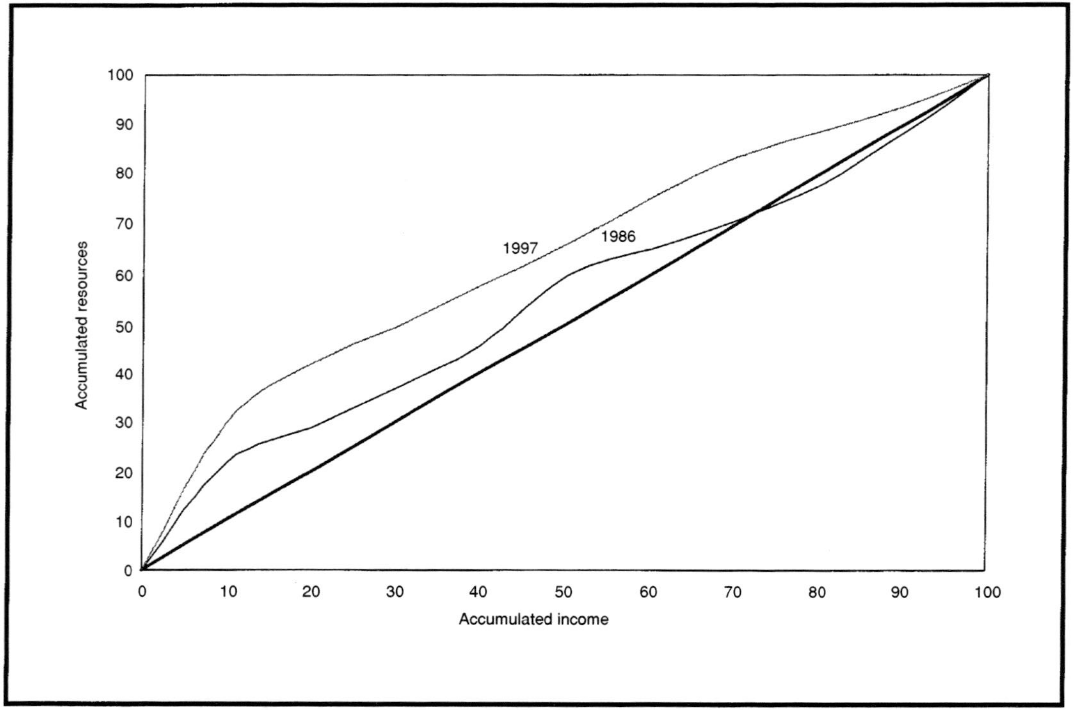

Figure 11.1 Concentration of resources received from the Community budget by EU countries*

* To compare the curves for 1986 and 1997 they were calculated for the countries which formed part of the European Union throughout the period. None the less, the curve for 1997 that includes all 15 members is very similar.

Source: European Court of Auditors: *Annual Report*; European Commission: *The Community Budget: The Facts in Figures*; OECD: *National Accounts*; vol. I: *Main Aggregates*; Departamento de Estudios Europeos, Fundación de las Cajas de Ahorros.

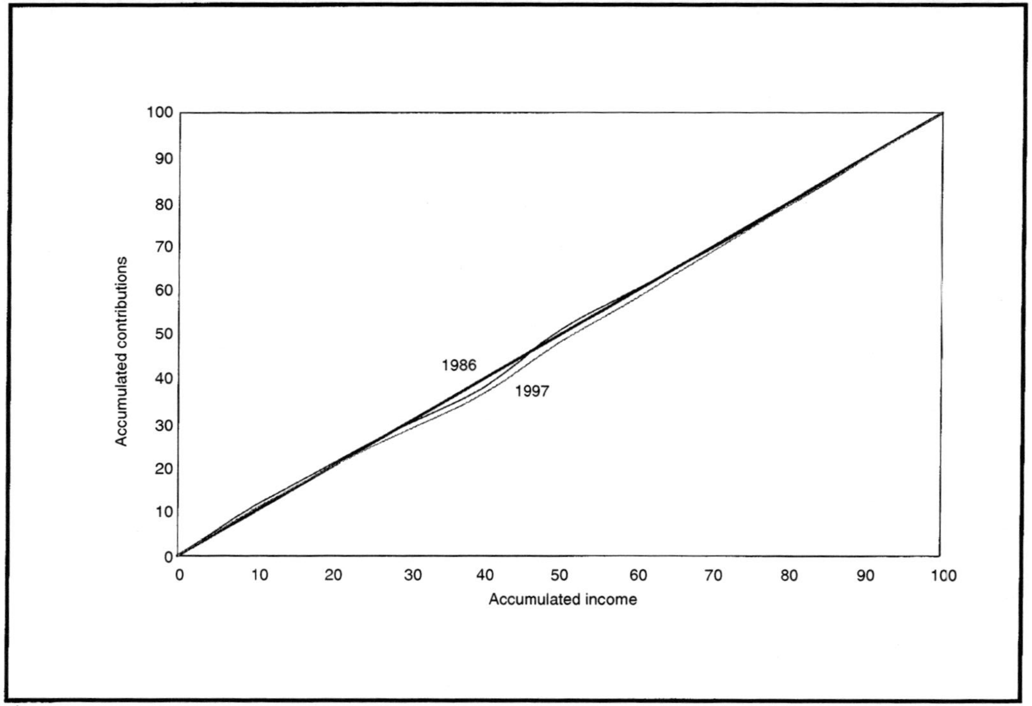

Figure 11.2 Concentration of contributions by EU countries to the Community Budget*

* To compare the curves for 1986 and 1997 they were calculated for the countries which formed part of the European Union throughout the period. None the less, the curve for 1997 that includes all 15 members is very similar.

Source: European Court of Auditors: *Annual Report*; European Commission: *The Community Budget: The Facts in Figures*; OECD: *National Accounts*; vol. I: *Main Aggregates*; Departamento de Estudios Europeos, Fundación de las Cajas de Ahorros.

After analysing the net contribution of each member country to the Community budget and evaluating it from the standpoint of equity, it would also be interesting to find out, from the same standpoint, what impact the main economic policy measures of the EU budget had in each specific case. A simple approach is to calculate the Gini coefficients of each country's contributions to and resources from the Community budget, breaking down the most relevant items as well as the distribution of these items among the member states.[21]

Examining the values obtained – shown in Table 11.5 – and beginning with those which refer to resources, we find a notable transformation in the resources from the EAGGF-Guarantee, which did not contribute to convergence at the beginning of the period[22] but in more recent years have been a favourable factor in the convergence process.[23] Structural measures are also found to be more effective now than 12 years ago in their objective of furthering economic and social cohesion. Finally, it is worth noting that the distribution of funds for R&D activities has not been guided by a cohesion objective. The result of the Gini coefficient (+ 0.09) derives from the specific case of the intermediate group in the ranking by per capita income, mainly comprising the so-called 'European archipelago' formed by 12 'islands of innovation', which alone absorb nearly 50 per cent of the funds of this type.[24] This concentration is illustrated in Table 11.5, which shows that this group receives 62.5 per cent of the assistance for R&D activities, even though it accounts for only 54.8 per cent of Community GDP.

As regards the countries' contributions to the financing of the European Union, several interesting conclusions may be deduced from the trends in the Gini coefficients of the various resources. From 1986 to 1997 the coefficient corresponding to VAT, despite its intrinsically regressive nature, showed a tendency towards cohesion, reflecting the ceilings on its base and uniform rate. None the less, it should be pointed out that this tendency is greatly distorted by the so-called 'British cheque'.[25] Agricultural levies and customs duties have had a negative impact on cohesion. Naturally, the fourth resource is neutral from the standpoint of economic cohesion.

Before concluding this assessment of the social and economic cohesion policy in terms of budgetary changes, several observations on future policy are in order. With this in mind, the following section examines the financial outlook for the next budget period – 2000 to 2006 – taking into account the possible accession of several Eastern European countries,[26] whose economic characteristics will make them eligible to benefit from the structural measures as they now exist.

Table 11.5 Distribution of resources from and contributions to the EU budget by groups of member countries

1986		Resources from:				Contributions to:			
	GDP in euro (%)	EAGGF Guarantee	Structural measures	R&D	Total	Agricultural levies and customs duties	VAT	4th resource	Total
Cohesion (P, GR, E, IRL)	9.4	13.1	29.3		21.0	5.2	13.3		10.8
Intermediate (UK, I, NL, B, F)	60.4	62.2	62.4		58.6	64.7	58.5		60.4
Higher income (D, DK, LUX)	27.8	24.7	8.3		20.4	30.1	28.2		28.8
Spain	6.4	1.2	8.7		7.9	2.1	9.2		7.0
Gini coefficient		–0.05	0.36		0.08	0.02	–0.01		0.00

1997		Resources from:				Contributions to:			
	GDP in euro (%)	EAGGF Guarantee	Structural measures	R&D	Total	Agricultural levies and customs duties	VAT	4th resource	Total
Cohesion (P, GR, E, IRL)	10.2	24.7	50.4	11.1	33.3	8.3	12.4	10.8	11
Intermediate (UK, I, NL, B, F)	54.8	52.6	31.5	62.5	45.3	59.9	46.5	52.7	51.3
Accessories (A, FIN, S)	6.8	5.4	3.4	5.4	4.9	5.4	8.2	7.2	7.3
Higher income (D, DK, LUX)	28.2	17.3	14.8	21.1	16.4	26.4	32.9	29.3	30.4
Spain	6.6	11.3	24.7	6.0	15.8	4.5	8.2	7.2	7.1
Gini coefficient*		0.19	0.44	0.09	0.28	0.04	–0.06	0.00	–0.02

* To compare the coefficients for 1986 and 1997 they were calculated by including the countries which belonged to the European Union throughout the period. None the less, note that the value of the coefficient calculated for 1997 that includes the 15 members is very similar.

Source: European Court of Auditors: *Annual Report*; European Commission: *The Community Budget: The Facts in Figures*; OECD: *National Accounts*, vol. I: *Main Aggregates*; Departamento de Estudios Europeos, Fundación de las Cajas de Ahorros.

11.6 Financial perspective for the budget and enlargement towards the East

On 1 January 2000 the new EU budget for the period 2000–6 will enter into force. Some time ago – in July 1997 – the Commission drew up its so-called 'Agenda 2000', in which it presented the future financial perspective for the budget and envisioned the possible enlargement towards the East as of the year 2002. The new budget was approved at the European Council in Berlin (24–5 March 1999) but proved to be a very difficult process, because the candidate countries have a much lower level of per capita income than that of the European Union on average and a much larger agricultural component in their economic activity, while at the same time most of the current EU member states are beset by high unemployment.

The fact is, the accession of Eastern European countries, as potential beneficiaries of the CAP and cohesion policies in particular, will require a substantial increase in the EU budget outlay, which will have to be financed by the current members.[27] In this respect, the new EU budget (outlined in Table 11.6) freezes the ceiling on resources at their present level (in other words, 1.27 per cent of the GNP of the Fifteen) and maintains a fairly similar expenditure structure. As can be seen from Table 11.6, this means that the budget cost of accession particularly affects the less developed partners, which are the beneficiaries of structural measures. This has naturally elicited criticism from the countries receiving structural funds. But this was not the only factor behind the heated controversy surrounding Agenda 2000, which was further fuelled by the demands of Germany and other countries that their net contribution to the EU budget be reduced. Further proposals included the elimination of the Cohesion Fund, the establishment of a lower ceiling for Community expenditure (the average of the 1993–9 budgets, which is lower than the ceiling of the year 1999); national co-financing of the CAP, until now covered exclusively by the Community budget; and the postponement of the entry of Eastern European countries until at least 2006.

Fortunately, however, this controversy has been resolved, and the necessary unanimity was reached for the budget's approval.

11.7 Conclusions

This chapter has analysed the budget policy of the European Union and, after seeing its limitations as regards stabilizing and allocative

Table 11.6 Composition of Community expenditure under the new financial framework for the period 2000–6 according to Agenda 2000* (% of total expenditure)

	2000	2001	2002	2003	2004	2005	2006
Agricultural guideline	**46.7**	**48.1**	**47.5**	**46.9**	**45.9**	**44.7**	**44.0**
Member states	42.0	44.5	42.4	41.3	38.5	34.7	33.2
Candidate countries	0.6	0.6	2.1	2.5	2.9	3.3	3.7
Margin	4.3	3.0	2.9	3.2	4.5	5.9	7.2
Structural measures	**36.0**	**34.8**	**35.6**	**36.4**	**37.4**	**38.7**	**39.5**
Member states	34.8	33.7	30.8	29.7	28.7	28.2	27.3
Structural funds	31.9	30.9	28.2	27.1	26.3	25.8	24.9
Cohesion funds	2.8	2.8	2.6	2.6	2.4	2.4	2.3
Candidate countries	1.1	1.1	4.8	6.7	8.7	10.5	12.3
Internal policies	**6.4**	**6.4**	**6.7**	**6.7**	**6.7**	**6.6**	**6.6**
Member states	6.4	6.4	6.1	6.0	6.0	6.0	5.9
Candidate countries	0.0	0.0	0.6	0.6	0.7	0.7	0.7
External actions	**4.9**	**4.9**	**4.6**	**4.5**	**4.5**	**4.4**	**4.3**
Administration	**5.0**	**4.9**	**5.1**	**5.1**	**5.2**	**5.2**	**5.2**
Member states	5.0	4.9	4.7	4.7	4.8	4.8	4.7
Candidate countries	0.0	0.0	0.4	0.4	0.4	0.4	0.4
Reserves	**1.0**	**1.0**	**0.6**	**0.4**	**0.4**	**0.4**	**0.4**
Total commitment appropriation	**100.0**	**100.0**	**100.0**	**100.0**	**100.0**	**100.0**	**100.0**
Total appropriations for payment	**97.4**	**97.5**	**97.3**	**97.8**	**97.6**	**97.6**	**97.7**
Appropriations for payments (% of GNP)	1.13	1.12	1.22	1.22	1.21	1.21	1.21
Margin for accession (% of GNP)	0.00	0.00	0.04	0.04	0.04	0.04	0.04
Overall ceiling for own resources (% of GNP)	1.27	1.27	1.27	1.27	1.27	1.27	1.27

* The hypotheses used by the European Commission for this scenario are: (a) average annual economic growth in the period 2000–6 of 2.5 per cent for present member states and 4 per cent for candidate countries, (b) GNP deflator in ecus of 2 per cent per annum, and (c) the year 2002 for accession. In addition, pre-accession assistance is included in the item for new member states.

Source: European Commission: *Agenda 2000* (European Council in Berlin on 24–25 March 1999); Departamento de Estudios Europeos, Fundación de las Cajas de Ahorros.

functions, the emphasis was placed on its impact on economic and social cohesion among the member states. The most important conclusions are set out below:

- The magnitude of total EU expenditure relative to Community GNP is very small, only 1.14 per cent in 1997. Although it has tended to rise in recent years, the increase has been insignificant. What is more, according to the financial perspective for the period 2000–6, it is expected to remain below 1.27 per cent.
- The European Union intervenes in economic activity more through regulatory measures in the form of decisions, directives and regulations, than through the budget. Judging by the above-mentioned financial perspective, this situation is unlikely to change in the near future.
- Given that the overriding objective of monetary policy in EMU is to control inflation, and that the member countries' use of fiscal policy to exercise a stabilizing function is constrained by the stability pact, the maintenance of a Community budget whose small size and scope leave it ill equipped to act as a stabilizing mechanism would seem likely to give rise to problems, particularly for the countries more vulnerable to specific shocks.
- The EAGGF-Guarantee is still the largest expenditure item, but it has been declining for many years, and this tendency will become more pronounced in the future. By contrast, economic and social cohesion policy, partly reflected in the weight of expenditure on structural measures, has gained momentum, as evidenced in the fact that the weight of structural funds in the budget's total expenditure rose twofold between 1986 and 1997.
- The expenditure items most closely linked to policies that promote jobs and research and development have risen only negligibly. As such, they have contributed, to some extent, to the fairly unsuccessful initiatives aimed at reducing unemployment in the European Union and improving the competitiveness of European firms vis-à-vis US and Japanese firms.
- The revenue structure has changed radically in the period, primarily as a result of the introduction of the fourth resource, which by 1998 had become the European Union's most important financing channel. Meanwhile, the weight of VAT, agricultural levies and customs duties has gradually diminished.
- The study – based on Lorenz curves, Gini coefficients and an analysis of distribution – of the data on the contributions of each country to the Community budget and the resources received, by their

separate headings, suggests that structural measures have increasingly contributed to the goal of social and economic cohesion. In addition, it shows that the EAGGF-Guarantee is no longer biased against equity, as it was in the mid-1980s. As to the other actions, however, and in particular those relating to the assistance for R&D activities, no positive influence is observed in terms of equity.

- Also, in the contributions by country, VAT stands out in particular, with the notoriously high regressivity that it introduced to the financing system tending to ease.
- The financial perspective for the EU budget for the period 2000–6, which envisages the possible accession of Eastern European countries, has created considerable tension among EU partners, once again demonstrating that one of the major challenges to the success of European integration is the attainment of higher levels of solidarity.

12
Unification of Monetary Policy in Europe

12.1 Introduction

The establishment of economic and monetary union (EMU) marks the culmination of the European integration process that began in the late 1950s under the Treaty of Rome.

Despite the lingering uncertainties over the economic implications of EMU membership for the member countries, progress on the theoretical side and the empirical experience of the process shed light on what may lie ahead.

The present chapter is structured as follows. It begins with an overview of the process leading up to monetary union, and discusses several of the doubts as to its final form. Section 12.3 describes the nature of the European System of Central Banks (ESCB), and identifies the main aspects of the startup of a European monetary policy and the fiscal policy regime that is likely to take shape.

The next section then briefly summarizes the theoretical costs and benefits of EMU, with an emphasis on the implications for the less developed members such as Spain. The closing section sets out the main conclusions.

Later, in the epilogue, these theoretical hypotheses will be compared with the empirical conclusions drawn from the analysis in the other chapters of the book in order to offer a fuller evaluation of EMU's implications for the Spanish economy.

12.2 The path to monetary union

The origins of EMU date back to 1962, when the European Commission drew up its first plan for achieving monetary union.[1] The only concrete result of this initiative, however, was the creation of the Committee of Central Bank Governors in 1964.

As long as the Bretton Woods system functioned smoothly, the pressure to fix exchange rates in Europe was minimal, because rates were already controlled through commitments with respect to the dollar. But when the system began to show signs of weakness, the project of monetary union was seen in an increasingly good light, and at the Hague Summit in 1969 a committee, chaired by Luxembourg's Finance Minister Pierre Werner, was asked to draw up a new plan for monetary union.

The Werner Report,[2] unveiled in 1970, contained a detailed plan for gradually attaining monetary union in Europe within a maximum of ten years. However, the plan was deemed too ambitious and difficult to apply in the situation of profound crisis in the international monetary system prevailing at the time. As a result, the only measure that was actually taken to achieve exchange-rate stability was the creation in 1972 of the 'European currency snake', which required that Community currencies be kept within a bilateral margin of 2.25 per cent.

The snake continued after currencies generally started to float freely against the dollar in the spring of 1973, marking the effective abandonment of the principle of fixed exchange rates envisaged in the agreement founding the IMF. None the less, serious problems immediately arose, including numerous devaluations and revaluations, as well as the recurrent departure and return of Community currencies, owing to the profound economic policy disagreements between European countries over the appropriate response to the oil crisis of 1973.

The next basic step towards monetary union was the launch of the European Monetary System (EMS)[3] in March 1979 in the form of an agreement between the participating central banks. Its objectives were to promote exchange-rate stability in Europe in an unstable international environment, to further economic convergence between the EMS member countries, and, by extension, to contribute to the process of monetary integration.

To what extent has it succeeded? Even though all the objectives proposed have clearly not been achieved, there is a fairly broad consensus as regards its considerable success – despite the crisis of 1992/3 – in several areas. The EMS has managed to bring about a certain degree of exchange-rate stability, which has contributed to the convergence in inflation rates, and it has also helped make cooperation between the participating countries a habit in the area of establishing economic policies compatible with the central parities.

In this way, the increasing consolidation of the EMS, coupled with the impetus provided by the entry into force of the Single European Act in 1987 and the resulting prospects for the formation of the internal market, led the European Council at the Hanover Summit in 1988 to reaffirm the goal of establishing monetary union. The liberalization of capital movements envisaged in the Single European Act was probably the chief catalyst of the conviction of the need to centralize monetary policy and to adopt a common currency. As Padoa-Schioppa (1994) points out, the liberalization of capital movements in a framework of free trade, fixed exchange rates and national autonomy in monetary policy made for an 'inconsistent quartet' of economic objectives. Accordingly, given that the Single European Act contained a commitment to the first three objectives, the fourth one would have to be modified.

The Hanover Council thus appointed a committee, chaired by Jacques Delors, President of the European Commission, to draw up a preparatory report. In April 1989 the Delors Committee unveiled its report on economic and monetary union in the European Community, which incorporated many of the ideas of the earlier Werner Plan and outlined a three-stage process for transition to the single currency. The report was approved at the meeting of the heads of government in Madrid in June 1989, and since then it has been the basic reference point for the subsequent steps towards monetary union. Indeed, the essence of the Delors Report was reflected in the Treaty on European Union approved by the European Council at Maastricht in December 1991, which set in motion the monetary union project and marked a milestone in Europe's integration process. The essential features of the plan formulated in the Treaty on European Union for the establishment of monetary union in Europe are as follows:

- The decision to reach the full establishment of EMU in three stages. In Stage One (begun in July 1990), the objective was to achieve the full liberalization of capital movements and financial and banking integration, as well as a narrowing in the differentials in inflation and interest rates and an increase in exchange-rate stability. Stage Two, to begin in 1994, called for a greater degree of convergence in national economic policies, in addition to the creation of the European Monetary Institute (EMI); the latter was assigned the task of coordinating, in collaboration with the Commission, the member countries' monetary policies, and of making the technical preparations to facilitate the transition to monetary union. Finally, the start of Stage Three, which was to be on 1 January 1999 at the latest, would see the transfer of the sovereignty of the member states participating in monetary union to the ESCB, formed by the European Central Bank (ECB) and the national central banks.

- To gain access to Stage Three of monetary union, the countries would have to meet certain economic criteria of nominal convergence.[4]
- An opting-out clause was included, allowing the United Kingdom – and later Denmark – to remain outside the single currency if they wished.
- An institutional framework, with a federal and independent central bank, was created for the application of monetary policy, while the centralization of fiscal policy was not considered necessary.

In Stage One of EMU, and especially after the final quarter of 1992, the economic and monetary scenario took an adverse turn. Largely as a result of the difficulties in ratifying the Maastricht Treaty and problems stemming from Germany's unification process, the EMS was hit by a major crisis. The two-year period 1992–3 saw the temporary withdrawal of the lira and the pound from the system's exchange-rate mechanism, successive devaluations of other currencies, and a widening of the fluctuation bands for the participating currencies to ±15 per cent.[5]

These events rekindled the debate on the timetable's viability and the complications involved in advancing to a single currency. Ultimately, however, the commencement of Stage Two of EMU in 1994, coupled with the impetus provided by the creation of the EMI and the entry of new Community members (Austria, Finland and Sweden), led to further progress in the negotiations, which crystallized at the Madrid Summit in December 1995. At this meeting of the European Council, the member countries confirmed their desire to move forward in the process of EMU; they also established the name of the new single currency, the euro, as well as the steps and the timetable for its introduction (summarized in Table 12.1).

The Madrid Summit marked a turning point from pessimism to optimism about the future of EMU, both in the political sphere and in financial markets, where opinion from then onwards increasingly warmed to the creation of economic and monetary union. In December 1996, the European Council in Dublin addressed two essential issues for the construction and operation of EMU. First, the content of the so-called stability and growth pact, aimed at preserving fiscal

Table 12.1 Plan for the introduction of the euro

Stage	Date	Measure

Preparatory period	Start: 'As soon as possible' at the beginning of 1998	• Selection of countries qualifying for EMU participation and announcement of the system for fixing the exchange rates vis-à-vis the euro
		• Establishment of the ECB
		  • Adoption of the ECB's decisions on the strategy and operational framework of the single monetary policy
		  • Final adjustments in the operational organization of monetary policy and the TARGET system
		• Preparation of the financial community for the execution of monetary policy in euro

Establishment of EMU and startup of the transition period	Start: 1 January 1999	• Irrevocable fixing of the exchange rates of national currencies vis-à-vis the euro • Entry into force of the Council's regulations on the introduction of the euro • Beginning of the ESCB's operations and conduct of monetary policy
	Late 2001	• Issuance of euro-denominated notes and coins
Period of exchange	Start: 1 January 2002	• Withdrawal of national notes and coins
Completion of EMU	1 July 2002, at the latest	• Abolition of national notes and coins as legal tender

Source: Banco de España (1997), p. 87; ECB.

rigour within EMU. And, second, the framework of the relations between the founding members and those EU countries which – either because of their failure to qualify or through their own choice – did not join EMU, the so-called 'pre-ins'.

As to the stability pact,[6] a provisional agreement was reached at the Dublin Summit to maintain after the formation of EMU the same requirement as regards the stability of public finances, stipulating to this end a series of sanctions – ratified at the Amsterdam Summit in May 1997 – for countries that infringe the agreement.

And, with respect to the relations between the EMU member countries and the pre-ins, the Dublin Council also approved an arrangement based on two essential elements: the creation of a new exchange-rate mechanism between the euro and the national currencies of the countries which have not adopted the euro, and the closer monitoring of these countries' convergence programmes. A consensus was also reached on the principle of equal treatment for the countries that accede to EMU after its startup, whereby the margins for interpreting the selection criteria must be the same as those applied to the founder countries.

In the first weekend in May 1998, the European Council in Brussels – known as the 'Euro Summit' – made a series of historic decisions in the process of European integration.

First, following the recommendation of the Economic and Finance Ministers Council and a report of the European Parliament, the European Council decided that only four EU countries would initially be excluded from the euro. In the final analysis, only Greece and Sweden failed to meet all the convergence criteria, but two other countries – the United Kingdom and Denmark – made use of the opting-out clause (introduced in the Protocols of the Treaty on European Union) and did not sign up for EMU.

Meanwhile, to ease the uncertainties which might arise between the time of selecting the member countries and the setting of fixed and irrevocable exchange rates, the bilateral exchange rates of each national currency were announced, coinciding with the central rates of the ERM's parity grid.

Finally, as several studies (Favero et al., 1995, and De Grauwe, 1996) had predicted, broad monetary union was achieved in the European Union. The contributing factors included a spectacular improvement in the degree of compliance with the convergence criteria approved at Maastricht, along with a certain flexibility in the interpretation of these criteria. Here, not only economic but also political reasons undoubtedly played an important role.

12.3 The monetary and fiscal policy regime of EMU

Since 1 January 1999, when Stage Three of monetary union began, the ESCB – formed by the ECB and all the national central banks of the EU member countries which belong to or are temporarily excluded from monetary union – has been responsible for defining and executing the single monetary policy. As envisaged in article 2 of the protocol on the Statute of the ESCB and of the ECB in the Treaty on European Union, its prime objective is to maintain price stability, and, in accordance with article 7 of the same protocol, it has full and formal autonomy from the governments.

This autonomy is a very important aspect, because, as seen in Eijffinger and De Haan (1996), the average inflation rate is generally lower in those countries whose central banks enjoy a greater degree of autonomy. However, a balance must exist between a central bank's formal autonomy and its political accountability, and although the former is clearly reflected in the Maastricht Treaty, the latter is not clearly specified.

The fact that the ECB enjoys great independence poses a twofold problem.[7] First, its objectives do not necessarily have to coincide with those of the member governments, and monetary policy therefore may not have the support or political consensus needed for its execution, and secondly, the external evaluation (except for the annual report, of a formal character, to the European parliament) is insufficient. In view of this, some studies have suggested that institutional changes should be made to secure the ECB's political legitimacy without sacrificing its autonomy.[8]

A knowledge of the ESCB's power-sharing and functions is key to understanding the way in which it designs and applies monetary policy in the EMU countries. In this respect, the European Central Bank is the ESCB's central governing institution. Based in Frankfurt, it has three governing bodies (see Figure 12.1): the Executive Committee (responsible for the day-to-day management and implementation of monetary policy), the Governing Council (responsible for the design and formulation of monetary policy), and the General Council (formed by the governors of the national central banks and responsible for relations with the EU countries not participating in the euro).

Each member of the governing bodies has one vote (plus the casting vote of the Chairman), and decisions are made by a simple majority, except for some which require a qualified majority (such as those relating to capital and reserves), when the votes are weighted in accordance

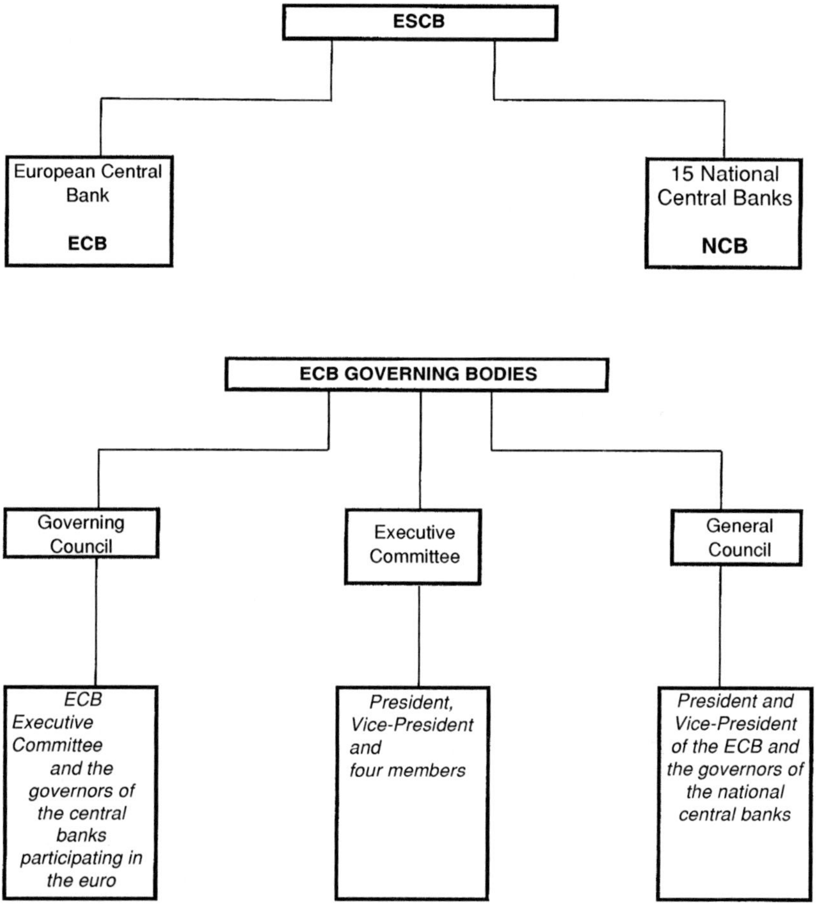

Figure 12.1 European System of Central Banks (ESCB)
Source: European Central Bank.

with the share of the national central banks in the ECB's capital. Each country's percentage of capital depends, in equal parts, on its population and its GDP with respect to the total of the European Union.

In the area of exchange-rate policy, however, sovereignty ultimately remains in the hands of the governments (through the ECOFIN). The fact that the treaty places the decisions on exchange-rate policy vis-à-vis the rest of the world beyond the bounds of the ESCB has led some specialists to warn that this may endanger the actual autonomy of the new institution.[9] However, the Treaty on European Union itself establishes a system for consultation between the two institutions to prevent conflicts.

As to the supervision of credit institutions, it is not yet entirely clear how the functions will be divided up and what form the operating structure for carrying out this task will have.

How is European monetary policy executed? Although the basic decisions on the single monetary policy are taken in a centralized way, its implementation (provision and absorption of liquidity) is the responsibility of the national central banks. In other words, the strategy is uniform, but it is implemented through instruments which are accessible to the financial institutions of all parts of the area on the same conditions. Moreover, a large-volume payment system known as TARGET (trans-European automated real-time gross settlement express transfer system) has been designed to transfer funds from one place to another in the European Union at the appropriate speed and cost.[10]

The system consists of a national component and a link between the national central banks (the interlinking mechanism). Each payment is settled individually and immediately upon notification. When a credit institution initiates a payment, the payment order is transmitted to the respective national central bank. Once the existence of the balance or of the relevant guarantees is verified, the interlinking system transmits the order to the central bank of the country of destination. Finally, the central bank makes the payment to the recipient institution. The four EU countries not participating in EMU also have access to the payment systems, subject to certain limits (intraday credit), but with the same guarantees as those required of the euro-zone countries. However, to ensure that banks outside the euro zone do not have the capacity to change the euro money supply when the ECB is closed, they will not be able to obtain overnight credit.

As we have noted, the strategy's basic objective is to achieve price stability (specifically established in article 105.1 of the Maastricht Treaty). As to the procedures for achieving this goal, five options were initially studied and three were rejected. Nominal income was not considered appropriate, because of the lag with which its magnitude becomes known and the sizeable revisions to which it is subject; a strategy based on interest rates is hard to articulate and, moreover, too little is known about the equilibrium level of rates compatible with the final objective; lastly, fixing the exchange rate would entail accepting the primacy of factors external to EMU. Thus, by elimination, only those strategies based on monetary targeting and direct inflation targeting were deemed feasible.

Taking the above observations into account, at its meeting of 13 October 1998 the Governing Council of the ECB agreed on the main features of the monetary policy strategy which the ESCB has implemented since 1 January 1999.

- First, the ECB has defined price stability as a situation characterized by an annual increase of less than 2 per cent in the harmonized consumer price index of the euro zone. Likewise, it has stated clearly that price stability must be maintained in the medium run and that the ECB's decisions will take into account the price trends in the euro zone as a whole, without taking account of specific regional or national conditions.
- Second, the ESCB's monetary-policy strategy assigns a prominent role to monetary aggregates. The ECB announces a reference value for the growth of a broad monetary aggregate that is consistent with the objective of price stability and assists in achieving it. The ESCB regularly analyses the relationship between the monetary growth observed and the reference announced, as well as the causes of any deviations which may arise, publishing the results of its analysis and the implications for monetary policy decisions.
- Third, in the ESCB's monetary-policy strategy, the evaluation of the forecasts of future trends in prices and of risks affecting price stability in the euro zone plays a central role. This evaluation draws on a broad set of information.

The Governing Council of the ECB systematically analyses all the available information and, in accordance with the principles of accountability and transparency regarding its monetary-policy strategy, it is committed to informing the public, in detail and on a regular basis, of its evaluation of the economic, monetary and financial situation in the euro zone, explaining its monetary policy decisions.

As to the implementation of the single monetary policy, the operational variable is the very short-term interest rate. There are basically three instruments available to control this variable: open-market operations (including regularly scheduled tenders and fine-tuning operations), standing facilities, and a reserve requirement.

The purpose of open-market operations is to steer interest rates, manage the market's liquidity and signal the stance of monetary policy. The second instrument, standing facilities (lending or deposit facilities, depending on whether the aim is to provide or absorb liquidity), is managed by the national central banks to absorb or provide overnight liquidity and bound overnight market interest rates. The third instrument, the reserve requirement, is aimed at stabilizing interest rates and controlling the expansion of the money supply, and requires credit institutions to maintain minimum reserves of 1.5 per cent and 2.5 per cent of their eligible liabilities in accounts with their respective national central banks (applied to the deposits and other issues of credit institutions, excluding those with agreed maturity over two years). Reserves are remunerated at the short-term interest rate (repo) on the main refinancing operations.

Note that under a monetary policy common to countries with disparate economic and financial structures, monetary impulses may have different effects in each country, either in terms of their different impact on prices and output or simply because of differences in the time it takes for the consequences of the policy measures to be perceived.

In the literature, three transmission channels for monetary policy are distinguished: changes in interest rates, in the exchange rate and in credit. These mechanisms, however, produce different effects in each country, depending on the degree of the use of long-term financing contracts, the degree of indebtedness of non-financial firms, and differences in the economies' foreign-trade ratios. These differences may appreciably complicate the ECB's tasks during the first few years of EMU. A recent study by Dornbusch, Favero and Giavazzi (1998) measures the potential differential impact of the ECB's monetary policy by constructing a model of the monetary transmission mechanism in six European countries. The results confirm the above-mentioned fears, since they indicate that changes in interest rates have a greater impact in Italy and Sweden than in Spain and Germany, owing to the differences in their financial markets. A second finding is that, given the different share of the EMU countries' foreign trade outside the euro zone, the ECB may need to control the euro's exchange rate to a greater extent than that of the US Federal Reserve. Finally, when considering economic-policy measures, the ECB will face the difficult task of judging to what extent the very creation of the euro is causing a change of regime in financial markets and in price- and wage-setting mechanisms. Nevertheless, these differences should gradually disappear over time in so far as the progress towards economic integration produces a convergence in financial markets and synchronization in the economic cycle.

Having described the monetary policy regime in EMU, we shall now go on to describe, albeit more succinctly, the fiscal policy regime.

We should begin by recalling that the Treaty on European Union does not envisage the creation of new institutions for the implementation of fiscal policy, nor are there any proposals for measures that might lead to the introduction of an even minimally significant centralized regime more in line with the radical change in the area of monetary policy.

Quite to the contrary, according to what has been agreed so far, the fiscal policy framework for the EMU member countries is quite similar to the existing one: autonomy of national governments, although within the strict margins permitted in the stability and growth pact (a ceiling of 3 per cent of GDP for the deficit).

In consequence, in the most likely scenario for fiscal policy in the Europe of the euro, there appears to be no room for any major change in the size or functions of the Community budget. By all indications, the budget will remain subject to the principles of balance and subsidiarity, which, together with its modest endowment (now 1.24 per cent of the GDP of EU partners and likely to increase to only 1.27 per cent, according to financial forecasts), appreciably limit its distributive capacity and inhibit its stabilizing function.

In short, the outlook for the EMU's macroeconomic policy regime is not entirely reassuring as regards the sufficiency of the available mechanisms to meet the specific or asymmetrical economic shocks which may arise.

In fact, as noted in other chapters (Chapter 5 in particular), the fiscal policy framework designed for EMU does not meet the prescriptions of economic theory on monetary unions, which affirm the desirability of a significant centralization of national budgets. Moreover, from the standpoint of economic rationality and of course solidarity, the Community's fiscal policy should be endowed with the instruments to implement efficiently a co-insurance function that would enable the regions affected by specific shocks to cushion the adverse economic and social effects. In this respect, some studies – for example, Pisani-Ferry, Italianer and Lescure (1993) and Goodhart and Smith (1993) – have put forward proposals on the nature of a system of transfers capable of carrying out a co-insurance function.

But, for the time being, the climate of solidarity in Europe does not appear to be strong enough for initiatives of this type. Moreover, there is a certain suspicion that such measures would give rise to an enlargement of EMU bureaucracy and problems of moral hazard, even though the existence of a no bail-out clause, which includes a solemn declaration by EU members stating that they will never support debt issued by other governments, makes it fairly unlikely that such problems would actually arise.

12.4 Advantages and drawbacks of EMU membership

In the cost–benefit analysis of EMU in the mid-1980s, it was widely believed that the economic benefits would amply exceed the costs, the latter being primarily macroeconomic in nature. This reflected the prevailing belief that the instrument to be renounced, the exchange rate, was of no great use in correcting imbalances between economies with a high level of international integration, and therefore that the changeover to monetary union would not involve higher costs than those already borne within the ERM. But the crisis of the ERM and the apparently beneficial effects of the relaxation of British economic policy after the pound's withdrawal from the ERM rekindled the debate in academic circles on the usefulness and sustainability of economic and monetary union. In fact, as noted in Viñals (1996), EMU should no longer be compared with a situation characterized by *de facto* exchange-rate stability, but rather with one in which nominal exchange rates may change.

For this reason, as a point of departure for evaluating the advantages and drawbacks of belonging to EMU, it is worth reviewing what the most recent economic literature considers to be the main economic benefits and costs derived from the creation of economic and monetary union.[11]

Beginning with the benefits, the main ones are the five described below.

The first is the *decrease in transaction costs* as a result of replacing the members' different currencies with a common one. According to the estimates in European Commission (1990), this could produce an annual saving of from 0.25 per cent to 0.5 per cent of Community GDP. But, as later noted in Eichengreen and Ghironi (1995), the quantification of the benefits derived from the elimination of transaction costs poses problems, both theoretical and applied, that are difficult to resolve and as such cast doubt on the above-mentioned findings.

A second advantage of the creation of EMU stems from the *reduction in the risks associated with exchange-rate swings*. In this respect, the common currency could improve economic efficiency and bolster investment and trade by eliminating part of the uncertainty in international transactions. Here, most of the empirical studies suggest that exchange-rate variability has a negative impact on trade. The underlying explanation for these findings appears to be the following: in so far as firms consider their market shares an important asset, in situations of exchange-rate volatility exporters and importers will attempt to delay the impact of changes in production costs on their prices until they are certain that they will not be offset by swings in the exchange rate, which implies a poor allocation of resources, at least temporarily, that will be avoided when the single currency is in use.

A third benefit of monetary union is *the increase in economic integration*. Even though the single currency is not essential to the workings of the single market, its introduction will reinforce the effects on competition and the allocative efficiency of the single market by making the differences between the prices of goods and services in the different countries more transparent.

Fourthly, EMU may also prove beneficial by *contributing to macroeconomic stability* and thus to the efficient allocation of resources and the achievement of a stable growth path. In this respect, the European experience of recent years has demonstrated the advantages for countries with less credibility on international markets that appear to be derived from linking the parities of their currencies to those of economies whose authorities have a better reputation. In this sense, the formal independence of the European Central Bank could help countries to achieve the objective of price stability, since the studies carried out suggest that a negative relationship exists between the degree of independence of central banks and the rate of inflation of their economies.

Fifthly, note that to a certain extent, in so far as the euro becomes an international reserve currency, it will be possible to *isolate the economy from the fluctuations of the other reserve currencies,* and of the US dollar in particular. However, this will largely depend on the conduct of the new European monetary authority and, by extension, on the reputation it acquires over time.

On balance, we find that the biggest benefits of monetary union will stem from the attainment of a climate of greater nominal stability and of a more propitious environment for exploiting the potential efficiency gains provided by the market's integration. In any case, it must be noted that it is very difficult, if not impossible, to arrive at a reliable quantification of these benefits.

After analysing the benefits, we shall now review what the recent economic literature considers to be the main costs of EMU produced by the loss of the nominal exchange rate as an instrument of economic stabilization.

The theoretical reference for analysing the possible costs of monetary union is the literature on optimum currency areas. The first research in this field was carried out in the 1960s, and in recent years the subject has gained fresh momentum due to the theoretical advances in macroeconomics and also to the process of monetary union in Europe.[12] Their objective is to ascertain what combination of conditions is necessary for a group of countries to be able to renounce, at no significant cost, the exchange rate as an instrument for achieving external equilibrium. In this respect, there is a broad consensus that these conditions are basically of two types. First, those which determine the probability of specific or asymmetrical shocks arising,[13] and, second, those associated with the availability of stabilization mechanisms other than the exchange rate for coping with these shocks.

As to the circumstances which may affect the probability that such shocks occur within a monetary union, the most cited ones are: the similarity of the member countries' productive systems, their diversification and foreign-trade ratio, and the flexibility of their goods and factor markets. Specifically, the view is that the greater all these circumstances are, the smaller the probability of shocks of an asymmetrical nature or effect.

As to the stabilizing mechanisms for counteracting the adverse effects of shocks of this type, two are considered especially important: labour mobility and the stabilizing and distributive capacity of the monetary union's fiscal policy.

These theoretical hypotheses have inspired numerous applied studies aimed at learning to what extent these circumstances exist within the European Union.

The approach taken by most of the analyses which seek to infer the degree of symmetry of the shocks within EMU is to compare the situation in the European Union with that in the United States, albeit focusing on different variables and using diverse methods.[14] Their findings coincide to a notable degree in pointing out that asymmetrical shocks tend to be more frequent in the European Union than in the United States. This conclusion is qualified, however, when only the group of countries which have traditionally had closer economic and monetary ties with Germany is considered; the degree of symmetry then proves to be more similar to that of the United States. In any event, what can be deduced from the studies as a whole is that shocks of a real nature will be more likely and more dangerous than those of a monetary nature.

As to the adjustment mechanisms other than the exchange rate available in European countries to relieve the economic and social costs of the shocks which may arise in a region or country in the area, we can only repeat what has already been said with respect to the insufficiency of these mechanisms. Here the available evidence on the European Union's low labour mobility is – as shown in Chapter 10 – very conclusive. Likewise, the absence of a centralized fiscal policy and the existence of but little leeway for the application of national anti-cyclical fiscal policies have already been underscored.

In short, there are well founded indications that EU countries do not satisfy the conditions for an optimum monetary union. As a result, there is a risk of economic shocks affecting several regions or countries in particular and which may not be adequately addressed owing to the inadequacy of Community-wide adjustment mechanisms. In this respect, two other considerations may be added. The first is that the risk of specific shocks is of course greater in economies with weaker productive structures. And the second is that the negative impact of these shocks will be all the greater the lower the flexibility and efficiency of the goods – and, above all, labour – markets of the countries affected.

From this it might be deduced that a multiple-speed approach would be the best way to achieve economic and monetary union, or in other words, that the union should be initially formed by a limited number of countries, with the others gradually joining when their economic conditions so advise. But this affirmation requires qualification, because the empirical studies on which it is based use historical data, while the structure which generates these correlations may change as the single market and monetary union advance further. Indeed, Frankel and Rose (1996a and 1996b) show how sharing the same currency stimulates trade, which in turn increases the correlation of economic cycles. The corollary would be that countries which do not meet the minimum conditions to form a monetary union *ex ante* may meet them more easily once they form part of it.

As to the specific case of Spain, on the basis of the comparative analysis carried out in the first part of this book, it could be concluded that at present neither the productive base nor the adjustment capacity of the Spanish economy appear to offer clear guarantees with respect to the risks posed by EMU, because, despite the liberalizing measures of recent years, not only are the rigidities still apparent in various goods markets and in the labour market but, even more important, the weakness of its productive structure and efficiency is also evident. And we have also seen how the recent history of the peseta has been marked by successive devaluations against other European currencies, owing to the Spanish economy's macroeconomic and structural imbalances.

From this it might be inferred that in the short run it would have been better for a country such as Spain to remain outside EMU until it had achieved a higher level of real convergence, or alternatively, greater flexibility in goods and factor markets that would facilitate its adjustments within the European Union.

Numerous considerations, however, argue against this option. In the first place, it should be borne in mind that the policy applied by the EU countries outside the euro zone must not differ substantially from that applied within the zone, because the coordination of economic policy will require that both groups of countries pursue orthodox budgetary policies and implement structural reforms in their markets.

Moreover, had Spain not joined EMU, it would still not have had any great margin for coping with competitive problems via nominal exchange-rate adjustments, because they would almost certainly have led to an increase in interest rates. At the same time, any diverging trends in its main macroeconomic variables would probably have unleashed a crisis of confidence and, in consequence, monetary turbulence.

In sum, although it is obvious that Spain's membership of EMU will mean having to adapt to major changes in economic policy and that this will require great efforts, from the viewpoint of economic – and of course political – rationality, self-exclusion was in no way a desirable alternative.

12.5 Conclusions

The creation of monetary union in Europe is unquestionably a difficult project, because it signifies the elimination of one of the most deep-rooted symbols of national sovereignty in the minds of a people: their currency. This marks the final step in economic integration and will very probably require a greater level of political union in the near future. The main conclusions drawn from the analysis in this chapter on the steps already taken, and those which remain to be taken, towards the establishment of EMU are as follows:

- The approval of the Treaty on European Union in 1991 by the European Council at Maastricht finally made it possible to carry out a project of monetary union after several failed attempts.
- Although the deep crisis that swept the EMS in 1992–3 cast doubt on the project's viability, with the widening of the maximum fluctuation bands to ±15 per cent, European currencies managed to maintain highly stable exchange rates, which helped restore

confidence in the startup of EMU on the scheduled date, 1 January 1999.

- Moreover, the very dynamics of the process of constructing the European Union, and the creation of the EMI in particular, contributed to the growing climate of macroeconomic stability in the European Union, based on the Maastricht criteria, which to some extent fed the expectations of the project's completion.
- According to the provisions of the Treaty on European Union and its implementing protocols, the design and execution of monetary policy in the Europe of the euro are the responsibility of the ESCB, formed by the ECB and the national central banks; policy is totally independent of the governments, and its almost exclusive objective is to achieve price stability within EMU.
- The achievement of higher levels of solidarity in EU fiscal policy is seen to be a difficult objective. For this reason, and taking into account the fiscal discipline required by the stability pact, it seems unlikely that national governments will have sufficient room for manoeuvre to undertake counter-cyclical measures.
- From the economic point of view, it is difficult to arrive at any clear-cut conclusion on the costs and benefits of belonging to a monetary union. The loss of autonomy in monetary policy may signify substantial adjustment costs, especially in those economies, such as Spain's, with less flexible goods and labour markets, while the gains are also difficult to quantify. But, when considering the risks involved in exclusion from the EMU project, participation is justified.

Conclusions: Prospects and Economic Strategies for the Spain of the Euro

This book began with a series of questions regarding the true extent of the Spanish economy's integration with its European partners – and its progress towards convergence with them – since 1986, when Spain joined the project to build a new, economically integrated Europe, with a common currency, the euro. As noted from the start, the book's more immediate goal has been to answer these questions as thoroughly and precisely as possible. But in the final instance, beyond shedding light on what these more than 12 years have held for Spain and its partners as they advanced towards a common goal, the book has also sought to provide useful information for the design of a feasible and suitable policy for adapting to the challenges that lie ahead – the deepening (consolidation of the recently created EMU) and the enlargement (accession of the Eastern European countries) of the process of European economic and, most likely, political integration.

By way of an epilogue, the closing pages of this book will review what we have learned from our evaluation of the past and present experience of the Spanish economy in Europe. From this vantage, we shall reflect on Spain's prospects and – even more important – economic policy options for securing a satisfactory position as a member of the European Union.

Broadly speaking, without repeating the conclusions drawn at the close of each chapter, the following points summarize what we have learned in our examination of how the Spanish economy has fared in the Europe of the Fifteen:

- We have found that, since joining what was then the European Community, Spain has significantly strengthened its ties with the countries which are now its partners in the European Union. The high level of interdependence of these countries is reflected in nearly all their economic dealings. From the standpoint of trade, the European Union has reinforced its position as the most important export market, a supplier of imported goods, and an area of origin and destination of international direct investment projects. During these years, only migratory flows have declined, within the general context of a sharply downward trend since the mid-1970s, and labour mobility is undoubtedly one of the areas where progress towards European unification has been least visible.

- The integration process is also evident in the area of coordination of economic policy, especially since the entry into force of the Single European Act and, above all, since the signing of the Treaty on European Union at Maastricht. The growing harmony in economic policy is apparent not only in the agreements implemented, among which the unification of currencies and monetary policy (as of 1 January 1999) marks the most important step, but also in the increasing coincidence in the countries' economic cycles, and in particular their common progress towards macroeconomic stability.
- The deepening of the integration of the economic policies and relations of Spain and the other EU members has been conducive to fairly broad convergence of the productive structure and conduct of economic and social agents in Spain with the averages of the other member states, although it varies sharply depending on which economic sphere is considered. And, as the variables indicate, much greater progress has been made in nominal convergence than in real convergence.
- Unquestionably, the Spanish economy has advanced spectacularly in achieving the price stability required for EMU membership; equally significant has been the progress in fiscal consolidation, albeit stemming to no small extent from measures – such as cuts in government investment and the rapid privatization of profitable public firms – that may prove counterproductive to economic growth in the future. Indeed, Spain was one of the countries that most comfortably passed the examination of the Maastricht requirements in spring 1998, qualifying for participation in the group of 11 countries forming the vanguard of economic and monetary union.
- Considerably less satisfactory is the verdict on the progress in the indicators that are used and analysed in this book to evaluate the level and path of real convergence, in particular taking into account the large negative differential that still exists between Spain's position and that of the EU average. Even though the gap between

Spain's GDP per capita and the EU average has narrowed by 6 percentage points since 1986; in 1997 it stood at only 78.7 per cent of that average. Moreover, Spain's relative position in terms of the unemployment rate is deplorable, although enormous improvement has been made in recent years. As regards expenditure on social benefits, the third of the indicators used to assess achievements in the area of real convergence, the situation is somewhat better: from 74 per cent of the EU average in 1986, Spain's ratio of social expenditure to GDP advanced to nearly 80 per cent in 1997, a higher proportion than that of Spanish GDP per capita compared with the EU average. None the less, the other two indicators used to estimate the Spanish economy's capacity to achieve real convergence – human capital endowment and the stock of technological capital, both indicators of an economy's potential for sustained growth – again paint a bleak picture; in spite of the tendency of these two indicators to converge, Spain still lags far behind: their values in 1997 represented only 66 per cent and 35 per cent, respectively, of the Community averages.

- The comparison of the performance and structure of the public finances of the Fifteen has revealed that, in addition to the above-mentioned convergence in their deficits, the relative levels (as a proportion of GDP) and the composition of government revenue and expenditure in the Spanish economy have moved closer to Community patterns. Improvements have been truly striking in the equity and flexibility of the Spanish tax system and in the greater alignment of the system of social expenditure, in terms of both benefits and free-of-charge services, with that in most EU countries. However, the delay in the modernization of Spain's public sector and the haste with which it was carried out – in the desire to redress as swiftly as possible the pitiful situation of public finances prevailing in the years before the return to democracy – gave rise to two other problems: a shortage of services which require investments that take a long time to mature (such as transport and school infrastructure) and an accumulation of various administrative deficiencies leading to a weak cost–efficiency ratio in some public activities.

In other respects, the progressive ageing of the population and the economic setting of moderate growth and high unemployment have produced a sharp increase in expenditure on social benefits, and, at the same time, have curbed the growth in revenue from social security contributions, making for increasing uncertainty about the future financial viability of the welfare state in Spain and in the other European economies.

- In addition, the comparative analysis has shown the existence in Spain of divergence in several other areas that also affects real convergence and – according to the economic theory on monetary unions – increases the probability of asymmetrical shocks, which in EMU cannot be dealt with through exchange-rate adjustments. Two areas of divergence stand out in particular. First and foremost is Spain's lower productivity, to a large extent associated with a shortfall of capital, which is particularly pronounced in those intangible assets that most affect productivity, namely technology and human capital. The second is the disparity in Spain's productive and trade specialization in relation to that of the core EU countries, with a much lower weight in the branches of activity with higher technological content and better growth prospects. In this respect, the detailed analysis of trade specialization has revealed that, within the large volume of trade of an intra-industrial nature, that which predominates is based on qualitative differences between the products sold, with Spain tending to specialize in lower-quality varieties.
- A further characteristic weakness observed in Spain's productive structure, which could impede exploitation of the opportunities provided by EMU, is the lower degree of internationalization of Spanish firms, reflected both in the ratio of exports to output and in the lower relative importance of direct investment abroad.
- In any case, the most distinctive feature of the Spanish economy is the extraordinary gravity of its unemployment problem, distinguished not only by an uncommonly high unemployment rate but also by the peculiarities in the composition of both the unemployed and the employed. Basically there is a greater incidence of unemployment among young people and women, a higher proportion of long-term unemployment and, above all, an exceptional rate of temporary employment (roughly three times the EU average). At the root of these disequilibria lie the rigidities and inefficiencies in the workings of the Spanish labour market, which are more pronounced than in the case of the other EU economies. Among others, the high cost of terminating contracts and the flawed system of collective bargaining stand out in particular. Moreover, there are good grounds for believing that the Spanish economy's extraordinary and persistent levels of unemployment are to a large extent attributable to the inadequate adaptation of Spain's economic system to the radical changes that have arisen in the techniques of producing and

distributing goods and services. It has been shown that the greater resort to imported goods incorporating new technologies, as well as the importing of the technical assistance and inputs required for their use, inhibits the job-creation mechanisms induced by technological change that could help compensate for the labour savings derived from the application of the new technology. None the less, it must be noted that both unemployment and the other relative weaknesses of the Spanish economy show very encouraging signs of progress.

So far we have listed the most salient features of the course of the Spanish economy since Spain's accession to the Community and its current position within the European Union. However, the analyses in the other chapters of the book have also revealed other developments, and together with the above points they provide an indication of the nature of the main economic challenges awaiting Spain and its EU partners in the years ahead. First, there is the challenge of adapting to the new economic policy regime involved in EMU membership. Secondly, our study suggests that the dynamics of the growing relations with the former communist countries that have the greatest possibilities of joining the European integration project constitute a further potential source of challenges that should not be underestimated. Lastly, though not least important, is the need to confront the changes in the forms of production and labour relations that will arise from the adoption of the innumerable opportunities that new information and communications technologies will continue to open up in the future. Let us look at each one in greater detail:

- Since the startup of EMU on 1 January 1999, the member countries have been subject to a new economic policy regime: on the one hand, a single monetary policy applied by the ESCB – and, more directly, by the European Central Bank – aimed at maintaining price stability, and on the other hand, an almost completely decentralized fiscal policy applied by the national governments, albeit subject to the strict fiscal discipline established in the stability pact, ratified at the Amsterdam Summit and, as such, characterized by little leeway for counter-cyclical measures. Under this economic policy regime, involving the disappearance of the exchange rate as a stabilization mechanism, EMU allows scant margin for the application of policies for dealing with the specific economic shocks that may affect particular regions or countries. In other respects, one of the most forceful conclusions drawn from the book's analysis is that, despite the clear headway observed in the years of Spain's membership of the Community, there are still flaws in its productive structure and efficiency that result in a greater probability of suffering specific shocks.

Hence, within EMU, there will still be a need for national policies to secure the consolidation of budget deficits but without impeding the growth of output and employment or undermining the core of the welfare state in Europe. This is certainly a difficult challenge, in particular for those countries, such as Spain, with a lower level of economic development and more serious unemployment problems.

- As regards the challenges posed by the likely enlargement of the European project to include Eastern European countries, this book has shown the existence of a series of tendencies that could endure, and even intensify, in the future. Since the arrival of these economies on the international marketplace after the bankruptcy of the communist system, their trade relations with the EU countries – including Spain – have grown at a very intense rate, as have the direct investment projects originating in Community countries, especially in countries, such as Germany and Austria, with which they had close ties in the past. Moreover, indications have been found of a tendency among the European firms of Central EU countries to move their productive activities to these emerging market economies, to the detriment of Southern European partners. Lastly, unless the funds earmarked for structural measures and the system for allocating them envisaged in the European Union's regional policy are changed, the integration of Eastern countries will put great pressure on the EMU budget, which is leading to an erosion in the assistance received by the beneficiary countries.
- Finally, the intensity and versatility of the technical innovations in the area of information and communications, and further advances in their dissemination, signal that in the years ahead substantive changes will continue to emerge in the methods of production and competitive strategies of firms, in line with those of recent years. Firms are therefore likely to persevere with their internationalization plans and in relocating certain stages of their production and distribution processes in order to benefit from the comparative advantages of different locations and the enormous possibilities for managing dispersed productive units opened up by the advances in communications. The demand for skilled labour, able and willing to adapt to the occupational and geographical changes required by these strategies, is also likely to continue.

In the light of this scenario, and bearing in mind the findings of the present study, outlined in the points above and described in greater detail in the conclusions to each chapter, several final reflections on the most appropriate *economic policy options* for Spain would seem in order.

- To begin with, it is worth repeating that, despite the great uncertainty about the extent to which Spain will share in the benefits that EMU is likely to generate for the member countries as a whole, its inclusion in the group of founding countries was the best option. In this respect, it seems clear that self-exclusion from the project would not have significantly increased its ability to apply different policies; in a world, such as the present one, marked by the strong globalization of markets, and especially financial ones, national policies that veer from the prevailing norms of fiscal discipline and price and exchange-rate stability are severely penalized. And, in fact, the Maastricht Treaty and the subsequent agreements supplementing it explicitly require that the pre-in countries pursue the same policies as those applied within EMU. Finally, it must be borne in mind that self-exclusion from EMU would leave the country sidelined from the decisions taken within the monetary union, but would not shield it from the consequences of these decisions.
- Secondly, it should be emphasized that, according to economic theory, it is not at all certain that, of itself, belonging to EMU will enable a country to exploit the potential advantages in efficiency and welfare offered by membership. It is true that EMU membership undoubtedly helps maintain a climate of macroeconomic stability that is conducive to productive investment and – by strengthening the integration of the European market – to its more efficient allocation. However, it is also true that these effects will not materialize without the active participation of economic and social agents, if only to counteract the distributive failures of the market system. In this respect, note that the existence of economies of scale, experience and agglomeration, so often found in most productive branches and even more in processes that generate technological and human capital, tends to produce an even greater polarization of economic activity. This suggests that countries, such as Spain, with a weaker starting position will have to work harder to take advantage of the potential benefits of economic and monetary union.
- In view of these considerations, we would advocate an economic policy that continues to give priority to maintaining macro-

> economic stability, but within a more ambitious strategy and a longer time frame, geared towards redressing the shortcomings in the structure and efficiency of Spain's productive system and, by extension, the worst of its negative consequences: unemployment. Fiscal consolidation policy should therefore be part of a plan of structural reforms and measures to boost growth in production and employment, and thus to improve the balance of costs and benefits involved in membership of EMU.

Although the detailed formulation of such a strategy is beyond the scope of this book, its findings none the less point towards the appropriateness of several possible lines of action.

Here the best point of departure is one of the aspects found – a common denominator as it were – in most of the factors of divergence and disequilibrium revealed in the comparative analysis of the Spanish economy in the European setting: the productivity gap stemming from Spain's lower capital stock, particularly as regards technological and human capital and, albeit to a lesser extent, infrastructure. Various sections of the book have provided evidence that this problem lies at the bottom of many other shortcomings, including: the Spanish economy's under-specialization in production and trade in the branches of goods and services with greater technological content and better growth prospects; the high income elasticity of the demand for imports; the low degree of internationalization of firms; and, last but not least, its more pronounced structural and technological unemployment.

If we accept this diagnosis as a starting point, it would seem clear that to enhance the Spanish economy's possibilities of sustained growth in output and employment – especially amid growing competitive pressures, such as those derived from EMU's consolidation and the likely expansion towards Eastern Europe – a substantial and sustained investment drive will have to be made in education, R&D and infrastructure. These areas are key to the proper application of the cumulative technological innovations generated in recent years – in many fields, but particularly in information and communications – and, by extension, to the development of the new productive activities and jobs which they make possible.

To achieve this objective, it would seem necessary for the public sector to take a more direct hand in promoting the investment efforts required, especially in the above-mentioned areas. Two types of measure would seem to be in order: reforms to the regulatory framework of markets and institutions, geared to creating a pattern of incentives to improve the efficiency of the economic system, and an increase in public investment in these areas.

As regards regulatory changes to improve the efficiency of markets, our analysis suggests that where they are most needed is in the labour market. In this respect, in Chapter 3, it was argued that the enormous relative weight of young job-seekers and long-term unemployed and the high proportion of temporary jobs together entail – along with other economic and social costs – a serious obstacle to the expansion and appropriate allocation of human capital. Youth unemployment implies a failure to make good use of a group that – given the more intense efforts in education in recent years – has a higher relative level of skills. Long-term unemployment, especially in an era of radical technological change as at present, leads to an obsolescence of the knowledge and abilities of the unemployed that undermines their job prospects. And finally, temporary employment discourages training initiatives by both workers and firms.

It would therefore seem appropriate to continue with the reforms aimed at overcoming the rigidities in wage structures and affecting job mobility that hinder the efficient allocation of human resources.

In addition to a more radical reform of the labour market, further progress is needed in deregulating the protected services sectors. At the same time – through a policy that actively promotes competition – measures would have to be taken to prevent market domination by a small number of suppliers and practices that are harmful to competition, situations which tend to arise after the application of deregulating measures such as privatization.

In any event, in addition to proposing the creation of a legal framework conducive to productivity growth, this book advocates the need for a more aggressive policy to stimulate output growth. This policy would involve boosting investment to enlarge, and improve the endowments of, those productive factors that, because of their special influence on growth and their significant positive externalities for firms, require government support, namely technology, human capital and infrastructure.

To reconcile the fiscal discipline required not only for the smooth functioning of EMU but also by today's globalized international markets with the increase in government investment associated with the policy proposed here, substantial changes would have to be made to the composition of the budget's revenue and expenditure, as well as major improvements in the way they are managed. In any event, this would appear to be the most appropriate way of ensuring the sustainability of fiscal consolidation over time, as required by the stability pact.

Beginning with the revenue side, it would not seem advisable to raise taxes, given the extent of the tax burden, although in some circumstances taxing the use of certain public services might be justified. In any case, the many signs of tax evasion and fraud suggest that further steps towards their eradication would not only be expedient but would also increase government revenue.

On the expenditure side, reforms in several areas of the welfare state are needed for many reasons, including the serious doubts regarding the system's financial viability and the inefficiencies observed in the management of social benefits. For the reasons adduced in Chapter 5, we believe these reforms should preserve the essence of the system, while introducing changes that would curtail expenditure, above all in the area that absorbs the most resources: pensions. Increasing the number of years included in the calculation of the base salary (used to calculate pension entitlement), the improvement of inspection systems to prevent fraud in the wrongful payment of pensions, and the promotion of private funded schemes are, in our view, among the best proposals for reducing expenditure.

As regards health benefits, it would also seem feasible and necessary to continue with the reforms aimed at restraining the spectacular growth in expenditure. This especially applies to the area of pharmaceuticals, where spending could be cut by reducing distribution costs, reorienting the consumption of pharmaceuticals towards cheaper products and brands, promoting the use of generic brands and, perhaps, increasing the consumer's share of the cost.

In the area of unemployment benefits, we have already explained the rationale behind reducing their size in favour of more intense and active employment policies. Here the objective is twofold: to remove the factors that discourage the search for a job, as well as the apparent abuses of the system, and to stimulate the hiring of the unemployed.

With respect to expenditure on education, however, there is little margin for cuts, although room does exist for a more efficient allocation. In this book we have argued (in Chapter 5) in favour of increasing government investment to improve the quality of teaching at the levels that are crucial in determining the eventual opportunities of pupils and which, moreover, generate a greater social return: primary and secondary education.

With this, we conclude the list of suggestions for Spain's economic policy deduced from our analysis. Before ending, however, it would seem appropriate to add several considerations regarding Community policies. Here we might note that one of the important challenges for EMU is to reinforce stabilization mechanisms to prevent the negative consequences of possible asymmetrical shocks. In this respect, we have argued in favour of endowing the Community budget with a stabilizing capacity.

In concluding, it is also worth noting that the problems associated with the difficult adaptation to new technologies and forms of international competition, so closely related to unemployment, are a phenomenon that – while especially harsh in Spain – affects all of Europe. This would suggest the need for stronger Community-wide policies. Moreover, not only from the standpoint of solidarity but also for the economic reasons discussed – in Chapters 11 and 12 in particular – attempts should also be made to ensure that economic and monetary union is more solidly underpinned by political and social integration in both the budget and the workings of the Community institutions.

Appendix I: Chronology of the European Integration Process

1950

- On 9 May, in a speech inspired by Jean Monnet, Robert Schuman, the French Foreign Minister, proposes that 'Franco-German production of coal and steel as a whole be placed under a common High Authority, within the framework of an organization open to the participation of the other countries of Europe.'

1951

- The **Treaty of Paris**, establishing the European Coal and Steel Community (ECSC), is signed by France, West Germany, Belgium, Holland, Luxembourg and Italy.

1952

- The **ECSC** enters into force in July.

1954

- The Brussels Treaty, establishing military cooperation between the United Kingdom, France, Belgium, Holland and Luxembourg, is enlarged with the accession of Italy and Germany, creating the **Western European Union (WEU)**.

1957

- On 25 March the **Treaties of Rome** are signed by the ECSC member states, creating the **European Economic Community (EEC)** and the **European Atomic Energy Community (Euratom or EAEC)**. Together, the EEC, the ECSC and Euratom constitute the European Communities.

1958

- On 1 January the **Treaties of Rome** enter into force.
- The Six agree to **abolish the tariffs** affecting their trade, except agricultural products, over a period of 12 years, and to create a **common external tariff (CET)** for trade with third countries. The **European Social Fund (ESF)** is established to improve employment opportunities.
- The Stresa Conference approves a **common agricultural policy (CAP)**.

1960

- In response to the creation of the EEC, at the initiative of the United Kingdom, the Stockholm Convention creates the **European Free Trade Association (EFTA)**, formed by Austria, Denmark, Norway, Portugal, Sweden, Switzerland and the United Kingdom.

1962

- **The CAP enters into force.**
- **Spain requests the start of negotiations for its association with the EEC.**

1964

- The **European Agricultural Guidance and Guarantee Fund (EAGGF)** is created to promote the development and diversification of the Community's rural areas.

1965

- The **Treaty merging the institutions** of the EEC, the ECSC and Euratom is signed, envisaging one Council, one Commission and a common European Parliament and Court of Justice.[1]

1966

- The '**Luxembourg Compromise**' is agreed, establishing the maintenance of the unanimity procedure when 'vital interests' of the Community are at stake. This brings an end to one of the European Community's most serious crises.

1968

- All **customs duties in internal Community trade are abolished** ahead of schedule, and the CET is established.

1969

- The **Hague Summit** studies arrangements to provide the EEC with its own resources. Value-added tax (VAT) and revenue from the CET are to be the main sources of financing for Community spending. It also mandates a committee, chaired by Luxembourg's Finance Minister Pierre Werner, to draw up a step-by-step plan outlining each of the stages leading to economic and monetary union (EMU).

1970

- **Spain and the EEC sign a preferential agreement**, marking the first link towards Spain's membership of the Community. The agreement, initially spanning six years, was extended until the entry into force of Spain's Treaty of Accession to the EEC in 1986.
- The **Werner Report** unveils a three-stage plan for the achievement of EMU, with the final stage to be reached in 1980.

1972

- The **first enlargement of the EEC**, with the entry of Denmark, the United Kingdom, Ireland and Norway, is agreed.
- The **EEC and EFTA sign a free trade agreement** to broaden their trade ties.

- Creation of the '**currency snake**'. The Six decide to limit the margin of fluctuation of their currencies against the dollar to ± 2.25 per cent.

1973

- The **first enlargement of the EEC comes into force** with the accession of Denmark, the United Kingdom and Ireland (a referendum in Norway rejects membership).

1974

- Amid an economic and monetary crisis, it is agreed to **postpone the process leading to EMU**.

1975

- The **Lomé Convention** establishes various mechanisms for aid to underdeveloped countries. The most important one is the **Stabex Fund**, whose purpose is to stabilize the trade revenue of the 70 African, Caribbean and Pacific (ACP) associated countries, to be financed from the European Development Fund (EDF).
- The **European Regional Development Fund (ERDF)** is created with the aim of narrowing the social and economic differences between the regions of the EEC.
- The **European Court of Auditors**,[2] one of the five institutions of the European Communities, is established.
- **Spain begins formal negotiations for accession to the EEC.**

1979

- The **European Monetary System (EMS)** starts up. It is structured around the European Monetary Cooperation Fund (EMCF), the forerunner of the present European Monetary Institute (EMI), and the exchange-rate mechanism (ERM). The pound does not enter the EMS, and the European currency unit, or *ecu*, is created.
- The **first election to the European Parliament by direct universal suffrage** is held.
- The **Second Lomé Convention** is signed, incorporating additional cooperation measures with the ACP countries.

1981

- The **second enlargement of the EEC enters into effect** with the accession of Greece.

1984

- The **Fontainebleau Summit** agrees to restrain agricultural spending and to correct the United Kingdom's excess contribution to the Community (known as the 'British cheque').
- In December the **Third Lomé Convention** on financial aid to the ACP countries is signed, including for the first time references to human rights.

1985

- The **Accession Treaties of Spain and Portugal** are signed.
- Belgium, Holland and Luxembourg join France and Germany in signing the **Schengen Agreement** on the free movement of persons across the borders of the signatory countries.
- The Milan European Council approves the **White Paper on the Internal Market.**

1986

- The **Community's third enlargement** becomes effective with the accession of Spain and Portugal.
- The **Single European Act**, containing the measures for the formation of a single market on 1 January 1993, is signed.

1987

- **The Single European Act enters into force.**

1988

- The **Hanover Summit** creates a committee, formed by the central bank governors and the President of the European Commission, Jacques Delors, to study the introduction of the single currency.
- The **Structural Funds are revised** and enlarged.

1989

- **The peseta joins the exchange-rate mechanism of the EMS**, with a broad-band fluctuation margin (± 6 per cent).
- The Madrid Summit approves the **report of the Delors Committee**.
- The **declaration of the fundamental social rights of workers** is approved by all Community countries except the United Kingdom.

1990

- In July the **first stage in the construction of EMU**, involving the coordination of economic policies, begins.
- The **free circulation of capital** comes into effect.
- **Unified Germany** is incorporated as a single state on 3 October.
- **The pound joins the EMS.**
- The EEC assigns substantial aid to the ACP countries within the **Fourth Lomé Convention**, which is to be in force for ten years.
- The five-year **PHARE programme** for financial assistance to Central and Eastern European countries begins.
- The European Council in Rome sets in motion the **inter-governmental conferences** (IGC) on EMU and political union.

1991

- The **European Economic Area (EEA)**, formed by the member countries of the EEC and EFTA, is created.

- The EEC signs the **European Agreements** with Poland and Hungary, which establish a new framework for economic relations and the transition to market economies as a prelude to their integration in Europe.

1992

- On 7 February the **Treaty on European Union (Maastricht Treaty)** is signed. It establishes the timetable for the formation of economic and monetary union and sets the criteria to be met by the countries seeking entry.
- The **Committee of the Regions** is created. This Committee and the Economic and Social Committee[3] are **auxiliary institutions of the European Communities**.
- The **Central European Free Trade Association (CEFTA)** is created, encompassing the Visegrad countries: Hungary, Poland, the Czech Republic and Slovakia.
- The Council of Ministers of Agriculture approves the **CAP reform**, based on the 'MacSharry Report', in which protection via prices is reduced and is replaced by a system of direct aid from the Community budget.
- The **Edinburgh Council establishes Cohesion Funds** to offset the possible negative effects of the process leading to EMU on the income distribution of the member countries.

1993

- **On 1 January the single European market enters into force**, although several directives relating to the free movement of workers are not yet in effect.
- **Delors unveils the White Paper on Growth, Competitiveness and Employment**. Among others, it contains a programme for trans-European networks to be financed by the European Investment Bank (EIB).[4]
- **A fresh crisis erupts in the EMS**, and the fluctuation band of the central exchange rates of the member countries' currencies is widened to ± 15 per cent.
- On 1 November, after a delay caused by the monetary crisis and the ratification by national parliaments, the **Maastricht Treaty comes into effect.**
- The criteria for granting **structural funds** in the years 1994 to 1999 are approved.
- New **European Agreements** are signed with the Czech Republic, Slovakia, Romania and Bulgaria, and the CEFTA becomes effective.

1994

- **The second stage of EMU begins**. During this stage the European Monetary Institute, precursor of the European Central Bank (ECB), is created, and the technical and organizational aspects to achieve monetary union are prepared. The statutes of national central banks, making them independent of their governments, are approved.
- **The EEA enters into effect.**
- The accession of Austria, Finland, Sweden and Norway marks the **fourth enlargement of the European Union (EU)**.
- The **European Agreements** with Hungary and Poland become effective, and the two countries also present their requests for EU membership.

- Following the failure of the job-creation policies set in motion by EU countries, at the **Essen Summit** a strategy is designed to achieve **a sustainable reduction in the high level of unemployment** on the basis of macroeconomic policies and structural reforms.

1995

- **The fourth enlargement of the EU becomes effective**, with the entry of Austria, Finland and Sweden. In a referendum Norway votes against accession.
- The **Cannes Summit agrees to postpone the start of the third stage of EMU** from 1 January 1997 to 1 January 1999, an alternative already contemplated in the Maastricht Treaty.
- The Spanish EU presidency promotes the **Mediterranean Conference** in Barcelona, whose purpose is to strengthen trade relations between Europe and the Mediterranean countries.
- The **PHARE programme** of financial aid to Central and Eastern European countries is renewed.
- The European Union signs **additional European Agreements** with the Baltic states (Latvia, Lithuania and Estonia), and the agreements with the Czech Republic, Slovakia, Romania and Bulgaria enter into force. Slovenia joins CEFTA.
- **The Schengen Agreement becomes effective.**

1996

- The European Council in Turin inaugurates the **inter-governmental conference** (IGC) that will revise the Maastricht Treaty.
- The Florence Council considers increasing the insufficient **resources for financing the programmes contemplated in the White Paper on Growth, Competitiveness and Employment**, which had set the objective of creating 15 million jobs.
- In December **the lira returns to the EMS.**
- The **European Council in Dublin** defines the terms of what is known as the '**stability pact**', requiring EMU member countries to maintain a policy of budgetary stability, with sanctions to be imposed on any country whose budget deficit exceeds 3 per cent.
- **Sweden, Denmark, Finland, Norway and Iceland join the Schengen Agreement** on the freedom of movement of persons across national borders; among the EU countries, by their own choice Ireland and the United Kingdom are not signatories of the agreement.

1997

- In June the **European Council in Amsterdam** postpones the institutional reform to be implemented prior to the enlargement of the European Union. The permanent nature of the stability pact is established, and it is agreed to include a section on employment in the new Treaty on European Union (Amsterdam Treaty), although no specific measures or financial channels for its implementation are contemplated.
- In late November an **extraordinary European Council on employment** is held.

1998

- The Council of the heads of state and government meet in Brussels on 3 May and approve the **entry of 11 EU countries into the third stage of EMU** in 1999. The United Kingdom, Sweden and Denmark are excluded by their own choice, and Greece because of its failure to fulfil the Maastricht criteria.
- On 31 December the governors of the **central banks fix the irrevocable parities of the national currencies vis-à-vis the euro**. The euro's value is set at:

Country	Currency	Exchange rate
Belgium	franc	40.3399
Germany	mark	1.95583
Spain	peseta	166.386
France	franc	6.55957
Ireland	Irish pound	0.787564
Italy	lira	1936.27
Luxemburg	franc	40.3399
Netherlands	guilder	2.20371
Austria	schilling	13.7603
Portugal	escudo	200.482
Finland	mark	5.94573

1999

- On 4 January, with the introduction of the single currency for the execution of monetary policy and its use in financial markets, the **third stage of EMU** begins. The **European System of Central Banks (ESCB)**, formed by the European Central Bank (ECB) and the national central banks, is constituted.
- On 24–5 March, in the Berlin Council, the Fifteen approved the **financial perspective** for the period 2000–6, contemplated in the **Agenda 2000**. This document also addresses one of the European Union's major challenges at the start of the millennium: its **enlargement to Eastern European countries**.

2002

- On 1 January the **circulation of euro notes and coins** will begin.
- On 1 July **national notes and coins will no longer be legal tender**.

Appendix II: Methodological Problems of International Comparisons

In analyses which draw international comparisons, as in the present study, very close attention must be paid to all aspects relating to the compatibility of the data. The essential questions to be considered are: (a) the homogeneity of the variables for the countries compared, and (b) the appropriateness of the system used for their valuation.

(a) With respect to the homogeneity of the information, at least two problems arise when dealing with international data: discrepancies in the definition of the variables, and differences in the form and periodicity in which they are gathered and published.

Even though international organizations have been making increasing efforts to harmonize the information provided by countries – the methodology used in the national accounts in the SNA and the ESA prepared by the United Nations and the European Commission, respectively, the labour market rulings of the ICLS, and the balance of payments in the IMF manuals, for example – differences still exist. These are explained by the exceptions introduced by individual countries in accordance with their needs and their ability to follow the statistical guidelines of international institutions.

At times these differences remain for legal reasons, as in the case of those relating to the working-age population (dependent on laws on the minimum ages for working and retirement), and are therefore difficult to avoid.

One constant source of problems for comparative analyses are the numerous sectoral classifications, which produce discrepancies in the branches of activity, even at high levels of aggregation.[1]

Because of these problems, arriving at a complete and homogeneous set of data proved a very difficult and painstaking task.

As to the second facet of the compatibility problems, those associated with the compilation methods and periodicity of international data are equally notorious. In this respect – and without going into the more technical methodological questions relating to data collection – it is worth pointing out that non-coincidence of the base years of many of the statistical series of the countries was a recurrent problem. Moreover, the periodicity, the degree of coverage and the updating of the data also differ greatly from one country to another.

These factors, together with the determination to offer complete information for the 15 EU countries and, in so far as possible, for the United States and Japan, over the same period (1986–97), made the task of checking and harmonizing a multitude of statistical sources particularly complicated. As these sources are indicated at the foot of the figures and tables, there is no point in listing them here. It would, however, seem worthwhile to comment briefly on the criteria used in their selection.

Whenever possible we have used information from Eurostat and the other Community institutions (European Commission, European Monetary Institute, European Central Bank, European Court of Auditors), selecting first the data compiled by the institution itself or, when they were not available, those collected and homogenized on the basis of the information supplied by national statistical offices.

None the less, the data provided by these organizations often had to be supplemented with information from other sources, particularly in the case of the three newest EU members (Sweden, Finland and Austria), because they still do not figure in many of Eurostat's statistics.

In these cases, we first searched the OECD's statistical databases and, when they too lacked the information needed, we explored others, primarily those of the IMF, the United Nations, UNESCO and the ILO.

It should also be pointed out that, even when the data for Spain were obtained from the same international organizations, they were checked and expanded with more detailed information from official Spanish sources.

Finally, even though the periodicity of the data employed in the analyses is annual, because of the time lag – longer or shorter depending on the variables in question – in most of the statistical sources, in some cases we had to use sources based on a shorter period (four-month, quarterly and even monthly data) to cover the information for 1997. This linking of the information provided annually with shorter-term statistics again required a major effort to harmonize the data.

(b) After considering the conceptual problems involved in harmonizing the data, we shall now turn to the valuation side. In theory, to establish comparisons between variables which, like those in this book, have both a geographical and a time dimension the four procedures shown in Figure A.1 can be followed.

These procedures – see Figure A.1 – are based on combinations of the two options for the treatment of each of the dimensions of the variables: time (valuation in nominal or real terms) and geography (harmonization of the values of the different currencies using the exchange rate or their purchasing power parity).

Before going on to justify the options used in this book, we shall illustrate the relevance of this question with an example (per capita GDP).

As seen in Figure A.2, the conclusions drawn from the analysis of Spain's convergence with the EU average in terms of per capita GDP differ substantially depending on which valuation procedure is used.

As expected, the differences are much more important in the two cases using the variables expressed in nominal terms. In fact, when comparing the results based on the exchange rate and PPP in nominal terms (procedures 1 and 2), differences arise in both their level and trends; however, the discrepancies arising from the analysis of the series in real terms (procedures 3 and 4) lie almost entirely in their level, as their trends are very similar. Indeed, it can be demonstrated that in bilateral comparisons – since the parity corresponds to that of the base year and is therefore invariant over time – the only difference between procedures 3 and 4 is that occasioned by the different values of the relative

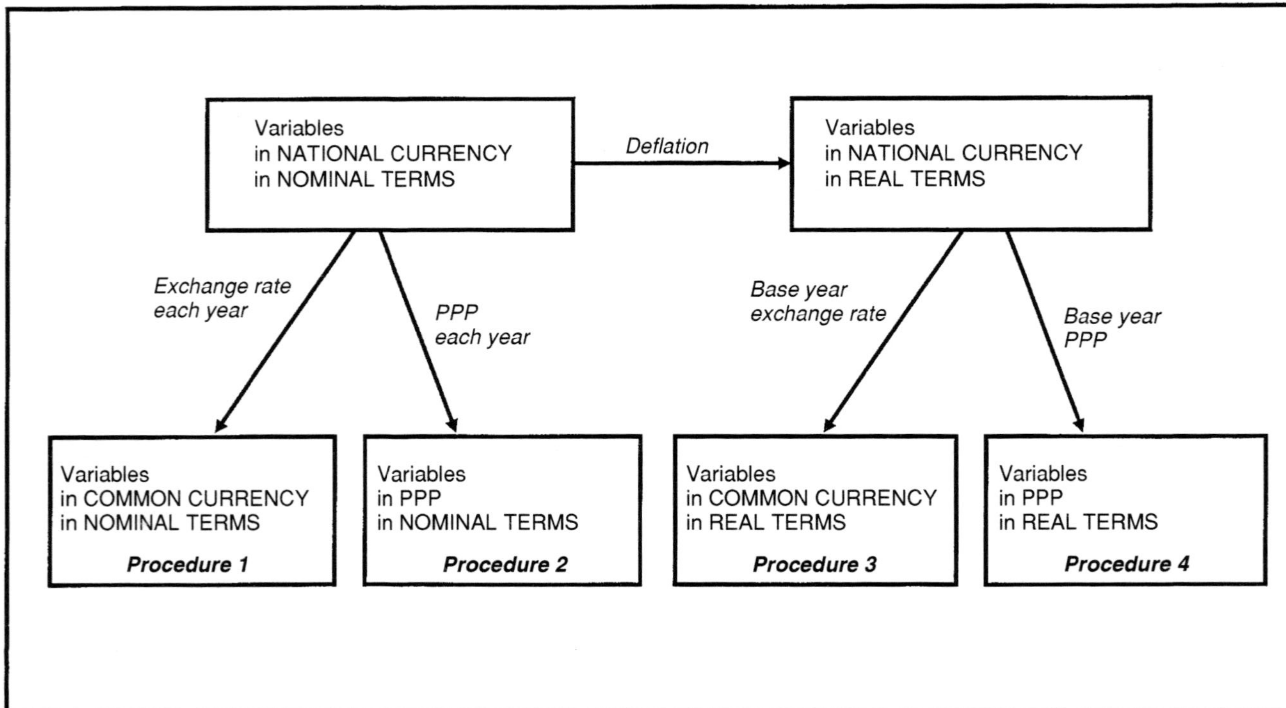

Figure A.1 Procedures for making international comparisons

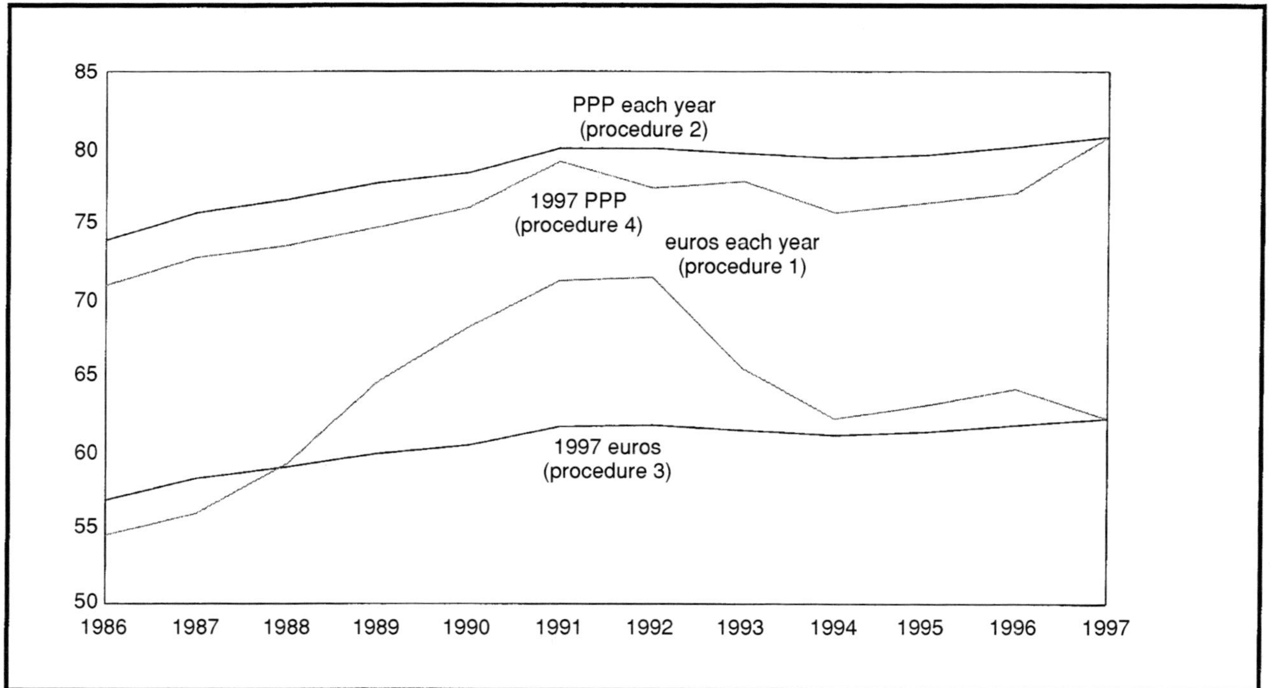

Figure A.2 Convergence of Spanish GDP per capita with the EU average according to the valuation system used (EU = 100)

Source: OECD: *National Accounts*; vol. I: *Main Aggregates*; OECD: *Quarterly National Accounts*.

procedures 3 and 4 is that occasioned by the different values of the relative exchange rate and PPP in the year in question.

Thus, if the following variables are defined:

Y_t^i	=	GDP in year *t* of country *i* in nominal terms,
P_t^i	=	Population in year *t* of country *i*,
D_t^i	=	Deflator in year *t* of country *i*,
T	=	Exchange rate (currency of country B/currency of country A) in the base year, and
PPP	=	*PPP* (currency of country B/currency of country A) in the base year,

the expressions for relative per capita GDP may be obtained by using valuation methods 3 and 4, which are:

(i) when the exchange rate is used:

$$\frac{(Y_t^A \cdot T)/(P_t^A \cdot D_t^A)}{(Y_t^B)/(P_t^B \cdot D_t^B)} \tag{1}$$

(ii) when PPP is used:

$$\frac{(Y_t^A \cdot PPP)/(P_t^A \cdot D_t^A)}{(Y_t^B)/(P_t^B \cdot D_t^B)} \tag{2}$$

Both expressions can be simplified, if we take into account that the real per capita GDP of country *i* for year *t* ($\text{GDP}pc_t^i$) can be defined as:

$$\frac{Y_t^i}{(P_t^i \cdot D_t^i)} \tag{3}$$

Substituting [3] into equations [1] and [2], we obtain:

$$\frac{\text{GDP}pc_t^A \cdot T}{\text{GDP}pc_t^B} \tag{4}$$

$$\frac{\text{GDP}pc_t^A \cdot PPP}{\text{GDP}pc_t^B} \tag{5}$$

Note, in this respect, that – as argued in Balassa (1964) and Samuelson (1964) and more recently in Heston, Nuxoll and Summers (1994) – the differences in price levels, and thus between T and PPP, will tend to be more pronounced the greater the economic gap between the countries compared. Thus rich countries, with higher productivity in tradable products, will tend to have higher price levels.

From this we deduce that procedures 1 and 2 should be ruled out. But we must still choose between procedures 3 and 4, in other words between the use of the exchange rate and PPP.[2] Here we should begin by pointing out that neither of the two represents the best option.[3] Thus, PPP – in expressing the value of a common basket of goods and services in the different countries[4] –

surmounts the problem which arises with exchange rates, owing to their failure to capture the differences in the purchasing power of currencies across countries.

PPP, however, is not without limitations. First, it reflects the discrepancies in prices attributable to differences in the systems of subsidies and indirect taxation in the countries, and it does not discriminate between goods imported or produced in the country at the time the data are collected. Moreover, the method for extrapolating PPPs used until recently for Community countries (based on specific surveys every five years with the values for the intervening years interpolated on the basis of the trends in GDP deflators)[5] led to substantial differences between the data extrapolated and those obtained from samples.

In sum, it might be said that the advantages of PPP over the exchange rate are, to some extent, offset by the limitations still involved in the complex process of its calculation. That said, it might be argued that it should be used when dealing with variables in whose interpretation it is important to reflect purchasing power. For this reason, we decided to use only PPP when it seemed essential to reflect this dimension, such as in the case of per capita GDP and welfare expenditure.

Before concluding this methodological appendix, we should explain the use of 1997 as the base year for expressing the variables in constant terms, as well as the parity used to convert the national currencies into euro. As regards the base year, we have used the last full year at the time of realizing the study in an attempt to make the interpretation of the data on the countries' relative position more attractive for readers by offering information based on updated prices. As to the euro parities, it should be noted that they represent the average annual exchange rates of each national currency vis-à-vis the ecu according to Eurostat's monthly bulletin: *Eurostat* 2, 1998 (p. 62).

Notes

Notes to the Introduction

1. The data have been updated as far as possible. While the book includes the most recent developments and even envisages the future horizon of monetary union in Europe, its prime concern is to analyse the events and economic relations of a more structural nature.
2. Appendix I gives a detailed chronology of the integration process.
3. Despite the growing signs of China's capacity to form another similar bloc.
4. Innovations of this type, which produce radical changes that affect productive processes as a whole, are what have recently come to be known as 'general purpose technologies' (Bresnahan and Trajtenberg, 1995).

Notes to Chapter 1: Growth and Structural Changes

1. To calculate GDP per capita for each of the countries, the values were obtained in constant 1997 terms, and the different currencies were then homogenized using the PPP with respect to the euro of that same year.
2. A more detailed analysis of the subject from a longer time perspective is contained in Fuentes Quintana (1995).
3. Exports plus imports of goods and services defined in national accounts terms.
4. See Alvira and García (1997).
5. For further illustration of this point, see Maté (1995) for the case of Spain in comparison with the European Union, and Ark (1996) for a set of eight European countries.
6. The productive structure was calculated without taking into account imputed bank services.
7. Sumpsi (1995) contains a more detailed analysis of the sector.
8. See, in this respect, the classifications used by Martínez and Muñoz (1995).
9. According to tourism receipts recorded in the balance of payments, Spain is in third place, with 23 569 million euro in 1997, behind Italy (26 387 million) and France (24 711 million). However, in terms of the number of overnight stays by non-residents, Spain ranks second after the United Kingdom, and fourth in terms of total overnight stays at tourist lodgings by residents and non-residents.
10. The similarity index is defined as $100 - \Sigma|p_i^1 - p_i^2|$, where 1 and 2 are the countries compared. This calculation was made on the basis of the NACE-CLIO (25) classification. For the economy as a whole, similarity indices of 74.17 and 75.51 are obtained for 1986 and 1996. For the manufacturing sector, these figures are 71.77 and 72.15.

Notes to Chapter 2: Productivity and its Determinants

1. Increased employment is also an important channel for correcting Spain's productivity gap, given the Spanish economy's low rate of employment in relation to the EU average.
2. More specifically, in 1995, the latest year for which information is available, the difference between the country with the longest working hours (Greece, with 43.6 hours per week) and the shortest (Holland, with 32.9 hours) was 10.7 hours per week.
3. Specifically, the measures of total productivity take as their point of departure the existence of only two productive factors: capital and labour. Moreover, most of the indicators used in its measurement introduce the hypotheses of constant returns to scale, perfect competition and long-term equilibrium.
4. Ruggles (1967) presents a summary of the main index numbers constructed for analysing total factor productivity.
5. For the theoretical discussion covering the Törnqvist-Theil index and the derivation of the final expression of the multilateral translogarithmic productivity index, readers are referred to Velázquez (1995a).
6. This is the appropriate measure of value added, because only capital and labour are taken into account as productive factors, and the sum of their remuneration is GDP at factor cost.
7. More specifically, the OECD publication *Flows and Stocks of Fixed Capital* presents data for the stock of physical capital for Belgium, Finland, France, Germany, Greece, Italy, Sweden and the United Kingdom within the European Union.
8. See OECD (1993) for an idea of how the findings are influenced by the differences in the methods used among EU countries to measure capital stock.

   A recent report published by Eurostat – *The Capital Stock in the European Union: Structural diagnosis and analytical aspects* – uses a homogeneous procedure for all countries, which in fact coincides with the one used in this chapter. In any event, unlike the present chapter, the report does not provide disaggregated information for the 15 EU countries.
9. Specifically, calculation of the capital stock under the perpetual inventory method requires data for the initial capital stock, a time series of the investment undertaken (from the year after the initial capital stock becomes available until the year for which the stock is to be calculated), a price series and a depreciation–obsolescence rate. The initial capital stock has been calculated for 1960 under the procedure proposed by Harberger (1978). The investment and price series are the series corresponding to gross fixed capital formation and its national accounts deflator. Lastly, the depreciation–obsolescence rate has been calculated as the sum of the obsolescence rate plus half the depreciation, obtained from Velázquez (1995b) – hence the reference to a hybrid measure – for all countries and years.
10. Martín (1995a) gives a brief overview of the main approaches to explaining growth and, specifically, of the endogenous growth models. A more detailed analysis is found in Grossman (1996).
11. Criticism of this indicator reflects two different standpoints. The first suggests that R&D spending is an overstated measure of the efforts in

technological activities in view of the high rate of failures. The second stresses the indicator's understatement, because it does not include the payments for external technology or the expenses incurred in assimilating technology that contribute to technological accumulation.

12. Here we have calculated the stock of initial technological capital under the procedure proposed by Harberger (1978). The investment series were estimated on the basis of information from the OECD and UNESCO, and correspond to the gross domestic expenditure on R&D since 1973, the first year for which data are available for all the countries. As a deflator we used that of gross fixed capital formation. A depreciation rate of 10 per cent was applied.
13. In this respect, it is worth bearing in mind that the least technologically advanced countries generally resort more to imports of technology as a way of creating technological capital. Since imported technology is not taken into account, the understatement which occurs in the countries with the lowest GDP per capita in the EU may cause a downward bias in the quantity of technological capital recorded. To assess the magnitude of this possible bias, we have calculated the EU countries' technological capital stock including expenditure on technological imports. In this respect, it is worth noting that the relative situation of the less developed countries improves, although not to any major extent. By way of example, according to this measure, Spain's technological capital stock ratio in 1997 was 43.2 per cent of the EU average.
14. Boscá, De la Fuente and Doménech (1996) review the main indicators used to measure human capital. They find that the indicator calculated here incorporates the principal corrections proposed in the literature on this type of indicator, although it may involve some sort of bias because it uses the accumulation of flows rather than an exact measure of a stock. None the less, it has the advantage of being simple to update, once the series for education dating from the 1930s is available.
15. The advantage of this procedure, in addition to its easy updating, is that it allows us to take into account that the disparities in expenditure per student across different educational levels and countries indicate different quality. Hence the measure presented here takes into consideration the most recent recommendations on measuring human capital, as shown in Gundlach (1997).
16. Specifically, it was assumed that if a job is not held, by the end of a working life the human capital acquired in primary education is reduced to 75 per cent of its initial level, in secondary education to 50 per cent, and in university and technical education to 33 per cent.
17. Biehl posits that infrastructure indicators referring to area and population are not exclusive, but instead represent complementary qualities, and he therefore proposes that they be considered in relation to a weighted average using the coefficients obtained in an estimation. Here we simply apply the same weighting to both indicators.
18. Specifically, 1 kilometre of motorway is assumed to be equal to 16 kilometres of national roadway, 32 kilometres of regional roads or 64 kilometres of local or town roads.

Notes for Chapter 3: Activity, Employment and Unemployment

1. By way of example, see Bean (1994), OECD (1994), CEPR (1995) and Viñals and Jimeno (1996).
2. The spectacular growth in temporary employment in Spain is largely explained by the numerous flexible hiring arrangements which arose after the labour market reform of 1984.
3. This hypothesis on the implications of labour market segmentation, increasingly backed by the empirical evidence, is formulated in the *insider–outsider* models of wage setting. Empirical evidence is found in Jimeno and Toharia (1993) and Bentolila and Dolado (1994).
4. See Jimeno and Toharia (1996) for evidence of the negative effects of the excessive use of temporary contracts on workers' productivity.
5. The unemployment rate used here follows the methodology of the International Conference of Labour Statisticians (ICLS) of the OECD and the ILO. Note, however, that some studies (see Toharia, ed., 1998) argue that this measure may give an upward bias to unemployment figures.
6. Naturally, the proportion of 'unemployed with no job experience' also declined, because the vast majority of this group falls within the age bracket (15 to 24) that defines youth unemployment.
7. For this reason, different financing strategies have been devised, and in some cases (the partial substitution of social security contributions by increases in value added tax) have been put into practice, albeit quite timidly. In this respect, the most far-reaching proposal – and in our view the most interesting one – was formulated by the EC Commission: the application of a 'green tax' (on CO_2 emissions) to offset the decline in government income stemming from the reduction in contributions.
8. More information on the characteristics of the systems of unemployment assistance in EU countries is found in Eurostat (1994) and European Commission (1997).
9. Although the latest labour reform of May 1997 opens up a channel for reducing dismissal costs – through a new permanent contract that entails a lower severance payment and also through the rewording of article 52(c), which clarifies the grounds for justified dismissals – it still seems insufficient.
10. By way of example, this would be the case of a small firm that is weathering a difficult period and finds itself forced to close because it is unable to cope with the labour conditions established in a sectoral agreement.
11. Chapter 3 of OECD (1996b) shows that wage disparity in the United States is much greater than in most European countries.
12. Specifically, the two legislative decrees of 16 May: one on 'Urgent measures to improve the labour market and promote permanent contracts', and the other regulating 'Social security and tax incentives to promote permanent contracts and job stability'.
13. Although these seem to be the most significant reforms, the legislative decrees contain other reforms which basically refer to collective bargaining and to the granting of tax credits on social security payments in permanent

contracts for jobless workers in groups with special difficulties in finding jobs.

14. This detailed report prepared by the OECD secretariat, under the direction of L. Soete, provides an in-depth review of the research carried out in recent years on the relationship between technology, productivity and employment.
15. A well documented discussion of the changes needed in the organization of companies and in the attitudes of employers and employees – in sum, in corporate culture – to make good use of the new technologies is presented in Sherer and Perlman (eds) (1992) and in Pérez-Díaz (1995a).
16. We return to this subject in Chapter 9.

Notes to Chapter 4: Costs, Prices and Competitiveness

1. Note that recent advances in international trade theory are grounded in these more complex notions of competitiveness. In fact, the new models of international trade – see Helpman and Krugman (1985), Krugman (ed.) (1987), Krugman (1990) and Grossman (1992) – introduce explanatory variables for trade in addition to the relative factor endowment of countries (the only variable considered in neo-classical international trade theory). In many of these models, it is acknowledged that there are disparities in the technological capacity of nations, which means that the differences in their relative prices do not depend solely on their relative endowments of capital and labour. Moreover, many envisage the existence of increasing returns to scale in productive processes and heterogeneity in products and factors, and, accordingly, most of them consider that imperfect competition exists in markets, giving rise to competitive strategies based on non-price factors.
2. A good example of this debate is to be found in a recent issue of the *Oxford Review of Economic Policy* (vol. 12, no. 3).
3. A detailed analysis of the problems derived from the creation of rankings under the aggregation procedure proposed by the World Economic Forum and the Institute for Management and Development is presented in Fernández (1993).
4. As readers will be aware, the export share indicates the relative position of a country or region as a supplier in a given market. It is defined as the country's exports as a proportion of the imports of the market of destination.
5. Thus, for example, Spain's share of the market where most of its trade takes place, the European Union, climbed from 2.0 per cent in 1986 to 3.7 per cent in 1997.
6. The European Commission (1995a) provides additional evidence of this phenomenon.
7. $$RCAI_{it} = \frac{X_{it} - M_{it}}{X_{it} + M_{it}} \cdot 100$$

   Where i = sector, and t = period.

8. Lafay (1991) presents a methodological discussion of the most appropriate way of obtaining a quantification of the structure of comparative advantages.
9. This hypothesis on the factor content of Spanish trade with its Community partners is tested under more formal procedures in Rodríguez (1993).
10. See Cañada and Carmena (1989).
11. The labour cost per wage-earner is obtained by dividing the remuneration of wage-earners, in 1997 euro, by the total number of wage-earners; the labour cost per hour worked is defined as the labour cost per wage-earner divided by the hours worked per wage-earner.
12. Specifically, when it is assumed, as is often the case, that the other production costs – of inputs and capital – evolve in a similar way to the trends in the labour factor.
13. This result is obtained in the econometric study found in Gordo and Sánchez-Carretero (1997), among others.
14. The fact that Spanish exporters act as price takers implies that they do not have the capacity to influence how prices are determined on international markets, and therefore, regardless of domestic cost pressures, they must adapt their export prices, after adjusting them for exchange-rate trends, to international prices if they do not want to see a decline in their market share. Thus, in circumstances of exchange-rate stability, domestic cost tensions will be reflected in a tightening in the operating margins of export firms if they decide to keep their export prices in pesetas – and, by extension, their market share – unchanged. In the same manner, devaluations of the peseta signify lowering export prices in foreign currency, which firms can absorb by raising their export price in pesetas, which would increase their operating margins, or by increasing their market share.
15. Other studies, such as Agenor (1997), use the ratio between the import and domestic prices of manufactured goods as an indicator of domestic competitiveness.
16. However, there are several appreciable differences in the positions occupied by the countries in the rankings calculated under the two labour-cost indicators, due logically to the differences in the hours worked in each country.
17. An approximate indicator of the trends in profit margins can be obtained by dividing the price index by the labour-cost index.
18. Producer prices take into account tradable goods, whereas the CPI considers these together with non-tradables and excludes capital goods.
19. Specifically, on 17 September 1992, the peseta's central rate against the ecu was reduced by 5 per cent. On 23 November, it was again lowered by 6 per cent. Finally, on 14 May 1993, it underwent a further reduction of 8 per cent.
20. Studies carried out by the Directorate General for Economic and Financial Affairs of the European Commission (see European Commission, 1995b) show how the pass-through strategies differ among the countries analysed. Gordo and Sánchez-Carretero (1997) provide a specific study of the importance of pass-through processes in the case of Spain.

21. The real effective exchange-rate indices have been calculated as usual in the following way:

$$REER_t = NEER_t \frac{P_t^E}{\prod_{i=1}^{15} (P_{it}^{EU})^{W_i}}$$

For:

i = each of the EU countries,
t = reference year,
W_i = weight given to each EU country on the basis of the relative importance of its trade relations with Spain.

and where:

P^E is the index of Spanish prices or costs,
P^{EU} is the index of the EU countries' prices or costs,
NEER is the nominal effective exchange rate defined as the foreign currency/peseta.

Given the way in which they are constructed, an increase in the indices represents a loss of competitiveness, either because of an exchange-rate appreciation or because of an increase in relative prices, while a decrease is interpreted as a gain in competitiveness for Spain.

Notes to Chapter 5: Public Finances and Fiscal Policy

1. Interested readers will find a very complete study of the stabilizing effects of fiscal policy in the main industrialized countries since 1960 in Marín (1997).
2. More detailed support of this line of argument is found in Lagares (1988) and Fuentes Quintana and Barea (1996).
3. These figures were obtained from OECD (1996a), pp. A33–4.
4. The 'primary gap' is calculated as the difference between the actual primary deficit (in other words: expenditure less government revenue after deducting interest payments) and the equilibrium primary deficit (defined as the deficit compatible with stability in the government debt/GDP ratio). Thus, the 'primary gap' = S – S^*, where S is the primary deficit and S^* the equilibrium primary deficit, and

$$S_t^* = -\left[\frac{r_t - g_t}{1 + g_t}\right] * b_{t-1}$$

where r = the effective interest rate paid on the debt, g = the nominal growth rate of GDP, and b = the debt/GDP ratio.
5. For the detailed arguments behind this assertion, see Raymond (1995).
6. Perotti (1996) gives an overview of these studies.
7. A summary of the main findings is presented in Alesina and Perotti (1995 and 1996).
8. Here we refer to the cases of drastic fiscal consolidation undertaken in Denmark between 1983 and 1986 and in Ireland between 1987 and 1989,

analysed in Giavazzi and Pagano (1990). In this respect, the case of Ireland is the most paradigmatic: between 1986 and 1996, it managed to reduce its debt ratio from 116.8 per cent of GDP to 75.4 per cent, while at the same time moving its per capita income closer to the EU average (from 65.2 per cent to 98.6 per cent in terms of PPP).

9. Although earlier precedents can be found, the welfare state is usually considered to originate in the Beveridge Report, published in 1942, in so far as it assumes government responsibility for dealing with five types of misfortune: old age, illness, lack of education, poor living conditions, and unemployment. Since then these have provided the basis for the institutional development in advanced economies of what has come to be known as the welfare state. Although its development in most European countries took place in the 1950s, 1960s and early 1970s, it was not developed in Spain until the 1980s when the return to democracy was consolidated.
10. See, as an example of the studies referring to the EU countries, the study commissioned by the Directorate General for Economic and Financial Affairs of the European Commission, whose results were published in 1994 in *European Economy*, no. 3, and with respect to the OECD, Oxley and Martin (1991).
11. Herce (1997) gives a good evaluative summary of the studies conducted in Spain on the pension system.
12. According to World Bank projections (see Bos, 1994), the ratio of the population aged over 64 to the working-age population (15- to 64-year-olds) is set to grow rapidly. For Spain this ratio is estimated at 19.8 per cent, 25.9 per cent and 41.0 per cent in the years 1990, 2010 and 2030, respectively, while the average EU figures are still higher, at 21.7 per cent, 27.4 per cent and 43.1 per cent in the same years.
13. The full text of the Toledo pact can be found in the *Boletín Oficial de las Cortes Generales* (1995).
14. In this respect, Segura (1996) proposes an updating system based on an index using a basket of goods and services representative of the consumption structure of the average pensioner.
15. The appendix in Antoñanzas and Pérez-Campanero (1992) summarizes the Abril Commission's report, and also includes a series of contributions by specialists in health economics, which provide an outline of the current issues involved in the reform of Spain's health system.
16. Toharia (1995) contains an historical analysis of the Spanish system of unemployment benefits with a more detailed explanation of the nature of these reforms.
17. In this respect, note that, on OECD data, Spain pays relatively less attention to active job-creation policies than its Community partners. Whereas the European Union assigned 1.04 per cent and 1.14 per cent of GDP in 1991 and 1995, respectively, to such polices, in the same two years Spain spent only 0.76 per cent and 0.72 per cent.
18. On problems relating to the quality of Spanish education, readers are referred to the incisive essay in Pérez-Díaz (1995b).
19. For more details on the arguments behind this proposal, see Corugedo (1995) and the references cited there.

20. When sanctions are imposed for the first time, they will include a deposit bearing no interest, which may become a fine if, after two years, the budget deficit of the member state in question remains excessive. The amount of the deposit will be calculated on the basis of a fixed component, equal to 0.2 per cent of GDP, and a variable component, equal to one-tenth of the amount by which the deficit exceeds the reference value of 3 per cent of GDP. The annual amount of the deposits will be subject to a ceiling of 0.5 per cent of GDP.
21. The stability pact is unnecessarily restrictive when fixing the extraordinary conditions under which it would be permitted to run a budget deficit of more than 3 per cent of GDP. These conditions will apply whenever growth falls below the average rate, less a standard deviation, based on the data observed in recent decades. In Spain the average growth from 1970 to 1995 was 3 per cent, and the standard deviation 2.5 per cent. The extraordinary conditions will thus apply if the growth rate is less than 0.5 per cent and not –0.75 per cent (see Marín, 1997).
22. This report, which inspired the text of the Treaty on European Union with respect to this question, was published in issue no. 53 of *European Economy*.
23. Chapter 11 advances additional arguments in defence of its distributive capacity.

Notes to Chapter 6: The External Sector

1. Note that the balance of payments on current and capital accounts, according to the definition in the IMF's *Fifth Balance of Payments Manual*, is the equivalent of the former current-account balance in the fourth edition of the manual.
2. Domestic absorption denotes the sum of government and private consumption and gross capital formation.
3. Naturally, a restrictive fiscal policy, by reducing public spending and investment or raising taxes, could restore the balance between income and expenditure. The same would occur with a restrictive monetary policy, which would signify an increase in the interest rate and, therefore, a decline in investment and consumption. Likewise, a currency devaluation, by reducing external purchases and increasing domestic ones, could help – even if only temporarily – to bring the trade balance into equilibrium.
4. Intra-Community trade represents more than 65 per cent of the volume of Spanish trade. Therefore, albeit with due caution, this result can be extrapolated to the total trade of the Spanish economy.
5. Specifically, these elasticities range from –0.92 (for Belgium–Luxembourg) to –3.58 (for Spain). For further details, see European Commission (1995b).
6. See, in this respect, the survey of Fagerberg (1996), spanning the Kaldor paradox and the more recent studies on the influence of non-price factors, and technological intensity in particular, on trade behaviour. For Spain, the result obtained is found in Martín and Moreno (1991).
7. See Walsh (1996) for a more detailed analysis of trends in Ireland's external sector and economy.

8. Maté (1996a), drawing on data from the Bank of Spain's Central Balance Sheet Data Office, shows the positive relationship between a better trade balance and the existence of firms which have made foreign direct investment.
9. For a more detailed description of Spain's energy sector, see Jiménez (1995).
10. Note that citizens of the European economic area generate nearly 92 per cent of Spain's tourism receipts. This explains why North Africa is in principle the main alternative destination to Spain. None the less, the development of alternative destinations in the Mediterranean area does not stand out as an important explanatory factor in the study conducted by Buisán (1995), in which the trends in international income and relative prices appear to be more relevant factors.
11. To illustrate the still minimal exploitation of tourism alternatives to the 'sun and beach' formula, the promotion of other natural resources is a case in point: Spain accounts for nearly half the European Union's green zones, but the share of activities exploiting these resources in Spanish tourism receipts was less than 9 per cent in 1995.
12. Note that, even though intra-Community current transfers are very significant, the development aid policy is also reflected in the capital account.
13. Boltho (1996) provides a summary of the principal effects of devaluations in several case studies, including those which occurred in various European countries in the 1990s.
14. The arguments supporting the influence of these factors are found in Bajo and Sosvilla (1996) and Martín and Velázquez (1996a), among others.

Notes to Chapter 7: Nominal and Real Convergence

1. For more details on the definition and measurement of σ and β convergence, see Baumol, Nelson and Wolff (1994), Sala-i-Martín (1994), and Grossman (1996).
2. Calculated as the standard deviation of the variables in Napierian logarithms.
3. For the comparison of price increases in the EU member countries since 1986, we have constructed indices for each country, using the national consumer price indices to 1993. For 1994 and 1995, we have used the interim indices of consumer prices in EU countries calculated by Eurostat on the basis of the national price indices. For 1996 and beyond we have used the harmonized indices of consumer prices published by Eurostat, which are fully comparable between the member states because they are calculated on the basis of a homogeneous basket of goods and services.
4. Also assumed are the countries' access to the same technology, the absence of economies of scale and externalities, homogeneity of goods and factors, and equality in consumer preferences.
5. Strong and sustained investment in different types of capital, above all human and technological capital. See Chapter 2 and the studies cited there.

6. The *1996 Annual Report* of the European Monetary Institute (EMI) highlights the worrying situation of unemployment in the Community and its structural cause; it calls on member states to intensify their labour market reforms, stressing that, to date, those carried out by most of the countries appear to be too marginal to produce any significant improvement in the trends observed in the labour market (EMI, 1997a).
7. Specifically, the human capital indicator was obtained through a formulation similar to the perpetual-inventory method: by adding up the number of students enrolled each year since 1930 (the year that allows us to consider the education of the entire population aged during the reference period – 1986 to 1996 – between 15 and 64) at all educational levels – primary, secondary, technical and higher education – previously weighted by the ratio between expenditure per student at each level of education and in each country, and the average total cost of educating a university student in the European Union. In addition, it was taken into account that the knowledge acquired depreciates in the event the person does not work (through inactivity or unemployment). The resulting indicator can therefore be interpreted as the percentage of the working-age population with the equivalent of higher education in relation to the average of the Fifteen. Finally, the results obtained were divided by the working-age population and expressed in terms of the average EU value in 1986. See Chapter 2, Section 2.3.3.
8. This indicator was constructed using the perpetual-inventory method, by calculating the stock of initial capital for 1974 and estimating the investment series on the basis of information from the OECD and UNESCO on gross domestic expenditure on R&D. The deflator used was gross fixed capital formation, and the depreciation rate used was 10 per cent. After the technological capital stock of all the countries and its relationship to GDP had been estimated, the results were expressed in terms of the average EU value in 1986. See Chapter 2, Section 2.3.2.
9. Social-protection expenditure includes spending relating to sickness, disability, industrial accidents, pensions, surviving dependants, maternity, family, job-promotion measures, unemployment, housing and other benefits.

Notes to Chapter 8: Trade Relations

1. Hine (1994) and Baldwin and Venables (1995) each offer revisions of the theory of economic integration and summarize the results of the main empirical studies in this area.
2. See Krugman (1990) and Grossman (1992) by way of example.
3. See Winters (1991).
4. The existence of external economies reinforces this hypothesis. Specifically, in the case of economies external to the national firm (in the sense that the firm's costs depend on the size of the industry in the country where it is located), trade integration might accentuate the tendency towards the concentration of production in countries with a more developed industrial base and larger markets and which therefore enjoy higher expected returns on

capital. Illustrative of this are the models of economic geography developed by Krugman (1991) and Krugman and Venables (1993) that emphasize 'economies of agglomeration', associated with the spatial concentration of economic activity, and the analysis of external economies of a temporary nature which derive from the accumulation of knowledge, known as 'economies of experience' (see Grossman and Helpman, 1991).

5. To a large extent this section follows the approach employed in Martín (1992) and Gordo and Martín (1995).
6. One of the characteristic features of international trade in recent years is the concentration of a significant volume in regions covered by trade agreements, due to the proliferation of intra-regional accords in the recent past, most notably NAFTA, Mercosur and ASEAN, among others.
7. See Cañada and Carmena (1989).
8. The data have been obtained from information provided by Spanish Customs and from the matching effected by the National Statistics Office between the classification of foreign trade (TARIC, or integrated tariff community) and the NACE-CLIO (56) classification of economic activities. The sectors have been aggregated into 15 branches of activity (NACE-CLIO 25), of which the 13 manufacturing sectors have been analysed. Finally, these 13 sectors have been divided into three groups according to the products' technological content, defined as the ratio between R&D expenditure and sales in the sector, in accordance with a classification prepared by the OECD. This grouping, as noted in other chapters, coincides with that obtained by applying the criterion of the relative vitality of demand.
9. A greater disaggregation of the trade flows in this branch indicates that automobiles are largely responsible for the growth in exports.
10. As explained in Chapter 4, RCAIs are defined as:

$$RCAI_{it} = \frac{X_{it} - M_{it}}{X_{it} + M_{it}} \cdot 100$$

11. A more recent study (Martín, 1995c) shows that in all other areas the factor content of Spanish trade with the European Union remained similar.
12. Fariñas (1992) analyses the relevant indices for the measuring of intra-industrial trade.
13. Unit value indices are obtained by dividing for each position of the five-digit SITC the value in pesetas of the exports (or imports) by the quantity or volume exported (or imported). However, the fact that each position encompasses a set of products, rather than a single product, means that the average values reflect not only the changes in the prices of the goods that make up each position, but also the changes in their domestic composition.
14. Note, however, that until 1992 there was an intensification in trade of a vertical nature, in which exports were of lower quality, and it was after that year that the shift towards intra-industrial trade of a horizontal nature took place (see Gordo and Martín, 1997).
15. Poland, the Czech Republic and Hungary are among the signatory countries most likely to gain admittance to the European Union.
16. Wang and Winters (1991) offer an analysis of the potential of these new markets for the expansion of the trade of industrialized countries. Hoekman

and Djankov (1996) analyse the trends and composition of trade between Central and Eastern Europe and foreign direct investment flows. In addition, Martín (1995c) evaluates the consequences for the Spanish economy of the opening up of these countries.

Notes to Chapter 9: Direct Investment Flows

1. The IMF's most recent guideline defines the ownership of more than 10 per cent of a company's capital as a controlling interest. None the less, it acknowledges the existence of cases in which a stake of less than 10 per cent may signify a controlling interest, as, for example, when shares are acquired in the company in return for the transfer of technology.
2. These hypotheses were initially postulated in Mundell (1957), in which direct investment is treated in the same way as any other international capital flow. Because of this, its trends are interpreted in terms of the differences in the countries' relative factor endowments.
3. According to the United Nations (1996), in the years 1990–95, the OECD countries received around 60 per cent of direct investment worldwide; of this, more than 60 per cent on average in these same years was concentrated in the group of nations which form the G-7.
4. On the theoretical side, there is a dispute as to which direction of flows is influenced by the presence of economies of scale, and empirical testing has failed to arrive at any conclusive result. Dunning (1993a) discusses this question in greater detail and describes the findings of various empirical studies.
5. International transactions in technology are indeed highly problematical – especially those involving the dissemination of knowledge which, as in the case of know-how, is hard to codify – not only because of the existence of asymmetrical information between the supply and the demand sides, but also because of the presence of other factors such as the question of moral hazard. For more details, see Markusen (1995) and the references cited there.
6. The existence of externalities associated with spatial concentration, together with the importance of transport costs, helps us to understand why those countries with higher capital endowment are able to offer larger returns to investors, and it is one of the reasons for the strong degree of concentration in production in the more developed regions (see Krugman, 1991).
7. The European Commission estimated that the creation of the single market would increase the annual growth rate of GDP in the European Union by 6.5 per cent. See Cecchinni et al. (1988) for further details.
8. Dunning (1997) compares the possible influence of the creation of the single European market and of NAFTA on foreign direct investment. Reference is also made to the way in which the successive steps towards the unification of the European market have affected the flow of foreign capital.
9. Examples of this type of operation are found in the centralization of R&D activities at many companies and in the specialization of a company's dif-

ferent establishments in a single production stage or product type. Likewise, in many sectors the minimum efficient size of firms has increased substantially due to the gradual elimination of market segmentation. This involves a need to grow, and for this purpose firms commonly resort to the acquisition of or merger with already installed companies, with a resulting increase in intra-Community direct investment flows. By way of example, in some productive branches the firms installed in the European Union greatly outnumber those located in the United States, a market similar in size to Europe's.

10. The current basic legislation on foreign investment in Spain is encompassed in Law 18/1992 of 1 July, Royal Decree 671/1992 of 2 July, and the decision of 6 July 1992 of the Directorate General of Foreign Transactions. The basic regulations on Spanish investment abroad consist of Royal Decree 1816/91 of 20 December, the order of 27 December 1991 (which implements the preceding decree), Royal Decree 672/1992 of 2 July, and the decision of 7 July 1992.

    For more details on the changes in the concept of direct investment, see Maté (1996b) and the references cited there. Álvarez and Eguidazu (1996) give a full historical list of Spanish legislation in this area and also describe the legal system governing capital movements in the European Union.
11. The Bank of Spain's data are used because they are more precise than the information provided by the Directorate General of Foreign Transactions. Note that the data of the latter source only reflect those investments which are subject to verification and authorization; moreover, the authorization granted in a given year does not necessarily mean the investment was carried out in that year – indeed, it may never materialize.
12. There are several breaks in the time series for direct and portfolio investment published in the balance of payments, primarily stemming from the legal changes in the concept of direct investment and from the modification of exchange-rate legislation. The most recent break is in 1991, owing to the decision of 25 October of the Directorate General of Foreign Transactions, under which a distinction is only made between acquisitions of unlisted securities and securities listed on stock exchanges. Notwithstanding, from 1992 onwards the balance of payments gives an estimate of the breakdown between direct and portfolio investments.
13. But note that this is mostly explained by a small number of large-scale operations, such as those of Telefónica in Peru and of Iberia in Argentina and Venezuela, and major transactions in the banking sector, such as those of Banco Santander and BBV.
14. For more details on the merger and acquisition data used, see European Commission (1994a).
15. Dunning (1997) comments on the findings of other empirical studies on the influence of the single market's creation on international direct investment flows from non-Community countries.
16. Although the empirical findings on the importance of labour costs as a location factor at the international level are not conclusive, Martín and Velázquez (1996a) show that for the Spanish case this factor borders on significance. Along these same lines, using the data for Great Britain and

Germany, Hatzius (1997) finds that the relevance of unit labour costs increases as international direct investment flows are liberalized, precisely what is now occurring in the European Union and the Visegrad countries.

17. In Hansen (1996), starting from a study of Danish direct investment abroad, the geographical proximity of this group of countries is found to be a relevant location factor vis-à-vis alternative locations, especially for smaller-scale transnational firms.
18. According to sources in the Eastern European countries themselves, international direct investment is primarily generated by EU countries, especially Germany and Austria, followed by the United States.
19. None the less, Dunning (1993b, 1997) gives a classification that groups sectors on the basis of their singularities and the degree to which they may prove attractive for the international direct investment undertaken as a result of the integration of the European market.
20. The figures for capital inflows with this disaggregation are available for 1987 and beyond, but those for outflows only exist as from 1988; for the sake of uniformity in the periods, we decided to forgo the year 1987 in our analysis of inflows.

    The information in this table is affected by two methodological changes: first, the changes introduced by the enactment of new legislation (see note 10), and, secondly, the use of a new National Classification of Economic Activities (CNAE in its Spanish acronym) from 1993 onwards.

    As to the changeover from the CNAE-74 to the CNAE-93, the lack of homogeneity in the data is minimized by reclassifying the information from the original three-digit CNAE to the NACE-CLIO (25). (For more details, see Maté, 1996b.)
21. Note, however, that technological advances are eliminating many of the existing obstacles to the trade of services: for example, all those relating to the transmission of information (see United Nations, 1996).
22. The large volume of investment using holding companies as financial intermediaries limits our knowledge of the true destination of investment. Campa and Guillén (1994) provide references to the sectoral trends in Spain's direct investment abroad for the period prior to that shown in Table 9.4, albeit with a lesser degree of sectoral disaggregation.

Note to Chapter 10: Migratory Flows

1. In Jordán and Sanchís (1997), readers will find a more detailed account of the Community legislation establishing the freedom of movement for workers, and of establishment and residence.
2. Zimmermann (1995) provides a summary of trends in European migratory flows since the Second World War.
3. In addition, a considerable portion of this percentage represents retired persons, who naturally do not signify an increase in labour in Spain.
4. Whereas the integration of the 'South' has not produced an avalanche of emigrants towards the more developed economies, the case of Eastern European countries is very different because of their greater cultural and

language affinities, in addition to the large disparities in living standards and much stronger social pressures.

5. Specifically, the per capita GDP of Greece, the least developed country in the European Union, is 9000 euro.

Notes to Chapter 11: The Community Budget and its Functions

1. In the European Commission (1992) document *From the Single Act to Maastricht and Beyond: The Means to Match Our Ambitions*, known as the Delors II package, an attempt is made to translate the objectives proposed into budgetary terms, emphasizing six in particular: the internal market, economic and social cohesion, consolidation of the European Monetary System, environmental policy, research and technology, and the social dimension.
2. Among the main factors behind these changes have been the integration of the EEC and Euratom – as well as several instruments of the European Coal and Steel Community (ECSC) – into a general budget; the development of several common policies – in particular, the common agricultural policy (CAP), economic and social cohesion, and research and technological development – and finally, the four enlargements undertaken to date, as shown in the chronology of the European integration process in Appendix I.
3. If we consider the countries with a federal structure, where responsibilities are decentralized, the findings are the same. Note, by way of example, that the level of expenditure of Germany's central government in 1995 was 20 per cent of GDP and that of the United States 20.8 per cent.
4. Reflected in article 199 of the Treaty of Rome: 'The revenue and expenditure shown in the budget shall be balanced.'
5. For a more in-depth treatment of these arguments, see Majocchi and Rey (1993).
6. The allocative function of the Community budget has been a topic of debate since the report of MacDougall et al. (1977) was published by the Commission.
7. For a closer view of the terms of this controversy, see among others, European Commission (1990), Masson (1996), and Hagen, Wyplosz and Zimmermann (eds.) (1998).
8. In fact, the disparity between the expenditure of EAGGF-Guarantee and EAGGF-Guidance narrowed during the period, with the latter representing 8.1 per cent of total agricultural expenditure in 1997, compared with only 3.4 per cent in 1986. Even so, it hardly lives up to the principle stated at the Stresa Conference (1958), when the CAP was created, aimed at ensuring that 'price and structural policies go hand in hand'.
9. The four operational principles envisaged in the coordinating and framework regulations are: concentration, cooperation, programming and additionality (see European Commission, 1996b).
10. The reform enacted in 1988 involved a substantial increase in the financial resources earmarked for EU structural intervention, concentrating intervention on five objectives (a sixth was added in 1995), as a way of simplifying

the management and monitoring of actions of this type. These objectives are:

1. To promote and develop structurally backward regions, through ERDF, ESF and EAGGF-Guidance.
2. To convert regions affected by industrial decline, via ERDF and ESF.
3. To combat long-term unemployment and to facilitate the integration of young people into working life, managed by the ESF.
4. To facilitate the adaptation of workers to industrial changes and to changes in production systems, also through the ESF.
5. (a) To speed up the adjustment of agricultural structures and to modernize and restructure the fisheries sector, via EAGGF-Guidance and FIFG.
   (b) To facilitate the development and structural adjustment of rural areas, through the EAGGF-Guarantee, FIFG and ERDF.
6. To facilitate the development and structural adjustment of regions with very low population density, in which the ERDF, FIFG and EAGGF-Guidance participate.

In turn, the reform of 1993 focused on the programme of structural measures for the period 1994–9, envisaging a certain increase. (An analysis of the effects of these reforms is found in European Commission, 1996a.)

11. The Cohesion Fund was created in 1992, but its definitive regulatory framework was established in 1994. Its objective is to provide financial assistance, in order to offset the adverse effects on income distribution, to countries whose per capita income is less than 90 per cent of the Community average, helping them to meet the convergence criteria. The distribution of cohesion funds from 1994 to 1999 among the eligible countries was as follows: Spain's share ranged from 52 per cent to 58 per cent, Greece 16 per cent to 20 per cent, Portugal 16 per cent to 20 per cent, and Ireland 7 per cent to 10 per cent.
12. In 1997, R&D expenditure represented 1.9 per cent of GDP in the European Union, whereas this ratio was 2.6 per cent in the United States and 2.8 per cent in Japan.
13. This figure has led some studies – See Goodman (1996) – to affirm that the European Union is not burdened by problems of bureaucracy.
14. The purpose of the ECSC funds is to provide social assistance to workers who have lost their jobs because of restructuring, and to finance research in the coal and steel sector. Other items not included in the general budget are, first, the credit and loan operations of the ECSC, Euratom and the New Community Instrument, and secondly, the projects of the EIB, which finances internal investments for the development of less favoured regions and projects relating to infrastructure and the environment. For more details, see Harrop (1996).
15. For the less affluent countries – Greece, Portugal, Spain and Ireland – this ceiling was lowered to 50 per cent of GNP in 1994.
16. The UK compensation was established at the Fontainebleau Summit of 1984, and it is justified by two factors: first, the United Kingdom has traditionally been a net importer of food, and has therefore contributed disproportionally – via regulatory tariffs – to the Community's own resources,

without receiving any great benefits from the CAP, and, second, it has a high VAT base rate in relation to GNP.

17. The specific measures were included in Decision 88/376/EEC.
18. The principle of social and economic cohesion is explicitly reflected in the Single European Act and is included in the Maastricht Treaty (article 130a).
19. The Lorenz curve showing the concentration of EU resources received by each country has been constructed in the following way: (a) accumulated income expresses the percentages of Community GDP that are gradually accumulated by the countries which make up the European Union, ranked by their per capita income from the lowest to the highest. The cohesion group accounted for 9.4 per cent and 10.9 per cent of the Community GDP of the EU Twelve in 1986 and 1997, respectively, and therefore occupies approximately the first decile of the abscissa, and b) the resources received from the European Union are also expressed in cumulative terms. Thus, in the same years this group represented 21 per cent and 33.3 per cent of the European Union's total expenditure in the member countries. The final result is that the curves of received resources located above the line of absolute equality – as opposed to those located below – indicate possible redressing effects. Moreover, the larger the area between the curves and the line of absolute equality, the greater the effect will be.
20. The Lorenz curve of contributions to EU financing is estimated in the same way as that of the resources received by each EU country, but in this case the final result is that the curves of contributions to the European Union located below the line of absolute equality – as opposed to those located above – indicate possible redressing effects. Moreover, the greater the area between the curves and the line of absolute equality, the greater the effect will be.
21. The Gini coefficient measures the area between the Lorenz curve and the line of absolute equality – the larger the area, the greater the degree of concentration. Therefore, in the case of the resources received from the EU budget by each country, a positive coefficient represents a redressing effect, as opposed to the case of contributions to the European Union, where this effect would be determined by a negative coefficient.
22. De la Dehesa and Krugman (1992), and the references to related studies cited there, present evidence on the lack of equity in this policy.
23. A similar conclusion is reached in Zanías (1994).
24. Under the definition of the European Commission (1996a) in the *First Cohesion Report*, the 'European archipelago' includes the research centres located between London and Milan, encompassing Amsterdam, Rotterdam, the Ile de France, the Ruhr basin, Frankfurt, Stuttgart, Munich, Lyon, Grenoble and Turin. This archipelago accounts for 28 per cent of Europe's population and absorbs nearly half the EU expenditure on R&D activities.
25. As explained in the section on the forms of financing, VAT consists of two tranches: the first introduces regressive elements, although these are not reflected in the Gini coefficient for 1996 owing to the existence of a second tranche, which is caused by: (a) the particular case of the United Kingdom, which obtains the 'British cheque' as a decrease in its contribution under this item – thus, while accounting for 15.9 per cent of GDP, it contributes only 6.9 per cent of the total VAT collected; and (b) the contribution from

the other members to cover what the United Kingdom does not contribute, established in terms of GNP. None the less, if we eliminate the distortion derived from the first cause, the Gini coefficient is 0.01 and –0.02 for 1986 and 1997, respectively, indicating much more negative results for convergence. An eloquent example of this is the case of the cohesion group, which in 1997 accounted for a total of 10.2 per cent of Community GDP and contributed 12.4 per cent of the total EU receipts from the VAT resource.

26. Specifically, Hungary, Poland, the Czech Republic, Estonia, Slovenia, and Cyprus.
27. Chapter 10 of Eichengreen and Frieden (eds) (1998) gives a penetrating overview of the economic and political tensions sparked by the issue of enlargement towards the East.

Notes to Chapter 12: Unification of Monetary Policy in Europe

1. For a description and broad analysis of the process of monetary union in Europe, see Gros and Thygesen (1992), Kenen (1992), and Camarero and Tamarit (1997).
2. For the full text of the Werner Report, see Monetary Committee of the European Communities (1986).
3. The classic paper by Ypersèle and Koeune (1985) describes the system in detail. Fratianni and Von Hagen (1992) provide an excellent analysis of the evolution of the system.
4. Recall that these criteria are:
   - Inflation: no more than 1.5 percentage points higher than the average of the three least inflationary member countries.
   - Long-term interest rates: the nominal long-term rate must not exceed by more than 2 percentage points the average rate of the three least inflationary member countries.
   - Budget deficit: no more than 3 per cent of GDP.
   - Government debt: no more than 60 per cent of GDP.
   - Exchange rate: the currency must not have been devalued or have exceeded the normal fluctuation band in the two previous years.
5. A more detailed description of this crisis in the EMS is found in the 1993 report of the Governors' Committee.
6. For the main features of the stability pact, see Chapter 5.
7. This aspect is known in the literature as the accountability problem.
8. See De Grauwe (1997).
9. See Goodhart (1996) and Kenen (1995).
10. A detailed description of the system is found in Banco de España (1997).
11. For an analysis of the costs and benefits of EMU, see among others the following studies: European Commission (1990), De Grauwe (1997), Gros and Thygesen (1992), and Masson and Taylor (1993).
12. A recent revision, which includes the credibility aspects, is found in Tavlas (1993), and an overview of the empirical literature on optimum currency areas applied to the case of EMU is found in Bayoumi and Eichengreen (1996).

13. A shock is asymmetrical if it affects certain countries in particular. If the countries' economic structures are different, even a common shock may have asymmetrical effects in the economies in question.
14. First, for an analysis of the variability of real exchange rates, see De Grauwe and Van Haverbecke (1993). Secondly, the studies of Bayoumi and Eichengreen (1993) and Erkel-Rousse and Mélitz (1995) distinguish between permanent and temporary shocks and, using the VAR method, analyse the correlation of shocks across countries and their effects on the real exchange rate. Finally, another group of studies, in particular those of Artis and Zhang (1995) and Bayoumi and Prasad (1995), analyse the correlation of economic cycles across countries and the degree of labour-market flexibility.

Notes to Appendix I: Chronology of the European Integration Process

1. The Council is the high legislative body of the European Union. It is formed by the national ministers of each ministerial branch. At least twice a year the heads of government of each country meet in what is called the European Council or Summit. Each country exercises the presidency by rotation for a period of six months.

   The Commission has various functions, including the right of initiative and the responsibility for safeguarding the fulfilment of the Community treaties, and, in a limited framework, it is the executor of the Council's decisions. It has 20 members elected for a period of five years.

   The European Parliament is an advisory body of the Commission under the cooperation procedure in certain matters, and, since the signing of the Treaty on European Union, it has for the first time acquired a legislative role in several specific matters through the co-decision procedure. With the entry of Sweden, Finland and Austria in 1995, the Parliament now has 626 members, elected in direct elections held every five years since 1979.

   The Court of Justice of the European Communities is responsible for ensuring that the law is observed in the interpretation and application of the treaties. It is composed of 15 judges, who are assisted by 9 advocates-general appointed by the member states.
2. The Court of Auditors oversees the legality and proper management of the revenue and expenditure of the European Union. It is formed by 15 members appointed by the mutual agreement of the member countries.
3. The Council, or the Commission, must consult the Committee of the Regions in matters concerning job training, cohesion policy and structural funds. It comprises 222 regional and local authorities of the member countries of the European Union.

   The Economic and Social Committee is an economic consulting body of the Commission and the Council, and is formed by 222 members who represent diverse segments of society, such as professional sectors and trade unions.
4. The EIB is the European Union's financing institution for the promotion of 'balanced and stable development'. It finances the cohesion policy, job creation and projects of common interest to various member countries.

Notes to Appendix II: Methodological Problems of International Comparisons

1. Note that there are even discrepancies in the definitions of the major branches of activity. An example is the delimitation of the manufacturing sector, which for the OECD includes oil refining and various mining industries, activities which Eurostat assigns to the energy sector.
2. In Camarero (1994) and Pérez and Vega (1994), for example, we find a more detailed discussion on the advantages and limitations of PPP, as well as a summary of the main empirical studies testing the appropriateness of using PPP to approximate the real long-term equilibrium exchange rate.
3. See Dollar and Wolff (1993) for an in-depth justification of this affirmation.
4. Two empirical approximations to this concept are distinguished according to whether the data on prices and quantities are obtained on the basis of the structure of output or demand. See Hooper and Larin (1988).
5. Since 1999, to calculate PPP, Eurostat has taken a new sample each year that encompasses a third of the goods basket, while the remaining two-thirds is estimated on the basis of national price indices.

References

Agenor, P. R. (1997) 'Competitiveness and External Trade Performance of the French Manufacturing Industry', *Weltwirtschaftliches Archiv*, vol. 133, pp. 103–33.

Alesina, A., and Perotti, R. (1995) 'Fiscal Expansions and Adjustments in OECD Countries', *Economic Policy*, vol. 21, pp. 205–40.

Alesina, A., and Perotti, R. (1996) 'Fiscal Adjustment', Working Paper 96/70, International Monetary Fund.

Alonso, J. A., and Donoso, V. (1996) 'Obstáculos a la internacionalización y políticas públicas de promoción: el caso de España', *Papeles de Economía Española*, vol. 66, pp. 124–43.

Álvarez, D., and Eguidazu, F. (1996) *Inversiones extranjeras* (Elcano: Aranzadi Editorial).

Alvira, F., and García, J. (1997) 'Actitudes de los españoles hacia el ahorro', *Papeles de Economía Española*, vol. 70, pp. 136–49.

Anchuelo, A. (1995) 'Sostenibilidad del déficit exterior español', *Información Comercial Española*, vol. 742, pp. 127–38.

Andrés, J. (1995) 'Aggregate Wages and Unemployment in Spain: A Review of the Evidence', in O. Blanchard et al., *Spanish Unemployment: Is There a Solution?* (London: CEPR) pp. 49–87.

Andrés, J., Boscá, J., and Doménech, R. (1995) 'Main Patterns of Economic Growth in OECD Countries', *Investigaciones Económicas, Segunda Época*, vol. XIX (1), pp. 35–63.

Andrés, J., and Doménech, R. (1996) 'La convergencia real en Europa', *Información Comercial Española*, vol. 756, pp. 33–49.

Andrés, J., and Hernando, I. (1996) '¿Cómo afecta la inflación al crecimiento económico? Evidencia para los países de la OCDE', Working Paper 9602, Servicio de Estudios, Banco de España.

Antoñanzas, F., and Pérez-Campanero, J. (1992) *La reforma del sistema sanitario* (Madrid: Mundi-Prensa and Fundación de Estudios de Economía Aplicada).

Argimón, I., et al. (1994) 'Productividad e infraestructuras en la economía española', *Moneda y Crédito, Segunda Época*, vol. 198, pp. 207–41.

Argimón, I., González-Páramo, J. M., and Roldán, J. M. (1997) 'Evidence of Public Spending Crowding-out from a Panel of OECD Countries', *Applied Economics*, vol. 29, pp. 1001–10.

Aristotelous, K., and Fountas, S. (1996) 'An Empirical Analysis of Inward Foreign Direct Investment Flows in the EU with Emphasis on the Market Enlargement Hypothesis', *Journal of Common Market Studies*, vol. 34, pp. 571–83.

Ark, B. Van (1996) 'Sectoral Growth Accounting and Structural Change in Post-War Europe', in B. Van Ark and N. Crafts (eds), *Quantitative Aspects of Post-War European Economic Growth* (Cambridge: Cambridge University Press and CEPR) pp. 84–164.

Artis, M., and Zhang, W. (1995) 'International Business Cycles and the ERM: Is There a European Business Cycle?', Discussion Paper 1191, CEPR.

Aschauer, D. A. (1989) 'Is Public Expenditure Productive?', *Journal of Monetary Economics*, vol. 23, pp. 177–200.

Bajo, O., and Sosvilla, S. (1994) 'Un análisis empírico de los determinantes macroeconómicos de la inversión extranjera directa en España, 1961–1989', *Moneda y Crédito, Segunda Época*, vol. 194, pp. 107–36.

Bajo, O., and Sosvilla, S. (1996) 'La inversión extranjera directa en la industria manufacturera española, 1986–1993', *Papeles de Economía Española*, vol. 66, pp. 176–90.

Bajo, O., and Torres, A. (1992) 'El comercio exterior y la inversión extranjera directa tras la integración de España en la CE', in J. Viñals (ed.), *La economía española ante el Mercado Único europeo. (Las claves del proceso de integración)* (Madrid: Alianza Economía, Alianza Editorial) pp. 167–228.

Balassa, B. (1964) 'The Purchasing Power Parity Doctrine: A Reappraisal', *Journal of Political Economy*, vol. 72, pp. 584–96.

Baldwin, R. E., and Venables, A. J. (1995) 'Regional Economic Integration', in G. M. Grossman and K. Rogoff (eds), *Handbook of International Economics*, vol. 3 (Amsterdam: Elsevier) pp. 1597–1644.

Banco de España (1997) *La Unión Monetaria Europea. Cuestiones fundamentales* (Madrid: Banco de España).

Baumol, W., Nelson, R., and Wolff, E. (1994) *Convergence of Productivity* (New York: Oxford University Press).

Bayoumi, T., and Eichengreen, B. (1993) 'Shocking Aspects of European Monetary Integration', in F. Torres and F. Giavazzi (eds), *Adjustment and Growth in the European Monetary Union* (Cambridge: CEPR and Cambridge University Press) pp. 193–240.

Bayoumi, T., and Eichengreen, B. (1996) 'Operationalizing the Theory of Optimum Currency Areas', Discussion Paper 1484, CEPR.

Bayoumi, T., and Prasad, E. (1995) 'Currency Unions, Economic Fluctuations and Adjustment: Some Empirical Evidence', Discussion Paper 1172, CEPR.

Bean, C. R. (1994) 'European Unemployment: A Survey', *Journal of Economic Literature*, vol. 32, pp. 573–619.

Benhabib, J., and Spiegel, M. M. (1994) 'The Role of Human Capital in Economic Development. Evidence from Aggregate Cross-Country Data', *Journal of Monetary Economics*, vol. 34, pp. 143–73.

Bentolila, S. (1996) 'Las decisiones judiciales sobre despidos en España: una perspectiva económica', Working Paper 9602, Fundación Empresa Pública.

Bentolila, S., and Dolado, J. J. (1994) 'Labour Flexibility and Wages: Lessons from Spain', *Economic Policy*, vol. 9, pp. 53–99.

Biehl, D. (1986) 'The Contribution of Infrastructure to Regional Development', document (Luxembourg: European Commission).

Biehl, D. (1988) 'Las infraestructuras y el desarrollo regional', *Papeles de Economía Española*, vol. 35, pp. 293–310.

Blanchard, O., and Katz, L. (1992) 'Regional Evolutions', *Brookings Papers on Economic Activity*, vol. I, pp. 1–75.

Boldrin, M. (1993) 'Public Education and Capital Accumulation', Discussion Paper 1017, Northwestern University.

Boletín Oficial de las Cortes Generales (1995) *Pactos de Toledo,* 12 April 1995 (Madrid: Boletín Oficial de las Cortes Generales).

Boltho, A. (1996) 'The Assessment: International Competitiveness', *Oxford Review of Economic Policy*, vol. 12, pp. 1–16.

Borjas, G. (1987) 'Immigrants, Minorities, and Labor Market Competition', *Industrial and Labor Relations Review*, vol. 40, pp. 382–93.

Bos, E. (1994) *World Population Projections* (Washington, DC: World Bank).

Boscá, J., De la Fuente, A., and Doménech, R. (1996) 'Human Capital and Growth: Theory Ahead of Measurement?', mimeo.

Bover, O., and Arellano, M. (1995) 'Female Labour Force Participation in the 1980s: The Case of Spain', *Investigaciones Económicas, Segunda Época*, vol. XIX (2), pp. 171–94.

Bover, O., Arellano, M., and Bentolila, S. (1995) 'Duración del desempleo en España: efectos de la duración de las prestaciones y del ciclo económico', Boletín Económico, November, Banco de España, pp. 71–7.

Bresnaham, T. F., and Trajtenberg, M. (1995) 'General Purpose Technologies: "Engines of Growth"?', *Journal of Econometrics*, vol. 65, pp. 83–108.

Buisán, A. (1995) 'Principales determinantes de los ingresos por turismo', Working Paper 9502, Servicio de Estudios, Banco de España.

Camarero, M. (1994) 'Aportaciones empíricas recientes de la paridad del poder adquisitivo', *Revista de Economía Aplicada*, vol. 2 (6), pp. 79–103.

Camarero, M., and Tamarit, C. (1997) 'La Unión Económica y Monetaria', in J. Jordán (coord.), *Economía de la Unión Europea*, 2nd edn (Madrid: Editorial Civitas) pp. 497–527.

Campa, J., and Guillén, M. (1994) 'Spain in the Investment Development Path', Working Paper 3740, Massachusetts Institute of Technology.

Cañada, A., and Carmena, A. (1989) 'La protección de la economía española: un análisis del período 1980–1986', *Boletín Económico, Información Comercial Española*, vol. 2195, August, pp. 3177–90.

Cantwell, J. A. (1992) 'The Effects of Integration on the Structure of Multinational Corporation Activity in the EC', in M. W. Klein and P. J. Welfens (eds), *Multinationals in the New Europe and Global Trace* (Berlin and New York: Springer-Verlag) pp. 193–230.

Carrington, W. J., Detragiache, E. and Vishwanath, T. (1996) 'Migration with Endogenous Moving Costs', *American Economic Review*, vol. 86 (4), pp. 909–30.

Caves, D. W., Christensen, L. R., and Diewert, W. E. (1982) 'Multilateral Comparisons of Output, Input, and Productivity using Superlative Index Numbers', *Economic Journal*, vol. 92, pp. 73–86.

Cecchinni, P., Catinat, M., and Jacquemin, A. (1988) *The European Challenge 1992: The Benefits of a Single Market* (Aldershot: Wildwood House).

C.E.P.R. (1995) *Unemployment: Choices for Europe* (London: CEPR).

Comité Gobernadores Bancos Centrales (1993) *Informe Anual* (Basle).

Corugedo, I. (1995) 'Productividad y empleo', *Información Comercial Española*, vol. 743, pp. 125–31.

Daveri, F., and Faini, R. (1996) 'Where do Migrants Go? Risk-Aversion, Mobility Cost and the Locational Choice of Migrants', Discussion Paper 1540, CEPR.

De Grauwe, P. (1996) 'The Prospects of a Mini Currency Union in 1999', Discussion Paper 1458, CEPR.

De Grauwe, P. (1997) *The Economics of Monetary Integration*, 3rd edn (Oxford: Oxford University Press).

De Grauwe, P., and Van Haverbecke, W. (1993) 'Is Europe an Optimum Currency Area? Evidence from Regional Data', in P. R. Masson and M. P. Taylor (eds), *Policy Issues in the Operation of Currency Unions* (Cambridge: Cambridge University Press).

De la Dehesa, G. (1995) 'Convergencia real y movilidad de factores de producción en la Unión Europea', *Papeles de Economía Española*, vol. 63, pp. 178–91.

De la Dehesa, G., and Krugman P. (1992) 'EMU and the Regions', Group of Thirty, *Occasional Papers*, vol. 39.

De la Fuente, A. (1997) 'The Empirics of Growth and Convergence: A Selective Review', *Journal of Economic Dynamics and Control*, vol. 21 (1), pp. 22–73.

De Rus, G., Román, C., and Trujillo, L. (1995) 'Infraestructuras de transporte y convergencia real', *Papeles de Economía Española*, vol. 63, pp. 234–51.

Decressin, J., and Fatás, A. (1995) 'Regional Labour Market Dynamics in Europe', *European Economic Review*, vol. 39 (9), pp. 1627–55.

Díaz de Sarralde, S., and Martínez, A. R. (1996) 'Factores explicativos de la inversión extranjera directa en España (1970–1992)', *Hacienda Pública Española*, vol. 136, pp. 19–31.

Dolado, J. J., and Viñals, J. (1992) 'El déficit exterior español: Sostenibilidad y objetivos en el proceso de transición a la UEM', *Papeles de Economía Española*, vol. 52/53, pp. 332–52.

Dollar, D., and Wolff, E. (1993) *Competitiveness, Convergence and International Specialization* (Cambridge, MA: MIT Press).

Dornbusch, R. (1996) 'The Effectiveness of Exchange-Rate Changes', *Oxford Review of Economic Policy*, vol. 12 (3), pp. 26–38.

Dornbusch, R., Favero, C., and Giavazzi, F. (1998) 'Immediate Challenges for the European Central Bank', in D. Begg, J. Von Hagen, C. Wyplosz, and K. F. Zimmermann (eds), *EMU: Prospects and Challenges for the Euro* (London: CEPR).

Dosi, G., and Soete, L. (1988) 'Technical Change and International Trade', in G. Dosi et al. (eds), *Technical Change and Economic Theory* (London: Pinter).

Dowrick, S., and Nguyen, D. (1989) 'OECD Comparative Economic Growth 1950–85: Catch-Up and Convergence', *American Economic Review*, vol. 79 (5), pp. 1010–30.

Duce, M. (1995) 'El impacto de la integración en Europa en la inversión internacional directa española', *Papeles de Economía Española*, vol. 63, pp. 192–208.

Dunning, J. H. (1974) *Economic Analysis and the Multinational Enterprise* (London: Allen & Unwin).

Dunning, J. H. (1980) 'Toward an Eclectic Theory of Internal Production: Some Empirical Tests', *Journal of International Business Studies*, vol. 11 (1), pp. 9–31.

Dunning, J. H. (1993a) *Multinational Enterprises and the Global Economy*, (Reading, MA: Addison Wesley).

Dunning, J. H. (1993b) *The Globalization of Business* (London: Routledge).

Dunning, J. H. (1997) *Alliance Capitalism and Global Business* (London: Routledge).

Eichengreen, B., and Ghironi, F. (1995) 'European Monetary Unification: The Challenges Ahead', Discussion Paper 1217, CEPR.

Eichengreen, B., and Frieden, J. (eds) (1998) *Forging an Integrated Europe* (Michigan: University of Michigan Press).

Eijffinger, S. C. W., and De Haan, J. (1996) 'The Political Economy of Central-Bank Independence', *Special Papers in International Economics*, vol. 19 (Princeton, NJ: Princeton University Press).

Erkel-Rousse, H., and Mélitz, J. (1995) 'New Empirical Evidence on the Costs of European Monetary Union', Discussion Paper 1169, CEPR.

Ethier, W. J. (1984) 'International Trade Theory and International Migration', Discussion Paper 5, Harvard University, Migration and Development Program.

Ethier, W. J. (1985) 'International Trade Theory and Labour Migration', *American Economic Review*, vol. 75 (4), pp. 691–707.

European Commission (1990) 'One Market, One Money', *European Economy*, vol. 44.

European Commission (1992) *From the Single Act to Maastricht and Beyond: The Means to Match our Ambitions* (Luxembourg: European Commission).

European Commission (1994a) 'Competition and Integration. Community Merger Control Policy', *European Economy*, vol. 57, pp. 1–77.

European Commission (1994b) *Libro blanco sobre el crecimiento, la competitividad y el empleo. Retos y pistas para entrar en el siglo XXI* (Brussels: European Commission).

European Commission (1995a) 'Highlights on Industrial Competitiveness: The Trade Performance of the EU Manufacturing Industry', in *Panorama of EU Industry, 95/96* (Luxembourg: European Commission) pp. 1–30.

European Commission (1995b) 'The Impact of Exchange-Rate Movements on Trade within the Single Market', *European Economy, Reports and Studies*, vol. 4.

European Commission (1996a) *First Cohesion Report* (Luxembourg: European Commission).

European Commission (1996b) *Structural Funds and Cohesion Funds, 1994–1999* (Luxembourg: European Commission).

European Commission (1997) *Social Protection in the Member States of the European Union* (Luxembourg: European Commission).

European Monetary Institute (1996) *Progress towards Convergence, 1996* (Frankfurt: EMI).

European Monetary Institute (1997a) *Annual Report, 1996* (Frankfurt: EMI).

European Monetary Institute (1997b) *The Single Monetary Policy in Stage Three: Specification of the Operational Framework* (Frankfurt: EMI).

Eurostat (1994) *Digest of Statistics on Social Protection in Europe: Unemployment* (Luxembourg: Eurostat).

Eurostat (1995) *Statistical Yearbook* (Luxembourg: Eurostat).

Eurostat (1997) *Labour Force Survey* (Luxembourg: Eurostat).

Fagerberg, J. (1996) 'Technology and Competitiveness', *Oxford Review of Economic Policy*, vol. 12 (3), pp. 39–51.

Faini, R. (1995) 'Migration in the Integrated EU', in R. E. Baldwin, P. Haaparanta and J. Kiander (eds), *Expanding Membership of the European Union* (Cambridge: Cambridge University Press) pp. 143–62.

Faini, R., and Venturini, A. (1994) 'Migration and Growth: The Experience of Southern Europe', Discussion Paper 964, CEPR.

Fariñas, J. C. (1992) 'La especialización comercial exterior: una tipología de índices para su cuantificación', in *Economía española, cultura y sociedad: Homenaje a Juan Velarde* (Madrid: Eudema).

Fariñas, J. C., and Martín, C. (1990) 'Ventaja comparativa y proporción de factores en el comercio español de productos manufacturados', *Investigaciones Económicas, Segunda Época*, vol. XIV (2), pp. 269–90.
Favero, C., Giavazzi, F., and Spaventa, L. (1995) 'High Yields, the Spread on German Interest Rates', Discussion Paper 1330, CEPR.
Fernández, E. (1993) 'La posición competitiva de la economía española: Una óptica global', *Papeles de Economía Española*, vol. 56, pp. 14–22.
Fernández, C. M., and Myro, R. (1995) 'Las migraciones de la actividad industrial en la Unión Europea', *Economía Industrial*, vol. 305, pp. 49–73.
Frankel, J. A., and Rose, A. K. (1996a) 'The Endogeneity of the Optimum Currency Area Criteria', Discussion Paper 1473, CEPR.
Frankel, J. A., and Rose, A. K. (1996b) 'Economic Structure and the Decision to Adopt a Common Currency', Working Paper C96-073, University of California, CIDER.
Fratianni, M., and Von Hagen, J. (1992) *The European Monetary System and European Monetary Union* (Boulder, CO: Westview Press).
Freeman, C., and Soete, L. (1994) *Work for All or Mass Unemployment* (London: Pinter).
Fuentes Quintana, E. (1995) 'El modelo de economía abierta y el modelo castizo en el desarrollo de la España de los 90', in E. Fuentes Quintana et al., *Problemas económicos españoles en la década de los 90* (Barcelona: Galaxia Gutenberg-Círculo de Lectores) pp. 61–176.
Fuentes Quintana, E., and Barea, J. (1996) 'El déficit público de la democracia española', *Papeles de Economía Española*, vol. 68, pp. 86–191.
García Solanes, J. (1995) 'Los márgenes de la política fiscal y presupuestaria en la Unión Monetaria Europea', *Presupuesto y Gasto Público*, vol. 17, pp. 67–84.
Giavazzi, F., and Pagano, M. (1990) 'Can Severe Fiscal Adjustments be Expansionary?', in O. Blanchard and S. Fisher (eds), *NBER Macroeconomics Annual* (Cambridge, MA: MIT Press) pp. 75–110.
Giavazzi, F., and Pagano, M. (1996) 'Non-Keynesian Effects of Fiscal Policy Changes: International Evidence and the Swedish Experience', *Swedish Economic Policy Review*, vol. 3 (1), pp. 67–103.
Goodhart, C. A. E. (1996) 'The Transition to EMU', *Scottish Journal of Political Economy*, vol. 43 (3), pp. 241–57.
Goodhart, C. A. E., and Smith, S. (1993) 'Stabilization', *European Economy, Reports and Studies*, vol. 5, pp. 417–56.
Goodman, S. F. (1996) *The European Union* (London: Macmillan).
Gordo, E. (1996) 'La apertura de los mercados internacionales y el déficit comercial español', *Papeles de Economía Española*, vol. 66, pp. 98–106.
Gordo, E., and Martín, C. (1995) 'El ajuste comercial de España en el mercado de la UE: inferencias sobre su impacto en la convergencia real', *Papeles de Economía Española*, vol. 63, pp. 164–76.
Gordo, E., and Martín, C. (1997) 'Integración económica, comercio intraindustrial y costes de ajuste', *Revista de Economía Aplicada*, vol. IV (12), pp. 151–64.
Gordo, E., and Sánchez-Carretero, M. C. (1997) 'El papel del tipo de cambio en el mecanismo de transmisión de la política monetaria', in *La política monetaria y la inflación en España* (Madrid: Alianza Editorial/Servicio de Estudios, Banco de España).

Greenaway, D., Hine, R., and Millner, C. (1994) 'Country-Specific Factors and the Pattern of Horizontal and Vertical Intra-Industry Trade in the UE', *Weltwirtschaftliches Archiv*, vol. 130 (1), pp. 77–100.

Gros, D. (1996) 'A Reconsideration of the Optimum Currency Area Approach: The Role of External Shocks and Labour Mobility', Working Document 101, Centre for European Policy Studies.

Gros, D., and Thygesen, N. (1992) *European Monetary Integration. From the European Monetary System to European Monetary Union* (London: Longman).

Grossman, G. M. (1992) *Imperfect Competition and International Trade* (Cambridge, MA: MIT Press).

Grossman, G. M. (1996) *Economic Growth: Theory and Evidence*, vols. I and II (Cheltenham: Elgar).

Grossman, G. M. and Helpman, E. (1991) *Innovation and Growth in the Global Economy* (Cambridge, MA: MIT Press).

Gundlach, E. (1997) 'Human Capital and Economic Development: A Macroeconomic Assessment', *Intereconomics*, January–February, pp. 23–35.

Hagen, J. Von (1992) 'Fiscal Arrangements in a Monetary Union: Evidence from the US', in D. E. Fair and C. De Boissieu (eds), *Fiscal Policy, Taxation and the Financial System in an Increasingly Integrated Europe* (Amsterdam: Kluwer).

Hagen, J. Von, and Harden, I. J. (1994) 'National Budget Processes and Fiscal Performance', *European Economy*, vol. 3, pp. 311–54.

Hagen, J. Von, and Harden, I. J. (1995) 'Budget Processes and Commitment to Fiscal Discipline', *European Economic Review*, vol. 39 (3–4), pp. 771–9.

Hagen, J. Von, Wyplosz, C., and Zimmermann, K. F. (eds) (1998) *Prospects and Challenges for the Euro* (Oxford: CEPR and Blackwell).

Hansen, M. W. (1996) 'Danish Foreign Direct Investment in Less Developed Countries and Eastern Europe: A Survey of the International Operations of Danish Companies', Working Paper, Series 9, Department of Intercultural Communication and Management, Copenhagen Business School.

Harberger, A. C. (1978) 'A Primer on Inflation', *Journal of Money, Credit and Banking*, vol. 10 (4), November, pp. 505–21.

Harrop, J. (1996) *Structural Funding and Employment in the European Union: Financing the Path to Integration* (Cheltenham: Edward Elgar).

Hatzius, J. (1997) 'Foreign Direct Investment, Capital Formation and Labour Costs: Evidence from Britain and Germany', Discussion Paper 336, CEPR.

Helpman, E., and Krugman, P. (1985) *Market Structure and Foreign Trade: Increasing Returns, Imperfect Competition and the International Economy* (Cambridge, MA: MIT Press).

Herce, J. A. (1995) 'Los servicios en la economía española', *Papeles de Economía Española*, vol. 62, pp. 213–25.

Herce, J. A. (1997) 'La reforma de las pensiones en España: aspectos analíticos y aplicados', *Moneda y Crédito, Segunda Época*, vol. 204, pp. 105–43.

Heston, A., Nuxoll, D., and Summers, R. (1994) 'The Differential-Productivity Hypothesis and Purchasing-Power Parities: Some New Evidence', *Review of International Economics*, vol. 3 (2), pp. 227–43.

Hine, R. (1994) 'International Economic Integration', in D. Greenaway and A. Winters (eds), *Surveys in International Trade* (Oxford: Blackwell).

Hoekman, B., and Djankov, S. (1996) 'Intra-Industry Trade, Foreign Direct Investment and the Reorientation of East European Exports', Discussion Paper 1377, CEPR.

Hooper, P., and Larin, K. A. (1988) 'International Comparisons of Labor Cost in Manufacturing', Discussion Paper 330, Board of Governors of the Federal Reserve System International Finance.

Hunya, G. (1996) 'Foreign Direct Investment and Economic Modernization in CEECs', Vienna Institute for Comparative Economic Studies, mimeo.

Jiménez, J. C. (1995) 'Sector energético', in J. L. García Delgado (ed.), *Lecciones de Economía Española*, 2nd edn (Madrid: Editorial Civitas) pp. 225–44.

Jimeno, J. F., and Toharia, L. (1993) 'The Effects of Fixed Term Employment on Wages: Theory and Evidence from Spain', *Investigaciones Económicas, Segunda Época*, vol. XVII (3), pp. 475–94.

Jimeno, J. F., and Toharia, L. (1996) 'Effort, Absenteeism and Fixed-term Employment', *Revista Española de Economía*, vol. 13 (1), pp. 105–19.

Johnson, G. E. (1980) 'The Labor Market Effects of Immigration', *Industrial and Labor Relations Review*, vol. 33 (3), pp. 331–41.

Jordán, J. M., and Sanchís, M. (1997) 'Los mercados de factores productivos', in J. M. Jordán (coord.) *Economía de la Unión Europea*, 2nd edn (Madrid: Editorial Civitas).

Kaldor, N. (1978) 'The Case of Devaluations on Trade in Manufactures', in N. Kaldor (ed.), *Further Essays on Applied Economics* (London: Duckworth).

Kenen, P. (1992) 'The Theory of Optimum Currency Areas: An Eclectic View', in R. Mundell and A. Swoboda (eds), *Monetary Problems of the International Economy* (Chicago: University of Chicago Press).

Kenen, P. (1995) *Economic and Monetary Union in Europe. Moving beyond Maastricht* (Cambridge: Cambridge University Press).

Krauss, M. B. (1974) 'Commodity Trade and Factor Mobility', *American Economic Review*, vol. 64 (4), pp. 797–801.

Krugman, P. (ed.) (1987) *Strategic Trade Policy and New International Economics* (Cambridge, MA: MIT Press).

Krugman, P. (1990) *Rethinking International Trade* (Cambridge, MA: MIT Press).

Krugman, P. (1991) *Geography and Trade* (Cambridge, MA: MIT Press).

Krugman, P. (1994) 'Competitiveness: A Dangerous Obsession', *Foreign Affairs*, vol. 73 (2), pp. 28–44.

Krugman, P., and Venables, A. (1993) 'Integration, Specialization and Adjustment', Working Paper 4559, National Bureau of Economic Research.

Lafay, G. (1991) 'The Measurement of Revealed Comparative Advantages', in M. Dagenais and P. Muet (eds), *International Trade Modelling* (London: Chapman and Hall).

Lagares, M. (1988) 'Niveles de cobertura del gasto público en España', *Papeles de Economía Española*, vol. 37, pp. 150–73.

Lucas, R. E. (1988) 'On the Mechanics of Economic Development', *Journal of Monetary Economics*, vol. 22 (1), pp. 3–42.

MacDougall, D., et al. (1977) *Report of the Study Group on the Role of Public Finance in European Integration* (Brussels: European Commission).

Majocchi, A., and Rey, M. (1993) 'A Special Financial Support Scheme in Economic and Monetary Union: Need and Nature', *European Economy*, vol. 5, pp. 457–80.

Marín, J. (1997) *Efectos estabilizadores de la política fiscal* (vols I and II) (Madrid: Banco de España).

Markusen, J. R. (1983) 'Factor Movements and Commodity Trade as Complements', *Journal of International Economics*, vol. 14 (3–4), pp. 341–56.

Markusen, J. R. (1988) 'Production, Trade and Migration with Differentiated, Skilled Workers', *Canadian Journal of Economics*, vol. 21 (3), pp. 492–506.

Markusen, J. R. (1995) 'The Boundaries of Multinational Enterprises and the Theory of International Trade', *Journal of Economic Perspectives*, vol. 9 (2), pp. 169–89.

Martín, C. (1992) 'El comercio industrial español ante el Mercado Único Europeo', in J. Viñals (ed.), *La economía española ante el Mercado Único Europeo* (Madrid: Alianza Economía, Alianza Editorial) pp. 119–66.

Martín, C. (1995a) 'La convergencia real en Europa: Un referente clave para la política económica española', *Papeles de Economía Española*, vol. 63, pp. 2–17.

Martín, C. (1995b) 'La industria española: Problemas estructurales y coyuntura actual', *Papeles de Economía Española*, vol. 62, pp. 188–205.

Martín, C. (1995c) 'El impacto comercial de los acuerdos de la UE con los países del Este', *Papeles de Economía Española*, vol. 63, pp. 269–85.

Martín, C. (1996) 'España en Europa: Convergencia real versus convergencia nominal', in J. Velarde, J. L. García Delgado and A. Pedreño (eds), *España en la Unión Europea: Balance de un decenio* (Madrid: Editorial Civitas) pp. 33–51.

Martín, C., and Moreno, L. (1991) 'Spain's Industrial Exports to the EEC: A Panel Data Approach', Discussion Paper 521, CEPR.

Martín, C., and Moreno, L. (1993) 'Determinantes de las exportaciones intra-comunitarias de las industrias españolas', in J. J. Dolado, C. Martín and L. Rodríguez (eds), *La industria y el comportamiento de las empresas españolas (Ensayos en homenaje a Gonzalo Mato)* (Madrid: Alianza Editorial) pp. 197–210.

Martín, C., and Velázquez, F. J. (1993a) 'Actividad tecnológica y competitividad de las empresas industriales españolas', *Papeles de Economía Española*, vol. 56, pp. 194–207.

Martín, C., and Velázquez, F. J. (1993b) 'El capital extranjero y el comercio exterior de las empresas manufactureras', *Papeles de Economía Española*, vol. 56, pp. 221–34.

Martín, C., and Velázquez, F. J. (1996a) 'Factores determinantes de la inversión directa en los países de la OCDE: Una especial referencia a España', *Papeles de Economía Española*, vol. 66, pp. 209–19.

Martín, C., and Velázquez, F. J. (1996b) 'Una estimación de la presencia de capital extranjero en la economía española y de algunas de sus consecuencias', *Papeles de Economía Española*, vol. 66, pp. 160–75.

Martínez Serrano, J. A., and Muñoz, C. (1995) 'Sector Servicios', in J. L. García Delgado (ed.), *Lecciones de Economía Española*, 2nd edn (Madrid: Editorial Civitas) pp. 267–82.

Más, M., et al. (1994) 'Capital público y productividad en las regiones españolas', *Moneda y Crédito, Segunda Época*, vol. 198, pp. 163–206.

Masson, P. R. (1996) 'Fiscal Dimensions of EMU', *Economic Journal*, vol. 106, pp. 996–1004.

Masson, P. R., and Taylor, M. P. (1993) 'Currency Unions: A Survey of the Issues', in P. R. Masson and M. P. Taylor (eds), *Policy Issues in the Operations of Currency Unions* (Cambridge: Cambridge University Press).

Maté, J. M. (1995) 'La productividad del trabajo en España y en la UE. Análisis comparado de la economía y de la industria', *Papeles de Economía Española*, vol. 63, pp. 112–25.

Maté, J. M. (1996a) 'Factores determinantes del comportamiento diferencial de las empresas industriales españolas que invierten en el extranjero', Working Paper 129, Fundación FIES.

Maté, J. M. (1996b) 'La inversión directa española en el exterior', *Papeles de Economía Española*, vol. 66, pp. 220–34.

Mauleón, I., and Sastre, L. (1996) 'An Empirical Model for Spanish Foreign Trade', *Economic and Financial Modelling*, vol. 3 (3), Autumn, pp. 101–44.

Mélitz, J. (1995) 'The Current Impasse in Research on Optimum Currency Areas', *European Economic Review*, vol. 39 (3–4), pp. 492–500.

Merino, F., and Moreno, L. (1996) 'Actividad comercial en el exterior de las empresas manufactureras españolas, y estrategias de diferenciación de producto', *Papeles de Economía Española*, vol. 66, pp. 107–23.

Monetary Committee of the European Communities (1986) *Compendium of Community Monetary Texts*, European Commission.

Moreno, L., and Rodríguez, D. (1996) 'La empresa industrial en la década de los noventa: Actividad exterior', Working Paper 9608, Fundación Empresa Pública.

Motta, M. (1992) 'Sunk Costs and Trade Liberalisation', *Economic Journal*, vol. 102, pp. 578–87.

Múgica, J. M. and Yagüe, M. J. (1993) 'Impacto del capital comercial en la competitividad empresarial', *Papeles de Economía Española*, vol. 54, pp. 242–76.

Mundell, R. A. (1957) 'International Trade and Factor Mobility', *American Economic Review*, vol. 47, pp. 321–35.

Munnell, A. H. (1992) 'How does Public Infrastructure Affect Regional Performance?', *Journal of Economic Perspectives*, vol. 6 (4), pp. 189–98.

Nickell, S., and Bell, B. (1995) 'The Collapse in the Demand for the Unskilled and Unemployment across the OECD', *Oxford Review of Economic Policy*, vol. 11 (1), pp. 40–62.

OECD (1992) *Technology and the Economy: The Key Relationships* (Paris: OECD).

OECD (1993) *Methods Used by OECD Countries to Measure Stocks of Fixed Capital* (Paris: OECD).

OECD (1994) *The OECD Jobs Study* (Paris: OECD).

OECD (1995) *The OECD Jobs Study: Investment, Productivity and Employment* (Paris: OECD).

OECD (1996a) *Economic Outlook*, vol. 59 (Paris: OECD).

OECD (1996b) *Employment Outlook* (Paris: OECD).

OECD (1996c) *The OECD Jobs Strategy: Technology, Productivity and Job Creation* (Paris: OECD).

Oxley, H., and Martin, J. P. (1991) 'Controlling Government Spending and Deficits: Trends in the 1980s and Prospects for the 1990s', *OECD Economic Studies*, vol. 17 (Paris: OECD).

Padoa-Schioppa, T. (1994) *The Road to Monetary Union in Europe: The Emperor, the Kings, and the Genies* (Oxford: Oxford University Press).

Pérez, F., Goerlich, F. J., and Más, M. (1996) *Capitalización y crecimiento en España y sus regiones, 1955–1995* (Bilbao: Fundación BBV).

Pérez, M., and Vega, J. L. (1994) 'Paridad del poder de compra: Un análisis empírico', *Investigaciones Económicas, Segunda Época*, vol. 18 (3), pp. 539–56.
Pérez-Díaz, V. (1995a) 'El largo plazo y el "lado blando" de las políticas de empleo', Research Paper 11, Analistas Socio Políticos.
Pérez-Díaz, V. (1995b) 'La educación en España: Reflexiones retrospectivas', Research Paper 10, Analistas Socio Políticos.
Perotti, R. (1996) 'Fiscal Consolidation in Europe: Composition Patterns', *American Economic Review*, vol. 86 (2), pp. 105–10.
Piñera, J., and Weinstein, A. (1996) *Una propuesta de reforma del sistema de pensiones en España* (Madrid: Círculo de Empresarios).
Pisani-Ferry, J., Italianer, A., and Lescure, R. (1993) 'Stabilization Properties of Budgetary Systems', *European Economy, Reports and Studies*, vol. 5, pp. 511–38.
Raymond, J. L. (1993) 'Acortamiento de distancias, convergencia y competitividad en los países de la Europa de los Doce', *Papeles de Economía Española*, vol. 56, pp. 78–97.
Raymond, J. L. (1995) 'El problema de la explosividad potencial de la deuda pública', *Papeles de Economía Española*, vol. 62, pp. 341–3.
Razin, A., and Sadka, E. (1995) 'Resisting Migration: Wage Rigidity and Income Distribution', *American Economic Review*, vol. 85 (2), pp. 312–16.
Rodríguez, D. (1992) 'Contenido factorial del comercio español de manufacturas: nueva evidencia', *Investigaciones Económicas, Segunda Época*, vol. XVI (2), pp. 317–26.
Rodríguez, D. (1993) 'Ventaja comparativa y competitividad empresarial', *Papeles de Economía Española*, vol. 56, pp. 100–11.
Romer, P. (1989) 'Human Capital and Growth: Theory and Evidence', *National Bureau of Economic Research*, Working Paper 3173.
Romer, P. (1990) 'Endogenous Technological Change', *Journal of Political Economy*, vol. 98 (5), pp. 71–102.
Ruggles, R. (1967) 'Price Indexes and International Price Comparisons', in W. Fellner et al. (eds), *Ten Studies in the Tradition of Irving Fisher* (New York: John Wiley) pp. 171–205.
Sakurai, N., Papaconstatinou, G., and Ioannidis, E. (1997) 'Impact of R&D and Technology Diffusion on Productivity Growth: Empirical Evidence for 10 OECD Countries', *Economic Systems Research*, vol. 9 (1), pp. 81–109.
Sala-i-Martín, X. (1994) 'La riqueza de las regiones. Evidencia y teorías sobre crecimiento regional y convergencia', *Moneda y Crédito, Segunda Época*, vol. 198, pp. 13–80.
Samuelson, P. A. (1964) 'Theoretical Notes on Trade Problems', *Review of Economics and Statistics*, vol. 46, pp. 145–54.
Schmidt, C., and Straubhaar, T. (1995) 'Maastricht II: Are Real Convergence Criteria Needed?', *Intereconomics*, September–October, pp. 211–20.
Segura, J. (1996) 'De ahora en adelante', *Economistas*, vol. 69, pp. 68–73.
Sherer, F., and Perlman, M. (eds) (1992) *Entrepreneurship, Innovation and Economic Growth* (Michigan: University of Michigan Press).
Stern, N. (1991) 'The Determinants of Growth', *Economic Journal*, vol. 101 (404), pp. 122–33.
Straubhaar, T. (1988) 'International Labour Migration within a Common Market: Some Aspects of EC Experience', *Journal of Common Market Studies*, vol. XXVII (1), pp. 45–62.

Straubhaar, T., and Wolter, A. (1996) 'Current Issues in European Migration', *Intereconomics*, November–December, pp. 267–76.
Straubhaar, T., and Zimmermann, K. F. (1993) 'Towards a European Migration Policy', *Population Research and Policy Review*, vol. 12 (3), pp. 225–41.
Sumpsi, J. M. (1995) 'Situación actual de la agricultura española', *Papeles de Economía Española*, vol. 62, pp. 172–87.
Tavlas, G. S. (1993) 'The "New" Theory of Optimum Currency Areas', *World Economy*, vol. 16 (6), pp. 663–85.
Toharia, L. (1995) 'La protección del desempleo en España', Working Paper 9504, Fundación Empresa Pública.
Toharia, L. (ed.) (1998) 'El Mercado de Trabajo en España' (Madrid: MacGraw-Hill).
United Nations (several years) *World Investment Report* (New York: United Nations).
Uzawa, H. (1965) 'Optimum Technical Change in an Aggregative Model of Economic Growth', *International Economic Review*, vol. 6, pp. 18–31.
Velázquez, F. J. (1995a) 'La convergencia desde la óptica de la eficiencia', *Papeles de Economía Española*, vol. 63, pp. 126–45.
Velázquez, F. J. (1995b) 'Medición y evolución sectorial del stock de capital de España y los países centrales de la Unión Europea', Working Paper 119/1995, Fundación FIES.
Viner, J. (1950) *The Customs Union Issue* (New York: Carnegie Endowment for International Peace).
Viñals, J. (1996) 'European Monetary Integration: A Narrow or a Wide EMU?', *European Economic Review*, vol. 40 (3–5), pp. 1103–9.
Viñals, J., and Jimeno, J. F. (1996) 'Monetary Union and European Unemployment', Discussion Paper 1485, CEPR.
Viñals, J., Vallés, J., and Canzoneri, M. (1996) 'El tipo de cambio como instrumento de ajuste macroeconómico: Evidencia empírica y relevancia para la Unión Monetaria Europea', December, Boletín Económico, Banco de España, pp. 49–56.
Walsh, B. (1996) 'Stabilization and Adjustment in a Small Open Economy: Ireland, 1979–95', *Oxford Review of Economic Policy*, vol. 12 (3), pp. 74–86.
Wang, Z. K., and Winters, A. (1991) 'The Trading Potential of Eastern Europe', Discussion Paper 610, CEPR.
Winters, A. (1991) 'International Trade and "1992": An Overview', *European Economic Review*, vol. 35 (2–3), pp. 367–77.
Ypersèle, J. Van, and Koeune, J. C. (1985) *Le Système Monétaire Européen, Perspectives Européennes* (2nd edn) (European Commission).
Zanías, G. P. (1994) 'The Common Agricultural Policy in the Process of European Integration and Convergence', in T. Georgakopoulos, C. C. Paraskevopoulos, and J. Smithin (eds), *Economic Integration between Unequal Partners* (Aldershot: Edward Elgar) pp. 110–22.
Zimmermann, K. F. (1995) 'Tackling the European Migration Problem', *Journal of Economic Perspectives*, vol. 9 (2), pp. 45–62.

Index

Note: page numbers in italic indicate figures or tables.